A CROWN OF FIRE

The Life and Times
of Girolamo Savonarola

FROM *Dialogo della verita prophetica* BY SAVONAROLA

A Crown of Fire

THE LIFE AND TIMES
OF GIROLAMO SAVONAROLA

by

PIERRE VAN PAASSEN

Charles Scribner's Sons
New York

Author's Note

This book stems in the main from watching the scene in Florence's Piazza della Signoria on the anniversary of Savonarola's martyrdom, and from observations made in a number of Dominican convents in Italy, Switzerland, Germany, and Austria in the course of the summer and autumn of 1958.

To Professor Giorgio La Pira, the former Mayor of Florence, and the Curators of the Florentine Archives and Libraries, goes my gratitude for having given me an opportunity to inspect the large collections of letters and copies of letters, minutes of the Grand Council, depositions upon the three false trials, theological tracts, and miscellaneous communications with the courts of France and Rome. Of my indebtedness to Professor Mario Ferrara of Lucca I can hardly say enough. With his scholarly transformation of the text of Savonarola's sermons from an archaic, outmoded language into modern Italian he has not only deserved well of the noble Friar's memory, but saved me from becoming bogged down in a mass of almost indigestible old scripts. The learned Dr. P. Dom. Planzer, O.P., of Lucerne, was kind enough to set me aright on the history of the Dominican Order and certain intricacies of Catholic doctrine. I also want to thank the Sindaco of Ferrara, the Honorable Spero Ghedini, for his exquisite courtesy in granting me an insight into the motives which inspired him and the municipal and provincial governments of Ferrara to set up a special section in the Ariostean Library devoted to Ferrara's greatest son. This very laudable enterprise by the Ferrarese is of a purely historical and cultural nature, and, contrary to press reports, has nothing whatsoever to do with contemporary Italian politics or polemics.

v

While I have endeavored to interpret the subject in his historical context, I also believe that, without turning this work into a compendium of names, dates, and statistics, I have brought to light some information on the Friar's life and times which has never before been published. In combining research with a feeling of deep sympathy for Savonarola, which goes back to my youth in Holland, I have, as Felix Timmermans once said of a book he wrote on Pieter Breughel, tried to "ferret and sniffle him out of his own works."

I cannot close without expressing my obligation to my dear friends Selma and Luise Steinberg who placed their pleasant home on the Lake of Zurich at my disposal for interviews and consultations with various Savonarola *Kenner* from all over Europe.

The book is lovingly dedicated to my wife who made the journey with me through the land of her Veronese ancestors.

Pierre van Paassen

Contents

By Way of Preface

Out of the Shadows of Night

DAWN came in that morning enveloped in a chill melancholy shroud making Florence resemble nothing so much as an enormous blank page. In the confused transition toward day the light was the color of white coffee, an undelectable mixture of gloom and sadness. The drizzle of the night had turned the pavement into rows of gleaming black mirrors. It was seventeen minutes before five o'clock. From far away across the Arno came the nervous tinkle of a monastery bell; a mere quiver of silvery vibration. When it stopped only the sound of the pigeons flapping their wings broke the stillness. The birds spent the night sitting on the heads and shoulders of the marble statues in the Loggia de' Lanzi, the magnificent open vaulted hall where Cosimo de' Medici posted his lancers on the occasion of great state ceremonials. Dim-looming through the floating haze a part of the grimy façade of the Palazzo Vecchio became visible. A thin frothy screen still concealed the slender top-heavy bell tower and the crenelated rampart on the palace roof. No human movement was as yet discernible. Only the haze rippled now and then like a lace curtain swaying in a gust of wind. When the veil lifted for an instant Michelangelo's gigantic statue of the boy David stood forth like a pale terror. Suddenly, and seemingly from all directions at the same time, a soft breeze blew into the Piazza causing whiffs and puffs of mist and vapor to race and dance back and forth like a myriad of ghostly wraiths and phantoms transforming the blank page of a moment before into a whispering pageant of past magnificence. . . .

In all ages and all seasons the Florentines poured into this Piazza in cascades now gay or somber, now raving mad or trembling with holy joy. In tumultuous demonstrations, brandishing their weapons and shouting their wild slogans, but also in solemn silent processions as serene as the hosts of the redeemed; in war and peace, amidst tears and laughter, to the sound of cannon thunder and sweetest hymns, the people of Florence made this square alternately a radiant hurly-burly and the dreariest of black spots, sinister with stake and gallows and writhing victims. Here they rose to a pinnacle of splendor unscaled since the Athens of Pericles. Here, too, intoxicated with fame and glory, they tripped on Fortune's treacherous dance floor.

They all walked here: the friends and the enemies of liberty, warriors of hot temper who filled the earth with clamor and woe, fervent mystics and smiling sceptics, atheists in pontifical garb, clerics wielding gleaming swords, popes, emperors, crusaders, and men of the sort called immortal: Dante, Leonardo, Machiavelli, Petrarch, the superman Michelangelo. Silently treading with ghostly step, the lacquered, gilt, and silvered Medici walked by; Pope Julius in unbelievably gorgeous raiment, a battle sword by his side, mounted on a white horse under a golden baldachin; Martin Luther returning to Wittenberg, his "eyes bloodshot with rage"; Pico della Mirandola who stunned mankind with the extent of his learning; the Angelical Doctor, St. Thomas Aquinas; St. Francis, God's troubador from Assisi; St. Catherine of Siena who bore on her hands, feet, and heart the impression of the wounds of the Crucified.

Intermingled like the soldiers of a routed army or trailing each other in utter disregard of temporal sequence came visions of Alaric and his Vandals on their way to the sack of Rome; Constantine the Great, the first Christian emperor, on the arm of St. Athanasius, the formulator of the Creed that bears his name; illiterate Charlemagne looking for still another site to build a school. . . Here is Mathilda of Canossa, who made an emperor wait barefoot in the snow before allowing him to enter her castle to beg Pope Gregory's forgiveness; Frederick Barbarossa, the German kaiser, who trained falcons, kept a harem, and wrote sonnets in Arabic; Napoleon, of all, the most systematic plunderer of churches and museums, whom Pius VII dismissed with the words: "Get out of my sight, *commediante!*" And then, his beard and hair bristling like the quills of a porcupine, the liberator Garibaldi accoutered in his blood-red shirt. "Have you ever seen a lion's face?" Mazzini once asked John Morley. "Isn't it a silly face? Isn't it the face of Garibaldi?. . ."

Then more saints and heroes, more scholars, artists, poets, natives of this city whose renown has not faded with the passage of time, now sleeping in the vaults and crypts of the churches and chapels round about the Piazza. And side by side with them "malign individuals of the scoundrel species": hotheads, cutthroats, bearing exalted names, all turned to dust; gone, gone into the final night that envelopes the destinies of man. . . .

It was in this square that the articles of luxury, known as the "Vanities" were piled in a huge pyramid and set on fire, and a whole nation vowed, like Joshua of old: "As for me and my house we will serve the Lord," only to remember its solemn pledge no more six months later. One day, in a vaporous dawn like this, 'tis said, repentant Sandro Botticelli, one of the masters of the Renaissance, climbed through the palace window to paint veils and drapes around his nudes on exhibition there. Another day, a seventeen year old boy dressed in cardinatial purple, Giovanni de' Medici, the future Leo X, upon learning that the members of his family were to be banished from Florence, stood sobbing out his heart against that Loggia wall. Leaving his mules, balancing baskets of books on their backs, in a side street, cautious Erasmus peered into the Piazza from around a corner not daring to enter lest he be recognized and taken back to Rome where his friend and admirer, Paul III, wanted to put a red hat on him.

From all possible sources come reports of cabals collecting in this square, imbecilities enacted, conspiracies hatched and smothered in blood; Guelph factions and Ghibelline factions at war; monks enlisting crusaders; an army of prostitutes doing penance; silver trumpets calling to the assault, red and blue panoplies waving in the breeze, and, occasionally, too, pans of incense sending up perfumed smoke in celebration of uneasy peace. One year Florence was a den of fratricidal discord, in another the people chanted the psalm of brotherly love: "How good and pleasant is it for brethren to dwell together in unity." One day upon the closing of the brothels by Savonarola it was *Te Deum Laudamus,* the day following his death the populace indulged in orgies so lewd and obscene as to make the debaucheries in ancient Daphne's grove seem innocent child's play in comparison.

A passionate people these Florentines, now kneeling in prayer, now storming the heavens in hellish rage and fury; like all peoples a mixture of good and bad, yet always something noble and beautiful shining through the soil and tarnish of their human condition.

Extinct for fifteen hundred years, divine prophecy was revived in this city on the Arno. Here a miracle of discipline was worked out by faith. Here the assertion was made of a discoverable and attainable paradise. In serious hearts the matter sank down deep, prompting attempts here and elsewhere to bring the messianic dream to realization. History has seen few explosions of faith such as that which once flared up in the Lily City. But here also happened things over which all Florence cried hot tears. . . and still weeps at times. . . .

In 1901 a memorial slab of bronze, replacing an earlier one of marble, was put down in the Piazza, just in front of Ammannati's fountain, on the spot where Savonarola was executed. "Here," says the inscription, "where with his brethren, Fra Domenico Buonvicini and Fra Silvestro Maruffi, on May 23, 1498, by an iniquitous sentence Fra Girolamo Savonarola was hanged and burned, this memorial has been placed after four centuries."

*　　*

It was five thirty when the first motor scooter roared across the square and up the Via Calzaioli, the Street of the Stocking makers, a noisy herald of a thousand others to follow. When the silence returned footsteps were heard. An old nun, nearly bent double with age, shuffled into view. From afar she seemed to glide behind frosted glass, unreal, shadowlike. In her left hand she carried a wicker basket, with her right hand she leaned heavily on a hawthorn stick. She halted and, as if to orientate herself, slowly looked around in all directions. Then she took from her basket a small bunch of flowers and placed it gently on the memorial slab. The violets lay there shy and lonely. For a moment the nun stood still with head bent so low that she seemed in danger of toppling over. After crossing herself she picked up her basket and with painful step shambled off, muttering indistinctly to herself, dragging her sandals through the puddles.

No sooner was the nun out of sight when more footsteps were heard. This time they tapped briskly and were counterpointed by the metallic click of an umbrella tip. A middle-aged gentleman dressed in a black cutaway, wearing a bowler hat, patent leather shoes and a glittering pince-nez, went through the same motions as the old nun. He carried a bouquet of red roses in cellophane. He unwrapped the flowers and deposited them by the side of the nun's violets. Stepping back, he cocked his head sideways like a painter surveying his own masterpiece, and swept off his hat in a broad gesture of salute. Probably assuming himself unobserved, he bowed, not inelegantly, to the flowers and said in a clearly audible voice: *Popolo e Libertà! Popolo e Libertà!* "The People and Freedom!" This was once the slogan of the *Frateschi,* the followers of *Fra* Girolamo Savonarola. The signor walked off scraping his throat and furiously swinging his umbrella.

Two men followed, both bareheaded, mufflers wrapped around their faces in deference to the old Italian superstition of breathing the moist morning air. Both men pushed bicycles and spoke rapidly through their mufflers. They may have been schoolteachers or clerks or minor officials of the *cristianodemocratico* party. They gave the flowers and the memorial slab a perfunctory nod as to a casual acquaintance and went their way but now mounted on their bicycles.

A pushcart rattled into the Piazza. It was piled high with flowers, the lilies, Florence's city emblem, standing forth like pale yellow candles amongst green ferns, red and pink roses, and carnations lying fresh and fragrant on the cart's edge. The woman pushing the cart halted, wiped her face with a red handkerchief, and got busy arranging the flowers. She smiled as a babel of children's voices came from the direction where the Via della Ninna debouches into the Piazza. The boys and girls bought one flower each. As they threw them on the slab of bronze they called out: *Viva Cristo!* That was the slogan of the Florentines when, upon Savonarola's nomination, they proclaimed Christ the king of their common-wealth.

Now a golden rim encircled the Piazza on high. The sky came through, a mixture of blue and vermillion, like a wide diaphanous garment overspreading the roofs. In the twinkling of an eye the last trace of mist dissolved and the humidity evaporated. From all sides, men, women and children could be seen coming into the square. A dozen nuns marched by like soldiers in step. Some people carried flowers, others made for the pushcart to buy. Still as a tomb an hour before, and perhaps as clammy and bleak, the Piazza now came to life inundated with sun and color. The whole city was awakening. The great bell in Giotto's Campanile hard by the Cathedral of St. Mary of the Flower, better known as the Duomo, led off the morning concert. From innumerable towers the bells rang in the 23rd of May in loving remembrance of Girolamo Savonarola.

In Flanders and Holland one gains the impression that the carillons answer each other. No tower sings out till its predecessor has finished. It is a mystic musical dialogue in which they engage, with an undertone of gravity, measured and solemn as the figures in Rembrandt's paintings. In Florence it's the other way around. No *voce velata* here, no veiled voices, no demitones, no carillons as a matter of fact; only chimes and bells. All the Florentine bells talk at once like men and women during the intermission in a theatrical performance. The bells of Florence clamor and clangor, they stutter and splutter. One moment they sound like a crowd of quarreling schoolboys, the next they burst into peals of laughter. And all at once all of them fall silent as if run out of breath or argument. . . .

"Es ist noch immer nicht ruhig um Savonarola!" soliloquized a vigorous broad-shouldered man with an impish smile on his red face. He wore the Dominican black mantle over a white robe and a round velvet hat. Through a pair of thick-lensed glasses he peered at the flowers on the pavement. "Things have never quieted down yet around Savonarola. . . It's nearly five hundred years since he died on this spot, and still all these flowers, all this excitement. . . Five hundred years is a long time! . . ."

Is it? In heaven five hundred years are but half "a watch in the night." To a people with a sense of historical continuity to whom the Church has communicated her secret of thinking in centuries, Girolamo Savonarola walked here only yesterday. Dante still stands at the end of Trinity Bridge gazing on the immaculate Beatrice. There are Florentines who tip their hats when they pass the spot. They still greet Cosimo, the father of their fatherland, high up on his bronze horse near the fountain of Ammannati to the left of the Signorial Palace. On Sunday afternoons they drop in on Fra Angelico, on Ghirlandajo, Donatello, and Da Vinci in the museums and churches as if visiting relatives or old friends.

Those bells are not tolling in mournful cadence for a departed soul. They are pealing in celebration of a birthday. They are expressing the joy which Savonarola experienced when he looked up at the gallows on May 23, 1498, and saw what St. Stephen the protomartyr saw, the gates of heaven open to receive him. Scholars, theologians, political parties, youth groups, and convents are still investigating Savonarola, discussing him, writing about him and inscribing his name on their banners. None ignores the victim of the trial which is universally regarded as an infamous frame-up. Even the most rabid anticlericals in Italy, who by force of habit minimize the religious significance of Savonarola's life and work, nevertheless express their admiration for the courage and the zeal with which he pursued his campaigns for moral purity and social righteousness. In February, 1959, the municipal council of Ferrara, Savonarola's birthplace, brought back one of his Bibles from a private collection in America at the fancy, though not exorbitant price of $31,000.*

There are more monasteries today than there were ten years ago in Italy, in Austria, and in Germany where Savonarola is venerated as a saint. In the San Romano Convent of Lucca, a few miles to the northwest of Florence, they have prayed for his intercession from the hour when his body fell from the gallows onto the flaming woodpile. *Beato,* Blessed Girolamo, they say with a note of endearment in their voices when speaking of the martyred friar. In the towering medieval convent of Wettenhausen, on the edge of the Black Forest in Bavaria, the Mother Superior Anselma, and the learned spiritual director, Sister Aquinata, spoke of him as *Unser Savonarola,* "Our Savonarola." As in Wettenhausen so in a score of monasteries his memory is cherished with exceeding love and reverence. In two Dominican churches in one single day was heard the Mass of Savonarola as a special office in his honor on the anniversary of his death.**

Books and pamphlets on Savonarola, controversial, eulogistic, and scholarly objective, continue to roll from the presses, not only

* Communiqué by the Municipality of Ferrara, April 31, 1959.
** *Officio del Savonarola,* with notes by Cesare Guasti, Florence, 1863.

in his birthplace Ferrara and in Florence, the city of his triumph and tragedy, but in France and Germany, in the Netherlands, Belgium, and Austria as well. The fire behind the five hundred years old controversy whether he was a saint, a heretic, or a revolutionary shows no signs of dying down. Instead of being allowed to slumber in the limbo of forgotten things, there is actually a rise in the market of Savonaroliana. At no time since the Jubilee Year of 1600 when pilgrims, with the high approval of Pope Clement VIII, bought the Friar's picture in Rome showing him with sainthood's aureole around his head and one of his prayers printed on the back, has the atmosphere around Savonarola and his memory been more agitated.

"There seems to be something stirring again around Savonarola," remarked one of the reverend fathers of the Birmingham Oratory, who is a member of the commission appointed to inquire into the life and work of John Henry Newman with a view to the great Oratorian's beatification and his ultimate canonization. "It should not be forgotten," he added, "that St. Philip Neri, Newman's patron saint, was canonized in 1622 despite the devil's advocate's objections. So ardent an admirer and devotee of Savonarola was St. Philip that all his life he carried a relic of the martyred monk on his breast. . . ."

Not once, but three and perhaps four times Savonarola seemed on the point of beatification, the first stage on the way to full sainthood. Once Giovanni de' Medici intervened when Julius II was about to issue a *Brief* elevating the Friar to the altars of the Catholic Church. Another time Clement VIII, who spent eight months in Savonarola's birthplace, assured the citizens of Ferrara that in so far as he was concerned the Friar's canonization was as good as certain. The Pope, however, died before he could pursue his plan to a successful conclusion.

Again in 1952, the five hundredth anniversary of Savonarola's birth when Ferrara and Florence led Italy in commemorating the name and the work of Savonarola, hopes ran high that the reigning Pontiff, Pius XII, would make an authoritative pronouncement. A petition to this effect was submitted to the Sacred Congregation of Rites. But again the attempt miscarried. It was rumored that the Pope had ordered a re-examination of Fra Girolamo's theological works.

Then Professor Mario Ferrara, the prefect of studies at Lucca, went to work and produced the first complete edition of the Friar's sermons and treatises with commentaries showing his "true aims and objectives," and unmasking the "many falsifications and the insults to the noble Friar's tremendous sincerity perpetrated by Jacobins and other enemies of the Church." According to the Luchese scholar all the old, and long since discredited, allegations such as Fra Girolamo's lack of charity,* his disobedience to the papal authority, his rebellion against the Church, melt in thin air when his works are read without prejudice or mental reservation. Professor Ferrara dedicated his work to "Catholics, honest Catholics only." In his opinion only such are capable and have the right to judge the "strict Catholic orthodoxy" of the one-time Vicar-General of Tuscany's Dominican province.

"Whether our hope of the proclamation of Savonarola's sainthood is realized or not," said Professor Ferrara, "he remains what he was, an apostle of the Christian spirit, a true prophet. . . If Rome and Italy and the world will at last acknowledge that Savonarola went down under an avalanche of calumny, filth and false accusations, we will see the pure and learned Friar step to the fore again and still lead us on. . . ."

"We *are* going back to Savonarola," emphatically declared the Lord Mayor of Florence, Professor Giorgio La Pira, who "in the spirit of Savonarola" has built an entire new city, Isolotta, consisting of pink and white low-cost workers' apartment houses along the shores of the Arno. Like George Santayana in his last years, Professor La Pira, though a layman, lives in a monastery. He is a deputy to the Italian parliament where he said, in speaking of the basic lines of Savonarola's five hundred year old political program as if it were an item in the morning's newspaper: "The Christian commonwealth as proposed by Savonarola is of the utmost significance and pertinency for our day. . . It is a free republic with its roots in the public spirit. It demands the religious regeneration of the individual. . . Savonarola's republic is like an oak, its roots go wide and deep in history. . . It rises from our collective conscience. . . The name of Savonarola will never die. . . The great Friar is once more poised to move forward."

* New York *Times,* March 2, 1959.

*   *   *

A serious, perhaps an impassable barrier to Savonarola's rehabilitation may be seen in the peculiar circumstance that a quarter century after his death he was virtually annexed by and integrated in the emerging Protestant movement. In one of his verbal hammer blows with which he shattered the supranational dream of a universal church, Luther called out: "Whereas Antichrist has damned Savonarola, God has canonized him in our hearts." In the group of statues known as the *Luther Denkmal* in Worms, the city where the rebellious Saxon monk appeared before the Diet, Savonarola sits at Luther's feet in the company of Wycliff, Huss, and Petrus Waldus. Protestants of Dutch, Scottish, Swiss, and German antecedents, will undoubtedly recall seeing Savonarola's likeness amongst these and other so-called "forerunners of the Reformation" in their church history books or on the walls of catechism classrooms.

By rights the Florentine prior does not belong in that category. There is no doubt that he was a champion of church reform, but which consecrated Catholic, we may well ask, was not in the fifteenth century? We always seem to overlook the fact that in the fifteenth century the issue was not for or against reform of the Church; everybody was for it. The question was how to bring it about, where to start, how far to go. All his life Savonarola showed a contemptuous indifference to sectarian quarrels and prayed and worked for a convocation of a Council of the whole Church. With much more justice Savonarola could be called one of the trail blazers of the Council of Trent where the Church did reform herself from within and with her own machinery. There is a difference after all between reform and revolt. Savonarola never seceded or threatened to go his own way. He never ceased to subscribe to the Church's articles of faith and the teachings of the Fathers. He was a reformer, not a rebel or revolutionary as was Luther who jumped overboard from St. Peter's bark and struck out for himself. Luther's breaching of the unity of the Church, which many regard today as one of history's major calamities and which Protestants themselves are striving to repair in their own way in and through the World Council of Churches, would have been unthinkable to Savonarola.

The process of Savonarola's rehabilitation extends practically over the same length of time as that of Joan of Arc. Joan was sentenced by an ecclesiastical court to be burned at the stake as a relapsed heretic in Rouen in A.D. 1431. Yet, in the lifetime of the Maid's own mother, that cruel verdict, which was prompted, if not dictated, by John Talbot, the commander of the Godons, as Joan called the English,* was set aside as a gross miscarriage of ecclesiastical justice. Nearly five centuries were to elapse before Joan of Arc was beatified in 1909 and canonized by Benedict XV in 1919. Evidently it takes time even for the Church to recognize a saint. Joan's rise to sainthood came up from the French people who would never admit that the "Saint of the Fatherland" was a heretic. If any person was ever canonized in a people's heart that person was Joan of Arc. The radical-socialists Joseph Fabre and Raymond Poincaré, anticlericals though they were, took the initiative in proclaiming Joan "the eternal symbol of French unity." Their proclamation was an act of faith which grouped the entire French nation around the memory of one of its greatest glories.

When the Church raised the Maid of Orleans to her altars a wave of reconciliation of all men and parties in France was set in motion. All the virtues and treasures of the race suddenly welled up from their subterranean sources. The Maid of Orleans, the "Phoenix of the Gauls," rose from her ashes as *Jeanne d'Arc, Sainte de la Patrie*. The greatest miracle attributed to her is the Battle of the Marne in 1914 when the seemingly irresistible German juggernaut rolled within a few miles of Paris only to be brought to as abrupt a halt as were Attila's hordes in A.D. 451 on St. Geneviève's prayer of intercession.

Will this century, which saw the canonization of Joan of Arc, also see the official rehabilitation of Savonarola? He, too, like Joan, was burned as a heretic. He, too, heard voices. He, too, saw visions. He, too, was the victim of political intrigue and savage implacable enemies. Many of the Friar's contemporaries, amongst them members of the Roman Curia, declared outright, as Joan's mother did in her daughter's case, that a ghastly mistake had been made in Florence's Piazza della Signoria on May 23, 1498.

* Godon, from the word goddamn, which was always on the tip of the Englishmen's tongues.

In A.D. 1962 the twenty-second Ecumenical Council will bring together, either in Venice or in Rome, 1600 bishops, cardinals, prelates, and heads of religious Orders. Pope John XXIII has renewed the tradition of convoking a Council of the whole Church. The mere mention of such a Council would have been deemed reprehensible as short a time ago as 1957 or 1958. The Council of Trent (1545-1563) put the Counter Reformation in motion, the Vatican Council (1869-1870), which was interrupted by the occupation of Rome by the Italian national army and put an end to the papacy's temporal power, set the Church's face in anger against the modern world and made the Pope a self-constituted "prisoner in the Vatican." The twenty-second Council seems designed to accomplish a vastly different purpose. The modern world does exist. It is in full process of evolution. That evolution, it is realized, can no longer be stayed.

John XXIII is determined that European civilization and culture shall no longer be programmatically endorsed or furthered by the Catholic Church in the foreign mission fields. Only the Gospel is to be preached and the universality of the Christian religion emphasized. In line with the trend of decolonization in Asia and Africa, the Church seeks to free herself from all links and ties with chauvinist-nationalist and imperialist policies. Her priests stand in the vanguard of the struggle against *apartheid* in the Union of South Africa. The French clergy, realizing the invincible folly of allowing the Communists always and again to step forward as the champions of the weary and heavy-laden wherever they may be, insists, in the teeth of the military cliques and the North African *colons,* that France, the eldest daughter of the Church, shall answer the cry for justice and freedom arising from Algiers.

Pope John who is said to have a conception of Christian unity as distinct from ecclesiastical uniformity, is not, as were his five or six immediate predecessors in the Chair of St. Peter filled with a secret nostalgia for the old days of the temporal power. He is not a Roman, he is not an aristocrat, he did not, as Pius XII, spend his whole life in the centralizing bureaus of the Vatican. In his youth, before becoming a priest, he walked in the picket line in front of a factory where the workers were on strike. As a student of history he knows that the notion of going back to the past or preserving the status quo is but a wishful dream, without hope or substance. Judging by the public lectures he delivered in Paris in 1954, the Pope, upon whom Christians of every name are beginning to trust for leadership and inspiration, will undoubtedly dare to look the advancing emancipation of natural science in the face with its silent but far more positive threat to all forms of supernaturalism and metaphysics than was ever presented by the spooky "gates of hell."

Some of the recent changes introduced by the Pope not only astonish but frankly bewilder a Protestant onlooker. For the first time in history the Roman Catholic churches in Germany use the vernacular in the liturgy. In Munich's cathedral where tens of thousands of pilgrims come annually to pray on the tomb of the valiant anti-Nazi champion, Cardinal Faulhaber, the priests read the Gospel with their faces turned towards the people, as was the custom during the first six centuries of the Christian era. That the reduction of Latin as a sacral tongue might unintentionally lead to something like a federation of national Catholic churches, does not seem to trouble the German clergy nor the Pope.

How long is it since Philipp Melanchthon, Luther's friend and collaborator, said: "Let us beware of quenching the spirit of God," and sat down at Regensburg with Roman Catholic theologians in an effort to heal the breach in Christendom? For the first time in four centuries groups of Roman Catholic and Reformed theologians gather week after week in the Netherlands and Germany for discussions and prayers for the Holy Spirit's guidance. In one Catholic church after the other congregations were heard to sing psalms in the German language and in the lovely plainsong cadences. In many places also went up the prayer, "Jesus Christ, Saviour and Redeemer, have pity upon us and upon the world. Have in remembrance thy Christian people everywhere, and bring together what is divided."*

On June 12,** Maurice Cardinal Feltin, Archbishop of Paris, was received in audience at the Vatican and met with him who, as

---

* *Jesus Christus, Heiland und Erloeser, erbarme dich ueber uns und ueber die ganze Welt. Gedenke deiner Christenheit und fuehre zusammen was getrennt ist. Amen.*

** New York *Times*, June 12, 1959.

Angelo Cardinal Roncalli of Venice, and with Professor Giorgio La Pira, "the Savonarola man," were the animators of the annual "Religious Conversations" in Paris. These men, curiously enough, were also amongst the most disconsolate over the censuring of the Worker-Priest movement in France in 1954 when the anguished cry went up from the midst of the *prêtres-ouvriers* themselves: "Are the historical mistakes of the Borgia era relating to Savonarola to be made all over again?"*

The expectations of the latter-day friends and followers of Savonarola are raised to new heights by events under the pontificate of John XXIII. It is their hope and prayer that a new breath of the Spirit may go forth from the Ecumenical Council to blow the smouldering embers into life again. Being very approachable the Pope will certainly be approached anew by "the Savonarola men" in the clergy and laity. To them, as to others, John XXIII is *Pontifex Maximus,* literally the Chief Bridgebuilder. Realizing that it is neither desirable nor possible to transfer the passions of one age to the controversies of another, they will nonetheless venture to ask whether Savonarola's life, teaching and martyrdom may not serve as building material in the bridge which the Pope is said to plan to throw towards the separated brethren? The Friar's beatification, frequently deferred but never definitely rejected, would, in their estimation, be a still stronger gesture of conciliation than Joan of Arc's canonization, the effect of which was restricted to the French national scene alone. . . .

In any case, whether the endeavors of "the Savonarola men" are brought to a prosperous consummation or not, it cannot be denied that the Friar continues his hold on the minds of men of the most diversified philosophies and antecedents. That hold is strong and enduring. Nothing weakens it, neither time nor distance, neither the revolution of opinion nor the fall of empires. However, since "the wings of all men's lives are plumed with the feathers of death," Savonarola cannot come to us, unless we make a reverent attempt, as here is done, to penetrate to him, bring him out of the shadows into the light of day, and show how strangely he was fitted for his great task.

* *Les Prêtres Ouvriers, Documents, Editions de Minuit,* Paris, 1954.

A CROWN OF FIRE

The Life and Times

of Girolamo Savonarola

Chapter I

Girolamo's Youth:
The Flight from Ferrara

WHEN Niccolo Savonarola, a prominent citizen of Ferrara, decided on a medical career for his third son, the still very young but precociously studious Girolamo, he followed a firmly established family tradition. Not only had there been at least one renowned physician bearing the Savonarola name in each of the preceding five or six generations, but the boy's undeniably superior mental attainments indicated him as the most promising successor to his grandfather, Ser Michele Savonarola, one of the ablest medical practitioners in all Italy.

Ser Michele's fondness for Girolamo and his delight in the boy's brilliance prompted him to take the education of his favorite grandson personally in hand. The result was that Girolamo wrote Latin as fluently at the age of ten as Erasmus of Rotterdam, that other nurseling of immortality who was his contemporary. He was an imaginative and reflective child, full of the wonder in which philosophy begins. His vast knowledge which was one day to astonish those two most wondrously erudite men of the Renaissance, Pico della Mirandola and Machiavelli, the boy acquired by endless reading. By sympathetic intuition too he always perceived a great deal more than the ordinary reader. In the formation of his mind, however, no influence was so direct, so persuasive, and of such lasting character, as his grandfather's. Girolamo's most impressionable years, up to the age of seventeen, were for the most part spent in

Ser Michele's library which, together with a small laboratory or pharmacy, was located in the rear of the house occupied by the Savonarolas in one of Ferrara's principal streets.

The widowed Ser Michele settled in Ferrara upon invitation of Duke Niccolo III of the ruling House of Este. He brought with him five sons, three of whom are known to have become priests. It was with his youngest son Niccolo and his daughter-in-law Elena, and their seven children, that Ser Michele eventually made his home. Before coming to Ferrara he practiced medicine in Padua and taught in that city's university whence his fame had spread throughout Italy and even beyond the Alps into Germany and France.

Called for a consultation to Rome one day, it was freely, though in a few instances grudgingly, acknowledged by the master physicians gathered at the Pope's bedside, that under Ser Michele's treatment the reigning Pontiff's perplexing illness had given way to a complete and permanent restoration of health. In recognition of these services the Holy Father, Nicholas V, bestowed on Michele Savonarola the grand cross of a knight of the Order of the Holy Sepulchre. When the Savonarolas shortly thereafter moved to Ferrara the Duke made a still more generous donation. He gave Ser Michele a house inside the city and another in the country on the left bank of the river Po.

In addition to occupying the post of court physician at a stipend of 400 ducats* a year, Ser Michele held the chair of medicine at the University of Ferrara. He was the author of a textbook on gynecology and on the maladies and treatment of infants. Strange to say, however, in the case of so eminent a physician, his most widely read book deals with a subject quite unrelated to medicine. It is a study of the prophetic vocation, the loneliness, and the tragedy of John the Baptist, who, as we are told in the gospel, was beheaded in the dungeon of Machaerus by order of Herod Antipas to please his queen whose adulterous conduct John had criticized.

Another work from Ser Michele's quill bears the title: *About the Therapy in Cases where Bodily Sickness is brought on by Mental Distress and vice versa.* Though written in the fifteenth century it is a curious blend of psychiatric ingredients and religious values

---

* A ducat, *ducato d'oro,* in the fifteenth century, had a purchasing value of approximately $25 today.

such as our own time begins to envisage in ministering to minds troubled by confusion, grief, or feelings of guilt. Ser Michele held that without investigating a patient's secret thoughts, his impulses, and his dreams a physician was unable to do his best work. The doctor was a priest-physician whose first care should be the diagnosis of the soul and only afterwards the body.

Ser Michele was a perfect teacher. Very learned, fervently pious, of a gentle patience with children, but a firm believer in the rigorous scholastic method at least for the first few years, he drilled and grounded Girolamo thoroughly in Latin, grammar, and probably in Hebrew also. For the rest he followed his own method and curriculum which consisted not so much in trying to make a good citizen of the boy as to equip him with what the teacher regarded as the highest good in life: a free and open mind. The wise old scientist's main object was to develop his grandson's intellect and help unfold the young man's own budding thoughts and ideas. By allowing and urging his pupil to talk freely, he taught Girolamo at an early age to respond to his own youthful visions. In other words, he "quickened the instinct of great questions,"—the truest service of all.

What did they study besides the classical poets and the great Roman historians? We know that on Ser Michele's table "always open" lay "certain books of cosmography and geography," and that on the wall of his study hung a universal map. The period in which Girolamo received the most intensive instruction from his grandfather falls between the years 1458 and 1468. It was an age of voyages of discovery. A quarter century was still to elapse before Christopher Columbus announced the discovery of a new continent. But Marco Polo had already written of his astonishing journey to the land of Cathay. The Savonarolas read Marco Polo, but they also read Giovanni Carpini whose recital of the Mongols and Tartars filled the whole world with marvel and curiosity. Although Carpini's explorations lay full two hundred years in the past, his book of travels did not become generally accessible till some years after the invention of the art of printing. This occurred in 1440, one decade before Girolamo Savonarola's birth. Carpini was now in print and grandfather Michele had a Latin copy of his *Book of the Tartars*.

Teacher and pupil read how Carpini, one of the companions of St. Francis of Assisi, having been sent by the Pope to the court of Genghis Khan in the tent-city of Karakorum, traversed what are now the lands of the Soviet Union as far as Turkestan. He saw great Mohammedan cities on the banks of a river "of which the name is not known" (probably the Volga). Skirting the northern shores of the Caspian and Aral Sea, he finally landed in the camp of Batu, the Tartar conqueror of the Slavs and all eastern Europe.

Fra Carpini's book is the chief literary memorial of European overland expansion before Marco Polo. It first revealed the Mongol world to Catholic Christendom. It is thought that Pope Innocent IV sent the Franciscan monk on his phenomenal mission with the object of trying to win the Tartars as allies against the followers of Mohammed who were ravaging the fairest provinces of Christendom. If such was the object, Carpini failed: the Tartars never again emerged from their Mongolian wilderness: their empire went to pieces. But the monk produced a book on the country, the climate, the women, the manners, the religion, character, history, policy, and military tactics of the Tartars which remains absorbing reading till this day. What interested Ser Michele most in Carpini's recital was the custom of the Tartars to take a cure of horse milk when afflicted by symptoms of what modern medicine suspects to have been anemia or tuberculosis. Girolamo, on the other hand, a doughty pedestrian himself, thought the speed with which Carpini traveled an uncommon feat of endurance: crossing mountains, fording rivers, facing sand and snowstorms, sleeping on the bare ground, and doing a full 3000 miles in 106 days; a man sixty-five years of age accompanied only by his interpreter, the Franciscan friar, Benedict Polonus.

Other author-explorers read by Girolamo during the geography lesson told of starting from the top of the Persian Gulf and sailing up the Tigris and Euphrates in search of the site of the legendary Garden of Eden. The most fantastic tales were current on the customs, the habits, the religions, and the rulers of but recently discovered peoples. With a typically amused shrug of the shoulders Marco Polo was commonly called *Il Milione,* "the million man," because of the astronomical figures he cited in connection with the Kublai Khan's treasures. If you could believe Marco Polo you might as well believe others who boasted that in vaguely identified or nameless countries in the mysterious East they had seen trees bearing precious jewels as abundantly as Bergamo's orchards bore apples and pears.

It was not only from books that Girolamo acquired his information about the wonders of the world. The mail service in those days was a monopoly of the great banking houses such as that of the Medici of Florence who had branch offices not only in Ferrara, but in most European and in several Eastern countries. Couriers went to and fro between these countinghouses and the Florentine mother institution bringing reports on conditions, events, and personalities in Egypt, Persia, Armenia, and from as far away as China and India. These reports could be read at the Ferrarese branch of the Medici bank, while the Franciscans and the Dominicans, who each had a convent in Ferrara, supplied news on political and religious conditions in the Far and Near East through the missionaries of their Orders laboring in those distant parts.

Then there were the traders and hucksters from Venice, Pisa, Amalfi, Brindisi, and Genoa who came to sell their wares in Ferrara's market place. Their imagination heated by the heady wine of the region, these men could and often did tell tales that made young Girolamo's hair stand on end. Sailing on great carracks and galleons, they had penetrated into forbidden cities and had returned, sometimes after torture and prison, their eyes still smouldering with the memory of the glamor, the greed, and the danger of it all.

Some of the adventurers brought back with them strange and wondrous animals, giraffes, zebras, elephants, ostriches, camels and the like which they exhibited at the fairs and kermess festivals. Young Girolamo saw men and women of yellow, black, and blue skin, creatures of unbelievable bodily size and of the weirdest exotic features and mannerisms. For instance amongst the blue-skinned Tuaregs of the Atlas region the men wore veils instead of the women.

Long before Columbus solved the riddle, grandfather Michele wondered what lay beyond the immense expanse of water starting from Britain's and Ireland's western shores. In every country men speculated why ships sailing to the farthest horizon did not fall off the earth which was supposed to be a flat disc. But Martin Behaim,

the Savonarolas knew, had already made his "earth-apple," and by
1490 this representation of the globe, in spite of fierce ecclesiastical
opposition, was recognized by all reasonable men as a correct representation of the earth.

Ser Michele and his pupil pored over their map searching for the
mysterious land of Ophir whence, according to Holy Writ, Solomon
imported the gold for Jerusalem's temple and which nobody has
ever since found again or identified. Icebergs had been sighted as
far south as the English Channel. How did they come into existence?
Why did Vesuvius and Stromboli spit fire only once in so many
years? What natural law or precision instrument set the time for
these eruptions? Did those belching flames really originate in the
nether world of fire and brimstone which popular imagination
identified as the dwelling place of Satan?

Private citizens spent fortunes in research and in subsidizing the
travels of scholars like Guarno of Verona and Francesco Filelfo who
passed a lifetime in ransacking the old temples of Greece and Asia
Minor for literary and artistic treasures; scrolls, codices, statues,
archaeological fragments, and utensils and ornaments once used in
the cult of the pagan gods. In Girolamo's youth the rage for
antiquity was at its height. As the Turkish danger loomed larger
many of the Greek scholars sought refuge in the West. Most of
them took up residence in Florence where the Medici furnished
them with dwellings and paid them a pension.

When one of these learned refugees arrived, his reception did
not in any way yield the palm in splendor to that accorded the
Pope or the emperor. Cities were decorated for the occasion;
churches and palaces were illuminated and the strangers escorted
through the streets amidst the singing of choirs and the playing of
musical bands.

The Greeks lectured at the various universities, including the
famous school at Ferrara. Ser Michele eagerly took cognizance of
their travelogues and in turn communicated the newly gained information to his grandson. It is reported that the local Ferrarese
scholars and the learned visitors more than once got into such
violent disputes that they engaged in fisticuffs, a not altogether
contemptible circumstance perhaps if it shows us that they took
their study of the classics seriously in those days. Francesco Filelfo's

hair turned completely white overnight upon learning that a ship-load of manuscripts from Constantinople was lost in a storm at sea. Another time the safe arrival of a great collection of literary treasures from the East was celebrated by a solemn *Te Deum* service in the principal churches of Italy.

The Medici of Florence were not the only purchasers. Many of the treasures came to Ferrara where the Duke of Este was a col-lector of precious stones and ancient feminine ornaments, such as bracelets, jewel-studded girdles, and necklaces. Young Girolamo and his brothers and sisters, as the other children in the community, inspected the Duke's treasures on Ascension Day, when the cham-bers where the jewels were on display, were open to the public.

Military events in what is now called the Middle East were a subject of abiding interest to the young student of political geog-raphy. It was an interesting time in which Girolamo grew up, but it was also a fearful time. A cloud blacker and more portentous of disaster than the almost forgotten depradations of the Huns, Goths and Vandals, had appeared on the eastern horizon. A year after Girolamo's birth something occurred of which the awful memory, instead of diminishing with the passing years, grew steadily and spread consternation in ever wider circles. Girolamo's whole lifetime lies under that cloud.

In A.D. 1453, Constantinople, the empire's capital, fell before the onslaught of the Osmanli Turks. A feeling of horror passed through Christendom as Genoese soldiers and sailors, who stood on the ramparts in defense of the city, drifted back, sometimes after years of slavery on the Turkish galleys, and told of having seen the victorious Sultan, Mohammed II, step over the lifeless body of the last Roman emperor, Constantine XI, and wade through the blood of the slain to the high altar in the Basilica of the Sacred Wisdom to spit upon Christ's golden image.

All of the Italian cities went into mourning when the magnitude of the outrage was realized. In Bologna the bells which customarily tolled only when there was a death in the community, rang for a week. In Ferrara the Franciscans chanted the penitential psalms as in the Office for Good Friday when the candelabra are extinguished at the moment when the Redeemer breathes his last on the cross. Since more than a thousand of her bravest sons had perished in defense of the empire's capital, Genoa sat in sackcloth and ashes. From the Roman Curia came the mandate to insert into the litany: "From the fury of the Turk, good Lord, deliver us!" The universal lamentation was prolonged from year to year as reports about the Grand Turk's power and the cruelty and the swiftness of his armies gained the remotest hamlets.

Girolamo's eyes followed Ser Michele's finger as it traced on the map the line of march of the Turkish legions and the probable course of their war galleys reported to be cruising amongst the Aegean Islands and in the Adriatic. Here he was, the Sultan Mohammed II, here in Constantinople, desecrating the noblest church in Christendom* by using it as a stable for his horses, while he and the women of his harem occupied the Golden Studium where the Ecumenical Patriarchs preserved their inestimably valuable collections of precious books and codices. What might be the foe's next objective in a campaign which avowedly aimed at the forceful conversion of the whole world to the religion of the Prophet? Country after country passed under the Ottoman's sway: Bulgaria, Serbia, Albania, Greece. Were the Hungarians still holding out? No word had come from the brave Magyars in a decade.

Ser Michele's finger moved north on the map and then in one sweep back to the south. "There lies Vienna," he said, "and here is Rome!" He showed his grandson how the defenses of the West lay wide open to the flying columns of the Turkish cavalry.

The people of Ferrara were perhaps more deeply perturbed about the trend of world affairs than the inhabitants of many another Italian city. The reason was that they saw and heard the Pope speak to them of Constantinople's fall and the consequences stemming from that calamity. In 1458 the gentle Enea Silvio Piccolomini, who was that year elected to the pontificate as Pius II, came to Ferrara. The Pontiff was on his way to Mantua where he had summoned a Council under his own presidency to rouse the Christian powers to make war against the Infidel.

Pius II stopped in Ferrara for a week. Girolamo and all his family were in the cathedral when the Pope impressed upon the assembled citizens the extent of the disaster which had overtaken the Christian East. The followers of Mohammed, said Pius, had

* The present St. Peter's basilica in Rome was not built yet.

obliterated more than four hundred bishoprics and laid waste thousands of Christian churches in Asia Minor and North Africa. The best part of Spain, most of Sicily, Rhodes and Hellas, and all the islands of the Mediterranean, languished under the yoke of the Moslem conquerors. Jerusalem lay in ruins. The Church of the Holy Sepulchre, containing the Saviour's tomb, had been turned into a brothel for the Janizaries.

Were the faithful Ferrarese aware, the Pope asked, that those countries where the Infidel had triumphed were the very vineyards of the Lord where once labored the holy apostles? In the great basilicas of Antioch, Alexandria, Salonika, and Athens, where St. Paul, St. Thomas, and St. Philip had gone before, where St. John the Divine, the beloved disciple had been a bishop, as well as the golden-tongued St. Chrysostom and St. Athanasius, the father of orthodoxy, everywhere in the East the light of the Gospel was extinguished. The voices of the sainted bishops and martyrs had been replaced by the raucous cry of the muezzin of Islam. Stilled was the sublime chant of the robed choirs in Constantinople's Hagia Sophia which, when they first heard it, made the heathen emissaries of the Duke of Kiev wonder whether they were in heaven or on earth.* The holy altars were bare or demolished, the golden lamps had ceased to burn. . . . Perhaps forever!

The Pope wept. The clergy and the congregation sobbed. Women wrung their hands in despair. But the silver trumpets blared, the gold-caparisoned mule was brought to the door and the Pontiff rode off to Mantua. The council convoked in that city was not less shocked than the people of Ferrara. But as in Ferrara nothing was done. Everywhere the Pope's appeal for a crusade fell on deaf ears. Not a single Italian city promised aid. Was this because the princes and the captains of the hosts were paralyzed with fear? Not so! The Italians never showed much interest in the crusades. They were merely waiting to resume doing business with the Grand Turk and preferred leaving the fighting to others.

Occasionally, it is true, a sense of impending doom swept through the country and the panic-striken multitudes streamed to the

---

* An incident of the highest historical significance in that it decided the Duke to introduce the Christian religion in Russia and to baptize his subjects in their tens of thousands in the Dnieper.

churches. Such was the case in A.D. 1485 when Girolamo was thirty-three years of age. In that year the Turks landed an army at Otranto and captured 15,000 citizens whom they immured and thus consigned to death by starvation. Before re-embarking they executed the city's archbishop in the public square by placing him between two planks and sawing his body in twain.

In later years Girolamo vividly remembered the Pope's visit. But he never made mention of the dramatic sermon he heard in the cathedral. Not that he was unmoved by the Pontiff's eloquence and tears. The boy was deeply impressed. He wept like everybody else. But one circumstance in connection with the Pope's visit inflicted such a lasting hurt upon his own and even more upon grandfather Michele's sensibilities that he could never refer to the incident without a sense of annoyance and shame.

This is what happened: when Pius II arrived in Ferrara he was met by a train of young girls dressed in white, singing a hymn of welcome. The maidens strewed rose petals on the Pope's path. Rich tapestries hung from the windows and balconies and the principal streets were carpeted with cloth. Headed by the Archbishop of Ferrara and followed by the clergy wearing their richest copes, the procession, which started from the banks of the Po, moved to the ducal palace, the Castello, in the center of the city.

After the massed banners of the people came the Pope under a canopy of gold brocade. What aroused Ser Michele's indignation was not the riot of color and pomp in the Holy Father's entourage. He knew that Pius II, the first of the humanist popes, loved luster and magnificence. But he did call it a scandal and a provocation that the municipality had stripped the palaces of their statues for the occasion and placed them along the route taken by the papal procession. These statues were the nude images of the Greek gods and goddesses of antiquity. One marble Aphrodite, the goddess of wanton love, a marvel of erotic allure, was carried right before His Holiness as he blessed the people.

Was this a thing to permit in the Christian city of Ferrara, in the presence of St. Peter's successor? Wasn't this an affront to the Christian conscience, this return of paganism under the most exalted auspices? Ser Michele was beside himself with resentment.

All his days Girolamo remembered the puritan sternness which lay at the root of his grandfather's anger on that occasion.

In later life Girolamo often referred with praise and reverence to his grandfather's methods of instruction. But he also made one surprising disclosure. In those nightly dialogues in Ser Michele's study, they had allowed their interest to roam freely from the history of Greece and Rome to the flowering of art and learning in Italy and from these points to nearly every subject under the sun, but of the possibility or the desirability of a medical career for his grandson the old doctor had never breathed a word.

Their attention had always been concentrated upon the one subject which really mattered in Ser Michele's estimation, that is, the Sacred Scriptures as the history of God's dealings with man throughout the ages. Usually they left their study of the Bible till the last because it was their chief delight. Many a morning their reading and discussions were not broken off till the first peep of dawn. At the age of twenty Girolamo knew the Bible so thoroughly that he was able to continue quoting by heart from any verse of which someone else had spoken the first three or four words.

It was not principally a love of learning which Ser Michele sought to inculcate. Belles-lettres, history, arithmetic, and geography merely served as a ladder to higher things. In that curious work on John the Baptist which the professor wrote only two years before his death he addressed himself directly to his grandson. His object was to instill a sense of vocation in Girolamo. Ser Michele did not live to see his grandson take up the religious life, but with that book he definitely set the categories of thought and action for the young man.

The professor wrote in a highly original manner* how John the Baptist left his father's house at the early age of seven to prepare himself to preach penitence to the Jewish people. His parents, Zachary and Elizabeth, were inconsolable to lose their only child. "But," wrote Ser Michele, "they should not have been inasmuch as the child was entering upon the service of God which should

---

* The amazing aspect of this book is Ser Michele's intimation that John the Baptist entered a convent. Was he aware of the existence of such monastic communities in the Holy Land of 2000 years ago as was brought to light by the discoveries near Qumram on the Dead Sea in 1950?

never be a cause for grief. Parents whose children take up the conventual life should rejoice rather than weep. . . ."

In his early manhood Girolamo felt himself called to the same prophetic task as John. His parents were distressed beyond words by his departure for the monastery. They were told to dry their tears and be glad that their son had become a knight of Jesus Christ . . . In the end Girolamo Savonarola suffered as tragic a fate as John the Baptist and virtually for the same reasons. . . .

All his life Girolamo carried on his person a small notebook containing a number of precepts written by his grandfather's hand. The words of one of these precepts which he was to repeat from the pulpit of Florence, may well have contributed more than any other circumstance or act on his part to his undoing and his disastrous end. "Neither the popes," wrote Ser Michele and Girolamo quoted, "nor their vicars have the right to teach anything contrary to the things instituted by God . . . I say this for those who pretend to find an excuse for their unworthy conduct in what they are pleased to call the broader view of life and doctrine . . . God's law is strict: 'strait is the gate and narrow is the way that leadeth unto life and few that be who find it. . . .' "

There was no doubt in his hearers' minds that Girolamo had his eye on the Borgia pope, Alexander VI, when he spoke these words.

Ser Michele's generous patron, Duke Niccolo III, died within a year after the professor's arrival in Ferrara. Although his illegitimate son and successor, Lionello, and after him Borso, continued the stipend of 400 ducats, the relationship with the court was no longer as friendly as it once had been. He may have been a phenomenal philanderer, but Duke Niccolo was also a scholar. He was as ardent a Bible student as Ser Michele. On the other hand, Borso was a knave and a fool, a blasphemer and a collector of pornographic books and pictures. The puritanical-minded Ser Michele could not get along with him. He asked to be released of his duties as court physician in order to devote himself wholly to his professorship and his writing.

In spite of the fact that he was loaded with honors, both by the Vatican and by a number of Italian ruling houses, none can recollect the slightest sympton of arrogance or vanity in Ser Michele. His bodily presence at eighty-three was still attractive, spare in build, his voice low and harmonious, his eye sympathetic and responsive. His evident love of truth and justice made him a great favorite with the poor from whom he never exacted payment either for his professional services or for the lotions, poultices, unguents and other medicaments which he and his grandson prepared in the little pharmacy in the rear of the house. His intellectual interests were ever widening and his study of the Bible never lost its intensity. He died in his sleep in the autumn of 1468 and was found with one finger wedged between the pages of the Book of Isaiah.

*   *

Unlike Ser Michele, his son Niccolo, Girolamo's father, followed no definite trade or profession. He appears to have been one of those men who, in Doctor Johnson's subtle phrase, hung loose upon society. He is reported to have carried a jeweled sword by his side and, like Joseph in the Book of Genesis, to have decked himself in a cloak of many colors. A good part of the family fortune and the totality of his wife's dowry were lost by Niccolo in reckless speculations. He also suffered a serious financial loss in a business venture of an undisclosed nature. The business may have been the wool trade since the Savonarolas, before coming to Ferrara, are known to have made their modest fortune in that line.

Niccolo and his wife and their family of seven children lived wholly upon grandfather Michele's bounty. After her husband's death, we find Donna Elena calling on her son Girolamo for financial help. A letter has been preserved in which she intimates that she feels quite unequal to the hardships and miseries besetting her. The house had been sold to pay her late husband's debts, the country home also had passed into the hands of moneylenders.

But all that comes later. In his lifetime, Donna Elena's husband enjoyed a reputation as a fine talker and a reciter of poetry, some of it, although trivial and lacking in talent and discipline, of his own composition. He frequently joined his father and his son Girolamo in the professor's study where his presence introduced a spirit of gayety and hilarity, a not unwelcome change perhaps from the habitually somber or at least grave tenor of the older man's animadversions. It was difficult to be dull in Niccolo's company for he was the prince of conversers. Girolamo was very fond of his father, as were all the children. It was, in fact, quite impossible not to conceive an affection for him. In spite of his oddities in dress and manner, perhaps because of them, Niccolo was and always remained a welcome visitor at the ducal court. For a brief time, probably not for longer than a year, he appears to have borne the title of poet laureate of Ferrara bestowed upon him by Duke Borso.

It is known that Niccolo Savonarola rushed into moods of exalted optimism and then just as suddenly fell into fits of despair. Yet, all the time he was eloquent. His pessimism was therefore hardly more than theoretical. Courtesy interpenetrated all that he said and did with a subtle fragrance. For what he lacked in industry he made up in ambitious projects. The only trouble with Niccolo was that he enjoyed life too thoroughly to concentrate upon the fulfillment of his plans, in other words, he was so busy that he virtually did nothing. . . .

His wife, Elena, sprang from the illustrious family of the Bonacossi of Mantua, which still survives and has given its name to one of the great printing houses of Italy. Donna Elena was a typical Italian matron, one of those strong masterful women of good education under whose influence the family was brought up in the atmosphere of traditional piety. She kept the fasts, went to church, read the Fathers and the lives of the saints, and gave hospitality to strangers. Donna Elena had the same russet colored hair as her son Girolamo and the same deep-set eyes. She was taller than her husband and carried herself with a dignity bespeaking her noble ancestry. From a perusal of Girolamo's letters it is clear that the son looked upon his mother as a woman of serene intellect, wide culture, and decided force of character. She taught all her seven children to sing, a not too difficult achievement one would imagine in a land where the flowers grow to extravagant beauty and the air is filled with the melodies of voice and instrument the lifelong day.

What songs did the Savonarola family sing? There were several popular song books in existence: the Hymns of Cortona, for instance, and the more plebeian collection called the Manual of Bologna. Ever since St. Francis of Assisi, the divine warbler, sang in sacred gratitude of the marvelous beauty of God's creation, the violas, the lutes, and the voices of all Italy thrilled in passionate harmony with his Hymn to the Sun. The people of Italy had become an immense choir of melodists and choralists. To St. Francis the Umbrian landscape was a true earthly paradise. He made all Italy sing of it. He spoke freely with the beasts of the field whom he called brothers and sisters. During winter he had pots of honey put out for the bees. A young hare caught in a trap and brought to him leaped into his arms and then, set free, followed his footsteps like a dog. A grasshopper chirping on a tree branch near his window, when called by him, perched on his head. "Sing my little sister grasshopper," said St. Francis, "and praise God with your happy song!"

What better songs could the Savonarolas sing than these canticles of joy and light, of beauty and nature? *Veni Maggio, regina di fiori!* "Come, O May, queen of flowers!" Every night they followed the advice of St. Francis: *Laudate sia, Dio mio Signore, con tutte le creature!* "Let praise be given unto thee, O Lord my God, by all thy creatures!"

Apart from the records concerning her third son, Girolamo, who was to achieve world celebrity, history is very sparing in details about Elena's other six children. All we know is that the eldest, Ognibene, followed a military career; the second son, Bartolomeo, was an architect; Marco became a priest and eventually took the habit of a Dominican friar in Florence under the name of Fra Maurelio, while the youngest, Alberto, rose to eminence as a physician and surgeon. Of her two daughters, the eldest Beatrice, remained at home unmarried, and the second daughter, Clara, after the early death of her husband, became housekeeper for her doctor brother Alberto.

* * *

Present-day visitors to Italy see a land of precise geographic limits and national union, a country of one people, one language, one single public authority using the same or very similar methods of law enforcement in every town and hamlet. In Girolamo Savonarola's time, the Appenine Peninsula contained a score of principalities, dukedoms, marquisates, republics, city-states, and kingdoms, some so lilliputian as not to exceed the present principality of

Monaco in size. In his writings Savonarola never speaks of Italy as one country or one people; he uses the plural: "Italian countries," or he says "these Italian peoples." Italy then was brimful of purely local patriotisms.

Because of the absence of a central authority, the Italian city-states were as self-centered as those of ancient Greece. They stood by themselves. A town like Ferrara did business and had diplomatic relations with all the other cities, but it lived a life of its own, had its own usages, customs, tastes, and traditions and even costumes. Ferrara was as proud and jealous of its own ways as Florence and Naples were of theirs. The one thing they had in common was their profession of a special recognition of the supremacy of religion. This does not mean, however, that they were not frequently at odds, and even at war, with the Pope.

All those Italian "countries" and "peoples" were mad with the delirium of nationality. They were armed to the teeth not only against foreign invaders but against each other. The cities themselves were often divided into mutually hostile camps; and, worse still, not only districts and boroughs, but neighboring houses and mansions were pitted against each other. For example, the ten or twelve so-called "fighting towers" in the community of San Gimignano, those square piles of brick standing no further apart than a few dozen yards, are all that remains of fifty or sixty similar fortified places from which fellow citizens and neighbors carried on regularly irregular hostilities against each other. But one glance at the great palaces of Florence, once the dwelling places of the Medici, the Strozzi, the Pitti, and other prominent families shows that these mansions were intended to serve as fortified strong places should the necessity arise, as indeed it did more than once in the course of the city's tumultuous history.

While Girolamo pursued his studies at Ferrara, the Duke of Calabria fought a long and bloody campaign against the papal army commanded by Roberto Malatesta. Florence was at war with Pisa, Genoa with Milan, Bologna with Mantua, while Ferrara itself was severely damaged by a Venetian expeditionary force. Not one of these endlessly warring principalities ever succeeded in establishing a complete predominance over the others. One Pope, the consummate diplomat Rodrigo Borgia, who succeeded to the tiara in the year 1492 under the name of Alexander VI, came nearest unifying the country in a league of Italian states. It was Girolamo Savonarola who frustrated the Pope's design by keeping the Florentine Republic out of the national alliance and taking the side of the King of France. Italy had to wait four hundred years before the genius of Cavour, the idealism of Mazzini, and the heroism of Garibaldi brought about the triumph of the brotherhood of all Italians and forged the peoples of the Peninsula into the nation one and indivisible we know today.

The two civil wars in Ferrara during Girolamo's youth were of such savagery and cruelty that contemporary chroniclers compare them with the times and methods of Nero and Caligula. Invariably these civil wars spilled over into the countryside where the Ferrarese had their farms and then the peasants had a hard time of it. If they fled, their poor hutches of twigs and loam were set on fire. If they mustered up enough courage to stay and see it through, they could never be sure that their lives would be spared by either friend or foe. The records show that before pulling out after victory or defeat the commanders of one or the other contending armies would give their troops full license to do with the peasants as they pleased. What this meant for the girls and women can easily be imagined. But the men scarcely fared any better. By way of sport the soldiers often flayed the peasants alive or smeared their bodies with pitch before setting them on fire.

But the dumb sheep were not always content with the manner of shearing. Sometimes the peasants took things in their own hands. When their homes and granaries were destroyed and their women kidnaped, those who managed to escape would band together and attack the nearest castle or monastery with pitchforks, flails, and firebrands. Though not permanently organized on a military basis in support of this or that rival bishop, as was the case in the Eastern empire, the monks would in turn retaliate. On all sides reprisals were as savage as the blood feuds of the Arabian desert. The spoils of war were the highest wages obtainable in that era. Of compassion or humaneness nobody seems to have had an inkling. Why take prisoners and have so many extra mouths to feed? Unless a good price could be obtained for ransom, a man's captors generally made short shrift of him. The country roads were so unsafe that one of Girolamo's contemporaries could truthfully write: "The roads are deathtraps full of ambushes and cutthroats; the country-side is a perpetual battlefield; one war doesn't end before another starts; it is almost impossible to distinguish friend from foe."

We do not need the testimony of Girolamo's father who complained that the streets of Ferrara resembled a cesspool. All the commentators and travelers of that age are in agreement on this point, and not only with regard to Ferrara. In London, Cardinal Wolsey walked around with an orange pressed to his nose. "I acquired the habit in Rome," he told his royal master, Henry VIII, thus inadvertently giving both capitals a malodorous reputation. An unimpeachable witness, Erasmus, the perennial traveler, avers that virtually the whole of Europe was filled with a detestable odor. He made an exception of the city of Basel where he found good air in a house on a cliff overlooking the Rhine.

In Ferrara the street cleaning was, in Lombroso's phrase, entrusted to the rains of heaven and the voracity of the pigs. Everything was thrown into the streets, dead cats, old clothes, household offal of all sorts. The privies, small stone cubicles built in on the street side of the houses, emptied through a slit in the wall into the streets. An odor of putrefaction pervaded all the public thoroughfares. When they could afford it, people burned incense or aromatic spices to neutralize or overcome the stench.

Except for the more or less new and spacious Corso Vittorio Emanuele, the Viale Cavour and the Corso di Porta Po, which were cut through a mass of structures dating from the Middle Ages, the outward appearance of Ferrara does not greatly differ from what it was in young Savonarola's time. In his day, however, the population numbered 100,000 souls, whereas today it has shrunk to half that size. According to William Ewart Gladstone, Ferrara was a ghost city in the middle of the nineteenth century with grass growing in the streets. Mussolini, who, among other things, made the trains run on time, also speeded up the industrialization of Ferrara. The city has a sugar refinery and a few small factories today. In the matter of taxation, however, Signor Mussolini dealt in as ruthless a totalitarian manner as once the Dukes of the ruling House of Este.

In Girolamo's time, the Ferrarese paid taxes on real estate, on footwear, on firewood, on salt, on horses and mules, on the number of windows in their houses, on chimneys, on spurs, on leather and silken belts; further, on bread, on linen and cloth, on vegetables, on wine, on grease, on candles, on bricks, on meat, and on the bordellos. If for some reason or other a citizen was unable to pay these imposts, all his goods were confiscated and the ducal sergeants carted off everything down to the last pots and pans and the bed he slept on. And still these people were expected to, and did, cry: *Viva il Duca,* "Long live the Duke!" when they caught sight of one of those monsters of the ruling family driving about in a jewel-studded carriage. That these princes owed any duty to their subjects never entered their minds.

At the palace they ate pastries of "the most marvelous hues and colors." But the bread the common people ate was black. The Savonarolas could and often did eat, like the peasants, from the intestines and the heads of sheep, cattle, and hogs which were slaughtered and dressed on the farms and delivered to the city for consumption by the members of the upper crust.

In order to escape the tax on chimneys, the country folk and the poor simply did without them. Like the *fellaheen* in the Arabian hinterland they made a hole in the roof or in the wall to let the smoke of the braziers and cookstoves escape. As a result the interior of the peasant huts and the dwellings of the urban proletariat turned pitch black with the fumes. Eye disease was a permanent scourge amongst the Italian peasantry as it remains in the Arabian countries till this day. Glass was a costly luxury and in most of the poorer houses in Ferrara the window frames were fitted with oiled paper or parchment.

Boys like Girolamo wore a coarse linen tunic or smock with a leather belt. Sometimes this jerkin was of cloth or velvet, depending on the financial circumstances and social standing of the wearer. Knee-length cloaks with wide sleeves generally black or brown in color were not worn by men till they reached the age of forty or fifty. The chroniclers are unanimous in awarding the *filles de joie* the prize for being the best-dressed persons in the community. In Ferrara these girls went so far that the municipal authorities felt obliged to draft and impose a set of "vestimentary regulations." Lest the harlots be taken for respectable women, they were forbidden to wear jewels, gold- or silver-colored belts, embroidered blouses and jackets, and garments lined with fur.

The temptation to look like a grand dame being stronger than the fear of punishment, the antiluxury bylaws were often broken. In 1475, the year Girolamo left Ferrara, a certain Yolanda Maria, surnamed *La Bella,* because of her "comely features" and "exquisite figure," was brought before the magistrates sitting under a cypress tree in the public square. She was forced to submit, says the old book kept by the bailiff, as the lace collar was cut from her gown and the fur from her jacket while her silver belt was confiscated and sent to the local hospital to be sold at auction for charitable purposes. La Bella was also warned to put less perfume on her hair. By way of helping her in this direction, her golden locks were clipped by the assistant hangman's scissors to the great amusement of a crowd of bystanders.

People take their amusement where they find it. The Ferrarese found theirs in the streets. Like everybody else the Savonarolas were very fond of clowns and trapeze artists, of jugglers, weight lifters, ambulant street singers, and the like. Monkeys, trained birds, and bears never failed to attract large crowds. Although the Church frowned on the exhibition of dancing bears on the principle that such shows tend to ridicule the human personality and inferentially make sport of the divine in man, no formal prohibition was ever imposed. Passing monks and priests laughed as heartily at the comical antics of the beasts as the laity.

In mid-Lent came carnival with jousts and games and masquerades. Booths ranged around the Grand Piazza dispensed wines and ale, white bread and sweets. Once or twice a year, generally around Easter or Ascension Day or some other church festival, the people were treated to a morality play. Scenes from the Passion or the Nativity were re-enacted. New Testament figures walked the streets of Ferrara and were greeted with respectful murmurs and deep curtsies, especially by the women. One of the members of the Savonarola clan, probably one of Girolamo's uncles, one year played the role of Joseph of Arimathea, the rabbi who asked Pontius Pilate for permission to bury the body of Jesus. The figure of Judas Iscariot, carrying around his neck the rope with which the traitorous disciple is said to have hanged himself, was hissed and copiously spat upon and not seldom pummeled with fists and sticks till he had to flee lest worse befall him. As everywhere else in Europe the most popular actor in Ferrara's morality play was the man made up to look like the devil. When he came in sight, black mask, horns, forked tail and all, and belching sulphur smoke from his mouth and nostrils, the joy of the spectators knew no bounds. A monk, walking immediately behind, belabored the fiend's padded posterior with a staff four feet long and three inches thick. At every blow the crowd roared its approval. It is recorded that one year, probably in sight of the Savonarola children, the actor representing the Saviour, bearing a huge wooden cross, collapsed under its weight and had to be taken to the hospital where he died in great agony a few hours after admission.

The court and the nobility, the prelates, the judges, and other persons of mark with their ladies, watched these performances from seats in the grandstand bedecked with banners and bunting and baskets of flowers. The Savonarolas stood in the streets and probably enjoyed themselves as well as their betters. Musical bands enlivened the proceedings, and in the evening, by the light of torches, a famous actor would declaim from Petrarch, Ariosto, or Boccaccio or a troupe of cantors sang those arias which are the forerunners of modern opera.

What the authorities were particularly on the alert for, but never succeeded in stamping out, was the practice of sorcery and necromancy. Love philters, aphrodisiacs, and magic powders such as mandragora and the root of belladonna were clandestinely peddled and widely used. A certain concoction named *rue* (ruta graveolens) which came in the form of pills was burned to make the shades of the departed come back and reveal themselves to the living. This stuff seems to have had a double-barreled effect, for it was also recommended for priests who wished to observe their vow of continence. There are trials on record where men and women were accused of having mixed the ashes of executed criminals with the blood of newborn infants or with the sacred elements of the Host which they administered to persons whom they wished to drive insane. Waxen dolls were sold by witches for the purpose of punishing conjugal infidelity. The purchaser merely needed to stick a pin into the doll and the absent husband, wife or lover would in the same instant feel an acute pain in the heart, the stomach, the head, or whatever region of the body corresponded with the place where the pin penetrated the doll.

As everywhere else, the heaviest punishment was reserved for those accused and convicted of witchcraft. It was not for soothsaying or fortunetelling that the witches were done to death, but for flying off on a broomstick to attend an obscene sabbath in the sky in the devil's company. Nor was it the Church which inaugurated the prosecution of witches. The common people feared that divine vengeance would descend on a community if diabolical arts were tolerated within its confines. For this reason it was the people who insisted that these poor women be tortured and dispatched with the fullest possible measure of suffering.

Learned, pious, and reasonable though he undoubtedly was, Ser Michele Savonarola placed great importance on charms and periapts or amulets. Every member of the Savonarola family wore an amulet. The charms were written on parchment and worn in a medallion around the neck as protection against evil spirits and dangers of travel, water, enemy, or arms. The words on the parchment were often the four Hebrew letters signifying the name of God or a quotation from the Cabala or the Bible. The ink was made of the ashes of incense and consecrated tapers mixed with holy water. Girolamo wore an amulet close to the skin containing the herb of heliotrope which was considered a most potent protection against black magic. Even contemporary rationalists like Lorenzo de' Medici and Pico della Mirandola paid a good deal of attention to astrologers, tokens in the sky, omens and forebodings, and good luck charms. Pope Alexander VI was greatly upset one day when, dining at a country villa, he discovered that he had left his jeweled amulet at home. "This means that I am in danger," he said. He wasn't wrong: he died after draining a cup of poisoned wine which, it is said, had been prepared for someone else.

*   *   *   *

Night life is the true life in the cities of modern Italy, but it was not yet so in the Ferrara of Girolamo Savonarola's youth. Except for father Niccolo, who spent an evening now and then at the court in the company of the Duke and his household wits, none of the members of the Savonarola family ventured outdoors after sunset. There were several reasons for this: for one thing the now ubiquitous *carabinieri* had not as yet made their colorful appearance on the scene. Secondly, there was no street lighting to speak of. An occasional votive lamp beneath a saint's statue on a street corner hardly illumed the façade of the house to which it was attached. When an open-air jollification or public festival was prolonged after dark, a few pitch torches or barrels were set on fire in the main square. For the rest the whole labyrinth of narrow and crooked streets, crossing and crisscrossing in all directions, remained steeped in stygian gloom.

Every door in Ferrara was locked and bolted and every window covered with heavy wooden shutters. When for unavoidable reasons a citizen was compelled to go out after sunset, he generally took a servant along who, walking backwards—as is still the custom in Addis Ababa and other African cities—carried a candlelit lantern to guide his master's footsteps. Other servants trailed behind armed with clubs to keep off footpads and cutthroats. The streets of Ferrara were no place for misunderstandings after dark, the knife decided promptly who was right or wrong. Citizens without servants simply took their lives in their hands.

Burglaries were so frequent that people laughed and joked about them, as well they might considering the robbers' original methods of operation. A gang would select a house, generally one whose owners were absent on a journey, and start to break down the doors or the shuttered windows. Such preliminaries took a little time and might be interrupted by a party of late homegoers. If anyone appeared on the scene, one of the burglars would promptly intone a tender love song, accompanied by the lute. A companion in crime, acting as lookout, would approach the strangers and explain to them that a certain nobleman was serenading his ladylove. But the nobleman must remain strictly incognito of course. If the chance passers-by continued on their way they would not only disturb the idyll, they might produce a social scandal by discovering and disclosing the lover's identity. So, please *signori,* have the goodness to observe discretion! As men of honor, show your understanding of the situation by going back or taking another way home.

Then there was a burst of laughter and much bowing and scraping, and the burglars resumed the honorable business at hand. Everyone in Ferrara was aware of this serenading stratagem. According to the old town records, the burglars usually did such a thorough job that they left nothing behind in the pilfered houses but the straw from the sleeping sacks. . . .

When an illness occurred in the ducal family or amongst the courtiers during the night, Ser Michele, the court physician, had to be fetched by an armed guard and did not go home till morning. He had a room in one of those famous towers of red brick in the Castello, the palace of the ruling House of Este (the provincial government building today), which looked more like a grim bastille than a royal residence.

At home Ser Michele seldom spoke of what he saw and heard in the ducal salons and bedchambers. As a Christian of the old stamp, he felt a strong distaste for the moral climate prevailing at the court. He could ill bear the sight, he once remarked, of bishops and cardinals diverting themselves and dancing *la gaillarde* with the ladies in waiting. Even more than his father, Duke Borso was crazily fond of festivities and hilarity, and his taste and money set the tone and the pace for a host of friends, courtiers and guests.

From six or seven o'clock onward, when the crystal chandeliers were lit and the chianti flowed in torrents, the palace was turned into a bedlam of music and ribaldry. The night brought no respite, the dancers were unwearied and the musicians showed no sign of exhaustion. Troubadours sang ballads of a phenomenal obscenity. In a cabinet next to the Chamber of the Dawn, so called because of its frescoes representing the four stages of the day: dawn, noon, evening, and night, may still be seen three huge paintings showing *The Bacchanalia* from the hand of Garofalo and his school. The scenes shown in these paintings are but a pale reflection of what once went on in the ducal palace.

Bands of harpists and lutists played in the Neapolitan chamber where boisterous crowds gorged themselves on the viands and wines from the Duke's well-laid tables and sideboards. On a stage set against a bucolic background the legends of the Greek gods and goddesses were re-enacted with breath-taking realism. Sometimes there were plays from Plautus or Terence or pantomimes from the

Apocryphal books such as *Susanna and the Elders* or from Solomon's *Song of Songs,* but the representations from Greek mythology were the most favored. The wives and daughters of the nobility vied with each other for the roles of the heroines and divinities of antiquity. Nymphs, fauns and satyrs danced and reveled in the nude. Actors and actresses revealed the secrets of the imperial alcoves and of the temples of sacred prostitution which stood in every major city before the advent of Christianity. The scenes of gallantry, eroticism, and perversion which disgraced the courts of a Tiberius or a Messalina were revived and the lascivious stories once current in the stews of ancient Rome were retold with utter frankness. The play acting at the Este court consisted in the perpetration of all that was impure and shameless and the renunciation of every lingering spark of decency.

That tale which, according to Ovid's Metamorphosis "was for a long time the talk of heaven" where Mars and Venus, tired from playing the game of love fall asleep in each others' arms, never failed to evoke the wildest applause. When Vulcan, the outraged husband steals up on the unsuspecting couple and traps them in a net "of fine links of bronze" and Mount Olympus shakes with the laughter of the gods over the plight of the helplessly imprisoned pair of lovers, the ladies and gentlemen of the Ferrarese nobility danced for joy.

As a physician Ser Michele could not always remain uninvolved in the conversations carried on in that milieu where sex was quite seriously regarded and spoken of as a sort of medication to be taken in large doses. In the correspondence carried on by the Ferrarese court with relatives and friends in Rome and Bologna occur words and indeed entire passages which by their turgid foulness would render a fishwife speechless. The scenes witnessed by foreign dignitaries in the palace of Ferrara pass credibility. Of Duke Niccolo III, Ser Michele's "pious benefactor," who made blasphemy punishable by death, it is recorded in the *Chronicles of the House of Este* by Ugo Caleffini, that the number of his mistresses amounted to no less than eight hundred. "Time alone," adds the historian with an almost audible sigh of regret, "prevented him from making the figure a round one thousand." One of the French princes of the blood, not exactly an ascetic soul himself, who visited Ferrara in

1461, told his Parisian friends how at the Este court he had blushed in shame upon seeing Italian gentlemen undress their young wives before the eyes of the Duke and his courtiers. . . .

To Michele Savonarola, who knew the classics as well as any scholar, these things were a revival of the wanton orgies of the imperial Roman court. Was the Duke, the father of the people, as he called himself, a Christian or a heathen? What was to become of the Christian people of Ferrara, Ser Michele asked, when they were set such an example of depravity? In the old doctor's opinion the Christian faith was being smothered in the filth and slime brought up from the pestiferous pagan past.

It is not surprising to find him warning his daughter-in-law one day to keep a strict watch over her children. He was aware that the Ferrarese army was about to return from one of those absurd little wars which the Italian city-states on the slightest pretext and sometimes for no apparent reason at all, constantly waged against each other. He feared a repetition of the disgraceful scenes enacted on previous occasions when the soldiers returning for a breathing spell from scorching and terrorizing the countryside, got out of hand and to all intents and purposes reverted to the animal state in their home town of Ferrara.

Nor was Ser Michele's warning superfluous. Within an hour after re-entering the city the following morning, the officers led their troops in a raid on the brothels. Scores of prostitutes and many respectable maidens and matrons who happened to be about in the streets and market places, were seized and forced to undress and then placed on the backs of oxen to lead off the victory parade.

Unless the Savonarolas kept their windows tightly shuttered they could not fail to see the tumult in the streets, for the ribald procession passed right by their house before proceeding to the grand square where the military commanders and the magistrates reviewed the returning heroes and their weeping captives from a gayly decorated stand.

It was the same when the civil war broke out in 1471 and two scions of the Este family fought each other over the succession to the throne. A dozen times the battle raged to and fro in the street where the Savonarola house was located. The memory of that hideous carnage haunted Girolamo all his life. He always referred to the civil war as "the bloody saturnalia of Ferrara." About evenly divided in their allegiance to the banners of one or the other princeling, the partisans, intoxicated with the fumes of blood, fought a veritable war of extermination. The wives and daughters of the leaders of the opposing factions were dragged from their homes to be publicly dishonored by the lowest plebs. People were pitched from the roofs of their houses where they had fled for refuge to be hacked to pieces in the streets below. Dwellings were set on fire and the inhabitants, prevented from coming out by their beleaguerers, perished in the smoke and flames. Every alley, every garret, every garden, even the churches of Santa Maria in Vado and San Giorgio, were turned into battlefields. For three days and three nights the slaughter went on. Both sides committed unmentionable atrocities.

What pained Girolamo most was the callous behavior of the new Duke, Ercole I, who, with the victors repaired to the banqueting halls, as soon as the fighting stopped. Caleffini reports that the bodies of two hundred of the leading citizens, after being stripped and mutilated, were nailed to the eaves of the ducal palace. There they hung for ten days rotting in the sun. Girolamo, then a university student, passed the spot every morning on his way to classes, a ghastly sight never to be forgotten. When he, quoting from Virgil, wrote in 1472: *Heu! fuge crudeles terras.* . . . "Oh, flee these cruel lands," the scenes he witnessed the year before were still vivid in his mind.

Today the electric light reveals the full extent and the depth of the Castello's dungeon under the Lion's Tower. In 1471 the dungeon was without any means of exit or entry but a slimy chute and a few iron grates to let in a feeble ray of light. Into these holes, aptly called *oubliettes** by the French, then steeped in gloom and stench, the survivors of the losing party in the civil war were dumped to decay and to be forgotten. All through the year 1471 these vaults were filled with prisoners, many of whom had lost all human semblance. The clanging of their chains, the cries of the violently insane and the groans of pain and despair could be heard plainly in the square through the gratings while in the marble halls

---

* From the verb *oublier*—to forget.

over the victims' heads the strains of music and the roar of revelry
continued night after night.

To the south of the ducal palace stands today a monument to the
memory of Girolamo Savonarola with an inscription that he was
born and lived *in tempi corrotti e servili dei vizi e dei tiranni
flagellatore,* "in corrupt and servile times of vice and scourging
tyrants." There is not one iota of exaggeration in that inscription.

*   *   *   *   *

By the time of Ser Michele's death his grandson had begun
the study of Thomas Aquinas, the saint upon whom the Church
conferred a title acknowledging both his erudition and his gentleness: *Doctor Angelicus,* the Angelical Doctor. In the *Summa* of St.
Thomas Girolamo found not only a new orientation for his heart
and mind but a spiritual home. The philosophy of the ancients, the
Platonic school, the skillful dialects of Aristotle, and the peripatetic
philosophers, in which he dabbled like every man of culture, suddenly lost their attraction. The discovery that St. Thomas made
the teaching of Scripture the touchstone of all doctrines and beliefs,
came to Girolamo like a ray of revelation. This was what grandfather had sought to convey in his precepts; the supremacy of the
Word of God and an unshakable adherence to the sacred texts.

To Girolamo it was like entering upon a new life. Day after
day he pored over the learned disquisitions of the great theologian.
In those days he would rather leave his meals untouched than miss
reading once more out loud and for the one hundredth time perhaps one page of the Angelical Doctor. He memorized every word
and in later years was able to quote St. Thomas verbatim without
looking up the text again. Three times, four times during the night
his mother would rise from her bed to see if Girolamo had at last
fallen asleep. Each time the sound of his voice or the sight of the
candlelight peeping from under the door of his room made her
retreat with a sigh of growing disquietude.

But still he sang. As long as he sang Donna Elena was not over-
anxious. Girolamo's singing was the gauge by which she measured
her son's mood and temper as well as the state of his health. Each
evening, in the hour of twilight, the young man would briefly tune

his lute and sing a song improvised on the instant, sad or joyous, solemn or light and gay, whatever the inspiration of the moment gave him to sing.

We are now in the summer of 1472. Girolamo is twenty years of age. From this time we have a somewhat sketchy but not wholly inadequate descriptive portrait of the young man. It is by one of his contemporaries, Francesco Pico della Mirandola, the uncle of the great humanist. Pico shows Girolamo to have been a person of pleasant countenance, lean of face and body and of average height. He had a habit of walking very erect, his head and shoulders thrown back, and vigorously swinging his arms. He was of a genial disposition, of ready wit and even jocose at times. His eyelashes were of a peculiar color, ruddy, dark orangelike, but much lighter than his eyebrows. He wore his dark red hair in curls falling to his shoulders. He had a strong aquiline nose, a large mouth, and a slightly receding forehead. It cannot be said that he was handsome: his thick lips were compressed in a manner denoting a stubborn firmness of purpose, but his smile, revealing a set of dazzling white teeth, softened his features with so benevolent a charm as to inspire confidence and warmth. When he smiled he seemed an entirely different person.

Two of Girolamo's physical attributes which, all his life, drew particular attention were his hands and his eyes. His hands were noble, long with thin tapering fingers, almost transparent. His eyes exercised a strong fascination upon everyone meeting him face to face. They were sea-green in color, the iris dotted with gold specks.

Girolamo's enemies have described his features as ugly, brutal and even repellent. But Caspar Lavater, whose gifts as a physiognomist none will deny, wrote of Savonarola's portrait: "Here is the face of a man made for piety, eloquence and intuition. It is not a face denoting a sharp critical sense, nor real spiritual freedom, but a face lit up by kindness and concern for others."

When Lavater made that analysis he based it on the famous painting by Fra Bartolomeo della Porta, in Florence's Academy of Fine Arts, which does not pretend to be a youthful portrait. It shows Girolamo at the end of his road of sorrows. He is a man of deathly facial pallor. His brow is deeply furrowed by sickness and care. The severe and solemn aspect can scarcely have belonged to a happy man. His shoulders seem bent like those of a tired old peasant. Just before the end, when Bartolomeo painted him, he slunk rather than walked through the streets of Florence. His rigorous fasts and self-castigations over a period of twenty-five years, the pain and fear which drain man's vitality, no doubt contributed their share to the physical deterioration so noticeable in Bartolomeo's portrait.

However, at the age of twenty, as we see him now, Girolamo looked quite a normal boy. He was neatly though inexpensively dressed. After Ser Michele's death the family fortunes dwindled so fast that Donna Elena was not always able to buy new clothes for her children and was often obliged to turn her son's clothing inside-out in order to give them a semblance of newness and freshness. Girolamo walked with a slightly dancing gait and was often seen speaking with children or acquaintances in the public square or by the fountains where all Ferrara lingered to chat and gossip in the hour before twilight.

His father was in the seventh heaven now that his brilliant son, after acquiring the degree of master of arts, had taken up the study of medicine. If Girolamo became a physician the family would soon be able to reassume the old train of life, not of abundance to be sure, for they were never rich, but of fairly well-to-do middle-class burghers. Who knows if the new Duke would not make Girolamo his private physician or place the young man in the chair of medicine formerly occupied by Ser Michele?

Expectations ran high in father Niccolo's mind when a number of incidents occurred which blasted his hopes forever. The first was Girolamo's fierce resentment over what he called the debasement and desecration of the Christian city of Ferrara on the occasion of the marriage of the new Duke with Eleonora of Aragon, the daughter of King Ferrante of Naples.

The bridegroom was Ercole I of the House of Este, who succeeded to the sovereignty after the civil war. The marriage ceremony was performed in Naples by Cardinal Pietro Riario. The festivities, also organized by Riario, were "the most stupendously sumptuous ever held in Italy." They were indeed of insane extravagance in a town of 100,000 population burdened under a tax load of bone-chilling severity.

One of the performances given at the wedding was *The Triumph of Venus*. The goddess seated in a golden coach was drawn by trained swans. The guests were informed that Jupiter, "the father of the gods," had descended from heaven to watch the spectacle. Jupiter was indeed pointed out seated among the guests in the form of a beautiful naked young man. Then Bacchus and Andromeda executed a dance the details of which, as the chronicler remarks, "had better be left undescribed." All this took place "under the eyes of the Pope without whose consent these festivities would have been unthinkable."

Upon the newly married couple's arrival in Ferrara a procession was staged through the streets ending in the banqueting hall of the palace, where the performances given the week before in Naples were to be repeated. It was in the Castello's Neapolitan hall that Girolamo Savonarola stood with a group of university scholars to welcome the Duke and his bride.

Preceding their Serene Highnesses, Girolamo saw the band of silver trumpets and the Duke's buffoons, whose waggish foolery and obscene quips and pranks have been preserved in small vellum-bound joke books which may still be inspected at the Museum of Ferrara. Some of the clowns held falcons or parrots in their hands or led strange exotic animals by chain or rope. The bridal couple were driven in an open coach of glass and silver. No show as lavish was ever given in Ferrara before; nothing was left undone to emphasize the high reputation of magnificence which the House of Este enjoyed throughout Europe and which gave rise to the saying long current in the country:

> "Who'er in Italy is known to fame
> This lordly House as frequent guest can claim."

But there, at the end of the procession, or rather at the head of a second procession, made up of the local clergy and the visiting prelates from Rome, came the nude statues of the Greek divinities with the dazzling Venus carried shoulder-high above the crowds. Behind Venus followed a statue of the Mother of God.

This mixing of the sacred and the profane proved too much for Ser Michele's grandson. Looking neither to left nor right, Girolamo tore through the crowd and the still marching procession back into the open air. For the first time his eyes flashed that terrible fire which the people of Florence were to see so often as he stood in the pulpits of their city. He was as indignant as his grandfather upon seeing a similar spectacle at the time of the Pope's visit to Ferrara. He clenched his fists and nearly choked with fury. All Ferrara talked of the incident for days, and all Ferrara was scandalized.

Girolamo rushed home and there alone in grandfather's old study, he wrote a so-called *canzone,* entitled *De Ruina Mundi,* "The Ruin of the World." This poem clearly reflects the state of mind induced by the scenes he had just witnessed in the street and in the ducal palace. The canzone—the word may be translated as sonnet or ode—begins with the words: "Seeing the whole world overturned: St. Peter is thrown down. His scepter has fallen into the hands of evildoers. Luxury and pillage abound on all sides. One cannot see how long heaven will put up with the injustices rampant in the universe. The earth lies crushed under so abominable a load of vice that she will never, it seems, be able to throw off the burden by her own strength . . . Rome which should rule the world and impose silence on the evil, has herself slipped into the cesspool . . . All values are reversed. All goodness and virtue have disappeared. Nowhere is there a shining light. No one in all the land is ashamed of his sin.

"Happy and honored is [judged] the man who lives by robbery and rapine, and feeds on other men's blood. He who despoils the widows and orphans entrusted to his care, who hastens the utter downfall of the poor, he who gains most by fraud and violence, he it is alone who is deemed gentle and noble of soul. He it is who stands to gain the highest prize that honor and glory can bestow. . . ."

Two hundred years before, Dante Alighieri wrote in the same critical and almost despairing vein: *Ahi, serva Italia . . .* "O slavish Italy, a huge tavern of sorrow art thou, a ship that has lost its captain, not a matron of virtuous modesty any longer, but a common harlot. . . ."

There follow a few sentences in Girolamo's canzone indicating that he intended to hide his opinion on the state of affairs from the public ken. *"O la mia canzone,* O my song, my song, take care

not to soil yourself with purple blemishes . . . Let your face not
be seen in the palaces of the mighty and in the public forum, but
act in such a way as to seem addressing yourself only to a small
number, lest you be denounced as the enemy of all."

Girolamo had offended the authorities, clerical and civil, by his
unseemly behavior at the palace. He realized that it would be
worse than beating his head against a wall if he, a youngster of
twenty, should try and set himself up as a censor to castigate the
prince and his courtiers. The Duke would not hesitate to crush
him as he crushed many others, or, what would be worse than
death, drive him from Ferrara to wander as an outcast in the highways and byways. There was no punishment the Italians dreaded
more than banishment from their native cities. Still, Girolamo was
confident that he had acted in the spirit of his grandfather who felt
that there must come a change, that society must either wholly
disintegrate or men must turn up another road. For the time being
Girolamo consoles himself with thoughts of the better land where
no sorrows ever dim the eye. The last words of his canzone seem
to be added as an afterthought: "Be calm my soul, be quiet and rest
in God . . . One hope at least remains: for now I know that in the
other life, 't will be seen whose was the fairest soul, whose wings
were spread to noblest flight."

Fortunately, no one knows what thoughts he harbors. Nobody
can prosecute or punish him for unexpressed opinions. He hides
the manuscript in a cupboard amongst the family's castoff clothing
where nobody will ever find it . . . Or, so he imagines! . . .

He went back to the study of medicine; he had one year to go
before he would be granted a license to practice. But would the
permit be given now that he had offended not only the Duke and
the clergy but virtually the whole city of Ferrara? Father Niccolo
thought that he could never live down the shame of his son's tem-
peramental flare-up. What was to be done? One thing was certain:
in order to acquire the position of court physician Girolamo should
without delay be taught urbanity and poise. Niccolo would call
on the Duke and humbly apologize for his son. He would ask that
the young man be invited to attend a gathering of the poets and
humanists which was held once a month at the Castello under Duke
Ercole's personal presidency. Those youthful outbursts of temper

would soon pass if Girolamo could get into the habit of mixing socially with the scholars, poets, and salon abbés. He must acquire polish and suavity and be done with such boorish incivility. "Once Girolamo sets his stubborn mind to it," Niccolo told his wife, "there is no doubt that he will move right to the top. What has happened is an accident. A young man of such phenomenal intellectual capacity must succeed. . . ."

Donna Elena was silent when her husband spoke of the awkward position in which their son had placed himself. It was early morning when the other members of the household were still asleep. She stared out of the open window. Her gaze swept over the roofs and chimneys and the castled towers of the palace till it came to rest upon a cloud of purest white drifting like a ship upon a sea of limitless blue. At last she spoke in the grave and sympathetic way to which she was accustomed. She never doubted, said Donna Elena, that Girolamo was predestined for an extraordinary life. She did not know this as one knows that one and one make two. She felt it in her heart. The boy's future lay in higher hands than either hers or Niccolo's. Like St. Peter, Girolamo might well be led into paths *not* of his own choosing. . . .

"Carissime," Donna Elena went on speaking to her husband, "you do not understand Girolamo's character. You have not looked into the depths of him. Of one thing you may rest assured; the boy will never occupy a high position in society. For that he will never learn to please the great and mighty sufficiently. In order to be a courtier, be it as a physician, a cleric, or a scholar, Girolamo should have less nobility of spirit and more charm, less talents and more aptitude for sycophancy and flattery, less conviction and more subtlety. . . .

"You remarked just now that Girolamo is stubborn. That word does not begin to cover the qualities of his heart and mind . . . He is as stiff-necked as the Old Testament Jews, as uncompromising as the prophets. And then," she added almost in a whisper: "Girolamo has a higher mission to fulfill than any other man now living in this world. He knows it not himself, though I think he is beginning to hear the call. . . ."

More Donna Elena would not say. Niccolo pleaded with her and stormed at her, challenging her to disclose the secret of Girolamo's future at which she had hinted. At last, in exasperation and pain, she called out: "His mission is a terrible one. . . ." Her voice broke off in a sob. Then Niccolo also grew pensive.

* * * * * *

What happened next seemed to make a mockery of Donna Elena's somber presentiments, at least for a time. Girolamo appeared quite unconcerned about the scandal he had caused and the tongues he had set a-wagging. He seemed to have overcome the moods of melancholy which sometimes oppressed him. He walked with a lighter step. He strummed new tunes on his lute, gayer, more worldly, some of ludicrous and unheard-of syncopation. He became more sociable, he participated in the games and athletics in which the other university students indulged. He played ball and even wrestled. And. . . . he fell in love!

There came to dwell directly across the street from his parents' house a man bearing the illustrious name of Strozzi. The Strozzi were one of the most influential families in Florence. They had given that city magistrates, scholars, and architects. But they were the rivals of the Medici and particularly of Lorenzo the Magnificent. In one of Florence's perennial factional squabbles the Strozzi and their partisans had been bested by the shrewdness of the prince and the overpowering repressional apparatus in the hands of his henchmen.

The head of one of the branches of the Strozzi family, who had been involved in the attempt to break Lorenzo de' Medici's hold on the life of Florence, was sentenced to banishment. He took up residence in Ferrara. He was the man who now lived in the mansion across the way from the Savonarola house.

As an exiled citizen from Dante's native city Roberto Strozzi had a special attraction for young Savonarola. Such a man, an opponent of the authoritarian Medicean regime, could not be other than a victim of persecution, a sufferer in the noble cause of patriotism and freedom. Girolamo took to watching the Strozzi mansion for a glimpse of the distinguished exile. What his glance met were the jet-black eyes of Roberto Strozzi's daughter staring at him from the window of the opposite house.

In the instant when his eyes met those of the damsel, Girolamo seemed transfixed by all the arrows from cupid's quiver in one fell swoop. He remained absolutely motionless. His arms, legs, even his tongue refused their customary service. He could not so much as bring his head to make a polite nodding gesture. He stood there as if he had been turned into a pillar of salt.

Though the exact location of the Savonarola house is no longer known, nor the site of the mansion occupied by Roberto Strozzi, we may safely assume that the street running between the two dwellings, was as narrow as the alleys still existing in the older parts of Naples, Florence, and Genoa. Yet those alleys were once the principal thoroughfares, the civic highways along which coursed the vitality, the commerce, and the luxury of great metropolises. Girolamo could easily have carried on a conversation with the young lady across the intervening space of fifteen or perhaps twenty feet. Still, he did not speak a word, nor, for that matter, did she. With wide open eyes, his body motionless in irresolution, he stared at the vision across the way.

However, it was not bashfulness or timidity alone which turned Girolamo into a mute. There were also certain social amenities involved, a certain code had to be observed. No well-bred young man in those days would venture to address a lady without having been introduced. Certainly, a young unmarried lady was not to be spoken to without permission having been asked and obtained from her chaperone.

It was from the Strozzi servants that Girolamo learned the young lady's name: Laudomia. The word Laudomia signifies: she who praises the Lord. Girolamo's heart gave an extra leap when he heard it. Such a beautiful and meaningful name he had never heard before. Laudomia! He repeated it with the chaste fervor of a nun reciting her rosary. Moreover, it was a name which lent itself perfectly to poetic fancy. Without a moment's hesitation Girolamo composed a canzone of greeting and admiration.

The next item of information from the Strozzi servants may well have been a little frightening to a young man of Girolamo's conventional upbringing. Laudomia's mother had not accompanied her daughter to Ferrara. The girl's mother was not Messer Roberto's lawfully wedded wife. She was a chance acquaintance, a mysterious visitor to his chambers one summer night now well-nigh seventeen years ago. If Girolamo wished to know the mother's identity, he had only to say the word. The servants were willing to tell everything. Laudomia's mother wore a black veil and a black mantle that cool summer night when she came to the Strozzi palace in Florence, but it was impossible to mistake the elegant figure and the sensuous walk . . . All Florence knew her. Even Lorenzo the Magnificent, it was said. . . . But here Girolamo shook his head. He had heard enough. Besides, what mattered the darkest rumors! He was in love for the first time in his life. He would prove that he was a man of the world and break through any and all barriers which fate or gossip might raise between Laudomia and himself. There was no law of Medes and Persians against writing one's beloved, was there? And even if there was! Off went the first *billet doux* to Laudomia Strozzi via the same gossiping servants.

For two months Girolamo wrote a poetic letter every day. He took good care that from a literary point of view his epistles were models of style. Didn't Laudomia hail from Florence, the city of taste and culture? The young man would now rush home from classes at the end of the school day to take up his position at the window on the first floor. He bought new strings for his lute and sang all the songs he knew. One song he sang so tenderly that passers-by in the street below stopped to listen: *Voglio invitar tutto 'l mondo ad amare* . . . I invite all the world to love . . . Let dales and hills and mountains, men and flowers, the sea and all the earth join in praise in the presence of my love. . . . Laudomia!

The song brought a sweet smile to the girl's lips. But that was reward enough. How adorable she looked! Girolamo's world was illumined by a new light. It was impossible to add one more grace to Laudomia's personality; she was perfect. How pellucid golden was her hair! What sparkle in her eyes! Tumultuous hopes were kindled in the young man's heart. He dreamed of blissful days at the girl's side. That Laudomia left his letters unanswered daunted him not in the least. That, he reflected, was just a clever woman's way. He had heard of such coy feminine tactics. She was probably trying him out, testing his constancy. Her servants told him that she questioned them continuously about the Savonarola family and all its members. A good sign if ever there was! All he had to do was to keep up his serenades and his letters. Perseverance does it, said Girolamo to himself. The man who holds out must win in the end. The end came sooner than he expected.

Before it came there were some precious hours spent in Laudomia's company. They walked hand in hand in the square, Laudomia's duenna following at a respectful distance. The girl was clad in a dress of so startling a design as was seldom seen in a provincial city. People stopped to look at the graceful young couple. When greeted by passers-by, Laudomia returned their salutation so courteously that they knew at once they had to do with a lady of quality.

Girolamo now sported a hat with peacock feathers. He had bought himself new clothes with money borrowed from father Niccolo who, for reasons not far to seek, did all in his power to encourage his son's friendship with the daughter of a house as proud and energetic and as wealthy as the Strozzi. A silken cloak, aquamarine in color, was the garment Girolamo wore when he went strolling with Laudomia. It was as gorgeous, he told his friends in afteryears, as that worn by St. Francis before his conversion when he walked in Assisi's streets at night surrounded by torchbearers to show off the magnificence of his costume. But what the two lovers talked about amongst themselves Girolamo never disclosed. In later life it seemed as if Laudomia had been only a vision he beheld once or twice in a dream.

One day, scarcely three months after he first caught sight of her at the window of her father's house, Girolamo walked with Laudomia on the flower-banked promenade on top of Ferrara's earthen ramparts. It was spring when all the world is green and the flaming sun has not yet scorched the Italian landscape to the hue of cinders. He had his lute with him and he sang a gay little song by Jacopone da Todi.* As he sang he felt that, for better or for worse, the blossom hour of fate had struck. He stopped singing and told his companion that he would soon take up the practice of medicine and had been encouraged to expect a professorship.

* Before the death of his wife Jacopone da Todi wrote a number of love songs.

With a gentle gesture he stopped Laudomia in her path. In a burst of boyish poetic eloquence he made known his feelings of love and honor.

Patiently she let him finish his declaration, though not a sign in her face betrayed her own feelings. When he had spoken he waited for her answer. It came, but it was so startlingly different from what he expected, that he felt as if struck by lightning. Looking him straight in the eyes, and raising her voice in haughty arrogance, Laudomia asked if he imagined for one instant that a daughter of so high and noble a family as the Strozzi would ever consent to an alliance with one so lowly and menial as a Savonarola. . . .

At first Girolamo blushed and then turned deadly pale. He could not believe his own ears. He was crushed with shame and mortification. For an instant the thought flashed through his mind to ask Laudomia a question in return, whether she thought that the Savonarola family would give one of its legitimate sons in marriage to a bastard like her? But he never asked that question, nor any one like it. He was too dumbfounded and thought, as he later divulged, that such a question would have shocked and humiliated the damsel too deeply. He pressed back the angry words that rose to his lips. Tears came to his eyes as Laudomia walked off holding her head high and humming the chanson which Girolamo had just taught her.

On his way home the young man vowed that he would never look upon a woman's face again. In his room he buried his head in his arms and wept bitterly. Never in afterlife did he smart as painfully under the insults and browbeatings of his enemies as under the beautiful Laudomia's sneer. In the first days after the incident Girolamo went nearly mad with grief. Laudomia's rejection literally seared his soul. It made him sink under the emotions which her callousness had produced. Her ice-cold words produced a shock detracting him for ever after from all desires of sensuous happiness. Ultimately it threw him into the bosom of God whence he never again wished or was able to escape.

Although she was not the kind of person to betray her emotions by idle talk or questioning, Donna Elena was now seriously perturbed about her son's odd behavior. Here was Girolamo, a master of arts, entitled to wear the velvet cap and gown of the schoolmen,

at liberty to stroll into the halls of learning and mix as an equal
in the brilliant, world-renowned academic circles of Ferrara, and
what did he do? He prowled around the countryside, his clothing
and general appearance scarcely distinguishable from a peasant's.
When acquaintances met him they asked themselves: can this be
the son of Niccolo Savonarola, the charming conversationalist and
poet laureate who, in spite of financial setbacks, still dressed in the
height of fashion? Girolamo did not even raise his head to acknowledge the greetings of friends. He was so preoccupied with the
struggle going on inside of him that he seemed both deaf and blind.
What had come over the boy? Had he lost his wits? Was the Strozzi
girl the cause of all this? Bah, said Niccolo, do you think that my
son will not be able to find another damsel as elegant and fair as
that vainglorious piece of Florentine snobbery?

He certainly could not find one in those squalid villages where
he walked day after day. The stench of the pigsties and dung piles
was enough to keep any civilized person away. Girolamo did not
study anymore; he no longer played the lute, he ate his meals in
silence. He scarcely spoke to his brothers and sisters when he came
home after a day of wandering. If it were not for the fact that he
still prayed as ardently as ever Donna Elena would have given up
hope altogether. . . .

Had he been asked what object he had in mind with those daily
walks along the river and in the huge monotonous plain around
Ferrara he would not have been able to answer. One day he was
seen in this locality, the next in another perhaps many miles away
in the opposite direction. Clearly there was neither plan nor method
to these escapades in the rural regions. It was plain sottishness.
The boy was losing his mental equilibrium. People pointed to their
heads and nodded knowingly. . . .

*   *   *   *   *   *   *

On a cloudless Sunday morning in April, young Savonarola
found himself in the market place of Faenza, twelve miles distant
as the crow flies from Ferrara. He heard the strains of a pipe organ
from the open door of the Church of St. Augustine; first the organ
music and then a clear tenor voice singing the *Agnus Dei,* "Behold,

the Lamb of God that taketh away the sins of the world." He entered the church and standing in the rear of a large crowd of worshippers, saw an Augustinian friar mount the pulpit to preach a sermon. That sermon, or rather one single sentence in it, changed Girolamo's life. The preacher's words went ringing into his head and into his heart and overpowered him. He was a prisoner of the Word of God from that moment till the end of his life.

For years Savonarola refused to disclose what was the word of grace and saving power which he heard in Faenza. He regarded it as a secret between God and his soul. No matter how much his friends pressed him, he, who never kept another secret in his life, stubbornly declined to gratify their curiosity. Not even the executioner and his henchmen who tortured him in the last days of his life, could extract an answer. Only in the very last extremity when death literally stood before the door of his prison cell and his confessor gently inquired when, on what occasion he had been first aware of God speaking to him, did Savonarola break a lifelong silence on the subject. . . .

The friar in St. Augustine's church that morning in April had chosen as his text a passage from the Book of Genesis, the commencement of the twelfth chapter where God speaks in a dream to the Patriarch Abraham, then still living in the city of Ur of the Chaldees: *Get thee out of thy country, and from thy kindred, and from thy father's house, into a land that I will show thee.* . . . When Girolamo heard the words of the text he stood as electrified. His mouth fell open with bewilderment. This, he realized, was no mere coincidence or chance or accident. This was God addressing him personally. It could not be otherwise but that a higher power had directed his footsteps that morning and on no other day to Faenza. . . .

Girolamo knew the text by heart. He had read it a hundred times. His grandfather had made him spell it out when he was just a beginner: *Egredere de terra tua,* "Get thee out of thy country. . . ." But there was a profound difference: in Ur God spoke to Abraham; in Faenza the word of the Lord came to Girolamo Savonarola. God had answered his prayers. For this he had prayed every night for days and months and years on end: "Make known to me, O Lord, the way in which I am to walk!" And now God had made known the way. It wasn't the friar in the pulpit who was saying these things. The preacher merely served as an instrument, as a voice pipe and mouthpiece of which God made use to speak to Girolamo Savonarola.

The Mass was over, the congregation walked out. The bells rang out their most joyous peal. As he started on the homeward journey, Girolamo's mood changed from pitiable uncertainty to an almost unbearable joy. The cloud was lifted, the perplexity dissipated. He saw the world with new eyes. Though they were the same flowers, the same trees, the same animals, the same people he passed earlier in the day, they now appeared other flowers, other trees, other people. . . . The birds which seemed song-choked and mute a few hours earlier, now sang with full throat. Their happiness communicated itself to his spirit. He felt like dancing. . . .

He had recovered his inner poise and found that astonishing peace of mind which would never again desert him, not even in afterlife's most trying circumstances. His understanding was illumined by a new light. Now he understood everything: why his grandfather had held the example of John the Baptist before his eyes, why he had been allowed to witness the violence and moral corruption of Ferrara, why Laudomia rejected him. It was all clearly part and parcel of God's purpose to prepare him and reserve him for a higher calling. From that day onward he was to devote himself to the great works for which so many forces within and without had been moulding him.

No doubt, Laudomia's haughty rejection came as a shock to Girolamo, but not as a shock in the ordinary sense of the word, as disappointment, regret, or blasted hope. It threw him into an anguish of introspection and self-reproach. Secret spiritual longings were activated. "I was always grateful to God for having placed me in this world," Savonarola once said. "I sought God from my earliest youth, but I did not always know that when I sought God it was God who was seeking me." What happened in Faenza was that the quest for self-discovery came to an end. He found what, subconsciously, he had always looked for. Henceforth he was conscious of being in contact with a living and personal spiritual power in which he recognized the Spirit of God. The

young man came under compulsion to translate into action a sub-
conscious desire to gather up, to concentrate, to combine all his
hopes, aspirations, and deeds into one harmonious unity and see
everything in life and in history from the point of view of eternity.
If God is a determinate living spirit in any sense personal, we may
say perhaps that there was a direct unmediated encounter between
God and Girolamo Savonarola. Faenza marks the beginning of that
intimate relationship with the Divine which continued uninter-
ruptedly till the hour when Savonarola fell from the burning
scaffold in Florence and was caught up in the everlasting arms. . . .

Did he have a presentiment in Faenza as to the cruel fate in
store for him? Ranke, the most erudite and objective of the Protestant historians, is of the opinion that Savonarola was "unquestionably endowed" with the gift of divination. True it is also that from
young manhood onward Girolamo often spoke of himself as
destined for martyrdom. In Faenza he may therefore well have
sensed that neither fame nor riches nor anything like worldly
glory lay in the offing, but that the rest of his road through life
would be the same lonesome trail trodden in all ages by all the
great spirits who have thought great thoughts and done great
deeds. . . .

He returned to Ferrara and in his room read one of the books
which grandfather Michele had left him. It was the manual of
monastic discipline, known as the *Mirror of the Monks,* drawn up
in the eleventh century by Arnulf of Beauvais. The monk, Girolamo read, ought not to concern himself with political events or
strangers or even his own relatives . . . Let the monk be like
Melchizedek, a priest of the Most High of whom we read * that he
was without father, without mother, and without descent . . . "Let
the monk," says Arnulf, "look upon himself as alone and upon God
as his Father. . . ."

Kneeling by the table, Girolamo repeated the prayer of the
Angelical Doctor: "Give me, O Lord God, a vigilant heart that no
idle thought can draw away from thee; a noble heart that no unworthy love can debase; a straightforward heart that no equivocal
purpose can cause to deviate; a firm heart that no adversity can
crush; a free heart that no violent passion can conquer or sub-

* Epistle to the Hebrews: 7:3.

jugate. And accord me, if it please thee, O Lord my God, an intelligence that knows thee, a zeal that seeks thee, a wisdom that
finds thee, a life that is pleasing in thy sight, a perseverance that
waits for thee, and a sure confidence of possessing thee in all
eternity. . . ."

Even so, he found it almost impossible to put his resolution to
become a monk into effect. He did not dare tell his parents what
the feeling was which preyed on his mind lest they burst into tears
and raise objections and he himself break down and abandon his
purpose. But what had to be done had to be done. On April 24,
Girolamo managed to convey his thoughts about leaving the dear
paternal home without the use of words. In the hour of twilight
when a beam of violet shot through the sky and the deep silence of
night was about to descend on Ferrara, he took his lute and standing by the window he played upon it a melody so sad and melan-
cholic that his mother turned upon him with a look of intense
sorrow on her face, and said: "My son, that was a sign of parting. . . ." By a strong effort Girolamo "kept his eyes on the ground
and continued with trembling fingers to pluck the strings without
venturing to answer."

On the following day, the festival of St. George, the people of
Ferrara were and still are in the habit of spending the day in the
open. Spring is then full upon the land and the open fields beckon
the Ferrarese to come outside and leave their gloomy houses. From
early morn the families could be seen moving through the streets
loaded with baskets of food and fruit and wine, heading for the
meadows and the forests for a day's excursion. His parents do not
seem to have thought it unusual that Girolamo did not come along.
They and the other children set out for the picnic and were joined
at the appointed hour and place by cousins and aunts and uncles.
In their haste to be off, nobody thought of saying good-by to Girolamo. But he stood by the upstairs window and saw them leave.
When the family returned in the evening Girolamo was gone.

There was no alarm the first night. As so often in the past
Girolamo was out, but he had always come back. In an hour, in
two hours, before morning surely, the boy would return. Niccolo
did not even trouble to look into his son's room. But when daylight came Donna Elena did. She confirmed what she had suspected

since the evening before, that her son was not off on one of his erratic wanderlust fits. "He is gone for good," she told her husband.

Niccolo paced the floor in growing anxiety, but he still refused to surrender to the evidence. Perhaps, he argued, Girolamo had wished to change his school for the last year of study . . . Padua had a better known medical faculty. The boy had probably inherited something of old Ser Michele's preference for the ancestral city. In order to reassure his wife and himself, Niccolo invented a hundred excuses for his son's absence. Who knows if there wasn't a new love involved? Who knows? . . .

But Elena shook her head. "He has taken nothing by way of food," she said. "He is wearing his oldest clothes. His books are all in order, neatly ranged on the shelves in his room where they always were."

"In that case, he will surely be back!" exclaimed Niccolo. "If Girolamo thought of departing for good, he would never leave his books behind."

"But he has taken one book," observed Donna Elena quietly.

"What book?"

"The Bible, the old Bible which grandfather gave him! . . . The Bible is missing. Look Niccolo, look, the Bible is gone! . . ."

On April 25, 1475, Girolamo Savonarola walked to Bologna. The distance is twenty miles. It turned out a warm day. The road was an endless trail of dust which the breeze threw up in thick yellow clouds.

Chapter II

The Time of Apprenticeship

UPON reaching Bologna Savonarola went straight to the Dominican monastery located in the heart of the city near the church where the body of the Order's founder lies entombed in solemn splendor. He knocked on the door and asked the brother-porter for admission. Without a word the friar beckoned the applicant inside and introduced him into a room where he was presently joined by three elderly monks. Facing the candidate across a plain wooden table on which lay an open Bible, the three proceeded to examine him as to his schooling, his family connections and his private life, going into the most intimate details and particulars. When this preliminary examination was over Savonarola was escorted to the chapter hall where all the brethren were assembled. Here the candidate knelt down and bowed his head. When the prior asked him what he desired, he rose to his feet and answered: "All I ask is God's mercy and yours. . . ."

In a brief allocution the prior told Savonarola that the monk's sole aim in life should be to seek holiness as demanded by Jesus in the Sermon on the Mount: "Be ye therefore perfect, even as your Father which is in heaven is perfect." From the pursuit of this, the Lord's supreme requirement, the prior went on to say, the monk should never deviate, though he must always bear in mind that total perfection in this life remains unattainable. In the quest for holiness he should direct himself almost exclusively to the formation of personal character. He was every day to examine his conscience and give himself an accounting of every act and every thought. All his psychological and physical energy should be concentrated upon and directed toward the one sole objective of personal sanctification.

The prior asked if Savonarola was prepared to enter upon such a life of renunciation, prayer, and study. Was he aware that going into the cloister meant saying farewell to the world and all its joys and desirabilities? Was he willing to carry out in strict obedience and to the best of his ability whatever task his superiors would set him to perform?

Savonarola replied that the sole object of his coming to Bologna was to find peace of mind. He had not applied for admission at the Monastery of the Angels at home in Ferrara for fear of complicating matters with his parents. He wanted to live wholly detached from his family. He was, he declared, not only willing but eager to give up everything dear and precious, and perform the humblest and most menial tasks to which the prior might assign him.

After Girolamo had thus spoken, the prior pronounced the formula used in such circumstances: "May the Lord who gave the beginning, also give a blessed end. . . ." Then the candidate received the tonsure and put on the white robe of St. Dominic and the long black mantle which is worn over it.

The prior of the convent in the year of Savonarola's admission was Dom Giorgio Vercelli. Speaking in later years of Savonarola's reception, he said: "Seldom has a young man brought so pure a body and soul into the monastery as Girolamo Savonarola, and none ever took St. Dominic's habit with more pious fervor."

It was past midnight when Fra Girolamo, as he was now called, was shown to his cell. Without waiting an instant he wrote his father. His letter reached Ferrara on April 27. A friend of the family who had been to Bologna on business, delivered it towards evening, when Niccolo, who had been rummaging all day among his son's papers, had just retrieved a Latin treatise by Girolamo entitled: *The Contempt of the World*. The tone and contents of both his son's letter and the treatise so upset father Niccolo that he placed the two documents under lock and key in the family strongbox. Here they remained for four hundred years till discovered by an Italian scholar in 1875.

When the treatise and the letter are read together, as father Niccolo read them that morning, we see the historical figure of

Savonarola take shape before our eyes: the boy is father to the man. Here is not merely a celebrated personality in the making or in formation; here is Savonarola full-grown and entire at the age of twenty-three, placing an uplifting moral ideal by the side of the cold intellectual activity of the Renaissance and the universal corruption of morals.

"Honored Father," he writes, "first of all I must give you the cause and reason which compelled me to take up the religious life . . . It is the abyss of misery into which the world has fallen; the wickedness of the men of our time, the moral decline, the adulteries, the robberies, the idolatries, the frightful blasphemies . . . Our age has arrived at a point where it is difficult to find one single man of entire good faith. This is why you heard me sing so often the stanza from Virgil beginning with the words: 'Oh, flee from these cruel countries . . .' I could no longer bear the perversities and the extreme evil of these blind Italian peoples amongst whom virtue is reduced to zero and vice triumphs on every hand . . . It is the general situation which is the source of my deepest distress. . . .

"Would it not be base ingratitude towards God if, after having prayed him to show me the way and he having revealed it to me, I should now refuse to walk in it? I would rather die a thousand deaths than behave in an ungrateful manner towards the Lord my God. My present condition is such, very dear father, that you should thank our Lord rather than weep, since he has given you a son and has preserved that son in good health for twenty-three years in order to make him a soldier of the cross. Do you not agree that it is a token of the divine grace to have a son who is a knight of Jesus Christ?

"Do not all of you [at home] believe me when I say that my separation from you is a sore and agonizing trial? Will you believe me when I say that since my birth I have not suffered any comparable affliction as that which compels me to tear myself away from those of my own flesh and blood, to go off and live among strangers and lay my life at the feet of men whom I have never seen before? . . .

"But consider again, beloved father; how could I do otherwise? How could I resist him who took upon himself the form of a servant to dwell among us? How could I harden my heart when I heard his tender voice calling: 'Come unto me all ye that are weary and heavy-laden, and I will give you rest . . . Take my yoke upon you and learn of me that I am meek and gentle of heart. . . .'

"Still, I know very well, father, that you are grieving over me as over a lost son. You wonder about the manner of my departure in secret, as if I were fleeing from you. Therefore, I must say, that the prospect of leaving you and my dear mother troubled me so much, that had I made my mind known to you, surely my heart would have broken and I would have renounced my purpose . . . I ask you then, dear father and mother, to dry your tears, so as not to cause me still greater pain than I suffer at present.

"I am not pained," he hastens to explain, "because I have taken this step. This step is irrevocable and I would not make it undone if I were to be compensated with the imperial dignity. The reason for my sadness is that my feelings as a human being are in conflict with the divine will. I am daily fighting to keep the devil off my shoulders as he whispers words in my ears to tempt me to retrace my steps.

"But one of these days, I am sure, honored and dearly beloved father, when the wounds of separation are healed, our sadness will also pass. Then, I trust, you and I will be comforted, in this world by grace abounding and in the life to come by glory everlasting. All I ask you for the present is to comfort my dear mother. And I ask you both to give me your blessing. . . ."

By way of postscriptum he adds a word of advice concerning his youngest brother. "Dear father, please see to it that Alberto stops idling his life away. It is your responsibility to set him to work and to study. To neglect this duty would bring a grave sin on your conscience."

This filial admonition was promptly taken to heart. Alberto soon took up the study of medicine which his older brother had just abandoned. In the end he became as accomplished a physician as grandfather Michele had been.

Niccolo's reading was not finished when he had perused his son's letter. There remained the document which he had found among Girolamo's papers that morning, although the writing was perhaps more than a year old. It can still be read in the National Library of Florence if only with the aid of a magnifying glass and with extreme care for the script is so minuscule as to be almost unde-cipherable and the paper has grown yellow and brittle.

Girolamo was angry when he wrote *The Contempt of the World*. But his wrath is creative. His pessimism throws a revealing light on contemporary society. There can be no amelioration unless stock is first taken of the extent and the magnitude of the evils rampant in the world. The wording of the essay is terse, unadorned, un-rhymed.

"Ferrara, and not only Ferrara," he begins, "but Venice, Flor-ence, Rome, all Italy, the whole world is gone astray." He turns with particular indignation against the humanists. "We call our-selves a wise and educated people, in reality we are but imbeciles. Are not the poor in spirit, the simple men and women, the common people whom we are told to regard as unpolished and crude, to enter first into the Kingdom of Heaven? . . . Why do we not follow Jesus and become like little children, simple, trusting, and pure? Our hearts dissolve into thought. [He means, our intellectualism stifles the real yearnings and aspirations of our hearts.] On the pretext that virtue is an eternal, imperishable quality, we neglect to practice it in the present. We say that virtue can wait. It is there all the time, within our reach, ready for the taking. We plan to take it up in a more propitious hour, at a more convenient time. Some day, some day we say that we will turn to virtue. . . .

"Do we not see that virtue is receding ever further into the background? Do we not realize that the world is filling up with iniquity and that virtue has well-nigh vanished? Why do we wait? Why do we tarry? What am I waiting for myself? Rise, O my soul, and flee from this Sodom and Gomorrah! Break away from the corrupt city [of Ferrara] from the youth without idealism, from the luxury-loving old men. . . .

"If you are assiduous in your studies, you are taken for an eccentric streaked with a queer twist. If you try to live chastely and modestly you are decried an idiot. If you are just, you are told that you are cruel. If you put your trust in God alone, you are labeled a fool or an old fogy. If you try to be charitable and try to love and respect your fellow men, you are called effeminate and people raise their eyebrows suspecting that you have some vile trick up your sleeve . . . When you place your hope in Christ, the whole world laughs at you. . . .

"No one is accounted a real man in Ferrara who does not use coarse language and spits out the most loathsome blasphemies. If you want to be considered wise and prudent, just strip the widow and the orphans of their last possessions. The more money a man hoards and covets, the wiser and more successful he is thought to be. Who is accounted a clever fellow in Ferrara? He who invents a still more fiendish way to torture human beings or who plots and executes a still more abject crime. No person amongst us is given credit for courage or manly conduct unless he assassinates a fellow creature or foments riot and revolution. . . ."

Father Niccolo was not ill-advised when, after reading his son's *Contempt of the World* to Donna Elena, he put the document securely away. Girolamo's denunciations would not have fallen on sympathetic ears at the Castello. The Duke would know full well whom the young writer had in mind. Ercole the Great—for he was the reigning prince since "the bloody saturnalia" of the civil war—had crushed men, the very friends of his youth, for uttering far less severe criticism of the moral state of Ferrara. It is true that the Duke had no jurisdiction over a monk residing in another principality, but he was powerful and shrewd and ruthless. One never knew. Girolamo's papers had better be kept out of sight.

Girolamo Savonarola passed seven years of his life in Bologna's monastery. "My only object in embracing the conventual life," he said afterwards, "was to seek peace and freedom." Did he find what he looked for? If it is borne in mind what monks in general and Savonarola in particular understand by peace and freedom, the answer must be in the affirmative. To Fra Girolamo peace had nothing to do with living a tranquil and easy life. On the contrary, it was a conscious search for the most laborious, the most irksome mode of existence. It could not in fact be called living at all, for in the monks' own words it was a constant process of "dying to this world."

To Savonarola freedom meant the right to impose upon himself all the constraints and disciplines which he thought necessary to humble his pride on the one hand and, on the other, to exalt and ennoble the sentiment of his vocation and mission in life. As he told Dom Vercelli he was willing to accept every servitude, every humiliation and hardship if only his mind was detached from worldly things and considerations. In afteryears he looked back on the time of his novitiate as the happiest in his life. "I found freedom and peace," he wrote, "for I did just what I wanted and had absolutely no desire to do anything else but what I was ordered. I was liberated from all desires save from prayer and obedience. In his quest for humility, he used all the means at his disposal, mental, spiritual, and physical, study and prayer but also rigorous fasting and self-chastisement. To be humbled, to be mocked or made the object of ridicule, to suffer physical pain and discomfort were not to be disdained or to be avoided, but to be gratefully accepted as part and parcel of a monk's means and methods to strive for perfection.

Such was Fra Girolamo's conception of peace of mind. Intrinsically it did not differ from what the man of Assisi regarded as the highest good in life. "When you," St. Francis once told his disciples, "return from a long and arduous journey on a bitter cold night and knock at the monastery door and you get no answer but are left outside in the snow and the ice-cold blasts of winter, then you may rejoice . . . But if the friar-porter should at last open the spyhole in the door and ask: 'Who are you?' and you reply: 'Here are two friars who have come home,' and he doesn't believe you but says: 'No, you are not friars but two vagabonds of evil intention,' and he seizes a cudgel and throws himself upon you and gives you a thorough beating, when that happens, my brethren, you may say to yourself: 'Now at last I have perfect peace and happiness. . . .' "

Many have spoken in a deprecatory vein, and passed severe judgment on monks and the conventual life in general. Criticism of the monks runs like an unbroken thread through the pages of the history of Christianity. In the era of the Reformation criticism turned into violent animosity. The monks were accused of all sorts of crimes. They were a pack of lazybones, gluttons, sensualists and above all worthless ignoramuses who held up the march of civilization. Erasmus had not one good word for the monks. His generalizations had the result that the role of the monks in keeping the torch of learning and culture aflame through the Middle Ages, remained largely hidden from the ken of history till a new evaluation of monasticism in later years slowly brought the other side of the coin to light.

Still, all the attacks were vain. Nothing could daunt the monks, neither persecution or suppression. After every storm they raised their heads again. "There will never be a time without monasteries." The longing for and the devotion to the monastic life is too deeply ingrained in the human heart for it ever to be wholly eliminated. Those who have visited monasteries testify that the inducements to leave the world and live in pious seclusion are as strongly felt now as ever they were. The monks are not as is often said, usually unhappy, though morbid conditions of one kind or another deriving from the repression of natural instincts are at times inevitable. According to Professor Walter Nigg of Zurich, who devoted one of his fine studies to *The Enigma of the Monks,* they have a secret which modern man with his purely utilitarian, this-worldly and secularist attitude to life is unable to grasp and must therefore perforce undervalue, misjudge, or even disown altogether. . . . Many monks, and Savonarola was one of them, derived a positive happiness from their strange manner of life. The English mystic Richard Rolle of Hampole wrote long ago: "Men suppose that we are in torture and in penance great; but we have more joy and more very delight in one day than they have in the world all their life. They see our body, but they see not our heart where our solace is. If they saw that, many would forsake all they have to follow us." The early Franciscans, we know, were generally in so merry a mood that they were known as *ioculatores Dei,* God's jesters. Of St. Francis, someone said, that he added one more beatitude to the Sermon on the Mount: "Blessed are those who laugh!"

During the first months in the monastery Savonarola still corresponded in a haphazard way with his father, but in the course of time the connection with Ferrara was broken off entirely. But this does not mean that Fra Girolamo passed his time in inert contentment. He worked in the communal kitchen, he waited at table, cleaned vegetables and fish, washed floors and dishes, and acted as general roustabout. He was a willing and cheerful worker, the brethren conceived a great liking for the somewhat swarthy yet florid novice who produced an impression of great physical energy and intellectual brilliance. The puritan sternness, which he inherited from grandfather Michele, was concealed by his good humor and gave zest to his conversation. Nothing was too much for Fra Girolamo. Night and day he was at the beck and call of his superiors as well as of his fellow friars. He seems to have done a good deal of nursing and attending to the needs of the sick and ailing amongst the elderly brethren. In the sickroom his medical studies, no doubt, stood him in good stead. At any rate, the house physician thought highly of Savonarola's medical skill.

On the other hand, these arduous physical labors did not cause him to neglect a monk's higher and principal duties. Savonarola, who was all his life to an almost incredible extent able to dispense with sleep, spent the hours of the night in his cell in prayer, in study and writing. Thus he was happy twenty-four hours around the clock. Perhaps he did not know very clearly what he expected, but that he felt at home in Bologna's monastery, of that there is no doubt. It was as if the last burden had rolled off his heart. He had arrived in the world of his dreams. He felt that in those cloistered halls the shades of the two greatest Dominicans of all time, St. Dominic and St. Thomas Aquinas, still hovered about. These saintly and learned masters were not dead; they were alive, they were near, and their presence filled the air. His mind, Savonarola reflected, had been a dark place into which the light filtered but slowly. In their company the light streamed in as if a great door had been opened wide. Under the watch and care of St. Dominic and St. Thomas he was growing up spiritually and intellectually. All that went before had been preliminary and preparation: in the monastery his real life had begun.

If the question were asked in what particular sphere of monastic activity, study, manual labor, teaching, or chanting Fra Girolamo engaged with fullest devotion and purest delight, the answer must be: prayer. To Savonarola prayer was the breath of life, a permanent state of mind rather than a single and deliberate act of faith. From his earliest youth he had been of the tenderest and most childlike piety. In the monastery, away from the world, without any obstacles or distractions diverting his attention, his piety unfolded and intensified with every passing day. He was a man who lived for religion and nothing else.

He eagerly participated in the rituals, the litanies, and the intercessionary prayers which were matters of regulation and discipline in St. Dominic's as in every other monastery in Christendom. But during the whole long day of work he looked secretly forward, and with keenest anticipation, to his private devotions in the night.

In seeking communion with God Savonarola really communed with himself. For he knew that God dwells in the inner parts of the man who prays. "We can only pray," he said once, "when we approach the great solitary One as solitaries." All the great men and women who were devoted to prayer, the mystics and the prophets, sought solitude, be it on the mountain top, in the depth of the forest, in the desert, or in the still upper room out of reach of the world's noise and clamor.

We learn from Marabotto, the father-confessor of St. Catherine of Genoa, that he once hid himself in the saint's room in order to see and hear her at prayer. Brother Leo, too, St. Francis' favorite disciple, is known to have crawled on his hands and knees to be near the Little Poor One of Assisi and hear his words as he prayed on a steep rock in the Alverner mountains in the middle of the night. Something similar must have happened in the case of Savonarola. Unknown persons took down what he said in the privacy of his cell and thus preserved many of his prayers. Even his bodily attitude during prayer became known though he was unaware of being observed. Some prayers he wrote down, but only when requested to do so. He warned his friends that a written prayer could never convey the spontaneity, the intimacy, and uplift which the word carried when spoken under the inspiration of the moment.

Mindful of the Lord's saying that real prayers are not spoken on street corners, Savonarola carefully locked his door and then did not kneel or fold his hands but stood up holding his hands before him as once was customary with the elders and presbyters in the primitive Church. Sometimes he is said to have placed his hands on his back and to have paced up and down his cell. To Savonarola praying was thinking and—thinking out loud. Prayer was an expression of everything that moved or stirred in his soul, all sentiments, joyful or sad, all psychological evaluations of himself, his longing for salvation, the passion for perfection, the conscious-

ness of sin, his striving for moral purity, the feeling of his own
unworthiness, his lack of faith, his sense of awe in God's presence,
feelings of ecstasy, of love, of resignation, of determination to
carry out God's will. Sometimes he began his prayer with the
words: "To thee I can tell everything . . . I do not understand my
own heart, but I will show thee what I feel . . . By confiding in
thee, my heart will be strengthened, my mind made wiser, my eyes
opened, and my soul set on fire . . . Only in speaking to thee do I
find peace. . . ."

From Dom Vercelli's household books, it appears that Girolamo's
superiors had to admonish him from time to time. Not, to be sure,
for any sin of commission or omission, for his conduct was exemplary, but to temper his zeal and to restrain him from living in a
manner well apt to wreck the health of an ox. The young monk's
fasts were far too rigorous. He would go without nourishment, save
for a drink of cold water on Sunday morning, for a whole week at
the time. These periods of total abstinence from food soon began to
tell on him. After six months in the monastery he was as thin as a
lath. He suffered from shortness of breath and pains in the chest.
They had to tell him to take more nourishment, especially in the
early morning when he had been seen swaying with faintness upon
leaving the chapel. Since the prior made it an order Savonarola
complied. He ate one more slice of black bread a day. But wine or
strong drink of any sort he would not take. Dom Vercelli, respecting the novice's scruples, mercifully refrained from making it an
order.

In consideration of his academic degrees, Fra Girolamo was
excused from attending the classes in grammar which for the other
novices, most of them country boys without much education, were
compulsory. This dispensation might have given him more leisure if
he had not at once applied for permission to attend the higher
courses in theology and rhetoric. The Bologna convent which, like
all Dominican monasteries, was principally a house of study, had
been elevated to the rank of a *Studium Generale,* a school of higher
learning. On its teaching staff in Savonarola's time were masters
and doctors who made a considerable name for themselves. The
lector principalis, or headmaster, was Peter of Bergamo. Bartholo-
mew of Bologna, Anthony of Trente, and Nicholas of Pisa, the

professors of theology and philosophy, were all well-known savants and authors whose works remained in honor amongst the cognoscenti for a long time.

It was the prefect of studies, Peter of Bergamo, who had his eye on Savonarola from the very beginning. It was he who made the prediction to his colleagues that Fra Girolamo would some day, perhaps in their own lifetime, be one of the brightest lights of St. Dominic's Order. "If he retains his health," said Brother Peter, "I foresee that this man will do a good deal for Christ's kingdom." As a result of this recognition, Fra Girolamo was put to the task of instructing the younger friars in reading and writing and in the historical books of the Old Testament.

Savonarola's seclusion was not so strict as to cut him off completely from all communication with the outside world. The Dominicans were not hermits nor were they under a vow of silence. There were townspeople, hucksters and tradesmen, who came to peddle or deliver their wares at the monastery. There was a steady coming and going of visitors from other religious houses in Italy. The General of the Order, Fra Giovacchino Turriano and the provincial vicars regularly passed through Bologna on their tours of inspection and to preside at examinations. Besides, the members of Bologna university's teaching staff, were not averse to dropping in of an evening for an hour of learned conversation with the friars or, as is more likely, just to gossip. In this way the brethren remained fairly well informed as to what went on in the outside world.

* *

Like the city of Bologna and the whole country in fact, the monastery went through a period of tense excitement in April and May, 1478, when Dominican friars who had been eyewitnesses brought word of the outbreak and suppression of the so-called Pazzi revolt in Florence. For a whole month the branches of the Medici bank in Bologna, Rome and other Italian cities remained closed and a financial disaster of world-wide ramifications seemed in the making as Lorenzo de' Medici was excommunicated and the papal army marched on Florence. Savonarola, no less than his superiors, shuddered at the prospect of an upheaval into which all Italy might be drawn.

Florence was then one of the richest and commercially one of the most important cities in Europe. The conduct of state affairs was in the hands of Lorenzo de' Medici and his brother Juliano, the scions of an enormously wealthy family of bankers. Successive generations of Medici had been in charge of the papal finances. In fact the family fortune was founded in A.D. 1414 by the antipope, John XXIII, and one Giovanni de' Medici in a deal which made the Medici collectors of the papal income in most European countries. The first year's transactions on behalf of the papacy brought the Medici one million and a half gold ducats in broker's fees, something like 37 million dollars in our money. The following years showed no decline in profits.

The Medici were treated as equals by the crowned heads of Europe though they carried no title nor held any office. They exercised authority by virtue of being the "first citizens" of the Florentine republic. There were branches of the Medici bank in London, Antwerp, Bruges, Paris, and Lyons and, of course, in all great Italian cities like Venice, Genoa, Rome, Bologna, Ferrara, and so on.

There had been several revolts and plots to break the Medici hold upon the life of Florence. Those revolts were nearly all led by the heads of rival banking families: the Strozzi, Bardi, Peruzzi, Spini and others. Roberto Strozzi, the father of Laudomia, the girl with whom Girolamo Savonarola once fell so passionately in love, was suspected of having been implicated in a former conspiracy against Lorenzo's life. He got off lightly: banishment to Ferrara.

The latest revolt, known as that of the Pazzi, broke out on April 26, 1478, which was a Sunday. While Mass was celebrated in the Cathedral, in the most solemn moment of the elevation of the Host, hundreds of conspirators, upon a signal from their leader, drew their daggers and advanced upon the Medici brothers. Juliano de' Medici was dispatched by a sword blow as he bent his head in adoration. Lorenzo, who stood at the other end of the choir, received a dagger wound in the neck. Though hard-pressed from all sides he managed to draw his sword, and wrapping his cloak around his left arm and using it as a shield, he fought his way to the sacristy.

The renowned Angelo Poliziano, a close friend of Lorenzo, who wrote a report on the bloody melee, tells us that he was able to save the ruler's life only by slamming the huge bronze door of the sacristy shut and bolting it from the inside. "The noise and confusion in the Cathedral was so great," adds Poliziano, "that it seemed as though the church itself was falling down."

Though the tumult came to be known as the "Conspiracy of the Pazzi," the members of the Pazzi family had but a minor share in the plot. They were mere tools in higher hands. Archbishop Francesco Salviati of Pisa, who celebrated Mass, was the organizer of the conspiracy. The knife to dispatch Lorenzo was entrusted to the archpriest of the cathedral. One of the Pope's nephews, Cardinal Rafaello Riario, who was the guest of Lorenzo at the Medici palace the night before, occupied the throne in the sanctuary when the fighting started. His brother Girolamo Riario, who made all the arrangements for the assassination of the Medici, and who was to be the chief beneficiary of their removal by succeeding them in the control of Florentine affairs, had taken care to remain out of harm's way in Rome. He and his uncle, Pope Sixtus IV, were the hottest promoters of the disturbance.

In the afternoon following Juliano's assassination word came that papal troops were standing at the Republic's borders ready to march into Florence and seize power in the confusion which was expected to follow the murder of the two Medici. The troops withdrew when it was learned that the plot had failed. But when Archbishop Salviati and other conspirators were hanged by Lorenzo from the windows of the archiepiscopal palace the Pope, in retaliation, seized the assets of the Medici bank in Rome and then excommunicated Lorenzo de' Medici and declared war on Florence. The whole bloody episode was but part of the Pope's unceasing struggle to enrich his rapacious nephews.

In Bologna's monastery the Pazzi revolt and the Pope's share in it were the subject of heated discussions. That Sixtus IV was implicated no one doubted. Every Italian knew with what "relentless ferocity the Pope pursued the members of the most prominent families in Rome in order to wring from them the surrender of their estates." The attempt on Lorenzo's life fitted exactly in that pattern. But some of the Bolognese brethren—Savonarola was one of them—condemned Lorenzo for the brutal fashion in which he had dealt with the conspirators after the failure of the plot. The war with Rome did not last long. In June, Lorenzo, a man of amazing physical courage, passed through the lines and called personally on the Pope who, in consideration of "the universal anxiety," lifted the excommunication, called off his troops and allowed the banks to resume business.

When the excitement over the Pazzi revolt died down, Fra Girolamo wrote a rhymed treatise full of symbolical imagery on the deplorable state of the Church. His superiors do not seem to have placed the slightest obstacle in his way when he set his ode on "The Ruin of the Church" to print, ran it off on the monastery's hand press and sent copies of it to the heads of convents in Italy and France.

In this ode he asks the Church whom he presents in the guise of a chaste and venerable virgin: "Where are the ancient doctors, the ancient saints? Where is the learning, the love and purity of olden times?" Looking upon the virgin's disheveled and sad appearance, he is prompted to exclaim: "Where are the precious stones, the white robes of purity, the burning lamps of faith, the sweet chants of devotion of former days?"

For answer the virgin takes Savonarola by the hand—as Virgil took Dante by the hand in the nether world—and brings him to a cavern, saying: "When I beheld proud ambition invade Rome and contaminate all things, I fled here for refuge. Here, where I spend my life in tears."

She then shows him the wounds disfiguring her body, and Savonarola turns in grief to the saints in heaven and bids them mourn over the misfortunes which have befallen the Spouse of Christ, the Holy Catholic Church. "Cast down is God's temple," he laments, "and the edifice of chastity." When he asks who has dethroned her, marred her peace and brought her to so lamentable a state, the virgin replies: "*Una fallace superba meretrice,* a false proud harlot!"

What Savonarola identifies as "a false, proud harlot," is not, as some commentators would have us believe, the Church of Rome,

but ancient pagan Rome, the Rome of the empire which the Book
of Apocalypse in the New Testament already called "the whore of
Babylon." Savonarola refers to the neopagan revival and other
aspects and accompaniments of the Renaissance. He specifically
has in mind the delight the most prominent men of his day take
in the lewdness, the impiety, and the inhumanity they find in the
newly discovered works of the ancient poets.

Rather than attacking the Church Savonarola is defending her.
It is because of the lack of faith, the contempt for religion, and
the general disregard of the Church's teaching, that he predicts
dire things for Italy. For the Church he prays: "Sweetest Lord
Jesus, greatest comfort of the soul in torment, turn thy face full
of love upon Rome. Look down with compassion upon thy holy
spouse and see in what trouble she is. . . ."

For his countrymen he has another word: "We must expect tor-
rents of blood if God's loving heart does not soon turn us to peace
. . . I see all Italy at war and ravaged by a terrible famine. . .
These countries will be smitten by a fierce pestilence."

And then the young novice, giving a foretaste of the spirit of
militancy which will one day animate him as he turns against the
pagan, unconverted world, exclaims: "O God, O Lady, that I might
break those spreading wings!" He means, of course, the fast-spread-
ing wings of evil.

In concluding his poem, he makes the Church address a word of
counsel, if not of reproof, to himself for his outburst of indignation: "*Tu piangi e taci; e questo meglio parme,* Weep you [Savona-
rola] and keep silent; that seems best to me."

He does indeed restrain himself, but his peace of mind is gone.
The vision of the disconsolate virgin robs him of the serenity and
cheerfulness which overspread his first years in the convent. Nor
will his peace of mind ever return. For the vision comes back
again and again in days and years to follow.

An incident of an entirely different nature, but no less sensational, which greatly upset the monks of Bologna, occurred a few
years later under the pontificate of Innocent VIII, when workmen
in demolishing some ruins on the Appian Way, uncovered a sarco-
phagus bearing the inscription, "Julia, daughter of Claudius,"
which contained the body of a young woman in a perfect state of

preservation. There was a positive surge of enthusiasm throughout the country when Julia's body was found. To Savonarola's intense dismay, the humanists were in ecstasy. They thanked the ancient gods for the discovery and there was "an upsurge of paganism throughout the land." From all over Italy the common people streamed to Rome to see the remains of their ancient compatriot who seemed to bear witness to the universal surmise that a fairer race than the present generation once lived in the Eternal City. The mummy's appearance must indeed have been extraordinary, "the parted lips revealed small white teeth, the black hair was caught up in a jeweled hair net and the perfectly tinted limbs had the semblance of life." People went wild as the body was transferred to the Capitol and the leading humanists day and night performed the rites which were once used to honor the passing of a deified emperor. To put an end to this revival of paganism the Pope had the body secretly interred outside the Porta Pinciana leaving only the empty coffin on view at the Capitol.

Five years previously there had been a similar outburst of enthusiasm in Rome, much to the horrified amazement and censure of the old-fashioned, nonhumanist clergy. At that time another antique, the Apollo of the Belvedere, was discovered on Cardinal Juliano della Rovere's estate. The statue was venerated as a holy relic by the multitudes, who poured into Rome as on a pilgrimage. Savonarola was as angry on that occasion as his grandfather had been when the Ferrarese carried the statues of Venus and the Virgin Mary in the procession welcoming Pius II.

Then again there was quite a stir in St. Dominic's convent when a few years later—the exact date is uncertain—a strange visitor appeared in the person of Doctor Yem, or as other historians call him, Dr. Isac Jemo, a physician by profession who had known Fra Girolamo's grandfather. This Doctor Yem or Jemo was in great trouble, and he seems to have sought sanctuary in the monastery where he knew his old colleague's grandson to be one of the friars. Dr. Jemo was charged with the old blood ritual crime which was first leveled at the early Christians in Rome who, in times of persecution, frequently celebrated their eucharistic services in the secrecy and relative security of the catacombs. The pagan imperial police accused them or their priests of drinking the blood of children from the chalice used in the sacrament of Holy Communion. When the Christian Church triumphed over paganism the blood ritual libel was transferred to the Jews. This is how Doctor Isac Jemo came to lie under suspicion, for he was a Jew and he was undoubtedly, though involuntarily, involved in the death of three Roman boys. Not that he was officially charged with any crime, it was the ignorant credulous mob which hounded him from pillar to post with the full intent of putting him to death.

Doctor Jemo's troubles started in the Vatican where he was summoned to examine Pope Innocent VIII whose bodily feebleness was so great that he was only kept alive by women's milk. Modern chroniclers of the Pope's last years have fallen into a serious error in relating that Doctor Jemo performed an operation for blood transfusion on the Pope, forgetting that such an operation could not possibly have occurred in a time when the circulation of the blood was unknown. Doctor Jemo, like every other surgeon in those days, took the veins for sinews, the blood for a stagnant in the body and the heartbeat as a pulsing of the bowels in the process of digestion. If the idea of transforming the blood from a healthy to a feeble body had ever occurred to the fifteenth century surgeons, "they would have filled up the whole weak body with blood through numerous incisions to be closed with red-hot cautery as usual," and the patient would certainly have died, "not from loss of blood but from too voluminous an acquisition of it."

At any rate, the Pope neither died nor improved, but the three boys who donated their blood to restore the Pope's health succumbed. Dr. Jemo had been unable to close the incisions. The Pope was given the children's blood to drink,* or, as the historian Stefano Infessura states, "the quintessence of their blood" which amounts to the same thing. When the boys died and the aged Pontiff continued to waste away the operation was first rumored, and then firmly established in the public mind, to have been a ritualistic act of the Jewish religion. Doctor Jemo was said to have drunk the blood himself or to have taken it to the synagogue where his fellow Jews—such was the popular superstition which cropped

---

* Drinking the blood of horses is still frequently prescribed in rural France for the cure of anemia in adults and weakness in children.

up time and again in the centuries to follow—had partaken of the sacrifice of three innocent Christian children.

The Roman mob wanted to torture the Jew to death and he fled to Bologna. As a medical man Fra Girolamo understood perfectly well what had happened and he convinced his superiors of Dr. Jemo's innocence with the result that the surgeon was allowed to hide in the monastery till danger was past and he walked off one day out of the ken of history.

*   *   *

The official name of the Dominicans is *fratres praedicatores,* preaching friars. Before the foundation of the Order priests and monks rarely appeared in the pulpit. Preaching was the prerogative of the bishops. When St. Dominic asked Innocent III to institute an order of preaching friars the Pope threw up his hands in a gesture of unbelieving surprise. But when St. Dominic pointed out that the people were growing estranged from the Church's teaching and that this neglect left the door wide open to heretical exhorters the Pope, recognizing the pertinency of St. Dominic's assertions, forthwith granted permission.

It was but natural therefore that Savonarola, as soon as he was ordained a priest, should be sent out to preach, first in small communities in the immediate vicinity of Bologna, gradually extending the range of his circuit to larger cities and more cultured and discriminating congregations. Some of the larger cities visited by Savonarola were Siena, Mantua, Padua, Brescia, San Gimignano, Florence, and Genoa. There is no record or report of how he fared in the capital of the Genoese republic, but in the other cities his preaching mission was a definite failure. Congregations accustomed to hearing the foremost orators of the day showed but little interest in a speaker whose provincial dialect grated on their ears. Savonarola early read Dante in Ser Michele's library, but he had not as yet acquired a fluency in the softly melodious Tuscan speech. Besides, he was nervous and ill at ease in the pulpit. His gestures lacked grace and dignity. In order to give greater emphasis he spoke louder and louder, till at last his voice turned into a shrill cry. Without pause or stopping to take a breath, he would hold forth for two hours and even longer heedless of the yawning, coughing, shuffling of feet, and other signs of the congregation's weariness.

Generally he selected an episode from Jewish history as his theme. The catastrophes, national defeats, and revolutions undergone by the ancient Hebrews were held up as prefiguration of what was in store for the Brescians, the Padovans, the Florentines, or whomever he happened to be addressing. In one pulpit Savonarola grew so excited in describing the horrors of war that the congregation became restless and then indignant.

The civic authorities and the guilds who had come out in a procession with trumpets and banners heard it said that not one stone of their fair city would be left upon the other. A foreign potentate, Savonarola predicted, would loot and devastate everything that would fall under his hands. "I see babes snatched from their mother's arms to have their heads dashed against the walls of this very church," exclaimed the preacher. "Half your city will go up in flames and all valuables will be carried off leaving you destitute and in tears. . . ."

For a time the congregation listened in shocked surprise, but when the *podestà* and his councilors angrily walked out, Savonarola lost the people's attention. By the time he started to say that the horrors of war could still be avoided if the people and their leaders would follow the example of Nineveh's inhabitants, who sat down in sackcloth and ashes on the Prophet Jonah's call for penitence and invoked God's mercy, the whole church was in uproar.

In Florence he had a similar experience, which was if anything rather worse. The very small congregations he addressed in that city's Santa Maria Novella [there were never more than fifty persons present] soon grew bored with his jeremiads. At one moment a titter was heard soon to be followed by gales of laughter. To the Florentines it sounded as if the young Dominican mispronounced certain words. Like a provincial he said "tee" when he should have said "tay" and "mee" for "may." A group of young men took up the refrain, tee-tee-teeing and mee-mee-meeing in a braying shouted chorus. Savonarola could not finish his sermon. Flushed and embarrassed he fled from the pulpit.

The city where the municipal authorities walked out on him may have been Brescia. At any rate, when Savonarola returned there a few years later and made virtually the same somber predictions it is recorded that the mood of the congregation had changed. Savonarola also had become a more accomplished preacher. Instead of hissing him, the people wept. Thirty years later in 1512, the Brescians saw Fra Girolamo's terrible prophecy go into fulfillment. Their city was ravaged and set on fire and the floor of the church where Savonarola preached was inundated with blood. Brescia, till then one of the wealthiest cities of Lombardy, never recovered from the sack by the French under Gaston de Foix.

Father Antonio Benevieni, one of the monks at San Marco's convent where Savonarola stayed during his preaching mission in Florence, took the young friar aside and said to him frankly: "Fra Girolamo, one cannot deny that your doctrine is true, useful, and necessary, but your delivery is faulty and lacks grace, especially when compared with Fra Mariano da Gennazzano. Why don't you go and hear Mariano preach? There is a man most worthy of emulation." But Savonarola knew all about Mariano. Everybody in Florence had spoken to him of the eloquence and the fine manners of this Augustinian friar to whose sermons in the Church of San Spirito the crowds flocked in such numbers that the church generally proved too small.

Angelo Poliziano, one of the great humanists in the entourage of Lorenzo de' Medici and a canon of the Duomo in Florence, the same who saved the Magnificent's life in the Pazzi revolt, wrote a letter of criticism. After chiding Savonarola's awkward and inexperienced preaching, Poliziano told of the tremendous impression Mariano had made on him: "I went to San Spirito," he wrote, "feeling badly disposed and mistrustful of the great praises I had heard of Fra Mariano. But no sooner did I enter the church than the preacher's appearance, his manners, and his face made a complete change in my feelings and I knew at once that I would hear great things from him.

"And indeed, I admit, that Fra Mariano soared to gigantic heights in the pulpit, far above all human proportions. I was all ears to his musical voice, the chosen words, the grand sentences. I was swayed by their perfect harmony and cadence. . . ."

When Poliziano's letter had been read to him, Savonarola re-

plied: "I thank you for your candor, but I, too, have heard Fra
Mariano. He preaches from Cicero and the poets and not from
Holy Writ. . . I do not deny that he declaims with great charm and
eloquence. But his phrases, gestures, the way he shows his teeth
or shakes the curls from his forehead, all of it is studied and
continuously rehearsed before a company of friends . . . What is
especially blamable is Mariano's carelessness in quoting from
Scripture. He only mentions those passages of which he knows
that they will charm the ears of his illustrious hearers . . . God's
word is not given to us to tickle our fancy. It is to convict us of
sin and to point the way of salvation . . . The verbal elegancies and
ornaments of Fra Mariano will have to give way to sound doctrine
simply preached. The main thing is to encourage men to act
rightly . . . You reproach me for my lack of style. What stuff
it all is! What has style to do with it? Have something to say, and
say it as clearly as you can. That is the only secret of preaching . . .
Let Fra Mariano preach the word of God. . . ."

At this point in Savonarola's career enters an element of uncertainty. Some sources will have it that he soon went out on a
new preaching mission. Others affirm that he returned to Bologna
to teach and but seldom left the convent in the years following the
failure of his first attempt. Certain it is that in 1485 he was appointed to preach in his native Ferrara and took up residence in the
Monastery of the Angels which stood within a stone's throw of his
parents' residence.

He made no objection when Dom Vercelli indicated Ferrara as
his next and perhaps permanent place of residence. He nonetheless
set out with a heavy heart. He had not the least desire to renew
former acquaintances and affections. Laudomia Strozzi and her
father still lived in Ferrara, and though she had remained unmarried the young lady now played a prominent role in court
circles as a friend and daily companion of Duchess Eleonora.

On the other hand, the Duke, Ercole the Great, from whose
wedding celebration Fra Girolamo once broke away to the scandal
of the whole town, was a changed man. He did not carry on the
tradition of licentiousness and shame which dishonored the courts
of his predecessors. He had become an ardent Bible student and
personally called at the Angels' convent to welcome Savonarola

back to Ferrara. Duke Ercole spoke to Savonarola about Donna Elena's penurious circumstances. He offered a gift of 400 gold ducats to provide a dowry for Beatrice and Clara, Fra Girolamo's sisters. When Savonarola politely declined on the grounds that his conscience would not allow him to be in anyone's debt, the Duke said: "No one needs to know, but if you ever change your mind, you only have to say the word."

During his son's two years' stay in Ferrara, father Niccolo was gravely ill and never left the house. The friar visited the paternal home only at nights since he was determined not to be seen in the vicinity of the Strozzi mansion. He admits that he did not make a favorable impression with his preaching on the members of his own family because, as he said, quoting the words of Christ: "No man is a prophet in his own country." Espying his mother and other relatives in the congregation, a fit of nervousness would seize him contracting his voice to a piping, almost hysterical dissonant. He was much better in private conversation and informal discussion.

A case is specially recorded of an encounter with a group of soldiers going to some war or other. Savonarola that time traveled by bark on the river Po, though as a Dominican friar he was required to go on foot. With his strong sense of providential guidance Fra Girolamo soon realized why he had chosen or rather why he had been made to choose the unusual mode of travel. It was predestined that he was to meet those soldiers who passed the time playing the game of *giocare diti* which Caesar's legionnaires were already playing during lulls in the campaign in Gaul and which Italian soldiers still played in North Africa in World War II. The game consists in a lightninglike sticking up of a number of fingers by one player while another guesses and just as rapidly calls out the number of fingers the first player keeps down. The soldiers on the bark interlarded their conversation with so many blasphemies and profanities that Savonarola could no longer bear it. He interrupted their game by asking them if as men of war they did not think that one who lays down his life for his friends shows not only immense love but is worthy of all praise. The soldiers readily agreed whereupon Savonarola told them the story of the Passion. The men were so touched by his searching appeal not to use the Lord's name in vain that twelve out of the eighteen who made up the group, threw themselves in contrition at the Friar's feet, crying for absolution.

From Ferrara he visited Florence again, and also Genoa, Venice, Mantua and Padua, though nothing has come down to us concerning his business in these and other cities in northern Italy. The reason must be that he had not yet acquired the phenomenal power as a preacher which drew men to him from all over the country a few years later. But a change was in the air. From Mantua he wrote a letter to his mother, who hailed from that beautiful city, saying that the people implored him to stay in their midst so impressed they were with his sermons. It was nothing less than a leap into fame when by order of his superiors he attended a Chapter General of the Lombard Dominicans in the city of Reggio. This was a gathering at which not only a large number of distinguished ecclesiastics and theologians, but many persons of note in the world of art and letters were present.

It is not specifically recorded what part Savonarola took in the proceedings. The most likely conjecture is that the reform of the Church, which was then the perennial subject of discussion amongst churchmen, gave him an opportunity to state his own views on the matter. Whatever it was that he said, he held the great assembly spellbound without the slightest trace of nervousness or vocal deterioration. Everyone present was impressed with the young friar's learning and versatility in theology and international affairs. He appears to have taken the floor several times by request of one or the other presiding prelates. Before the Chapter General adjourned the hitherto obscure monk was the most conspicuous figure in Reggio. Through the dispersing delegates he was lifted into notice throughout Italy as a man of extraordinary talent and unusual promise. Two future popes, Cardinals Rodrigo Borgia and Juliano della Rovere, took particular notice of what Savonarola said in Reggio and were to refer to his remarks more than once in afteryears.

One of the persons who heard him speak in Reggio was the Count Giovanni Pico della Mirandola, who has been called the wonder of the world because of his vast knowledge and learning. He spoke and wrote twenty-three languages fluently, including Chaldean, Coptic, Armenian, and Hebrew. He had studied in Paris, Oxford, Salonika, and Padua and had traveled over the entire Euro-

pean continent, spending one year in Constantinople. Endowed with
a phenomenal memory, Pico may be said to have amassed in his own
mind the sum total of human knowledge then available. A favorite
of Lorenzo the Magnificent, "this gifted man with his gracious bearing, long golden hair, and open countenance excited admiration
wherever he went," except at the court of Rome where he was
suspected of heresy.

There is no doubt that Pico della Mirandola was not an orthodox
Christian, perhaps not a Christian at all, at the time of the Reggio
assembly. He felt nonetheless so strongly attracted to Savonarola
that he entered into conversation with him and ever after, till his
premature death at the age of thirty-one in 1494, remained one of
the Friar's strongest supporters. It was Savonarola who brought
Pico back to the Christian faith and administered the last rites.

On his return to Florence, Pico called on Lorenzo de' Medici to
tell him of his discovery of a monk who "has more theological insight and sincerity than a hundred Fra Marianos put together." He
urged Lorenzo to bring Savonarola to Florence by securing him a
place in the Dominican Monastery of San Marco which was heavily
endowed by the Medici family. At first Lorenzo demurred. He did
not like to mix in church affairs. "And besides," he said, "we have
three thousand monks as it is in Florence, what do we need him
for?" In the end he gave in to his friend's solicitations. "But,"
said Lorenzo, "you, Count, write the letter asking Savonarola's
transfer yourself, and I will sign it." Some years were to pass before
Pico's request was acted upon.

In 1487 war clouds were gathering over Ferrara. The Venetians
dispatched an army with the object of seizing the city and making it
tributary to their domain. In the ensuing anxiety, the Vicar-General,
Fra Turriano, ordered the monastery closed. Some historians will
have it that the building was damaged by gunfire. The monks were
ordered to disperse and Savonarola was sent back to his old convent at Bologna. In 1489 he was again ordered to change his
residence. He remonstrated with his superiors. Since he had not
met with a favorable reception in Florence and he dreaded a repetition of the unpleasantness he had experienced in the Arno city, he
preferred to stay in Bologna. It was then that he learned that Pico
della Mirandola had been active on his behalf and that the order for

his transfer to Florence's San Marco came from "the highest authority" which could not be other than the General of the Order or perhaps the Pope himself.

So he left Bologna. Parting did not come easy with Girolamo. He wept on the shoulders of Prior Vercelli who accompanied him as far as the city gate. Eighteen miles from Bologna in the broiling heat of the Appenine foothills, Savonarola, exhausted by fatigue, sank down by the roadside and lay gasping for breath. As was not unusual with him he had refused or neglected to bring either food or drink. He could not muster the strength to rise to his feet. It was high noon and the sun stood directly overhead. His tongue was parched and, thinking that the end had come, he felt himself fainting away.

He awoke in a village hostelry to discover that an unknown wayfarer had lifted him on his mule and brought him to the tavern. The stranger bent over him and plied him with food and drink. After a night's sleep Savonarola felt able to resume his journey. The stranger walked by his side till shortly before twilight when they saw Giotto's Campanile and the Tower of the Signoria in the distance.

"Go now into Florence," said the man, "and do the work God has called you to do in this city." With these words the stranger vanished. Savonarola regretted all his life that he had not asked the good Samaritan's name.

Chapter III

In the Florence
of Lorenzo the Magnificent

SAN MARCO's monastery, where Savonarola took up residence in the latter part of 1489, dated from the thirteenth century, but had been completely renovated by Cosimo de' Medici, the grandfather of Lorenzo the Magnificent. The buildings do not at present serve any religious purpose. In the wave of anti-clericalism sweeping Italy in 1863, the monastery was suppressed and the edifice made over into the present Museum of San Marco. The interior, however, has remained virtually unchanged so that in cells number 12 and 13 on the upper floor, once occupied by Fra Girolamo, his wooden crucifix and rosary, his writing table and chair, seem to be still waiting for his return. In the corner of one of the rooms stands the staff from his itinerant preacher's days, a pleasant strand to the thread of memory which joins the past years. In fact the whole place seems invested with an aroma of pious remembrance. The famous Bible which Girolamo inherited from his grandfather lies in a glass case in the hall, the margins of its pages covered with commentary notes and references in the Friar's printlike perpendicular handwriting. The museum's library, once the private property of Lorenzo de' Medici, was purchased by Savonarola after the Magnificent's death, a venture that proved of immense value to posterity but which plunged the Friar head over heels in debt.

On the same floor with Savonarola's old cells is one that was originally set aside for the monastery's patron and renovator, Cosimo de' Medici, who intended to spend the eventide of life within San Marco's walls. Death came before the "Father of the Fatherland" could carry out his pious design, although he often visited the convent in his last days to sit and meditate in his cell, in order, as he said, to accustom himself to being alone with God.

Most of the monastery's art treasures remain in the same places and in the same excellent condition as the Friar found them in 1489. Several of Savonarola's fellow friars were artists of world renown. One of them, Fra Bartolomeo, has left a portrait of the Friar in the last year of his life, reproductions of which are scattered far and wide in the Christian world. The aureole of sainthood around Savonarola's head was added by Bartolomeo within a few hours after the Friar's death. The master painter of the monastery, Blessed Fra Angelico, who died before Savonarola came to Florence, ranks with Gozzoli. Donatello, Lippi, Da Vinci, and other great artists of the Renaissance. He adorned the walls of the refectory and cells with a number of frescoes depicting the life of Christ of which Michelangelo remarked that "no scenes more true, more noble, or more exquisitely rendered can be imagined."

It was not long before Savonarola discovered that the social condition of Florence bristled with the sharpest contrasts. There were hideous slums and infinite misery, public ethics had sunk to a low level, and in no other city perhaps was so much evil spoken, though "nowhere else did people speak with so much wit and elegance." The popular quarters were beehives of vice and crime, but the fine arts were cultivated with a zeal that seems almost incredible today. The immense wealth accumulated in the foregoing generation and the energy of the leading families were applied to artistic and literary ends alone. Many men then living won immortality. The epoch of the Medici had reached its zenith and no age since that of Athens has produced in the whole earth so much of such lasting merit.

Florence was a small city then with a population not exceeding 120,000. Lorenzo de' Medici had no difficulty in keeping accurately informed as to the movements and activity of the most conspicuous of his fellow citizens. Why, he wanted to know, wasn't the new Friar at San Marco's like a good shoemaker sticking to his last? When he could spare an hour from his duties of teaching and lecturing at the convent Savonarola was reported to be wandering about the city's popular quarters. Was there nothing else to see? Had he no eye for the monuments, the churches, the shops, and art treasures in the public squares and buildings?

Indeed, he had, but he who was to become known as "the preacher of the starvelings and the wretched" took more interest in the condition of the common people. Lorenzo's vigilantes reported the Friar to be asking questions, to be inquiring at the hospitals and the leprosery, conferring with apothecaries and physicians. He called at eleemosynary institutions like that of the Good Men of St. Martin where bread and clothing were distributed to the poor. His chief concern seemed to be to find out how the poor lived, what their homelife was like, and what was the state of public morality.

It was clear enough what the Friar was up to: he was searching out the evils of Florentine society. Here was a strange monk, a monk whose spirituality took a material form. "Feed my sheep," said Jesus, give food and water to hungry and thirsty bodies. Fra Girolamo was a shepherd in the full sense of the word to whom the material and physical welfare of the flock was of primary importance.

Every afternoon he strolled in the market places or in the San Marino quarter of the artisans watching the weavers and wool carders at work, the cloth dyers, the sword smiths, the stonecutters, the furriers, and the shoemakers. As soon as he left the Piazza della Signoria behind and the center of the city with its churches, countinghouses, foreign embassies, and municipal offices, and its well-dressed crowds of merchants, customers, and visitors he was appalled by the number of beggars. There were so many blind in Florence that they had formed corporations to pool their resources for the employment of guides. As the grandson and confidant of a specialist in women's diseases Fra Girolamo more than suspected that venereal infection lay at the bottom of the prevalence of blindness.

Crime, vice, destitution, and filth on all sides: how could the Florentine commoners live the good life and care for their souls' welfare? What good was the building of cathedrals and palaces when so many were reduced to the barest necessities of life and sometimes less? A great number lived in holes in the wall, in leaky garrets and musty cellars which the Medici would have declared unfit for their greyhounds and race horses.

Most willingly Savonarola would have stopped at one or the other street corner to speak to the perennially congregating crowds. Only he soon became aware that whenever he approached the people would instantly fall silent and quickly disperse in all directions. The reason was that they took him for one of Lorenzo's spies. His Dominican garb gave him away. The people knew very well that the Dominicans were the favorites of the Medici. "Pst! Watch out, here comes a dog, *un' cano!*" someone would call out when Savonarola hove in sight. That was the way the people, with a play on the word Dominicans, referred to the members of the Order: *Domini canes,* the Lord's watchdogs. Nothing dismayed Fra Girolamo so much as to be even remotely identified with the Medicean regime which was to him the personification of the world's injustice.

He was shown the ruined mansion of the Bardi, said to have been destroyed by popular rage, which meant that it was sacked and ruined by a rioting mob at the instigation of one of the Medici. The owners were banished or had fled, counting themselves fortunate not to have been thrown into the *carnaio,* a dungeon so vile and horrible that none ever left it alive. Other mansions to the right and left along the banks of the Arno owned by distinguished exiles had been stripped of their valuables and furniture. Their dilapidated interiors were cluttered up with a hundred half-famished, destitute families.

The market places were as picturesque and hilarious as those in Bologna, Genoa, Ferrara, and the other large cities which Savonarola had visited, but in Florence he paid particular attention to the flagrant contrasts of wealth and poverty; of carefree abandon and body- and soul-killing misery; of magnificent, sophisticated living on the one hand and the most sordid, venal, human wretchedness on the other. One moment he was enraged till his blood boiled, the next instant rendered him almost speechless with wonder and admiration. Churches, private palaces, elegant monuments were arising on every hand. Every day new books appeared or new paintings were exhibited. The most brilliant processions wended their way

through the narrow streets, to be followed by hordes of refugees
from the rural regions, haggard with sorrow and sickness.

One of the many poor art students who enjoyed Lorenzo de'
Medici's hospitality plus five gold ducats pocket money, frequently
accompanied Savonarola on those sight-seeing escapades. The lad's
name was Michelangelo Buonarroti. He was only fifteen years of
age, but of such phenomenal understanding of art that one could
not have wished for a better guide. Michelangelo lived at the
dormitory and worked at the studio which Lorenzo had built in
"the most marvelous garden in the world," located near the
Palazzo Medici and also in close proximity to San Marco's convent.
The garden which Lorenzo and his lady Clarissa had personally
laid out, drew visitors from all over Europe. Along the sides the
Magnificent had ranged statues, columns, vases, bronzes, fragments of pagan altars, and other treasures excavated by his
archaeologists in Greece and Asia Minor. In this pleasance where
popes, emperors and kings loved to linger, Michelangelo lived and
worked and saw those statues of the immortal Greek sculptors
Pheidias and Praxiteles "than which," as he said, "art cannot be
purer and more perfect because there is a living soul in these
marbles."

Although Fra Girolamo had visited Florence in the past and
once spent a whole year in the city, he had never paid much attention to his environment. In this respect he resembled Desiderius
Erasmus before whose eyes the greatest works of art passed un-
noticed. On his previous visits Savonarola's thoughts had been
concentrated, to the exclusion of everything else, on the ultimate
questions. Now Michelangelo showed him the bronze doors of
the Baptistry, and explained how the artist, Ghiberti, had been six
years in the designing and casting of one door alone. "Here, reverend father," said the boy, "you look upon the beauties of
paradise itself. There," he pointed to Giotto's Campanile, "is not a
tower, but a lily* more gracious than Solomon in all his
glory." They looked up at Brunelleschi's *duomo* on top of the
Cathedral, then considered the eighth wonder of the world, with
its sweeping curves eclipsing the hills, little suspecting that the
same Michelangelo in his old age would build a still loftier one on

* The lily is Florence's municipal emblem.

St. Peter's in Rome. When they entered the so-called Baptistry, really the Church of St. John the Baptist, which Ruskin was one day to call "the most perfect building on earth," Savonarola was overcome with a sense of awe in the presence of so daring and all-embracing a conception.

It was Michelangelo who told Fra Girolamo that the tower on the Palazzo della Signoria, now called the Palazzo Vecchio or Old Palace, soared aloft as an expression of the Florentine people's aspiration for freedom. Then through the Por' San Maria street leading almost directly to the Ponte Vecchio, the Old Bridge, then as now bearing on either side a myriad of jewelry shops. Across the river they could see the mass of the Pitti palace, and the red roof of Messer Niccolo Machiavelli's mansion and, far beyond, the mystic purple of Tuscany's great lonely hills. Back through the buzzing Old Market where singing birds, rabbits, cats, and dogs and tripe and fish were for sale, they would inspect the churches of San Miniato, of San Spirito, Santa Croce, and the gracefully spired Badia, the marvels of Orsanmichele, Santa Maria Novella, and Santa Maria Nuova, great building projects, more spires and towers, more palaces, more splendor. Seldom did the two sight-seers end their promenade without halting a moment before an inconspicuous three-story house bearing the inscription: *Qui Nacque Il Divino Poeta,* "Here was born the divine poet": Dante Alighieri, the greatest and unhappiest of their countrymen.

In the afternoon, when the stalls and the booths of the hucksters, the greengrocers, butchers, and vintners were taken down and put away for the night, the streets filled with ambulating musicians and ballad singers, acrobats and soothsayers, sellers of charms and obscene pictures. Thieves and robbers tried to dispose of stolen wares. Forbidden elixirs, drugs and aphrodisiac concoctions were openly peddled. There were gaming houses on every street, taverns with darkened interiors, dives and stews of the lewdest kind. "And yet this is Florence," Fra Girolamo said to Michelangelo, "this is the city of taste and culture, of fine manners and famous cuisine, of wealth and brilliancy in art and letters renowned through the length and breadth of the earth."

As he spoke he was shocked to see the nuns of St. Mary Magdalen's convent, arms akimbo, leaning in the window sills, hailing passers-by and engaging in gallant conversation with young men and boys. More than once the two wayfarers were accosted by prostitutes. As a contemporary visitor from Bologna relates, the Florentine harlots were so impertinent that they habitually jostled and pushed respectable bourgeois matrons from the middle of the street into the gutters.

On the basis of what he had seen, Savonarola was soon to speak of Florence as another Sodom and Gomorrah and of Lorenzo de' Medici as an enemy of Christ. While readily admitting the "incontrovertible": Lorenzo's brilliant intellect, his genuine poetic gift and fine taste for art, Savonarola nevertheless held him responsible for encouraging the worst tendencies of the age and the multiplication of its corruptions. "Abandoned to pleasure himself," it was said, "Lorenzo urged the people to ever lower depths of abandonment and depravity in order to plunge them into the lethargy of intoxication" and continue undisturbed in the shameless arbitrariness of his rule.

If certain of his biographers may be believed Lorenzo was a ruthless tyrant. He had many crimes on his conscience. There is a long list of eminent citizens put to death by him for political and other reasons. He had swindled the custodian of the public domain and robbed the Monte delle Fanciulle, a charitable institution for providing respectable poor girls with a marriage dowry, thus forcing an untold number of young women into a life of shame. The responsibility for the sack of Volterra and putting its population to the sword must be squarely laid at his door. But he was also, and this not even his bitterest foes denied, amiability personified. His manners were of such kindliness and refinement that men did not notice his hard face and its crushed nose when they came in his presence. Never were the gates of the Palazzo Medici guarded. Every citizen of Florence from the wealthiest to the poorest could enter freely. Like his father Piero and grandfather Cosimo before him, Lorenzo possessed the rare quality of being able to deal with all manner of persons as an equal and on the friendliest terms.

Lorenzo was twenty years of age when, two days after his father's death, the principal men of the city and of the state came to his house to ask him to take charge of public affairs. No election took place, and, like his ancestors, Lorenzo de' Medici held no title. He was not of noble birth and filled not any specific office. The Medici belonged to the class of the *popolani grassi,* the fat, wealthy moneybags. By profession they were bankers and possessed as much energy and resourcefulness, as prudence and boldness. Of Lorenzo it is said that he went straight to his ends, trampling over all considerations whether human or divine if he thought his personal interests were at issue or some advantage was to be gained for his family. The Medici epitomized the principle of power without responsibility.

During the first nine years of his rule he acquired the surname of *Il Magnifico,* by reason, as one of his well-wishers writes, "of his extraordinary abilities, his great liberality, the lavish expenditure of his wealth for the public benefit, and the general splendor of his life in which Florence participated."

The Florentine Republic stood at the top in world commerce. The banking house of the Medici controlled or influenced the finances of most of the Peninsula's principalities. There were powerful branches of the bank in the lands of the western Mediterranean, Spain, France, Morocco, Tunis, and, in northerly direction, Flanders and the Netherlands. Representatives of Florentine business houses resided in Lyons, Paris, and London, in Salonika, Constantinople, Alexandria, on Cyprus, in Persia, Armenia, China, Egypt, even in Timbuktu beyond the Sahara desert in the heart of Africa. Lorenzo, as the head of the Medici bank, sat on the interlocking directorates of all these great commerical enterprises.

It was but inevitable that a man wielding such power and influence should be the object of fierce envy on the part of other, almost equally wealthy merchant princes in Florence and abroad. Several attempts were made by force of arms to upset his dominion and eliminate him personally. All failed, but the historians have taken sides and judged him, not impartially, but according to their own prejudices and perhaps their personal interests and predilections.

To some Lorenzo was a son of Belial, "a monster of depravity" who roamed the streets of Florence at night in the company of a band of perverts in search of adventure. Others say that the charge of profligacy and of debasing public taste by introducing licentious-

ness into arts and letters is without an atom of foundation. Whom
are we to believe?

Some facts about his daily life are indisputable. Lorenzo was an
early riser. Before leaving the Palazzo Medici or one of his country houses, he rode horseback with his two young sons, Piero
and Giovanni, or played ball with all of his seven children, or took
them to see the animals in his private zoo at Careggi. The morning
hours he spent in his office at the Palazzo della Signoria with the
municipal clerks, receiving delegations and embassies, discussing
home and foreign affairs with diplomats and financial experts. In
the afternoon he busied himself with the art students to whom he
freely extended the hospitality of his palace. Il Magnifico personally
helped Michelangelo, who was one of these wards, in fashioning
the wax models for the "Madonna of the Steps," "The Battle of
the Centaurs," and "Apollo," the first productions of the young
master's chisel. In the early evening musicians and young poets
played and recited verses at the Medici table. He helped and encouraged them by every means at his command. For the great
artists Lorenzo built villas in the vicinity of his country house at
Fiesole. There scarcely passed an evening without a session of
the Platonic Academy where his genius shone in a company of the
most eminent philosophers, theologians, and poets.

Where then did Lorenzo find the time to accomplish the multi-
farious turpitudes with which he has been charged?

*   *   *

> *Quant'è bella giovinezza*
> *Che si fugge tuttavia.*
> *Chi vuol esser lieto, sia;*
> *Di doman non c'è certezza.*

> "Fair is youth and void of sorrow;
> But it hourly flies away—
> Boys and maidens enjoy today;
> Nought ye know about tomorrow."

Thus sang Lorenzo de Medici in his "Triumph of Bacchus" at
the beginning of his career. And Simonetta Cattaneo, the dream girl

of the Renaissance, responded: "How glorious is it to be alive in this age!" Simonetta, the brightest star in the Florentine heavens, was the dearest friend of Lorenzo and also of his brother Juliano who perished in the Pazzi revolt. She was the center of the festivities, the balls, masquerades, jousts, and costume contests which the Medici brothers organized. The whole of Florence lay at the feet of this sixteen year old girl from Genoa who inaugurated the brief epoch when youth and beauty reigned supreme. The young people who gathered around her were fairly intoxicated with joy and enthusiasm in the presence of the accumulating masterworks of art, sculpture, poetry, and painting.

The oldest in the circle of her admirers was the philosopher Marsilio Ficino; thirty-six years. Verrochio, the chief pupil of Donatello, whose work is represented in the Vatican by "The Adoration of the Magi," was thirty-three; Botticelli, twenty-two; Ghirlandajo, twenty; the poet Angelo Poliziano, who lived in the Medici palace, was but sixteen; while Leonardo da Vinci, who worked as an apprentice in Verrochio's studio, was seventeen years old. Sandro Botticelli could not stop gazing at Simonetta, "the star of Genoa," "the heavenly apparition," "the most pure angel." All were in love with her. Juliano de' Medici was never from her side. What Beatrice was to Dante Simonetta was to Lorenzo, the object of mystic love and veneration.

The high point in the adoration of this young woman came on her birthday when Lorenzo staged a show in the Piazza Santa Croce where his brother Juliano appeared in a coat of mail entirely of silver riding at the head of a procession to do homage to her whose portrait by Botticelli on the silken banner in Juliano's hand was inscribed with the words *La Sans Pareille,* "The Unequaled." It was Simonetta who, as queen of the festival, in the sight of all Florence, pressed the laurel wreath on the kneeling Juliano's brow.

And yet she was not beautiful in the true sense of the word. She was wonderfully gentle and charming, her hair honey-blonde, her voice golden, her simple but delightful gestures ineluctably drew everyone's attention. The masters Piero di Cosimo and Ghirlandajo present her with rather coarse features: high cheekbones, an upturned nose, a pointed chin, and feverish blue eyes. But Botticelli painted her as "Cleopatra," as "Venus rising from the

Foam," and as the principal figure in his composition "Primavera" (Spring.) Verrochio immortalized her in his "Tobias with the Angels" where Simonetta is represented as the matchlessly graceful archangel Michael. In the magnificent ode which he wrote for her birthday celebration. Angelo Poliziano compared her with a wood nymph.

Simonetta's triumph lasted seven years, then she was taken to Piombino on the Riviera where she died of galloping consumption. On the eve of her death, Lorenzo, who happened to be walking with a friend in Pisa, seeing an unusual bright star in the sky said: "Look, there goes the soul of this precious woman!" The Magnificent composed a sonnet to "The Dear Departed One." Juliano was inconsolable. And Sandro Botticelli, whose real name was Filipepi, forty years later in the hour of death, urged his friends to be sure to bury him in the family chapel of the Filipepi in All Souls Church, "because there lies dearest Simonetta."

Soon after Simonetta's death the entertainments resumed with even greater ostentation. "It was their wont," says Il Lasca, speaking of the Medici and their friends, "to go forth after dinner, and often they lasted till three or four hours into the night, with a multitude of masked men on horseback following, richly dressed, exceeding sometimes three hundred in number, and as many men on foot with lighted torches. Thus they traversed the city, singing to the accompaniment of music arranged for four, eight, twelve, or even fifteen voices, supported by various instruments."

Lorenzo had written a bundle of fanciful Carnival songs. The best artists and poets collaborated with him in setting them to music and making the songs popular, something in which they succeeded so well that the ballads have not been forgotten till this day. These splendid songs dealt with such subjects as the Frog-catchers, the Furies, Old men and Young wives, Old wives and Young husbands, Jewelers, Gypsies, Penitents, Devils, Nymphs in love, Nuns escaped from convent, and a hundred abstractions on Death, Madness, Calumny, and, of course, Love, Love, Love. . . . They were brilliantly written, but their tone and content were uniformly and deliberately immoral.

The greatest connoisseur of the Renaissance said of Lorenzo's Carnival Songs that "one might fancy them composed for some

ancient phallic festival." An amazing spectacle it must have been
when Florence "ran wild in Dionysiac revels proclaiming the luxury and license of the senses." Day after day, except in Lent, these
cavalcades and processions passed through the streets adorned
with triumphal arches, decorated with flowers, banners and cloth
of gold. There were hailstorms of confetti, torches flared on the
famous bridges and the façades of the palaces and churches. The
air rang wild with the music of lute and cymbal and the voices of
trained singers, male and female.

Passing through the Piazza or arrived beneath Giotto's Campanile and the Duomo of Brunelleschi, the singers were joined by
the multitudes in the chorus of Lorenzo's "Triumph of Bacchus,"
"Fair is youth and void of sorrow; Boys and maidens enjoy today.
. . ." As in Ferrara, but on an infinitely more elaborate scale, al-
legorical representations were given. Beautiful women posed as
the goddesses of pagan divinity in tableaux from the classical poets.
These fabulous shows, say all the chroniclers, were made as perfect
and dramatic as possible under Lorenzo's personal supervision. . . .

*   *   *

It almost goes without saying that Savonarola did not approve.
To him all these boisterous manifestations of public rejoicing were
a sham and a deception, a screen obscuring the ugly reality of a
people deprived of its freedom and compelled to take the semblance
of contentment for a genuine and healthy joy of life which could,
in his estimation, be found only in striving for the realization of
generous and noble ideas. He saw the hollowness of the image
that had been set up, a substitute presentment which turned the
people aside from their libertarian aspirations. Prevented by Lorenzo from participation in the making of policy and from mixing
in the affairs of state, a paralyzing inertia had settled on the intel-
ligentsia. The energies that would ordinarily have infused a new
spirit in the people and benefited them, were sidetracked, deliberately in Savonarola's opinion, in the pursuit of private enjoyment.
From his grandfather he had inherited a strong aversion to all
forms of tyranny. It swelled into bitterness now that he came face
to face with Lorenzo's autocratic procedure. The ruling family's

iron grip on all of Florence's intellectual and commercial activity filled Savonarola with a secret rage.

No doubt Florence's cultural state was still unbelievably high. Everybody of any consequence spoke and wrote Latin and Greek. Women composed verses and books in the classical tongues. There were more painters, sculptors, and architects of surpassing merit than at any other time. In Lorenzo's salons, amid his fabulous and forever unparalleled art collections, philosophers, poets, musicians, and classical scholars gathered to listen to his sparkling conversation. But to Savonarola it was all a flaunting of class selfishness, indifference to the people's condition, an after-us-the-deluge attitude. So long as the ruler showed no sense of responsibility in matters touching the common weal, the learned were unable to make their knowledge available for loftier aims. What Florence lacked in Lorenzo's day was principle and a regard for the teachings of Christian morality. The old virtues and the traditions of simple piety were no longer practiced save in the remotest villages which had no contact with the corruption and depravity of the glittering city.

To a religious purist like Savonarola the attitude to the Christian gospel in Lorenzo's entourage appeared downright blasphemous. Each year on the 27th of November, the supposed anniversary of Plato's birth and death, Lorenzo staged a solemn service of commemoration. His friend Marsilio Ficino kept a votive lamp burning in his study before Plato's bust. This man's whole life was devoted to an attempt to reconcile the irreconcilable: classical antiquity and the Christian revelation. He spoke of a universal religion in which honors to Venus and the Virgin Mary would be equally divided. Though a canon of Florence's Church of St. Lorenzo, Ficino declared that there was no specifically Christian truth. In all its forms, in the pagan as well as the Christian, truth was divine. The testimony of the Hebrew prophets and seers concerning Christ's advent, were superseded by the Fourth Book of Virgil, where the coming of a world saviour and the dawn of a golden age are announced. Ficino asserted that Plato testified "very benignantly" of Jesus as a highly religious and pious person. He insisted that Plato taught the truth of Christianity by means of strange and subtle allegories. For this reason he and his friends proposed that the Pope be asked to canonize Plato as a saint of the Church.

What must a rigorous orthodox Christian like Savonarola, to whom Christ was not just a pious good man but, in the words of the Creed, "very God of very God," who believed in the uniqueness of the Christian revelation and the inerrancy of the Sacred Scriptures, have thought of a priest like Ficino, who dreamed of wiping out all dogmatic differences and institute a universal religion based on Platonism?

At his own expense Lorenzo brought some of Europe's most brilliant intellects to teach at Florence's Academy, men like Landino, Bisticci, and Grocin, afterwards professor of Greek at Oxford, and Thomas Linacre, the most eminent physician of England. Angelo Poliziano, who occupied a canon's stall at the Cathedral, wrote such perfect Latin verse that his works were placed on an equal footing with Virgil, Horace, Ovid, and other poets of the Golden Age. When he preached he used the most edifying language, but in private he declared that the creeds were absolutely meaningless.

Poliziano was the tutor of Lorenzo's two eldest children, Piero and Giovanni, the first an execrable creature who incorporated in his person all the vices of the age, the second a boy of sweet and lovable habits who was ordained to the priesthood at the age of seven, became a cardinal at fourteen, and was elevated to the supreme pontificate as Leo X in 1513. "He is so strictly bred," wrote Master Poliziano in a report card, "that never from his mouth comes a lewd or even a light expression. He does not yield to his teachers in learning, nor to old men in gravity of demeanor." Poliziano made a perfect linguist and art connoisseur of him so that Leo knew no greater joy in later life than to receive a letter in Greek from Erasmus or to be invited to see a new painting in Raphael's studio. As Pope he spent a colossal fortune in the promotion of art and letters. But like his teacher, Leo cared little for religion. "He would have made a perfect Pope," remarked one of his Cardinals, "had he believed in God." From Poliziano he learned to speak of the New Testament as "the book of the fables of Jesus Christ" and of the doctrine of transubstantiation as "a juggle to deceive the vulgar." The first act of Leo's pontificate was to bestow the purple on Julio de' Medici, the illegitimate son of his uncle Juliano who died in the Pazzi revolt. "Look, Julio," said Leo X, "Let us enjoy the Papacy now that God has given it to us."*

Luigi Pulci, one of Lorenzo's bosom friends, was the author of a graceful invocation to the Virgin, followed by another to Venus, and this again by a satire on the immortality of the soul. Lorenzo himself refused to read the Bible, lest its poor Latin and many inconsistencies affect or spoil his perfect command of the language. Pico della Mirandola, the finest scholar of the age, reports that the Magnificent's expenditure for books in one year alone came to the fantastic equivalent of half a million dollars. Personally Lorenzo was the author of a volume of fables entitled *Ambra,* a work that was praised to the sky by his friends as the equal of Petrarch's *Laura.* It showed indeed an uncommon intellectual refinement and a deep feeling for nature. . . .

For a few months Fra Girolamo went on quietly with his work of instructing the novices at San Marco. However, soon the lecture hall became too small as outsiders, members of the city's regular clergy and professors from the Platonic Academy, amongst them Poliziano and Pico della Mirandola, began to drop in. In the summer of 1490 when he started a new course on the Book of Revelations, Savonarola moved his lectern into the shade of a rose bower in the cloisters. Before long even that proved inadequate. During Lent in 1491 he received a summons to preach in the Duomo so that the common people might hear him on Sundays when they were free from work. On Sunday, August the 8th, he made this strange remark in the Cathedral pulpit: "I shall preach in Florence for eight years and no more." This was precisely the length of time that his ministry in the Arno city lasted, for he died in the spring of 1498.

"Italy," he said, "this paradise on earth, has become a spiritual wilderness." It was a country of idols and abominations. In the plainest terms he condemned the scepticism and the corruption of the most celebrated literati and philosophers. Turning to the Church, he charged that the clergy was not combating evil by holding up their sins before the mighty, but was merely flattering the princes and the rich in order to stand in their good graces.

* *Godiamoci il Papato poichè Dio l' ha dato.*

"If there is no change soon," he warned, "the Church of Italy will be punished for not preaching the pure gospel of salvation." He cautioned the congregation not to be deceived by the peace which, for once, reigned undisturbed in Italy. It was a false peace, said the Friar. It was a lull before the storm. There was a terrible war in the making, a war to be followed by famine and pestilence. He added that he did not make this prediction because he wanted to pose as a prophet of gloom. "Like Amos, I say to you: 'I am not a prophet!' My reasons for announcing these scourges and calamities are founded on the Word of God. The Church will be afflicted with great sorrows and humiliation. The State will be punished for the injustices inflicted on the poor."

Savonarola has fired the first shot in the warfare which he is to wage for the rest of his life: for renewal of the faith and the alleviation of the people's misery. He is the champion of popular liberty in the pulpit. From now on the city is divided, although the lines are not yet sharply drawn. On the Friar's side stand all those who are dissatisfied with the Medicean autocracy, the small businessmen who are crushed by taxes, the families whose relatives and friends were banished or perished in prison. With this host of malcontents and those avid of novelties stand the truly pious who are dismayed over corruption in the highest ecclesiastical circles and the general decline of faith amongst the masses.

On Lorenzo's side are the nobility and the wealthy, the scholars and the high clergy, and all those, and their number is legion, who in one way or other are beholden to the Medici. The leader of the budding anti-Savonarola movement is that same Fra Mariano, the Augustinian friar whose gestures, voice, and citations from the poets Savonarola had characterized as more suited to a variety theater than to the house of God.

The most irksome obstacle to good relations between the Magnificent and Savonarola was the fact that San Marco served as a sort of *Hofkirche* or palace church to the Medici family. In emulation of his father and grandfather, Lorenzo generously supported the Dominican monastery. Nothing chafed so much on the incorruptible Savonarola's sensibilities as this relationship upon which he looked as that of master and servants. It hampered his full freedom to speak out against the abuse of power by the monastery's patron.

Originally the Dominicans were an Order of mendicants. They lived on and by the charity of the faithful whose oblations were once and still should have been collected at the monastery's door, preferably on Sundays. When Savonarola came to Florence the brethren had long since dispensed with this old custom. From Lorenzo came the bread for their tables, as well as the oil, the eggs, the macaroni, the cheese, and the wine, even the firewood for the kitchen stove and the open hearth in the chapter hall. Several rooms, such as those of the Prior and the librarian, were luxuriously furnished. The Prior's meals were served in his chamber on dishes and plates bearing the Medici crest. By Lorenzo's decree imported foodstuffs destined for San Marco passed untaxed through the custom service. The woolen cloth and the silk for the monks' gowns and priestly vestments were supplied and tailored by the Magnificent's personal purveyors and craftsmen.

Apart from the fact that such abundance and luxury seemed to him contrary to and even subversive of monastic discipline, Savonarola looked upon this display of generosity with a suspicious eye. He thought it a conscience-salving expedient on Il Magnifico's part, another trick to divert attention from the extortions practiced on the Florentine people.

When Lorenzo learned of Savonarola's opposition to the patronage system he said to Pico della Mirandola: "This monk whom you brought to Florence seems to be bent on throwing things upside down. He predicts the end of the world and unheard of catastrophes . . . But he also calls the people to penitence and conversion. This is very good. There is no law against doing penitence or being a Christian. Everyone in Florence is absolutely free to convert himself or to remain in his sin. There are no constraints in this city. Whether a man sings or drinks or amuses himself by hearing a sermon or watch a comedy, it makes no difference to me . . . There is no reason for anyone in Florence to be dissatisfied. There is peace at home and abroad. We give the populace excellent theatrical shows and processions. Florence is a beautiful city and grows more beautiful every year. What more do men want? Haven't we the essence of liberty here in Florence?

"Perhaps you could hint to your friend," continued Lorenzo, "that he should not dabble in politics. I don't like interference in that domain. I do not like to hear of anyone talking politics in the pulpit or anywhere else. . . ."

"Fra Girolamo," said Pico to his friend, "do try to be more moderate in your sermons. Why scare the daylight out of the Florentines? They are a fickle and naive people: they are easily swayed. You are perhaps not aware of it but you are raising a storm. Can you not confine yourself to general subjects? Don't go so fast, don't force the issue! If you continue on your present course, you will make enemies, powerful enemies. If you could preach with less violence, you might touch the hearts of your hearers more effectively and do their souls more good. . . ."

Lorenzo was seriously alarmed. Yet, in spite of his usual clear insight in men and affairs, he could not make up his mind. His conscience troubled him and he was both fearful of and fascinated by the preacher of penitence. "I respect the Friar," he said once, "but I do not think his piety and poverty sufficient guarantees for religious or political infallibility." Lorenzo did not speak only to Pico della Mirandola. He sent a delegation of five influential citizens to San Marco. The delegation was made up of men of whom a great deal is to be heard in days to come, Domenico Bonsi, Guidantonio Vespucci, Paolo Soderini, Francesco Valori, and Bernardo Rucellai, all of them in the service of or associated with Lorenzo in some business enterprise or other.

At first these men tried to make Savonarola believe that they had come on their own initiative. Like Pico they urged him to moderate his tone and take a less severe attitude in denouncing abuses. He should refrain, they advised him, from criticizing the existing state of affairs and above all not play politics.

Fra Girolamo listened in silence, but when Messer Soderini, after an embarrassing pause, hinted that the Friar ran the risk of banishment if he should continue his sweeping charges, the monk looked up in surprise. "You are acting on the bidding of another," he told the deputation. "You are not here on your own accord, but have been sent by Lorenzo de' Medici.

"I do not fear your threat of banishment," he added. "Not I, but Lorenzo will be the first to go. I will stay where God has sent me, and speak what God gives me to say . . . And the first thing I say to you is this: Lorenzo should without delay repent of his sins . . . The Lord is no respector of persons. Even the mightiest must appear before the divine judgment seat. . . ."

He went on to tell the astonished deputation of a strong assurance he had of a coming change in the affairs of Italy and Florence. "I see disaster upon disaster descending on these Italian countries and on Florence and Rome especially."

He did not go into particulars. He would rather speak of them in the pulpit, he said, for he intended to keep to his present course of preaching no matter what threats were made. He then predicted that Lorenzo the Magnificent, Pope Innocent VIII, and Ferrante, King of Naples, were soon all three to depart from the land of the living.

When Lorenzo heard the report of his delegation, he decided to speak to Savonarola himself. He had expected to see Fra Girolamo at the Palazzo Medici on the occasion of the Friar's election to the priorate of San Marco which occurred in July, 1491. It was customary for a newly elected prior to pay his respects to the monastery's patron and protector. Lorenzo had waited in vain. "See now," he said, "here is a strange man who has come into *my* house and will not deign even to visit me!" The Magnificent bore the discourtesy with dignified forbearance. He went further: he humbled himself by attending a service at the convent chapel. But Savonarola took no notice of him. When the service was over Lorenzo sat down in the monastery garden. The monks informed the Prior that the Magnificent was still about. They urged him to go out and greet him.

"Did he send for me?" asked Savonarola.

"No, but he is evidently waiting for you to join him in the garden."

"I shall not go out," Savonarola replied.

"But he brought you to Florence, reverend Father," the monks insisted. "It's a matter of elementary courtesy. . . ."

"He did *not* bring me to Florence," the Friar spoke back heatedly. "God brought me to this city and to God alone I owe an accounting."

While they were talking one of the novices ran into the Prior's cell to tell him that there had been a hundred gold ducats deposited in the collection box that morning. Savonarola ordered the money forthwith sent to the Good Men of St. Martin for distribution amongst the poor. "I can neither be terrorized nor bribed by Lorenzo," he said.

Never in his life had the Magnificent met with so stinging an affront. Here he was, the despot of one of the noblest cities in Europe, who had overcome all his enemies, to whose court traveled foreign embassies to deliver flattering orations and precious gifts, whom the finest scholars of the time loaded with praise for his literary and philosophical effusions, and such a man was virtually shown the door by a monk from nowhere.

The city buzzed with gossip. In the shops, the taverns, the monasteries, and the countinghouses people talked of nothing else. Wagers were laid as how long the Prior of San Marco would last, whether he would simply be expelled or escorted to prison some dark night to be locked up and to be forgotten. One counselor after the other came to Lorenzo with the advice to get rid of the monk as quickly as possible. Why wait till this Friar, this outsider, inflame all the people? What authority had this Savonarola to set himself up as a reformer of church and state? Wasn't the incident in the monastery garden a plain enough case of provocation? Such disrespect, such insolence!

Lorenzo was not angry over the affront in the monastery garden. He was saddened and pained by Savonarola's lack of courtesy. The matter required reflection and prudence. The people were evidently on Fra Girolamo's side. Moreover, it was generally taken for granted that Lorenzo had brought Savonarola to Florence. If the Medici should withdraw his protection, it would only make the Prior more popular. If Savonarola were forbidden to speak in public, it would make him only more intransigent and inflexible. Lorenzo knew men and he readily granted that he had never yet crossed arms with so baffling an opponent. "As a rule," he said, "I prefer injustice to disorder, but in this case I can do neither the one nor allow the other."

How about trying some charm and flattery then? They sometimes prove more effective than bluntness and force. After all, Savonarola was human. There must be some weakness in his character, some little flaw in his armor. Could he not be corrupted? Could he not be won over by honors and preferment?

One day Fra Girolamo received an invitation to come and
preach in the Palazzo Medici's private chapel.* "If Lorenzo wants
to hear me," grumbled the Prior, "let him come to the convent
church like everybody else. I won't go to him!"

The monks sought to temporize with him. "Do not pile insult
upon injury," they told Savonarola. "The invitation is couched in
most courteous terms. What will it cost you? You need only to go
across the way, and the thing will be done. Why incite the Magnificent to anger? You have friends in the palace . . . Besides, we
will all accompany you. You need have no fear. . . ."

Nothing can make Savonarola change his mind till an old
monk remarks: "Father Girolamo, as a priest you cannot refuse.
Who can tell if Lorenzo is not a soul in distress? You may not
withhold the message of salvation from anyone, rich or poor, man
or woman . . . You must go, it is your duty. . . ."

On hearing this perfect plea Savonarola consents. He walks to
the Via Larga one Sunday morning into the palazzo of which the
interior resembles a pagan temple. The walls of the grand hall and
of all the other chambers are covered with paintings and frescoes
by the great masters. As he proceeds to the chapel he traverses a
gallery which is on either side adorned with a row of statues. Side
by side with the pagan divinities are images of the Madonna, the
holy apostles, and exquisitely wrought crucifixes. A heavy perfume
of aromatic spices hangs in the air. There are too many boys with
painted lips and eyebrows. The women are too extravagantly at-
tired. Savonarola lets his eye travel over their costumes and ornaments: glittering jewels, golden necklaces, sparkling bracelets, the
costliest velvet and silken gowns, girdles set with emeralds and
rubies meet his glance on every hand. At the entrance of the chapel
a choir of girls welcomes him with a hymn of salutation. The
maidens are dressed to resemble the Graces of Greek mythology.

Savonarola waits till the regular clergy has celebrated Mass.
Then he ascends the pulpit. Lorenzo occupies a golden chair immediately in front. Next to the Magnificent sits Angelo Poliziano,
the poet. As he announces his text from the Book of Judges

* The Palazzo Medici is now called the Palazzo Riccardi after its later
owners.

(3:20), Fra Girolamo looks Lorenzo straight in the eyes: "I have a message from God unto thee. . . ."

At once Il Magnifico's brows contract. He looks away and stares at Gozzoli's painting representing the journey of the Magi to Bethlehem. The faces of the Magi are those of his own Medicean ancestors.

At the outset Savonarola makes a few cautionary remarks. "I am aware," he says, "that today I must speak with forbearance and moderation. I find myself somewhat in the position of our Lord Jesus Christ when he was a guest in the home of the Pharisee." In other words: this is not the occasion to touch on controversial subjects, nor to shock anyone with inconsiderate or critical remarks.

No sooner are the words out of his mouth than Savonarola throws all caution to the wind. "Everything in a *città* [the word means both city and state] depends on the chief magistrate," says the Friar looking directly at Lorenzo. "If the head of a state walks in the strait and narrow path that leadeth unto righteousness, a città may become a reflection of the heavenly kingdom, of the City of God. On the other hand, if the chief of state does wrong, everything goes wrong, and great is his sin.

"I know a city where the tyrants are incorrigible. They do not walk in the light, but in darkness. They are haughty and vain. They listen to flattery. They do not restore their ill-gotten gain to those whom they have despoiled. Arbitrarily they impose ever heavier taxes on the population . . . They exploit the peasantry . . . They buy up votes and are guilty of dishonesty when they debase the coin of the realm. They make the tax on salt so heavy that the common people are wholly deprived of this vital necessity in their diet. . . ."

It is true, Savonarola mentions no names, but there is no mistaking his references to the situation in Florence and to the abuses of Lorenzo's dictatorship. One concession to Lorenzo and his learned friends Fra Girolamo makes: he speaks in Latin. It is in that language, which the Magnificent loves so dearly, that he proceeds to denounce and execrate all the tyrants and dictators of history, showing by chapter and verse how they all came to a bad end.

An admirable discourse! But wasn't the theme in that milieu

somewhat reckless, foolhardy even? Was the man mad? Was this naiveté or plain, calculated pugnacity? It would not have been surprising if Lorenzo or one of his officers had interrupted the preacher and put an end to his diatribe.

When Fra Girolamo has finished, Lorenzo gives the signal, there is a burst of applause. The Magnificent compliments the preacher on his excellent Latin. He thanks him for having pronounced a sermon of sound doctrine, a truly edifying, encouraging homily. If there is any sarcasm or insincerity in these remarks Lorenzo does not show it. The choir intones another anthem and Savonarola, after saluting the Magnificent with a curt nod of the head, walks out.

"There goes a brave man," Lorenzo says to Poliziano, "a brave man and an honest one. But he must be broken. . . ."

The instrument to break Savonarola will be Fra Mariano da Gennazzano, the fashionable Augustinian, an admirer of Lorenzo and so much admired in turn that the Magnificent has built a convent for him just outside the San Gallo gate.* Fra Mariano receives secret instructions to refute Savonarola, to show up the absurdity of his prophecies of the wrath to come, to unmask him as an imposter and rabble rouser, in a word: to demolish him by compromising him in the popular mind. For Mariano this will be an easy matter, for Italy is at peace, there is not a cloud on the international horizon. So fair are the prospects that Lorenzo the Magnificent and the Pope, the no less magnificent Innocent VIII, plan to translate the eternal dream of Italy into reality: they are negotiating the establishment of a national union and set up a joint army.

Fra Mariano promises to make a fool of Fra Girolamo and do it publicly. He needs no coaxing for he is insanely jealous of Savonarola who has captured the people's attention while Mariano's own congregations have dwindled to the vanishing point. Fra Mariano vows to throw Savonarola into the dust. Lorenzo may count on him.

And so the stage is set: the next Sunday Fra Mariano is to preach after the vesper service in his own Church of San Gallo.

---

* It was at this convent that another Augustinian monk, Martin Luther by name, stayed in 1511 on his way back to Wittenberg from Rome.

The church is crowded to the last nook and corner for the occasion. There are people sitting on the pulpit steps, in the choir loft, and even within the altar rail. All Florence, ever avid for a novelty, has turned out to witness the first round in a verbal joust between the two most eloquent preachers of the day. The doors and windows have to be opened so that the people standing outside may hear the voice of him who is compared with Cicero and Demosthenes for the grace of his delivery, for the musical cadence of his rolling sentences, and for his marvelous quotations from the poets.

Lorenzo arrives in the company of his friends Poliziano and Pico della Mirandola, followed by dignitaries and some distinguished foreign visitors. Savonarola is represented by Fra Ubaldino, the future historian of San Marco. Fra Ubaldino is the inventor of a system of shorthand which will enable him to take down Mariano's every word.

The first impression Mariano makes as he appears in the pulpit is overwhelmingly in his favor. He wears a blue velvet gown set off with an ermine collar. His hair is freshly waved and shines like an aureole around his head. In his right hand he holds a golden crucifix which he kisses fervently to the edification of everyone present.

As he announces his text, a murmur of satisfaction runs through the congregation. How clever! How apt! How well-chosen! How straight to the point! Savonarola is as good as ruined. The text is from the Book of the Acts of the Apostles (1:7) where Jesus, just before ascending to heaven, tells his disciples: *Non est vestrum nosse tempora vel momenta.* . . . "It is not for you to know the times or the seasons which the Father has placed in his own power."

The preacher attacks Savonarola's prophecies as delusions and deceptions. We are told, he says, that the Pope is about to die. Would the Florentines believe him if he told them that he had seen the Holy Father with his own eyes but two weeks before celebrating Mass in his Church of St. John Lateran? The Pontiff looked the picture of health. Where was the threat of war coming from of which Savonarola spoke so menacingly? The Emperor was at peace with every Italian potentate, and so was the King of France! The Turks, perhaps? But nobody knows what the Turks are doing. When last heard of they had been decisively checked near Belgrado. Mariano shrugs his shoulders: "Fra Girolamo either sees spooks or he drinks too much."

Mariano calls Savonarola's prophecies gibberish. He holds him up to scorn and ridicule. He tells Aesop's fable of the locust which sat on the hub of a carriage wheel and called out: "See, how much dust I throw up!" Several times he makes the congregation laugh with his verbal sallies. He imitates Savonarola's gestures. He wrinkles and tweaks his own nose as if to remind the congregation of Fra Girolamo's prominent proboscis. And then Mariano overshoots the mark. In the heat of temper and argument he engages in personalities. His vituperation becomes coarse. He calls Savonarola a worm, a cockroach, a snake, a wolf in sheep's clothing. His invective turns scurrilous. He uses indecent language and makes one particularly indecent gesture. When Fra Mariano exclaims that Savonarola is but an ignorant monk from the provinces who cannot even read his breviary in Latin, Lorenzo shakes his head. When Mariano, heedless of the Magnificent's silent admonition, adds that Savonarola never studied the Bible, Pico della Mirandola calls back in Latin: "Do not bear false witness in the presence of the sacraments!" Everybody in church is shocked. Even Fra Mariano's admirers are deeply disappointed. Lorenzo to whom the least vulgarity in speech and manners is the unpardonable sin, leaves without speaking to Fra Mariano.

But that is not the end in so far as Fra Mariano is concerned. Stenographer Ubaldino had not only taken down the sermon word for word, he has also made extensive notes of a conversation between Fra Mariano and Savonarola. This conversation took place at San Marco's when Fra Mariano paid a visit to the Prior only a week before. In his interview with Savonarola, at which several monks were present, Mariano spoke in exceedingly complimentary terms of Savonarola's learning and of his marvelous voice which enthralls the Florentine multitudes. Everything Savonarola did since coming to Florence carries away the extravagant praises of Fra Mariano. It is no wonder, said he, that so many novices had entered the convent since Savonarola became the Prior. They are drawn to Fra Girolamo's reputation as a great biblical exegete who in addition shows himself thoroughly conversant with the writings of the Fathers. "If I were a younger man," adds Fra Mariano, "I would like nothing better than to come to San Marco and sit at the feet of so renowned a scholar and theologian as Your Reverence. . . ."

On the following Sunday Savonarola preached in the Duomo to a congregation estimated at 15,000. He took for his text the same passage which Mariano used the week before: "It is not for you to know the times and the seasons." But in his introductory remarks he took care to read Ubaldino's verbatim reports of the conversation with Mariano. "How is it," asked Savonarola, "that after covering me with his silly flatteries one day, he poured out the vials of his wrath and invective on me a few days later?" Had the conversation at San Marco slipped Fra Mariano's memory? If he was sincere at the monastery he lied in church. On the other hand if he spoke the truth in church he prevaricated on the occasion of his visit to San Marco. "What happened in the interval to make Fra Mariano change? Was he really speaking his own mind when he made those outrageous charges against me? Or did someone put him up to it to attack me from ambush?" Savonarola needed say no more. Everybody in the vast assembly understood what had transpired.

After that public exposure Fra Mariano did not stay long in Florence. He realized he had lost Lorenzo's esteem. He obtained an appointment at Rome and was not heard of till five years later when Savonarola was in trouble with the Pope. Mariano then made himself conspicuous at the Vatican by his hatred of Savonarola.

But there was a change on the way. Business in Florence declined as Lorenzo kept more and more to himself and but seldom showed himself in the streets, at the public festivals, or at the Signorial palace. He had never been the same since Simonetta died and two years after her flight to heaven, his brother, the beloved Juliano, was assassinated. The true traits of his character came to the fore: melancholy and sadness. There scarcely passed a day without his horoscope being cast. The astrologers made him very conscious of the fact that he was born under the sign of Capricorn with its saturnian influences of gloom and despondency. He spent long hours sitting in his garden staring vacantly before him fingering his rosary.

A vague uneasiness spread from the Palazzo Medici into the

city and the country as word passed that the sun of Lorenzo's life was about to set. On top of this the winter of 1491-1492 turned out uncommonly severe. There was snow on the ground and ice floes crashed and splintered against the pillars of the bridges. In the spring the Arno overflowed its banks. The flood waters caused havoc in the farmlands and great suffering amongst the peasants. People took these accidents of nature as an indication that the bad spirits in the air were threatening them with still greater calamities. The rationalist Ficino changed his amulets several times a day in the hope of staying the portents. The signs remained definitely unfavorable.

In the spring of 1492 Lorenzo the Magnificent was struck down by a disease which baffled human skill. He was carried to his country home at Careggi, about two miles to the northwest of Florence, where he had his zoological and botanical gardens. There, with a view of the green meadows and in the shade of his olive plantations, hoping to be soothed and healed, he suffered unendurable pain. From Angelo Poliziano, who wrote down the history of Lorenzo's last days, we have a few details on the circumstances at the Villa Careggi. He says that the house was filled with physicians and surgeons who had been summoned from all over Italy. Night and day these specialists held consultations and did their utmost to relieve the patient's distress. It was all to no avail. And small wonder!

Amongst the doctors was the famous chirurgeon Juan de Vigo who had hit upon a cure for the ulcers suffered by Cardinal Juliano della Rovere by "boiling together in a brass kettle for three hours, old rags cut in pieces, crumbs of fine bread, plantain, and a fomentation of arsenic sublimed in rose water." This brew "cured the Cardinal in a very short time, to the admiration of all concerned." Fortunately, Juan de Vigo did not need to try his skill on Lorenzo, who did not suffer from ulcers but from gout, or as is more likely, from circulatory trouble in the toes and feet.

The do or die therapy applied to Lorenzo was the invention of the renowned Lombardy physician, Lazaro of Pavia, whom Ludovico Sforza, Duke of Milan, had sent over. Doctor Lazaro crushed and dissolved a fortune's worth of diamonds and pearls, and after mixing the pulverized stones with red wine, gave this potion to the sick man to drink. The remedy seems to have hastened Lorenzo's end rather than to have effected his recovery. A violent quarrel broke out between Doctor Lazaro and the Magnificent's personal physician, Pier Leoni, whose body was found after Lorenzo's death at the bottom of a well in the garden.

On the morning of April 8, Lorenzo de' Medici was sinking so rapidly that the last rites of the Church were administered. All the doctors had been dismissed, only Pico della Mirandola and Angelo Poliziano remained in the sickroom. To these friends, Lorenzo said: "What I regret most is that death has not spared me to finish your libraries." Then he became very agitated and asked that Savonarola be sent for. "I want to speak to a truly religious priest," he whispered, "pray Fra Girolamo to come."

Savonarola came at once to Careggi. What happened at the bedside is difficult to ascertain with precision. There are different versions of what took place. According to a *Life of Savonarola* by Fra Pacifico Burlamacchi, Savonarola asked Lorenzo if he would restore their liberties to the Florentines, whereupon the Magnificent is said to have turned his face to the wall and refused to answer, and Savonarola then went out without giving absolution.

But Burlamacchi was not present in the sickroom and his allegation that he heard the story from Savonarola himself is gravely suspect. Savonarola took his priestly vocation too seriously to have disclosed the secrets of a deathbed confession. Poliziano, who was present at Careggi, knows nothing about a last minute clash or harsh words between Lorenzo and Savonarola. Poliziano says that Lorenzo was extremely restless till Fra Girolamo arrived. To the monk he expressed deep regret over his sins.

"God's mercy is boundless," replied Savonarola. "Your Magnificence must not doubt for a moment . . . The divine love enfolds you in its arms even now and always. . . ." The Friar exhorted Lorenzo to amend his life should he recover. "And this he promised most diligently to do," adds Poliziano. On the other hand, should death be near, Savonarola urged the Magnificent to meet it with resignation. And the reply was: "Nothing would please me better if it be God's will."

Then Pico and Poliziano were asked to leave. When Lorenzo had made his confession they re-entered the sickroom. Lorenzo noticing that Savonarola was about to depart, called him back: "Dear Father Girolamo give me your blessing before you go!" Once more the Friar knelt by the bedside and offered up the commendatory prayers for the dying. The Magnificent by now utterly calm and without pain for the first time in months, "joined earnestly in the responses." The Friar blessed the dying man and stooping down kissed him on the forehead and then walked out unable to hold back his tears.

Lorenzo de' Medici died on April 8, 1492. He was 43 years of age. When Pope Innocent VIII heard the news he remarked: "This is the end of the era of peace in Italy."

Chapter IV

Rodrigo Borgia in St. Peter's Chair:

Savonarola Reforms His Convent

Just before Lorenzo died the dean and chapter of St. Mary of the Flower, Florence's cathedral church, extended an invitation for the second year in succession to Savonarola to deliver a course of Lenten sermons. The historian Guicciardini remarks that the people of Florence so "quickly tired of everything" that they had never before invited the same Lenten preacher twice. From this general attitude of blasé impassiveness, he infers that Savonarola must still have been regarded as a curious novelty in that his sermons provided a refreshing change from the boring and monotonously optimistic discourses of the humanists. But this was surely not the only reason for bringing Savonarola back to the Duomo.

Not the people but the canons extended the invitation. It was principally the clergy who wanted to hear Fra Girolamo. Among the 3000 monks and 2000 regular clergy in Florence there were certainly other preachers of brilliant and supple talent, but their preaching, according to the fashion of the times, was frequently overrun with pedantry and quotations or swelled up to a false sublime. Savonarola, on the other hand, was a man of deep convictions and simplicity. The Duomo canons knew that he pursued no selfish ends. When he spoke out as boldly as he did he gave utterance to the apprehensions and the indignation lying more or less latent in every thoughtful cleric's heart. Someone said of the Friar: When Fra Girolamo denounced the corruptions, the life of obscenity, of lying, treachery, oppression, and murder of the majority of the Italian ruling houses it was as if he conveyed hour-by-hour bulletins on the rising temper of God's wrath.

But that was not all: the Friar also deplored the Church's bogging down in externals and the contamination of the papacy itself with the blight of neopaganism. Never before in history, he said, had the Church been so deeply humiliated as it was then. Papal enthusiasm for the revival of art and learning appeared to Savonarola as unnecessary extravagance and love of display, totally alien to the spirit of the Gospel. Beginning with Pius II, who visited Ferrara in Savonarola's youth, the popes sought to place themselves at the head of the cultural and artistic revival, with the result that they squandered so much of their time and strength that they had none to spare for their office as teachers and apostles. They were occupied day and night with hunting after properties, with law suits, with the worldly enrichment of members of their own family, and with the ceremonials of the papal court.

If able and honorable men were not promoted to the spiritual office it was because their good sense or shame prevented them from coming forward and stooping to the usual means of buying benefices and engaging in other simoniacal and corrupt practices. It was no secret that persons unworthy in character and wholly incompatible with the spiritual task, but possessed of much money and brazen impudence, had pushed themselves into the leading situations. Fashionable preachers of Fra Mariano's type passed over the evils of the time with averted eyes. But Savonarola, whose mind was permeated with the prophetic writings of the Old Testament, burned with indignation over the bad example set in the highest quarters. With the Friar it was always the people who came first: the people, he feared, were not being guided into paths of righteousness but led astray and, what is not surprising, to despise a clergy which itself disregarded the commandments of Christ.

Long before Luther there were in every city and country of Europe noble and well-disposed priests and laymen, men of calm and good sense, occupying positions of the greatest dignity in the universities and the Church who openly deplored, no, who uttered the bitterest complaints over the rude ignorance, the debauchery, and the avarice of the priests and pastors of their time. Nor were they blind to the fact that gross irregularities in the clergy were not effectually combated by Rome but, on the contrary, sanctioned by notorious examples on the chair of St. Peter. On all sides men were saying, if only a vigorous and reforming pope could secure election to the chair of St. Peter, a man with the zeal and determination of a Hildebrand, there might yet follow a restoration of the religious authority of the Holy See and with it a general spiritual revival. For it was the religious authority of the papacy which declined in such measure that the princes and potentates of the many contending civil states in Italy regarded the papacy and the Church as just another set of puppets in the diplomatic and military chess game called the balance of power.

The canons of the Duomo as well as the Archbishop of Florence and the virtual totality of the city's clergy were as distressed over the increasing secularization of the papacy and its absorption in political intrigue and diplomacy as was Savonarola. That is why they wanted to hear the Friar. Besides—and here Guicciardini was undoubtedly right—Savonarola spoke from the Bible, a most welcome departure from the manner of preaching of the humanists who based their discourses just as lief on irrelevant though marvelously euphonious passages from the classical poets or Plato.

To Savonarola the Bible was not merely a record of the past but a mirror reflecting the trend of future events. He found that it was applicable to almost every situation in public and private life. He came to this view by a realization that in the Bible everything in history is seen as part of a great world plan. He saw that the course of history is laden with historical decisions and that it would terminate with a crisis. The running of affairs, he felt, should not be left any longer in the hands of cliques for the distribution of plunder and power, but be turned towards the welfare of the common people everywhere. Coming down to brass tacks, Savonarola always correlated the Scriptures' utterances with the contemporary scene and brought the Word of God to bear on the social and religious conditions of his own times. The Bible spoke clearly as to what lay in store for the Jewish people if and when they disobeyed the precepts of the divine law and went "whoring after false gods." But even as God abundantly pardoned the Jews their transgressions when they turned to him with a broken heart and contrite spirit, so the Florentines would not be rejected if they repented and invoked the divine forgiveness.

In the course of the two years he had been speaking in Florence, first at his own convent church of San Marco and then at the Duomo, he had overcome all the impediments and difficulties which formerly beset him in the pulpit. When he appeared in the Duomo in the Lenten season of 1492 the sound of his voice penetrated to the furthermost corner of the immense structure with its dim religious light and austere simplicity. His gestures were measured, calm, and dignified. His voice was a rich tenor, most pleasing to the Italian ear. He had acquired so perfect a command of the Tuscan manner of speech and intonation that Michelangelo who never failed to attend made the same remark that men still living make today when they recall the preaching of John Henry Newman: "Oh, that voice, that voice! . . . It can never be forgotten by anyone who once heard it."

On Good Friday Savonarola informed the Duomo congregation that he and his monks had spent the two weeks since Lorenzo de' Medici's death in mourning, prayer, and meditation. In the course of those two weeks, he said, he also beheld a strange vision. From the midst of the city of Rome he saw an enormous black cross rise slowly in the sky. On the cross appeared the words: *Crux Dei Irae,* "The Cross of God's Wrath." When the top of the cross reached the sky, the heavens were darkened, thunder and lightning broke forth, a violent hail storm swept over Italy, and "a great multitude was slain."

When the skies cleared, a second cross appeared. This bore the inscription: *Crux Misericordiae Dei.* "The Cross of God's Mercy." But the second cross did not issue from Rome. It appeared above the city of Jerusalem. The whole world was bathed in a celestial glow by the light streaming from on high. In an instant the flowers budded, bloomed and brought forth blossoms. A perfume of unbelievable suavity was wafted through the universe while the sound of hymns, as if sung by angels, seemed to come from every direction.

Savonarola's communication of his vision produced incredible excitement in Florence. That his words, as he said, were faithful, none doubted. But the meaning of the vision escaped high and low alike. In a week's time all Italy talked of the two crosses with bated breath as matters of grave and ominous portent.

The suspense was not broken till two months later when word came that the Pope, Innocent VIII, after long years of illness, had gone the way of all flesh. Thus the second death predicted by Savonarola had now occurred: both Lorenzo de' Medici and Innocent VIII were no more. As a result Savonarola's reputation as a seer filled Italy with wonder and consternation. But soon a new anxiety filled the city and a good part of Europe: who would be the next pope? Had Savonarola's vision of the black cross above Rome anything to do with the deliberations of the cardinals gathered in the apostolic palace on Vatican hill?

* *

In the night following August 10, the Conclave chose Rodrigo Cardinal Borgia to fill the vacant chair of St. Peter. The new Pope took the name of Alexander VI, and his coronation with unlimited magnificence followed on August 26.

By that time the Pope's rival and implacable enemy, Cardinal Juliano della Rovere, had quit Rome and was on his way to Florence. Fearing Alexander's vengeance he did not feel safe anywhere on Italian soil. He stayed in Florence but a few days and then hastened to France where he took up residence in the town of St. Germain-en-Laye near Paris where the mansion he erected stands till this day on the Rue de Poissy. St. Germain was then and for many years after one of the royal French residences. It was under the protection of King Charles VIII that Cardinal della Rovere placed himself. He spent the next ten years plotting the downfall of Pope Alexander and embroiled Savonarola in his machinations. But he did not directly succeed his enemy on the papal throne. The pontificate of Pius III, which lasted only one month, falls between the two. In 1503 Juliano della Rovere became supreme pontiff under the name of Julius II. He is the Pope who, "inspired by God," called Michelangelo to paint "The last Judgment" on the ceiling of the Sistine Chapel.

While in Florence Cardinal della Rovere stayed with Piero de' Medici who had succeeded his father Lorenzo. He gave his host and the principal men of the city assembled at the Palazzo Medici some details on the new Pope's private life and character. According to the Cardinal, Alexander VI was not a Christian and had not even been baptized. For years he had lived in concubinage with Donna Giovanna dei Cattanei who had already been married three times and by whom he had four children, Cesare, Giovanni, Lucrezia, and Goffredo. The conclave, he told the Florentine merchant princes, had been a concatenation of intrigue, bribery, and terror, a plain case of bidding and counterbidding, threats, and promises ending with the purchase of the papal throne by Alexander and the demoralization of the cardinals who lent themselves to such venality. Ascanio Cardinal Sforza who promoted Alexander's election had received four mule loads of gold for his trouble plus the magnificent palace on the Banchi Vecchi in Rome, the income of the diocese of Agria in Hungary, and the town of Nepi. Other cardinals, whom Della Rovere named, had been similarly richly rewarded for casting their votes in Alexander's favor. He added that the cardinals had been terrorized by Sforza and gnashed their teeth in fury when Borgia's name came out at the head of the poll.

The truth of the matter is quite different. That the Pope, after his election, wished to reward his supporters was but natural. To give preferments was one of the duties of his office and he remembered all his friends but not his single envious rival, Cardinal Juliano della Rovere who, in revenge, alleged simony. Della Rovere had personally spent 200,000 ducats, placed at his disposal by the King of France, to bring about his own election. Alexander Borgia, who was "the richest of rich men in a time of riches," easily outmaneuvered his rival in the Conclave. He won the race by the large majority of twenty-two votes out of twenty-three. One vote only went to Della Rovere, his own. We have it on the authority of Johan Burchard, the master of ceremonies at the Conclave, but no friend of Alexander VI by any means, that instead of a gnashing of teeth, there was seldom seen such an outburst of genuine almost boisterous rejoicing in the Sistine Chapel as when Alexander Borgia was elected. The Pope was deeply moved and for a moment sat in bewildered surprise when he saw his colleagues lower their green or purple canopies to his. He sat so long in silence that the gigantic seven feet tall Cardinal Sanseverino ran over and, lifting him in his strong arms, seated him squarely on the altar. The Pope jumped down like a boy, and, amidst the laughter of the cardinals, ran behind the altar to put on his new robes of office.

All the world is familiar with the story of Alexander Borgia's life. Books and books have been written on the subject in every civilized language. In the annuary of the popes, occurring in the official Church publication *Ecclesia,* he is called "an unworthy man," and "a scandalous pope." But as head of a temporal state, as a prince among princes, as a statesman and diplomat he was certainly not worse than any of the heads of the contemporary ruling houses. He played what he called the game of the world according to the rules and standards of the time. Machiavelli highly approved of Alexander's realistic statesmanship.

The tittle-tattling Della Rovere never ceased defiling Alexander's name, but he never disclosed the real reason for his malevolence. He charged Alexander with simony, nepotism, adultery, incest, murder, and gluttony. What he did not say was that Donna Giovanna dei Cattanei, better known by the endearing name of Donna Vannozza which the Pope gave her, had been his, Juliano della Rovere's mistress. Not Pope Alexander VI, but Cardinal della Rovere, was the father of the mass murderer Cesare Borgia who passed for Alexander's eldest son.*

The most virulent attack shortly after Alexander's elevation, was an anonymous pamphlet called a "Letter to Silvio Satelli." It gave a list of all the crimes which Alexander was said to have committed. They were in the main the same filthy charges which Juliano della Rovere peddled. The Pope read the "Letter to Silvio Satelli" and laughed heartily over the exaggerated absurdity and the coarseness of the satire. But he took no offense. "There is liberty of

---

* According to the Catholic historian Varillas, the whole truth came out in 1503 after Alexander's death, when Cesare Borgia's support was sought by the Cardinal della Rovere in his candidacy for the tiara. Della Rovere informed Cesare that he was his "father after the manner of men, and further alleged this to have been the cause of his [the said Cardinal's] enmity against Pope Alexander VI, deceased." If Cesare would support him, the Cardinal promised to acknowledge him as his son and confirm him in all the offices which he then held. Cesare duly exerted his full influence in a filial manner, but once elected, Juliano della Rovere went back on all his promises.

speech in Rome," he commented, "and we care nothing for libels against ourself. If they are witty and well-written, they are amusing, if not, we take no interest." Cesare Borgia, the Pope's soi-disant son, was less tolerant. He traced the authorship of the booklet to a certain Girolamo Manciano of Naples. The writer confessed and his right hand was cut off and his tongue pierced with a red-hot iron.

There is no use going into details about the various accusations launched against Alexander. That the man lived an immoral life is certain enough. The Cardinal Pallavicino, writing some years later, says of Alexander: "The memory of him cannot be recalled without horror and indignation." One particular charge, however, requires some airing for it was the same that was brought against Savonarola. Della Rovere alleged that the Pope was descended from a family of Marranos, that is to say, Spanish Jews, who under threat of death, abjured their religion and accepted Christian baptism, but secretly still adhered to the religion of their fathers. It is true that Alexander VI was born Rodrigo Lançol, and that he took the name Borgia from his uncle, Pope Calixtus III (Alfonso Borgia) who called him to Rome. He was unquestionably a Spaniard, but he was not a Jew or a Marrano.

The allegation of Alexander's Jewishness was first made by Ferdinand and Isabella, the sovereigns of Spain who expelled the remainder of the Jews from their domains in 1492 after years of a persecution the most hideous till Adolf Hitler went into that paroxysm of inhumanity which we beheld in our own time. Alexander wrote to Isabella that the sufferings of the Jews in her kingdom were so extreme as to fill him with commiseration. The Pope condemned the Spanish Inquisition as a diabolical atrocity and welcomed the Jews who managed to escape from Spain. Under Alexander's pontificate they had security of life and limb in the whole of Italy. The Queen of Spain suspected, or at least pretended to suspect, Alexander's toleration of the very people whom she pursued as though they were mad dogs as partiality for his own coreligionists.

This does not mean that the Jews were exempt from discrimination or serious hardships in Italy. In the fifteenth century and long after hatred of the Jew was nothing less than an article of faith.

Even so advanced a thinker as Pico della Mirandola could write that "the divine justice delights in the sufferings of the Jewish people." To have anything to do with them socially or to help them in their tribulations laid one open to the charge of favoring their perfidy and unbelief. Even the study of Hebrew, the language of the Old Testament, without which no real Bible study is possible, rendered the Christian student suspect. Both Pope Alexander VI and Girolamo Savonarola were at one time or another denounced as Jews, the first for extending a welcome to Jewish refugees, the second for studying the Bible in the original.

In his youth in Spain Alexander studied law and when elevated to the supreme pontificate set to work reforming the Roman legal system and court procedure. From this point of view the first years of his pontificate were models of prudence and organizational ability. During the seventeen days that intervened between the former Pope's death and the election of Alexander VI, some two hundred and twenty assassinations took place in Rome. Alexander acted with decision to end this state of lawlessness. An assassin was caught red-handed on the second day of the new pontificate. He and his brother were forced to look on while their house was razed to the ground, the worst disgrace possible to a Roman, and then were ceremoniously hanged among the ruins. A commission was set up to decide all quarrels which formerly had been settled by cold steel. Official inspectors of prisons were appointed, arrears of official salaries paid, and a bench of four judges established for dealing with capital crime. The first act of Alexander's pontificate was the restoration of public order. The admiring Romans said that this vigorous administration of justice was evidently due to the guidance of divine providence.

Della Rovere may have spluttered all the vituperation he liked, the Roman people were extremely fond of Alexander VI. They liked him for his generosity, his frank and open speech, his love for his children, and for the novel appearance he made in his costume as a Spanish *hidalgo* or when his tall and handsome figure in full pontifical garb moved about on St. Peter's altar.

To the immense delight of the Roman populace Alexander dismissed the charge of nepotism with the remark: "I am an honest man. I frankly admit that my children are not my nephews. I love them dearly."

Whether Savonarola personally met Cardinal della Rovere on the occasion of the latter's passage through Florence is not known. At his trial in 1498, one of the main charges leveled against him is that he plotted with the Cardinal against Pope Alexander. Although this charge was not substantiated, true it is that Alexander's elevation filled Fra Girolamo with the gravest forebodings. Since all Florence was repeating and enlarging upon Della Rovere's allegations Savonarola cannot have failed to have heard of them. The Friar soon connected his vision of the cross of God's wrath with the advent of the Borgia pope. He prayed publicly that God should soon send "a good shepherd" to his Church, so that the flock of Christ might be fed spiritual food and be saved, the implication being that spiritual food could not be expected from so worldly a man as Alexander VI.

When Savonarola addressed words of reproof to the dignitaries of the Church not only the huge congregations in the Duomo listened but the whole country was now on the alert, all Europe in fact. Copies of his addresses and treatises were found in every monastery, parish house, and theological school. The résumés of the Friar's sermons were frequently pasted up on the walls of their warehouses by Florentine businessmen residing in Paris, Lyons, Antwerp, and other foreign cities. Pope Alexander, too, gave orders to be kept closely informed on the content of Savonarola's sermons. Not, to be sure, to find fault or traces of heresy, as some historians contend, but because the subject matter of the Friar's homilies interested him intensely. There is not the slightest indication of ill will or suspicion on the part of Alexander towards Savonarola in the first years of the new pontificate. Several times the Pope expressed a wish to hear the Friar personally. Before long we will find him sending an invitation to Fra Girolamo to come and preach at the Vatican.

One day the Pope was discussing a cover of chased gold for his breviary with Francesco Castoro, the renowned goldsmith who was to become the teacher of the still unborn Benvenuto Cellini. Master Castoro had been summoned from Florence to carry out a number of the Pope's pet projects in miniature sculpture and metal work.

In addition to making the book cover, the Pope asked him to submit a design for a golden chalice to be set with rings of rubies, amethysts and sapphires. For Donna Julia Farnese,* who had succeeded Donna Vannozza in the Pope's affections, Master Castoro was to cut a cameo brooch depicting Leda with the Swan. For himself the Pope ordered a gold medallion and a silver casket to hold his breviary when not in use.

At the Pope's interview with the Florentine goldsmith were present: Donna Julia Farnese; the Pope's daughter Lucrezia; and Cardinal Oliviero Caraffa of Naples. The Pope's chalice for his private chapel was the chief subject under discussion.

A few weeks later the same company found itself in the Holy Father's apartments when Cardinal Caraffa read the Pontiff some excerpts from the latest of Savonarola's sermons, the manuscript of which had just arrived from Florence. With the 73rd Psalm for his subject, Savonarola dwelt with particular emphasis on the corruption of the clergy and the vices of the Italian princes, and had also something to say about chalices. "The clergy," he said in that sermon, "take no interest in the salvation of souls. They speak against pride and worldly ambition, yet are plunged in both up to their eyes. They preach chastity and keep concubines. They prescribe fasting and gorge themselves on choice and expensive food.

"There you see the great prelates with splendid miters of gold and precious stones on their heads, and silver croziers in hand; there they stand at the altar, decked with copes and stoles of brocade, chanting those beautiful vespers and Masses, very slowly and with so many grand ceremonies, so many organs and choristers, that you are struck with amazement . . . Men gaze upon these vanities and rejoice in these pomps, and say the Church of Christ was never so flourishing, nor divine worship so well conducted as at present. Likewise (they say) that the Church's first prelates and bishops were inferior to these of our time . . .

"The former, it is true, had fewer gold chalices, for, indeed what few they possessed were often broken up to relieve the need of the poor; whereas our prelates for the sake of obtaining chalices, will

---

* She was know as *Giulia Bella,* the Beautiful Julia. Her nude portrait-statue by Guglielmo della Porta stands on the sepulchre of her brother, Pope Paul III, in St. Peter's.

rob the poor of their sole means of support. The truth is this, in the primitive Church the chalices were of wood but the prelates of gold. In our day the situation is reversed: the chalices are gold, but the prelates are of wood. . . ."

Alexander gravely nodded his head. "Shall we countermand the order for Your Holiness' chalice with Master Castoro?" asked Cardinal Caraffa. The Pope burst out laughing. "There is no need for such drastic measures," he replied.

"The great Alexander is not afraid of a little monk, I trust?" interjected Donna Julia.

"No," replied the Pope, "we are not afraid. But let us hear if Fra Girolamo has anything else to say." And so Caraffa read on and the Pope heard the rebukes which Savonarola addressed to the political rulers of the land, the pompous little despots who held sway over the numerous Italian principalities. He heard it said that the princes with very few exceptions made their courts a place of refuge for wantons and pederasts. "The princes show favors to flattering philosophers and poets, who pander to their vanity by lies and fables, but the righteous are oppressed in these cruel countries . . . The princes are devising ever heavier burdens to oppress the people. The righteous men of Italy are longing for the scourge of God to smite the earth . . . And for truth, they will not have long to wait. The cup of suffering is full to overflowing. It will not be long till all Italy hears the footsteps of God's messengers hurrying from the North. Over the Alps one is coming, sword in hand, against Italy to chastise her tyrants and prelates. His coming will be in the storm and the whirlwind and the fire . . . I have seen a sign in the heavens. Not a cross this time, but a sword. It's the Lord's terrible swift sword which will strike the earth!"

"This is very serious," remarked the Pope, rising from his seat. "But whom can he mean? Who is about to make war on Italy? We are at peace with the world. There does not seem to be the least cause for worry on that score."

"The monk is either lying or he was drunk when he preached that sermon," spoke up Donna Julia.

"But this monk is neither a liar nor a drunkard," the Pope replied. "We all know that he is a fine theologian. Do you not recall how he astonished Pico della Mirandola and the bishops with his erudition and eloquence at the convocation in Reggio a few years back? Do you realize that the greatest scholars of the Florentine Academy, Poliziano, Ficino, and Pico sit at his feet, and that the most consummate artists, Michelangelo, Botticelli, and Bartolomeo are his friends and admirers? We cannot lightly dismiss this man's words. . . ."

Savonarola soon brings himself anew to the Pontiff's attention, though not with any passionate protestation. He will propose a reform in the regulations governing the monastery of San Marco. The Friar was very much aware that one who criticized the moral laxity and the luxurious living of his superiors as severely and consistently as he did must be a man without blot or blemish himself and above the least breath of suspicion. This, Savonarola realized, he was not and never could be in the eyes of the common people as long as he and his monastery remained under the protection and patronage of the ruling family. After Lorenzo's death, his son Piero de' Medici, continued to exercise an effective though benevolent supervision over San Marco. The monks lacked nothing; their food and clothing were supplied and their splendid buildings were kept in repair by Piero's workmen. It was not at all unnatural therefore that the people of Florence looked upon San Marco as a privileged community. Some, as Savonarola knew well, went further and despised the monks as tools of the hated authoritarian regime, as a sort of spiritual police force, or worse still, as a corps of secret agents disguised in clerical garb to spy upon the private lives of the citizens.

The Florentines had a saying: "Whose bread and cheese I eat, to his tune I dance." When this saying was applied to himself and his monks, it cut Savonarola to the quick. He found his relationship as pensioner and ward of the ruling house a hateful plague and, what counted much more with him, felt that it prevented him from preaching as freely as he desired. In Lorenzo's time, when he was a simple friar, Savonarola could not do much about it. Now that he was Prior of San Marco he decided to put an end to the system of compromise and half-and-half measures. Like the prophets of old, Savonarola was never a man of the middle mind.

To his brethren he proposed to close San Marco, leave everything behind save for the library, and take up a world-forsaking life of absolute poverty in a new convent. This convent was to be a humble, one-story barracklike structure which the brethren were to put up with their own hands in the neighborhood of Careggi. At Careggi the brethren would live what Savonarola and the founder of the Dominican Order before him, regarded as a godly and holy life under the sole yoke of Christ. With his last breath St. Dominic had pronounced a curse on anyone who should dare attenuate his order of utter poverty by acquiring property in any form for the religious houses he had established. At Careggi Savonarola and his brethren, who were in enthusiastic agreement with him, were to be mendicants, that is, they were to live solely from the alms of the faithful and concentrate on tasks for which they were destined by their founder: study the Word of God, preach the Word of God, hear confessions, administer the sacraments, call the people to repentance, and combat heresy.

Savonarola soon ran into opposition. His plan to abandon San Marco was rejected outright, not only by Piero de' Medici, but also by Dom Giovacchino Turriano, the General of the Dominicans and by the Pope himself. No permit to build a new house, however low the cost and humble its appearance, would be forthcoming. He was ordered to drop his plans for Careggi.

"Why cannot Fra Girolamo," asked the Pope, "leave well enough alone and be satisfied with what he has? He wants to embrace poverty and go into the wilderness? Does this mean that he plans to deprive us and the people of Florence of those excellent sermons? We will not hear of it. For his own good and the good of the Florentines we desire Fra Girolamo to stay where he is and to perform the duties to which he is called as Prior of San Marco."

Savonarola obeyed the Pope but did not cease his efforts to institute certain reforms at San Marco. He suggested to Piero de' Medici that, having failed to obtain the Pope's consent to abandon the old monastery, he be nonetheless empowered to sell the valuable landed properties. Piero agreed to this proposition in which he would be the chief beneficiary, and in turn apprised the Pope who, though at first adamant, was brought around by Cardinal Caraffa.

On Savonarola's request Cardinal Caraffa had drawn up a Brief ordaining the separation of San Marco and certain other Dominican monasteries from the province of Lombardy. The matter was discussed at a consistory held at the Vatican in May, 1493. Caraffa expressed the belief that the separation of the Tuscan monasteries would add to the dignity of the Pope's friend Piero de' Medici. But the Holy Father was impatient: "We do not want to hear any more talk about Savonarola and his schemes," he said. "We will sign no Brief today, the assembly is closed."

The other cardinals went out, but Caraffa stayed behind. In playful conversation with the Pontiff, it is said, Caraffa drew the signet ring from the Pope's finger and sealed the document while Alexander VI looked on "highly amused."

The effect of this Brief was to give Savonarola a liberty of action which he had not formerly possessed. He was re-elected Prior of San Marco and at the same time appointed Vicar-General of the new Tuscan congregation. He was now independent of all ecclesiastical authority save that of the Pope and the Father-General of the Order.

As soon as Savonarola became master in his own house in the full sense of the word, he proceeded to carry out a program of reform, his first step being the restoration of the rule of St. Dominic. The last words of the founder to his disciples had been: "Have charity, preserve humility, observe voluntary poverty; may my malediction and that of God fall upon him who shall bring pos-sessions to this Order." This meant that all properties which the convent had acquired in disregard of St. Dominic's injunctions, were now disposed of by Savonarola. The costly furniture which the Medicean patrons had installed and renewed from time to time, was put up for auction and the money received distributed among the poor. The funds from the sale of the land went of course to Piero de' Medici. The monks were forbidden to wear fine clothes and their cells were stripped of all ornaments. They were to eat but the simplest food and that in extremely small quantities while no drink save water was tolerated. Longer hours of prayer and fasting and a more severe form of penitential mortification were prescribed.

The brethren accepted the new regulations gladly with the excep-tion of one man, a certain Francesco Mei, who had been the fore-most orator of the Dominicans till Savonarola's coming to Florence. Brother Mei accused Savonarola of secret arrogance and of being solely concerned with increasing his own prestige and influence in the city of Florence. Francesco Mei left San Marco in a bitter mood, went to Rome and, in the course of time, rose to a high position. But he never ceased pursuing Fra Girolamo with a deadly hatred. Fra Francesco made it his life's task to give San Marco and its Prior a bad name, an undertaking in which he succeeded only too well. When Savonarola later clashed with the Pope and was excommunicated and finally burned at the stake, Francesco Mei openly boasted of having brought about the Prior's downfall.

To the common people of Florence the transformation at San Marco was a cause for joy and gratitude. Now that the monastery was no longer part of the Medici's private domain its doors were open night and day. Anybody could come in and talk with the brethren on religious and secular matters or what not. Savonarola kept their books for several small businessmen who did not know their way about with figures. Not seldom did he act as matchmaker in line with a custom which is still in vogue in French and Italian rural parishes where the priest often plays the role of honest broker in the elaborate negotiations preceding a marriage.

San Marco's brother-porter was under instructions never to turn away any man or woman no matter how lowly or however loathsome or repulsive their features corroded by leprosy or other disease. Drawing upon his store of medical knowledge, the Prior set up a small clinic and a pharmacy from which he dispensed medication, pills, lotions, and salves free of charge to the indigent sick and ailing. Many a night he spent copying apposite passages on the care of newborn babes from the textbook which his grandfather published on the subject. One of his counsels to the Florentines was: never hesitate or be ashamed to talk to your priest, for he is the physician of both your soul and your body, a bit of advice to which grandfather Michele was no stranger either.

There were days when no less than five hundred persons, grownups and children, passed through the gates of San Marco. Boys who showed a special aptitude for study, but whose financial circumstances precluded their going to a higher school of learning, were always welcome. They had the freedom of San Marco's splendid library and the assistance of the monks in their studies. It goes without saying that the spiritual needs of the visitors came before everything else. Whether winter or summer, day or night, Savonarola was never too weary to pray with persons of troubled conscience or discuss difficulties of an intimate religious or psychological nature with those afflicted by doubt or other impediments to their peace of mind.

All Italy was talking of the changes at San Marco's convent and many visitors, both lay and clerical, came to Florence to see with their own eyes "the wonders wrought by God and Fra Girolamo." One of these visitors was Duke Ercole, the ruler of Savonarola's home city of Ferrara. In order to escape detection, the Duke had disguised himself in peasant's garb, but the Friar recognized him at once, and sat with him talking throughout the night. When one of the novices came to call Fra Girolamo for early Mass he found the Duke and the Friar in prayer.

Savonarola's relations with his own monks and with the visitors were of a most cordial and friendly character. The natural austerity of his disposition was softened by a gentle graciousness. There was a flavor of saintliness about the man. He was the true priest in whose simplest words and acts men felt something of God's presence. Though lined and wrinkled by care, his face was so pure and his smile so spiritual that people were often moved to tears. He was loved almost to distraction, worshipped would perhaps be a better word, by the young novices who flocked to San Marco in ever larger numbers and from the most distant regions in Italy and Europe. Drawn by the high reputation of Savonarola's scholarship, one monk, Fra Anton of Zwolle, had come all the way from the Netherlands. In Zwolle Brother Anton had known a fellow friar Desiderius Erasmus by name. There were several Germans and Frenchmen amongst the new friars, and at least one Englishman, Fra Thomas of Exeter.

Savonarola seems to have known every child in Florence by name. More than once he was seen sitting on the steps of some church or in the garden of the monastery with a host of children round about him, telling them such stories "as they had never heard before." The tales he invented and told were not always of a serious nature. Eyewitnesses report having seen and heard his child audiences scream with laughter and rolling on the ground in merriment.

How he kept up the killing pace in which he lived must forever remain a riddle. There were weeks when he scarcely slept. In the daytime his main occupation was teaching. At nights he withdrew to cell number 12 and wrote those treatises on *Prayer, The Love of Christ, The Widowed Life, Humility, Family Worship,* and other subjects which have all been preserved. In the course of three years he published ten volumes on moral theology. His tractates were widely used as religious handbooks, especially in families and prayer circles. His sermons, too, which were all written out before delivery in the pulpit were set to print, some in his lifetime, others after his death. Michelangelo had the entire collection and read a portion every day in the eventide of his life.

Since the disestablishment of San Marco signified the end of the Medicean patronage and bounty, the monks were now entirely dependent upon the alms of the faithful. St. Antonine, who was prior fifty years before Savonarola, had requested a lifting of the rule which forbade the Dominicans to own property collectively or privately and to receive endowments and donations. Antonine's reason was that the alms of the faithful were insufficient to provide his monks even with the barest necessities of life. It was then that Cosimo de' Medici took over and supported the monastery from his private purse. With the separation from the Lombardy province, San Marco's community was now back where it was before Cosimo's generous intervention. Many predicted that the new-old situation would not last; in his distress Savonarola would be compelled to appeal for aid either to the Pope or to the General of his Order or to Piero de' Medici.

Savonarola did nothing of the sort. The funds came in ever growing volume. When there was need of money the monks went begging from house to house in Florence and vicinity. They met "everywhere with the utmost kindness and generosity" in spite of the fact that general conditions were far worse than they had been in St. Antonine's time.

Soon begging was no longer necessary, people brought their gifts to the convent in such abundance that there was often a surplus which was at once distributed amongst the poor. With the days on which the monks formerly went begging Savonarola did an unheard of thing: he made them days of sport. The young novices were to spend at least one day a week in carefree abandonment, in games, running, jumping, playing ball, and even wrestling. The Prior took them on hikes or picnics in the forests along the road to Pisa and Pistoia. Savonarola in front, his cassock hitched up in his cincture, the friars, sometimes as many as two hundred, marched through the streets of Florence into the open country like a company of soldiers. And the songs they sang! A male choir two hundred strong, this was something no Italian could resist. No wonder that men, women, and children, teachers, clerics, bankers, magistrates, roustabouts, and hucksters, literally everybody, interrupted whatever they were doing and ran out into the street to see this new Christian militia, this monkish hallelujah army march by.

Alleluya, alleluya, altore di gloria,
Che venisti et descendisti a noi per tua gratia,
Alleluya!

"Hallelujah, hallelujah, king full of majesty,
Who came down from heaven to us through thy great
   mercy,
Hallelujah!"

After a day of frolicking it was back to work for the friars. The laziness of the monks—Savonarola knew well that this was so much the object of popular criticism that it had become almost proverbial—found no encouragement at San Marco. Under his administration the convent became a hive of artistic industry. Not every friar's taste or abilities qualified him for intellectual studies or spiritual work. So it was to wood carving that he would be put or to plain simple carpentry work, or to the writing of illuminated manuscripts or to sculpture or painting, whatever suited him best. No man was permitted to be idle nor did anyone desire it. They were all volunteers.

And Fra Girolamo himself? Was there anything else he could do? Twice a week he conducted a course in dogmatic theology, one in the early morning for the novices, and one just after the half-hour noon recess for the elderly students and scholars. As always the study of the sacred Scriptures was the Prior's chief concern. To this he devoted two full hours in the afternoon, everybody not otherwise occupied being required to be present. There was nothing the brethren liked better and the Prior carried out with more zealous devotion and joy. After the two hours of Bible study came the courses in Greek, in Hebrew, in Chaldean, in Syriac, and in Aramaic. Savonarola did not teach these subjects but he attended the classes nevertheless. His appetite for learning was insatiable.

He who expects to awaken interest in the bosom of others must first feel it in his own. We do not know what the other friars thought of it when Savonarola, who, in addition to everything else made the regular rounds of a watchman at nights, would suddenly awaken his brethren and urge them all to come out into the garden with him to look at the stars. There were clear frosty nights when Fra Girolamo was moved to tears in contemplating the stars sailing like luminous ships in the ether. On those escapades in the rural regions with his monks or at the botanical garden at Careggi he would almost go into ecstasy at the sight of one particularly beautiful tree or flower.

In order to win other Dominican priors to his educational system and to persuade them to follow his example of taking an independent stand, i.e., loose from all property and patronage ties, Savonarola set out for Siena first, then to Pistoia and Pisa, which were all three located in or very near the Florentine Republic's territory. In this undertaking he had the full support of Piero de' Medici who, in that era when the spiritual and the temporal were inextricably bound together, looked for an increase of his own power in the measure that Savonarola extended the authority of his vicar-generalship.

However, Fra Girolamo's mission was not very successful. Only the prior of the convent in Fiesole agreed to come into the new province. Of this man, Fra Domenico Buonvicini, we will hear again, for he went to the gallows with Savonarola in 1498. At Siena the friars would not even discuss the subject of changing their obedience. In the other cities the priors received him with all honors and promised to follow the example of San Marco in reverting to mendicancy and divesting their houses from the bounties of patronage.

But no sooner had Savonarola turned his back than the Pisans and

Pistoians went back to the easier life. What Fra Girolamo called putting on the yoke of Christ was too onerous for them. By that time the Friar had continued on his journey to Bologna and was lodging once more in the Monastery of St. Dominic where he made his first vow. Here were old friends and he gained a sympathetic hearing. His curriculum of theological studies was adopted by the Bolognese, but that was all. In administrative matters they politely refused to follow suit.

Savonarola stayed nearly two months in Bologna. The authorities, profiting from the presence of so renowned a preacher, invited him to deliver a course of sermons in the Cathedral of Saints Peter and Paul. It would be the last time he spoke in the city which had been his spiritual home. Before he got through with his sermons all Italy was in uproar and Florence was calling him to return in all haste. In the Bologna cathedral he escaped an attempt at assassination by an amazing display of coolness and sangfroid.

The church was full to overflowing: burghers, peasants, men and women of note, the civic magistrates, and the regular clergy, all were attracted by the reputation of his forceful preaching. One of his regular hearers was the wife of Giovanni Bentivoglio, the despotic lord of Bologna. She was a woman of great beauty but of towering arrogance. She came habitually late to the service with a whole train of attendants. Since seats had been reserved for herself and her retinue near the pulpit, her arrival and progress through the crowded church caused considerable disturbance. At first Savonarola paid no attention or tried to shame her ladyship by pausing in his sermon and waiting till she and her suite had settled in their seats. It didn't help; the following Sunday they came still later. Then Savonarola, addressing the court party in general, asked for more decorum and reproached those who, by their late arrival, disturbed the devotions of the congregation.

But with that remonstrance the preacher's patience was at an end. When the Lady Bentivoglio on the next occasion arrived with her train of attendants and had her armed escort clear a passage for her and her ladies in waiting through the massed congregation and thus disrupted the entire service, Savonarola, after a silence, suddenly exclaimed: "Now we can see what manner of tactics the devil adopts in order to disturb the Word of God!"

Enraged by such an affront, the Lady Bentivoglio shouted back that she would not tolerate Savonarola another minute in *her* cathedral. Turning to her cavaliers, she ordered them to draw their swords and strike Fra Girolamo dead in the pulpit. There was an outcry as some peasants raised their fists and advanced menacingly on the armed courtiers. Though the Lady Bentivoglio repeated her order several times, the noblemen thought caution the better part of valor and remained motionless.

Two hired assassins were sent to the convent the same evening with orders to make short shrift of Fra Girolamo. They were admitted in his presence, but when he addressed them in the friendliest manner and pointed out the gravity of the crime of murder they went away mortified. Twice more in the week that followed suspicious persons knocked at the monastery door asking to see the Prior of San Marco. Each time Savonarola talked them out of whatever evil design they were sent to accomplish.

The following Sunday Fra Girolamo announced from the pulpit that he would leave for Florence at six o'clock the following morning. "I shall be alone," he said, "and I shall bear no arms. I will have nothing on my person but my wooden water flask and my staff. At noon I shall rest for an hour in the village of Pianora . . . If anyone wishes to speak to me before I set out, let him or her come now!" And then he added with significant emphasis: "I shall never return to Bologna. It is not my fate to die here. I am going to Florence to receive the martyr's crown. . . ." He had a great work to do, and till it was done, he felt, nothing could harm him.

Chapter V

The French Invade Italy:
Savonarola in the Role of Mediator

IN THE SUMMER of 1494 the third of Savonarola's predictions went into fulfillment: Ferrante, King of Naples, followed Lorenzo de' Medici and Innocent VIII into the grave, and the era of peace in Italy came to an end. Ferrante was succeeded by his son, Alfonso II, but the young monarch had scarcely taken possession of his throne when the King of France, Charles VIII, let it be known that he intended to dispute the succession. Under an old charter the French ruling house of Anjou held a claim to the Neapolitan kingdom. That Charles VIII fully intended to enforce this claim became evident when he ordered his army to assemble in the neighborhood of the city of Bourg where the French court maintained a summer residence. Here Charles made preparations to cross the Alps, traverse nearly the entire length of the Italian Peninsula, seize Naples, depose Alfonso II, and put one of the French princes of the blood royal on the throne.

In order to get to Naples by the overland route the French army would have to pass through the territories of the Duke of Milan, the Florentine Republic, and on the east side of the Appenines such city-states as Mantua, Bologna, and others. Had the Italian princes in that moment followed Pope Alexander's advice to combine in a confederation or league, unify their armed forces, place them under a single command and notify the French King that they would together resist his advance, Charles would in all likelihood have given

up the idea of invasion. However, Charles and his advisers, counting on the mutual hostility and intrigue of the different Italian ruling
houses, believed that no serious obstacles would be placed in
their path.

They were not wrong in this surmise. To begin with Ludovico
Sforza, Duke of Milan, offered the French unopposed passage
through his domains. The Genoese Republic promised Charles a
financial subsidy on the understanding that the French army by-pass
its territory, while Florence was thrown into a quandary whether to
side with the King or oppose him. Ludovico Sforza went furthest;
he had his own reasons for wanting to see Charles dethrone the new
King of Naples. Sforza kept the rightful heir of the Milanese dukedom chained up in prison. This man, Giovanni Galeazzo, was the
brother-in-law of Alfonso, the recently crowned King of Naples.
If the French succeeded in deposing Alfonso, the Neapolitan threat
to liberate Galeazzo and restore him to power in Milan would be
nullified at the same time. Sforza entered into a formal alliance with
the King of France and made a contribution of 200,000 gold ducats*
towards the expenses of the expedition.

Pope Alexander immediately suspected that there was more to
the French King's plan to seize Naples than the enforcement of
an ancient claim by the House of Anjou. "If only Naples were involved," remarked the Pontiff, "King Charles would never stir from
his court at Bourg . . . It is the Cardinal della Rovere who is behind
all this. The Cardinal entertains close relations with the French
court. The French army cannot avoid passing through Rome on its
way to Naples. Cardinal della Rovere has probably convinced King
Charles that it will be an easy matter to drive us from St. Peter's
chair, call a Conclave, and put Della Rovere in our place. . . . However, my Lord Cardinal will discover that we are not as helpless as
he thinks. For a start we will take the side of Alfonso, the King of
Naples. We will place our two kingdoms in a state of defense and
the Lord Cesare Borgia will unify and command our forces."

When Charles VIII learned of the Rome-Naples alliance he
halted his army, which had already marched from Bourg to
Grenoble, and announced that lack of funds compelled him to give
up further thoughts of the expedition. This news brought the Cardi-

* Approximately 5 million dollars.

nal della Rovere in all haste from his residence in St. Germain-en-
Laye to the royal camp for the purpose of persuading the King to
change his mind. At first Charles proved adamant: he had not
counted, he objected, on fighting so powerful a combination as
Naples and Rome so far away from his military base depots. Once
he crossed the Alps and penetrated some distance into the Italian
Peninsula, his lines of communication might be endangered. Without a regular flow of supplies he might be defeated and trapped
south of the Alps.

Della Rovere brought all his powers of persuasion and flattery
to bear on the King. Charles listened with growing amazement as
the Cardinal unfolded a plan that amounted to nothing less than
world conquest. Naples, the Cardinal observed disdainfully, was
scarcely worth troubling about by so powerful a monarch as Charles
VIII. What the King should do was march straight on Rome before
the Pope and Alfonso II had time to consolidate their forces. The
Pope was to be imprisoned and a Council of the whole Church
called to investigate the simoniacal methods employed by Alexander
VI in his election. Thus would the way be cleared for his own,
Della Rovere's elevation to the chair of St. Peter.

By decision of the Council of Constance in 1417, the Pope was
obliged to convoke a Council of the whole Church once every ten
years. If the Pope refused or procrastinated, the way was open for
either the German Emperor or the King of France to call a Council. "Let the Most Christian King," said Cardinal della Rovere to
Charles, "do his duty. The whole world will applaud Your Majesty's
action in calling a Council and depose the fraudulent Borgia who
usurps the seat of Blessed Peter."

When Charles still hesitated, the Cardinal pulled out his trump
card. Once in the chair of St. Peter, Della Rovere promised the
King that he would crown him Emperor of the West and thus revive
the glorious epoch of his ancestor, Charles the Great, Charlemagne.
Then he, Juliano della Rovere, would preach a new crusade. Together they would drive the Turk from Europe, liberate Constantinople, end the schism between the Eastern and Western Church,
restore Jerusalem and the basilica containing the Saviour's tomb,
and dominate the universe in a holy alliance of Emperor and Pope.

The whole of Christendom, he predicted, would rally to their side and no power on earth would be able to resist them.

Such was the proposal of high adventure, of military and ecclesiastical triumph with which Cardinal della Rovere sought to bring the French King around. He minimized the hazards of the French expedition by saying that if Charles would make a public announcement of his intention to depose Alexander VI, all the Italian princes would not only come to his side, but would press him to execute his project with the utmost speed.

In spite of the artful and designing policy and the glittering prospects, the French King could still not be persuaded. Naples, yes! It was eminently just, he held, to unseat King Alfonso since he had no right to the throne of Naples. But to lay his hands on the Pope's sacred person was another matter. To Cardinal della Rovere the Holy Father may have been a usurper of St. Peter's throne, a base intriguant, an unbaptized infidel, a scandalous adulterer, and all the rest of it, to Charles he was the Pope, the Vicar of Christ, the Father of the Church, the rightful lord and monarch of the whole world, from whom emanated all power and jurisdiction even of a temporal kind, and who was consequently the supreme and transcendent authority in all the earth. There was a certain indwelling power in the Pope in the presence of which Charles, like all Christians of that time, stood in solemn awe. The Pope's sacrosanctity derived from the doctrine that Jesus Christ had invested St. Peter and his successors, the Roman pontiffs, with a plenitude of power, in virtue of which the Pope had at his disposal all that the earth contained, and even the angels in heaven had to obey his commands.*

In the end Cardinal della Rovere prevailed though not by persuasion or flattery. While he was conferring with the King, information reached Grenoble that the Florentine Republic had joined the Rome-Naples alliance and that other Italian principalities were about to follow suit. Instead of depressing the French monarch this intelligence roused him to fury. "My house," exclaimed Charles, "has always entertained the friendliest relations with the Medici and the Republic of Florence. Why then this treachery? I have neither offended nor threatened them. I had not the least intention to enter Florence. I planned to by-pass the city and follow the

* . . . *Cum etiam ipse Papa Angelis habeat imperare.*

Mediterranean coastal road, perhaps resting my army for a week at Pisa, and then proceed directly to Naples . . . But now," he added angrily, "after this shameful betrayal of an old friendship, I shall certainly enter Florence. I shall sack the city and collect all the funds needed for my expedition . . . I promise that I will pursue the vile Medici brood to the ends of the earth. . . ."

And so, the French army set in motion once more. Charles crossed the Mount Genèvre and stood on Italian soil on September 3, 1494, at Susa. A week later he made his triumphant entry in Asti where his ally, Ludovico Sforza, Duke of Milan, bade him welcome and organized a sumptuous reception in his honor. Sforza urged the King to make all haste in marching on Naples where Cesare Borgia was said to have arrived to take command of the Neapolitan armed forces.

King Charles, with whom hesitation was a normal state of mind, wavered again when word reached him that the people of Florence had forced Piero de' Medici to renounce his alliance with Rome and Naples. "The Florentines have changed their mind," the King remarked to his commander in chief, the Seneschal de Beaucaire, "who will vouch for it that the Duke of Milan will not do the same? These Italians are as changeable as water. Their pledged word means nothing . . . If I move further south into the Peninsula leaving Ludovico Sforza in my rear, what prevents him from stabbing me in the back? He needs but to occupy the mountain passes and I will be cut off from France . . . Might there not be a secret understanding between these Italian princes to lure me on and starve my army into submission? I do not feel safe, I do not feel safe. . . ."

The French army cautiously moved a few miles to the south and occupied the town of Piacenza. In that city the King had a new surprise, perhaps the most painful of the many he experienced in the course of the campaign. Within a few hours after Charles quit the Duke of Milan, that prince had caused his nephew, Giovanni Galeazzo, the rightful heir to the dukedom to be strangled in prison. Charles was so upset by this news that he forthwith ordered his army to make about turn. The campaign was now definitely off. The King had lost faith in his Milanese ally. Not a ducat of the promised subsidies had been forthcoming. Venice and Genoa had not even sent ambassadors to greet him. Bologna was silent, so were Mantua,

Padua, and Ferrara. Charles felt himself surrounded by invisible foes. Any moment, he feared, the Italians might descend upon him from their strong places in the mountains. Hadn't the German hero Herman once ambushed and destroyed the vastly superior Roman legions under Varus that way in the fastness of the Teutoburger Forest?

Charles retraced his steps towards Susa. He had regained the passes of the Alps and was about to cross the border back into his own country when Cardinal Giovanni de' Medici caught up with him. Giovanni informed the King that Florence was impatiently awaiting his arrival. More than that, he, Giovanni, was empowered to offer the King a substantial financial contribution to bring the campaign against Naples to a successful conclusion.

Cardinal de' Medici was in perfect good faith when he made this offer, yet he sadly exceeded the terms of his ambassadorial commission. He was indeed to do his best to dissuade the King from carrying out his threat to sack the city of Florence. But he was not to bring the King back home with him. When Giovanni saw that Charles and his army were heading for France, he should have left well enough alone and thanked his stars that the French threat was finally averted. But now, upon receiving Giovanni de' Medici's hopeful message, the French King ordered his troops to make about turn once more.

The further King Charles penetrated into Italy the more feverish grew the atmosphere in Florence and in the rest of the country. The most fantastic rumors were current about the size of the French forces and the deadly power of their equipment. The French were said to have cannons that could demolish the strongest fortresses in an hour's time. It was bruited about that in spite of the change of heart in Florence, the French King planned to wreak revenge for the affronts offered him by Piero de' Medici. He was determined to sack not only Florence but every city on his way as far south as Rome and Naples. Cardinal della Rovere, who was in the French King's retinue, according to the rumormongers, would be allowed to deal personally with his enemy Pope Alexander VI by crucifying him on Vatican hill.

Savonarola's visions were coming true: the Lord's terrible swift sword was now suspended over all Italy. In every city and hamlet the people were seeing signs and tokens of approaching doom. In Apulia three suns shone forth in the middle of the night and tainted the sky with the color of blood. In Arezzo it snowed and thundered at the same time. In half a dozen cities a heavily armed phantom cavalry was seen riding across the nocturnal heavens. The clatter of their arms and the thud of the horses' hoofs made the earth quake in Calabria. In Novara a monk preaching in the cathedral went further: he identified the apocalyptic horsemen and frightened his congregation to the point of hysterics by saying that the invading armies were made up of Spaniards, Greeks, Turks, and Blacka-moors. In a score of churches throughout the land the statues of the saints began to sweat. In Naples an image of the Mother of Sorrows, on the testimony of the Archbishop himself, was seen shedding tears of blood. One woman in Florence was delivered of a child with a dog's head. Another had a baby with two heads and four legs.

In the measure that the French army came nearer, the tension in Florence degenerated into a sickening dread virtually putting a stop to the usual day-by-day activities. The streets were no longer swept. Shops opened but for one hour in the morning. Hoarding of grain and wine drove the prices up to an unheard-of pitch. The Floren-tines, always so valiant in the defense of their fatherland, had lost heart. Never in living men's memory had there been such abysmal despondency. The people saw no way out from the terror bearing down upon them. The Signoria was in permanent session, but the doors of the Palazzo Vecchio remained shut to the stunned and stupefied crowds milling about in the great square. Instead of raising confidence the calling of every citizen to the colors had the opposite effect in that it only served to heighten the sense of dread and alarm. The Signoria gave out no instructions, and the reports which carriers and spies brought in from time to time were left unpublished.

The peasants stayed away from the markets for fear of being shut up in the city in the event of a siege and undergoing the usual fate of the inhabitants of a captured place. Convinced of the futility of forging halberds, pikes, and swords, in the face of the French army equipped with the latest type of artillery, the smiths and iron-mongers laid down their tools and extinguished their furnaces.

In mid-October it became known that Charles VIII had divided
his forces in two equal parts; one column ten thousand strong, under
the Seneschal de Beaucaire, was marching down on the east side of
the Appenines for Bologna in the vicinity of which Cesare Borgia
was preparing to make his stand. Another column, with the King
at its head, came straight down the west coast. Any day, any hour,
the blue banners with the royal fleur-de-lis might appear under the
walls of Florence. The signal fires on the mountaintops were still
burning indicating that King Charles had not reached these points.
But Piero de' Medici, the ruler of Florence, was nowhere to be
seen. His residence, the Palazzo Medici, was deserted. At the
session of the Signoria where he should have presided, Piero had
not put in an appearance for days. Where was he? Had he fled?
Could a Medici desert his city in the hour of danger? To distress
was added confusion. There were no leaders. Nobody knew what
to do.

The feast of All Souls was approaching and Savonarola would
occupy the cathedral pulpit once more. The Friar announced that
on the indicated day he would begin a series of sermons on the
Psalms and the Prophet Haggai. All Florence was invited and all
Florence turned out. Nearly twenty thousand people squeezed into
the Duomo while other thousands stood outside. Savonarola did not
in any way minimize the city's danger. There was no denying the
peril of Florence.

"O *Firenze,* O *Firenze,* O *Firenze,*" he called out to the immense congregation gathered at his feet. "O Florence, repent, repent, repent! Our God is the Lord God of hosts. He it is who
marches at the head of the armies bearing down upon our city. If
you want God to help you, you must begin by opening your hearts
to him . . . For a long time, O Florentines, I have been warning you
that God would send these afflictions . . . Believe me at last now
that you can touch calamity with your hands. . . .

"O *Italia,* it is because of your transgressions that this evil has
come upon you!

"O *Firenze,* it is because of your iniquities that this adversity
stares you in the face.

"O clergy, clergy, clergy, it is because of you that the storm of
God's wrath has risen!

"O you magistrates and bankers and prelates, it is because of your neglect of the people that these things are coming to pass. Neither your wealth, nor your cleverness, nor your flight can stay the divine judgment. There is no escape! . . ."

And then in a gentler tone, he continued: "The hand of God is upon you *not* in order to destroy you. The hand of God is upon you, O Florentines, because he wants to show you his great mercy and loving kindness . . . On the other hand, if you do not turn to the Lord God now, in this hour of dire extremity, he will hide his face from Florence forever. The time has come," said Savonarola, "for each of us to forgive and forget the harsh words we have spoken to each other, the jealousies we bear in our hearts, the impure desires we have nourished, the thought of revenge we have cultivated, the possessions of our neighbor we have coveted . . . Let each citizen go to his fellow citizen and ask forgiveness! Then come back here and we will pray together that the cup of God's wrath be turned from our lips. . . ."

Before dismissing the congregation with his blessing, Savonarola announced that a three days' long prayer service would be held in the Duomo. During that time the people were to fast on bread and water. Only the children and the sick were exempt from this ordinance. The fast was to be repeated every Friday till the following spring. Three times a week, he said, he would preach in the cathedral and discuss the current situation.

"Now, *Fiorentini, figliuolini, fratellini,* my dear Florentine children and little brothers, go home and pray. And know this for sure: We shall not die! We shall live! God is merciful! God is merciful! God is merciful!"

Thousands of voices in and outside the cathedral took up the cry "till the roof of the Duomo shook": "God is merciful!"

With the approval of the Archbishop the Signoria issued a proclamation the same afternoon ordering all churches, chapels and convents in and around Florence to hold prayer services for the next three days and three nights.

At the end of the three days of penitence came the shattering news of Piero de' Medici's betrayal. He had secretly left Florence on the last day of October in order to meet the King of France at the Republic's borders. On his march through the region of Lunigiana to Pisa, Charles VIII had run into a trap between the Mediterranean shore and, for his cumbersome artillery, the impassable mountain ranges to the east. The French army had come to a halt in a narrow passage. Straight ahead in its path lay the heavily fortified Florentine fortresses of Sarzana and Sarzanello. A handful of men could hold the French at bay at this point. The Florentine garrisons were on the verge of launching a sortie when Piero de' Medici appeared on the scene and ordered the two cities to hoist the white flag of surrender. Then he approached the King of France and offered him not only the two fortresses but also the fortified towns of Librafatta, Pietrasanta, the citadel of Pisa, and the harbor of Livorno. Without striking a blow, Charles had the whole of Tuscany in his hand and he looked upon Piero as an angel from heaven who had extricated him from a sore predicament.

But that was not all: Piero promised the King of France 200,000 gold ducats and . . . granted the French army permission to enter Florence and for three days pillage and debauch to its heart's content. The only reciprocation demanded was the security of his own person, that of the members of the Medici family, and its properties. Piero heaved a sigh of relief when Charles willingly granted this request. He had saved his own skin and complimented himself on being henceforth safe and sound under the King's protection. He did not suspect that in reality he was lost forever.

When the Florentines learned from the refugees streaming from the war zone that Piero de' Medici had surrendered the fortresses and, besides, had virtually handed their city over to the loot-hungry French army, the pent-up tension exploded in a burst of indignation and fury. Thirty thousand crudely armed citizens marched through the streets tearing the heraldic emblem of the Medici family from public buildings, convents and eleemosynary institutions endowed by the members of the ruling house in the course of the past seventy years. Wherever the hated name appeared on monuments, memorial tablets, or façades it was erased with ax blows or blotted out under a layer of tar. The mob shouting revolutionary slogans proceeded to break into the Medici bank in the center of the city. To the dismay of the rioters it was found to be empty. Piero had taken the precaution of secreting all his money and valuables before leaving for the French camp. Florence deemed this proof abundant that the Medici treachery was premeditated.

Since nothing could be gained at the bank, the mob stormed up the Via Larga in the direction of the Palazzo Medici. Flaming torches were carried along to set the palace on fire and burn it to the ground. However, the excited crowd was intercepted by Savonarola whose convent stood in the immediate neighborhood of Piero's residence. "What can you gain by burning down the palace?" the Friar asked the rioters. "The owner is absent and the poor servants certainly have no share in his misdeeds. They are as much the victims of his treachery as you. If you destroy the Palazzo Medici and its treasures you only empoverish yourselves and the city of Florence!"

For a wonder the crowd allowed itself to be persuaded. Savonarola now held the confidence of the Florentines to such a degree that he could tame even a mob intoxicated with the thought of revenge and plunder. They knew him to be an enemy of tyrants and a partisan of the popular cause. *Popolo e Libertà!* the crowd roared at him. "The People and Liberty!" he replied.

Meanwhile, the Signoria deliberated on the political problem that had arisen by the absence of Piero de' Medici. In the session of November 4, a citizen of the highest repute, Piero Capponi by name, stood up to declare that the Medici were no longer fit to govern the state. By an unanimous vote Piero de' Medici was banned from Florence, and he and his successors, for all time to come, declared unworthy to occupy any position of authority.

This decision, however, did not dispose of the French threat. What was to be done with regard to the French army which was known to have entered Pisa, Florence's chief tributary city? The Signoria decided to send an embassy to Charles VIII with an invitation to enter Florence peacefully. If the King consented to desist from violence he was promised a royal welcome and the Florentines were prepared to enter into an alliance with France. Again on the motion of Piero Capponi, Savonarola, "known to all of us as a man whose probity of character and devotion to liberty are beyond dispute," was asked to be one of the ambassadors.

When Savonarola accepted the commission he took the first step on the slippery road of politics and took part in the first stages in a

major revolution. Four years later, when the political wind veers
around, his acceptance of the embassy will be held against him as an
act of high treason. His defense will be that, although his membership in a monastic order barred him from participation in political
affairs, he found the Florentine Republic in November 1494 a ship
without compass or rudder and its people in the gravest danger.

The Friar set to work at once. Before leaving for Pisa, he advised
that all funds, treasures, and valuables in the public domain be
shipped out of the city and hidden in the mountains with a strong
guard over them. Secondly, all females under the age of twenty-five
were to be placed beyond the grasp of the French soldiers who could
be expected to enter Florence any day. The nunneries in the vicinity
of Florence were notified to get ready to receive, lodge, and feed
several thousand women and girls. At the end of the crisis the
mothers superior were promised a liberal reward for extending hospitality to the matrons and daughters of Florence. In order not to
lead the French troops into temptation and to avoid incidents,
Savonarola made a further proposal to close the brothels for the
duration of the emergency and to disperse the licensed prostitutes
over the neighboring villages. His proposals were deemed "wise and
bespeaking a high sense of patriotism," and the female exodus got
under way without delay.

Savonarola's chief task was to dissuade the French King from
carrying out his intention to sack and loot the city for which the
pusillanimous Piero de' Medici had given the foreign troops full
license. Since he could not foresee that he would be successful in
his effort Savonarola's last suggestion was for the Florentine soldiers
to be collected in secret places in the city, and for all citizens to
provide themselves with arms and to be ready to issue forth and
fight in case of need. The Cardinal Giovanni de' Medici, who had
returned to Florence after gauging the mood and temper of the
French troops, thought it safer to remove certain highly valuable art
treasures from his mansion. There was no better place than the
cellars of San Marco's convent and there, with Savonarola's consent,
they were stored. Though San Marco was the virtual headquarters
of the popular anti-Medici party, the integrity of Savonarola and
his friars was so universally acknowledged that the Cardinal de'
Medici entrusted his valuables to their care.

But still Fra Girolamo could not leave for Pisa. His friend, Count
Giovanni Pico della Mirandola, sent for him. For some time Pico
had been giving lessons in Hebrew and Syriac to the monks of San
Marco. He was now dying at the early age of 31. Though he had for
long, under some excuse or other, sought to postpone his adherence
to the brotherhood of San Marco, Pico now asked to be buried in the
chapel in the habit of St. Dominic. He had believed in the fulfillment of all of Savonarola's predictions but one. He could not believe that a foreign potentate with a large army would one day
appear before Florence. Now he surrendered to the evidence. Fra
Girolamo hurried to the stricken man's side and sat with him during
the last twenty-four hours of his life, hearing his confession and
giving absolution.

From Pico's bedside the Friar sent a proclamation to the citizens
of Florence imploring them to be steadfast in mercy and peace. "If
you would have the Lord continue his mercy towards you," he
wrote, "be ye merciful towards your brethren, your friends and
even your enemies. Do not soil yourselves with an act of revenge or
vandalism during my absence. . . . The Lord be with you!"

Then at last he set out on his errand to Charles VIII. The other
ambassadors, who had preceded him, informed him, on his arrival
in Pisa, that the French King refused to commit himself on the conduct of his troops. His men had left their wives and sweethearts behind in France, explained the King, they had been on hard rations
since the beginning of the campaign and had experienced enormous
difficulties in transporting the baggage and heavy artillery across
the Alps. If the troops had cheerfully borne and overcome all these
hardships, it was because they looked forward with keenest anticipation to the delights awaiting them in the friendly city of Florence.
It would be contemptible on his part, the French monarch told the
Florentine ambassadors, and perhaps destructive of his royal authority if he should go back on his word now that his army had
come in sight of the promised paradise. In fact, the King said, he
could hardly wait himself to see and taste the joys in store for him.

"His Majesty needs money desperately," the Florentine ambassadors reported to their colleague when Savonarola arrived in Pisa.
"'He may forego the looting of our city in return for a substantial
financial subsidy. See what you can do!"

Before calling on the King Savonarola conferred with Guillaume Brissonet, overseer of the treasury of France and Archbishop of St. Malo, who was the chief of the King's brain trust. The Archbishop warmly complimented Savonarola on his sermons and taking the Friar's hand in his own urged him to sit down and discuss the Italian political situation. Brissonet praised Fra Girolamo's foresight in announcing the coming of a herald from God to deliver the Italian peoples. This messenger had now arrived in the person of Charles VIII. The primary object of the French expedition was to curb the power of the despots and tyrants in the various city-states, beginning with Alfonso II who had no right to the throne of Naples.

As to the Church, Archbishop Brissonet favored a thoroughgoing reform, but he would not go as far as the Cardinal della Rovere: no harm was to come to the reigning Pontiff. On the other hand, Cesare Borgia, the Pope's son, would undoubtedly be imprisoned or taken as a hostage to France upon the King's return.

"If a Council can be called in Rome well and good," said the Archbishop, "but it must not be forgotten that the convocation of a Council is the prerogative of the Supreme Pontiff. King Charles is of a very uneasy mind on this subject. He does not want to exceed his authority. Before doing anything in the line of ecclesiastical reform His Majesty wishes to consult the Cardinals resident in Rome. Having obtained their view, the King will communicate with the doctors of canon law in his own university of Paris.

"Perhaps," continued Brissonet, "the King might set up an interregnum during which Pope Alexander is to be asked to move his residence from the Vatican to the Castel Sant' Angelo while a committee of Cardinals carries on the administration of the Holy Catholic Church till the day when the Parisian canonists reach a decision on the validity of Pope Alexander's election."

"But might not the Holy Father," asked Savonarola in turn, "be urged to put himself at the head of the reform government? Would the Pontiff not acquire greater freedom of action if the papacy's ties with the Italian potentates are severed and the Pope placed under French protection?"

"His Majesty, my master," replied Brissonet, "would like nothing better than to see the Pope freed from Italian political intrigue, but he does not want to dictate the Pontiff's actions. The King acknowledges the Roman Pontiff as his suzerain . . . Reforms there must be. The Church is in grave danger as long as the present situation continues . . . I approve most heartily your protestations against the well-known abuses. I trust you will not relax in your vigilance for the good of the Church. . . ."

Archbishop Brissonet presented Savonarola with a copy of a book of prayers of his own composition, entitled *Enchiridion precum,* and then introduced him into the royal presence, leaving the King and the Friar alone.

As usual Savonarola went straight to the point. He did not talk to King Charles of church reform, this subject lay outside the terms of his embassy. His sole task was to dissuade His Majesty from dealing harshly with the city and people of Florence. Accordingly he told the King that if he seriously considered Florence a friendly city it should be the more reason to treat the people with forbearance and kindness. If Charles VIII was indeed a herald of God he should not degrade the nature of his mission by permitting the commission of ungodly acts by his soldiers. God would surely hold him responsible for their conduct. Yes, undoubtedly, God would visit the sins of the soldiers upon their father and King. . . .

Charles started to tremble as the meaning of Savonarola's admonition penetrated his feeble intelligence. The Friar was deeply disappointed not only in the French monarch's evident intellectual limitations but in his physical appearance. Savonarola had spoken to the Florentines of Charles as a son of the great crusader St. Louis, as a descendant of Charlemagne, the liberator and unifier of Christendom; what he saw was a dirty little man, with a bulbous head and puny limbs. The King's face twitched as he spoke, the eyes were lusterless, his nose looked like the beak of a bird of prey and his mouth hung wide open as he listened to Savonarola. The ambassador of Venice, who saw the King right after the Friar, reported that Charles giggled like an idiot.

Piero de' Medici, the deposed ruler, although not present at the royal interview, was gravely perturbed over Savonarola's appearance in the role of ambassador at King Charles' headquarters. He realized that something had gone wrong with his dominion over Florence when the Friar did not even take the trouble to greet him. As his nervousness increased, Piero informed the French King of his intention to make preparations for the royal entry in Florence. He hastily collected some troops and returned to the city on the evening of the eighth of November. The next day he presented himself at the Palace of the Signoria with a bodyguard and let it be known that he had come to take the government of the Republic personally in hand. The Signoria sent out word that Piero would be permitted to enter, but alone and unarmed and not through the main entrance but through the rear door. When he came into the hall of deliberation he was received with studied coldness and told outright to dismiss his troops in order to avoid a senseless struggle with the citizens. Boiling with rage, Piero turned away, saying that he would take counsel with his friends and then return to let the Signoria know his decision.

He called the commander of his troops, Paolo Orsini, and the officer of the city guard, Lorini, and gave orders to occupy the towers of the San Gallo gate. Then he returned to the Council with some trusted soldiers and drawing his sword was about to enter the Palace when three of Florence's most distinguished citizens, Corsini, Nerli, and Gualterotti, came outside and barred his way. He tried to take an arrogant tone and waved his sword, but the doors were shut in his face. The populace who had witnessed the scene began to riot. The street urchins pelted Piero with a volley of stones and several citizens menaced him with their staves. Then the Captain of Justice and keeper of the arsenal, one Pico dell' Aquila, appeared on the scene with his men. Aquila attempted to protect the Mediceans but he and his men were disarmed by the mob and compelled to open the Bargello, the city prison, and release all the prisoners confined there. The crowd then poured into the arsenal and after seizing the arms, re-appeared in the streets. The great bell in the Signoria tower began to peal and all Florence collected in the Piazza.

Piero de' Medici withdrew into his palace and put on his armor. He was determined to fight it out. With a troop of cavalry he came thundering into the square scattering the crowd to right and left. Just at that moment Francesco Valori, one of the ambassadors to Charles VIII, returned from Pisa riding on a mule and covered with dust. The crowd pressed around him and asked for news, and in a moment he was in the thick of the riot. He confirmed the rumors that Piero de' Medici had betrayed the city and disgraced the name of his family. Valori was an old partisan of the Medici. It will be recalled that he was one of the five sent by Lorenzo to Savonarola to ask the Friar to moderate the tone of his sermons. But he was now so disgusted with Piero's contemptible transactions with the King of France, that he called on the citizens to fight the Medici troop. Piero saw him coming and raced towards the San Gallo district where he tried to rally the rabble in that slum quarter by scattering gold and silver coins. But the people would not move. They hissed, insulted, and attacked him. After a brief skirmish, Piero de' Medici galloped through the San Gallo gate and the doors were immediately closed behind him.

This left Piero's young brother, the Cardinal, still in town. Giovanni came riding down from the Palazzo Medici towards the grand square shouting: *Palle! Palle!* "The balls, the balls!" a reference to the balls in the Medicean escutcheon and the family's rallying cry. But meeting Francesco Valori and the armed mob, he beat a hasty retreat and learned at the mansion that his brother had fled without waiting for him.

Giovanni threw off his cardinal's gown and put on the hair shirt and the rough cassock of a monk and ventured out once more. He appeared before the Council in the evening while that body was drafting a law putting a prize of 2000 ducats on Piero's head. The Cardinal, a mere boy of seventeen at the time, pleaded to be allowed to remain in Florence as a private citizen. "If you drive me out," he expostulated, "you will break my heart . . . I ask you as Christian gentlemen to grant me your forgiveness . . . Do not commit an irreparable act of cruelty . . . I was born in this city. I grew up in it. My dear mother whom I lost as a child is buried in your midst. I love every one of you as my very own brothers. Have pity on me! Have pity on me for the sake of Cosimo and Lorenzo who brought this city to greatness. Believe me when I say I cannot live without Florence, my Florence, my home. . . ." Giovanni fell to the floor sobbing like a child.

Suddenly he rose to his feet and with tear-choked voice and arms outstretched, he asked the Signoria: "Where shall I go?"

"We do not care where you go!" they shouted back. "Go to your brother! Go to the Pope! Go to the devil! Get out of our sight! . . ."

In the interval Piero de' Medici and a handful of cuirassiers still loyal to him, spurred their horses to all speed, hoping to reach Bologna before daybreak. He feared that if the peasants recognized him he and his men would be taken captive and murdered on the spot. But in Bologna he met with a humiliating reception. The Lord of Bologna, the haughty Giovanni Bentivoglio, said to him: "I would rather be hacked to pieces than abandon my state in this fashion." Hearing these words, Piero pursued his journey to Venice where, exhausted and covered with mud though he was, he received the honors which were usually accorded to fallen potentates.

Giovanni de' Medici did not go out as ignominiously as his brother. After the Signoria dismissed him he knocked on the door of San Marco calling on Savonarola to let him in. But the door remained closed. The Friar had not returned from his embassy to Pisa. Had he been home he would most certainly have allowed the Cardinal to enter. For no man, whatever his condition, said Fra Girolamo, is ever to be turned away from the gates of mercy.

The night watch allowed Giovanni to pass through the San Gallo gate. In a driving storm of rain and sleet he took the road to Bologna on the night of November 11, 1494. Twenty years were to pass before he returned to Florence, but then he came as Pope Leo X, arrayed in his white robe of office. His first stop in his native city was at the Convent of San Marco. He entered cell number 12 and, as is recorded, "stood for a long time with bowed head in deep thought remembering the martyred Fra Girolamo."

Thus the rule of the Medici in Florence was overthrown after seventy years during which successive members of the house lifted the city to a pinnacle of wealth and renown it was never afterwards to attain. Not even Savonarola could now prevent the mob from breaking loose and looting the properties of the Medici and their partisans. All memories of the past despotism were destroyed. The houses of the manager of the Medici bank, Antonio Minati, and of Giovanni Guidi, the chief tax collector, were thoroughly sacked. Both these men and their families were banished as having been tools of the Medici in devising and imposing various methods of burdensome taxation on the people. The residence of Cardinal de' Medici was ransacked from top to bottom and the famous garden which Lorenzo had adorned with valuable antique statues and which he had personally tended for years with his lady Clarissa, was laid waste. On the other hand, many citizens were recalled from exile, in the first place those who were banished by Lorenzo, many of them unjustly, at the time of the Pazzi revolt. From Venice, Bologna, Ferrara, from Genoa and Mantua, from nearly every large city, the banished families streamed back.

At the same time measures for defense were pushed with the utmost speed. The French King's intentions were still unknown. Beyond saying that he would certainly come to Florence, he had not made any reassurance with regard to the behavior of his troops nor had he revoked his promise to let them pillage for a period of three days. Piero Caponi, the right-hand man of the Republic in those days when there was no one with executive authority, was stocking all the houses with war material. Stakes and planks with long sharp spikes driven through them and piles of cobblestones lay ready in courtyards and cloisters to barricade the streets at a moment's notice.

French officers and men had begun to enter the city in small parties. They were of the commissariat department and went around marking with chalk the houses in which the French troops were to be billeted. What struck the Frenchmen with amazement was not only the sight of so many splendid buildings, but the grim severity of the palaces which could, without any difficulty, be turned into so many impregnable fortresses. On November 15 the officers of the French advance guard witnessed a scene that sent a pang of apprehension through their minds. A rumor suddenly spread through the town that Piero de' Medici had turned around and was nearing the walls of Florence with a considerable body of hired troops.

Instantly the alarm bell rang its hellish clangor and the streets swarmed with the infuriated citizens. The city gates were closed, the fighting towers were manned, the windows of public buildings were covered with thick iron bars, barricades sprang from the ground as by magic. Thousands of archers took up their position on the roofs. The French saw that every house was a fortress and that there were several thousands of well-armed men ready to spring to the city's defense.

Within a few hours it became known that the rumor of Piero's return was false, and the Florentines repaired to the taverns to drink to their victory. But the French officers were forced to acknowledge that their tactics and stout battalions would be almost powerless, hemmed in those narrow streets, against a mode of warfare as baffling as it was intractable. They sent word to the French camp advising the King to come in peacefully and to avoid a clash at all cost since his situation would at best be hazardous in a city bristling with invisible defenders.

In the late afternoon of November 17 Charles VIII made his entry in a downpour of rain. The Signoria met the King outside the San Frediano gate and one of the judges made an address of welcome which was cut short by the downpour. Inside the city awnings had been spread out all the way to the Palazzo Medici to protect the King and his grand seigneurs against the weather. The city was superbly decorated with banners and bunting. From the windows and balconies hung brilliant, multicolored draperies and costly tapestries. A thousand torches illuminated the façades of the principal buildings and churches. But the people looked on with mingled wonder and fear as they saw the huge brass cannons, each drawn by twenty horses, roll over the Ponte Vecchio and onwards through the Piazza where the Signoria's great bell was ringing like mad.

First came the artillery, then the Swiss guard, bearing halberds of burnished steel, their uniforms parti-colored and rich waving plumes on their helmets. These Swiss troops had discarded the armor they formerly wore preferring to fight with their chests bare. The center of King Charles' army consisted of Gascon infantry, small men, light of step, who carried short, unsheathed swords which, in the manner of Caesar's legionnaires of old, they clashed on their shields in rhythm with every fourth step of their marching feet.

What followed next made the people of Florence stand back with feelings of dread and wonder, here was the French cavalry. It comprised the flower of the aristocracy, earls, dukes, barons, preceded by their banner bearers and followed by their retainers, all seated on horses which were much taller than any the Florentines had ever seen. The French horses looked like prehistoric monsters covered with mail and armor, their tails clipped and ears cropped. The sight

of the nobles was the most dazzling spectacle ever witnessed in
Florence; gleaming cuirasses and silver helmets, velvet banners embroidered with gold, chains of gold, and other glittering ornaments
clustered around the Burgundian and Norman banners. The royal
standard passed by in the midst of a forest of lances and a blaze of
martial pomp.

What the Florentines saw that day was Europe's first regular
army, very different from the usual slovenly Saturday afternoon
militia or mercenary hordes employed by the Italian potentates.
The French troops had discipline. They marched in step. The
horses remained in line. There was precision and confidence in the
soldiers' movements, the result of endless training and drilling. The
cavalry was followed by the archers who were armed with extraordinary long wooden bows. These men came from Scotland and
were of so huge a bodily frame that in the words of a contemporary
historian *parovano uomini bestiali,* "they seemed beastlike men."
Marino Sanudo, who wrote the history of Charles VIII's Italian
expedition, tells us that "the French weapons seemed better suited
for splitting doors than for fighting." At the head of the archers
marched "a monster of a man with a polished sword like a spit for
a roast pig, and then four drums played with both hands, accompanied by droning bagpipes making an infernal noise." The pi-
brochs were indeed wailing one of the most savage war songs of the
Highlands. And then more infantry; Flemings, Picards, Bretons,
and Alsatian *Landsknechten,* sturdier than the Gascons, bearing
lances and arquebuses and long swords, all in tight-fitting uniforms,
stepping so perfectly in unison that the ground shook.

A blare of silver trumpets announced the King himself to be
drawing near. Preceded by a bodyguard of young noblemen re-
splendent in bright-dyed cloaks, seated on a white horse which
bore a saddle of scarlet and cloth of gold, Charles VIII rode under
a canopy held up by four princes of the blood royal. The princes
wore the blue sash of the Order of St. Louis over their scarlet tunics
and the silver grand cross. By the King's side rode the Cardinal
Juliano della Rovere, and immediately behind him the Cardinal
Gurgins, the royal chancellor, and the Archbishop of St. Malo,
Guillaume Brissonet.

The people's expectation of the French King as a prince of im-

perial grandeur and an ambassador from heaven had been raised to
the fabulous by Savonarola's descriptions. The actual appearance
of this hunchbacked man with the enormous feet (he had twelve
toes), half-shocked and half-amused the Florentines. The glittering
crown on Charles' doddering head sagged sideways nearly hiding
his left eye. He wore a black velvet robe and an ermine collar sym-
bolic of the imperial dignity. In his left hand he held a golden scepter
set with jewels. The Florentines noticed at once that Charles VIII
carried a lance in his right hand and that the lance was held in a
horizontal position signifying that the King entered their city, not
as an invited royal guest, but as a conqueror. This frightened the
people, but Niccolo Machiavelli, who stood among the spectators
in the Piazza, looked with a cold eye on the royal procession and
said to those standing about: "The Florentines need not fear this
army of France. If called upon we can annihilate this troop in an
hour's time."

After an impressive service in the Duomo, Charles VIII, the
Cardinals and the princes of the blood, were conducted along the
Via Larga to the Palazzo Medici which had been prepared for their
reception, while the troops were quartered in the houses of the
people. More than a thousand years before St. Jerome had sounded
his warning to all mothers to keep their daughters indoors during
a city's occupation by foreign troops. To their astonishment and
no small disappointment, the French soldiers discovered that the
mothers of Florence had gone St. Jerome one better by sending
their daughters out of reach. There wasn't a female in sight.

For the next two days, Florence was ordered to feast and be
merry. At the Medici palace King Charles and his barons spent the
time in banqueting, receiving delegations and listening to extravagant eulogies by the one Florentine dignitary after the other. The
King was compared with Nebuchadnezar, with Cyrus the Great,
with Alexander the Great, with the great and immortal Augustus,
and, of course, with his ancestor and namesake Charles the Great.
History, it was predicted, would know him as "Charles the still
Greater." "Blessed is he that cometh in the name of the Lord,"
exclaimed Marsilio Ficino, the renowned Platonist, in his address
of welcome. "One day history will say of Charles VIII what Caesar
said after crossing the Rubicon: *Veni, vidi, vici.* I came, I saw, I

conquered." Charles, who did not understand a word of these Latin orations, was said to be endowed with Abraham's faith, with Job's patience, with Solomon's wisdom and with the Saviour's gentleness! When Jesus said: "Suffer the little children to come unto me," it was Charles VIII speaking to his children of Florence and Italy . . . The Most Christian King was destined to become the ruler of the world.

Only when the last Florentine orator ended his discourse by lifting his cup to *"Francia, Francia aeterna!"* (Eternal France), did the King come to life, and rising to his feet, declared that Florence would henceforth be regarded as a French city with the right to carry the royal fleur-de-lis in her official escutcheon and on her martial banners.

Early in the morning of the third day of the French occupation a quarrel broke out between some soldiers and the inhabitants of the Porta Gallo quarter over a woman who claimed that she had been molested. Half a dozen French soldiers who were pointed out as the perpetrators of the outrage, were disarmed and had their throats slit. Their bodies were dumped into the Arno.

When the King learned of the affray he sent the Swiss infantry in. The halbardiers were met by a hail of stones and roof tiles and other missiles flung from windows and house tops while barricades jumped from the ground like mushrooms. In a few minutes' time the Swiss were inextricably trapped and could go neither backwards nor forwards. Then the artillery was sent to the rescue with orders to demolish the entire quarter by gunfire.

This was exactly what the Florentines were waiting for. In a flash a thousand pots and pans crashed in the streets. The frightened French horses stampeded, tore loose from their harness, trampling their drivers and the cannoneers. The horses were cut down with scythes and sickles as they reared before the barricades. The French retreated in the utmost disorder and took shelter in the cathedral. What the Florentines' ancestors had done to Hannibal's trained elephants their descendants did to the horse-drawn French artillery.

To the reproaches of their commanders that they had given away before a mob of unarmed burghers, the soldiers replied that they could not fight an invisible foe or venture into those labyrinths of narrow streets where every house was a silent fortress manned from cellar to garret with knife-bearing desperadoes. "Our artillery is no match for ten thousand stilettos," they complained. "We are in an intolerable situation . . . Where are the women? What of the King's promises of a looting spree? Did we come here to be stabbed in the back by greengrocers and beardless cowards?"

In the meantime relations between the French King and the Florentine magistracy took a grave turn. Obliged to abandon all thought of restoring the Medicean ruling house, Charles was still determined to regard and treat Florence as a conquered city. He demanded that he be formally recognized as sovereign and that a Frenchman be appointed as King's lieutenant whose presence and assent would be necessary to the validity of the proceedings of the Signoria. In addition Charles wanted immediate cash payment of the 200,000 ducats promised him by Piero de' Medici.

In vain did the magistrates seek to moderate the French terms. The negotiations dragged on for days without any compromise coming in view. They were not a conquered people, the Florentines protested, under no circumstance would they barter away the independence of their republic. They consented to conclude a formal alliance with France, but it must be an alliance of equals, not an arrangement imposed by virtue of the French military occupation of their city.

In the end the King summoned the Signoria to appear before him in a body at the Medici palace. He spoke to them rudely, "as if they were menial servants," and then posed his terms anew. When the Signoria demurred and brought its own proposals to the fore King Charles flew into a rage. He ordered his chancellor, Cardinal Gurgins, to read the ultimatum: Either the Florentines accept his conditions, or, the King's patience being at an end, he would. . . . The chancellor got no further: Piero Capponi interrupted him coldly with the word: *Impossibile!*

King Charles, rising to his feet, screamed at Capponi: "We will blow our trumpets for the assault!"

Capponi snatched the ultimatum from the chancellor's hand and tore it in shreds. Looking the King straight in the eyes, he declared: "If you blow your trumpets, we will ring our bells!"

Capponi's proud rejoinder made a devastating impression on the King. He sank back in his chair, his face blanched, his mouth twitched, and his hands were seen to tremble as if struck by the palsy. Charles knew well enough that the city of Florence, at the first clangor of the alarm bell, could be turned into a seething cauldron in which he and his forces, despite their superior armament would be in extreme danger. The King was given some water to drink to calm his nerves. When the negotiations resumed all traces of his former obstinacy and rudeness had disappeared. The discussions, which had dragged on for days, were brought to a satisfactory conclusion to both sides in less than an hour.

The terms of the treaty provided that the King of France would receive the title not of sovereign, but the more or less meaningless byname of "Restorer and Protector of the Liberties of Florence." Secondly, the Florentines were to pay him 120,000 ducats in support of his campaign to cleanse Italy of usurpers and tyrants, while the fortresses in the north which Piero de' Medici had surrendered, were to be returned upon termination of the French expedition. The only concession King Charles obtained was the revocation of a signorial decree putting a price on Piero de' Medici's head. On the other hand, however much he tried, he could not prevent the insertion in the treaty of the decree of banishment of the members of the former ruling family to a distance of 100 miles from the Tuscan border. After the signing of the treaty the high contracting parties met in the Duomo where the Cardinal della Rovere conducted a service of thanksgiving and the King vowed eternal friendship to the city of Florence.

There was no reason now for the French to linger any longer in Florence and everybody expected that upon payment of the first installment of 40,000 ducats of the war subsidy, which took place on the morning following the signing of the treaty, they would take their leave. But on this point the Florentines grievously miscalculated. When he received the treasury officials bearing the coin, Charles reverted to his old characteristic surliness. There was an ugly frown on his face and he spoke improper language. He made a coarse pleasantry on Piero Capponi's name* and made known his intention to stay in Florence for some time to come so that his

* "But one *capono* (capon) amongst so many *galli* (roosters), what's the meaning of this?" The word Galli also means Frenchmen.

troops might have a proper rest before setting out on the arduous enterprise of subduing Naples. From this royal remark the magistrates concluded that they were not out of danger yet. "I love Florence," said the King, "I intend to enjoy my stay in your midst."

The situation was as strained and confused as before. The shops remained closed. The peasants, still fearful of the foreign troops, stayed away with the result that there was a great scarcity of foodstuffs, especially meat and vegetables. Night and day the streets were crowded with rowdy and brawling French soldiers who had found the Tuscan wines immensely to their taste. One quarrel wasn't settled before another broke out. It looked as if the French troops were seeking a pretext to break loose from all disciplinary restraint. Ten, twenty times a day, the magistrates were called out to settle disputes or stop fights and restore peace. And all the time every able-bodied Florentine stood ready in his house to sally forth at the least provocation. To this must be added that there was quite an epidemic of burglaries and murders. The French soldiers, who were perforce on short rations on account of the scarcity of provisions, broke into houses, robbed the occupants, and in parting gave them a beating. The general suspense was heightened by the impossibility of persuading the King to set a date for his departure.

On November 25th there was a new explosion. This time the riot started in the Borgo Ognisanti, the All Saints borough. Here a party of French soldiers was seen dragging a dozen or so Italian prisoners of war taken a few weeks earlier in the fortresses up north. The French were forcing their prisoners, who were tied with ropes, to beg money from door to door to pay for their ransom under threat of death if they should not obtain enough. The Florentines were so enraged at this barbarous spectacle that they intervened. They cut the prisoners' ropes and set them free. Furious at seeing their prey escape, the French made use of their weapons. But the citizens stood their ground and the tocsin began to ring. The Swiss infantry thinking, or more likely having been falsely informed that King Charles was in danger, rushed to the Medici palace, that is, in the opposite direction from where the melee took place. When after considerable delay they arrived in the Borgo Ognisanti, they were met by a salvo of stones and a flood of boiling oil and water poured from windows and house-tops. Flaming pitch-drenched hoops of straw were thrown around the horses' necks. Once more the French were forced to withdraw in disorder.

Somebody had to tell the King that the presence of his troops would sooner or later lead to a major clash if not to open warfare. Savonarola was chosen to carry out this errand, and he accepted, though realizing that the task was difficult and full of hazard. Before setting out for the Medici palace, the Friar warned his brethren that the future of Florence hung upon the outcome of his being allowed into the royal presence.

When he reached the palace the guard jostled him and carousing Gascons tried to pull the robe off his shoulders. "This is the friar," the soldiers cried, "who prevents us from getting our hands on the girls." Finding the King in his bedchamber, Savonarola told the astonished Charles that his stay caused great injury to the city. The King was wasting his time and neglecting the duties laid upon him by Providence. "Hear now," said Savonarola, and it is as if we hear one of the prophets of Israel addressing his royal master, "hear now the voice of God's servant! You are an instrument in the hands of the Lord who has sent you to relieve the woes of Italy, as I have for many years foretold. He has sent you to raise up his Church which now lies prostrate in the dust. Go your way without procrastinating and do not bring ruin on this city lest the Lord's anger be kindled against you, and he chooses another instrument to carry out his design. I warn you solemnly that if you neglect to carry out the mission upon which God has sent you, he will smite you with a terrible scourge . . . These things I say to you in the name of the Lord. . . ."

King Charles, his generals, and the Cardinal Gurgins, who were all present, were so impressed by Savonarola's grave manner of speech, that orders were forthwith given to break camp and to march southward. On November 28, 1494, King Charles VIII left Florence and the city awoke as from a nightmare.

In the night before their departure, however, the French were guilty of an act of vandalism of which the sorrowing echo comes sighing down the ages. They wrecked the Palazzo Medici. With the exception of a few articles of precious value earlier brought to safety in San Marco's convent by Cardinal Giovanni de' Medici, all the treasures which the assiduity and the wealth of Lorenzo and his ancestors had accumulated in half a century, the most magnificent art collection ever gathered under one single roof, was lost that night. What could not be carried off, was broken to pieces. Paintings were ripped from the walls or slashed to ribbons. Nor were common soldiers or inferior officers alone implicated in this dastardly spoliation. Philippe de Comines, the French historian, who saw it all, reports that "the hands of generals and barons were equally busy and the King himself carried off objects of the greatest value: vases, cameos, and gems of such superb workmanship as to make one catch one's breath with wonder."

And so the French occupation of Florence came to an end. Rome was next on Charles' list. Pope Alexander said to his cardinals: "Now come the barbarians who promise the Italians *libertà,* what they bring is nothing but *calamità!"* The French campaign up north had been totally devoid of chivalry and humaneness. The troops turned out as cruel as the Saracen hordes. Those Florentine soldiers in the fortresses of Sarzana and Sarzanello whom Piero de' Medici ordered to surrender, were massacred to the last man. Unless a captive was able to put up a large sum of ransom money he was killed on the spot. The French dispatched not only the enemy's wounded but their own as well. On his way back from his embassy to Pisa Savonarola counted more than 300 bodies lying by the roadside. These peaceful citizens had been done to death by French soldiers to amuse themselves or just pass the time of day. Pope Alexander had good reason to be alarmed.

Chapter VI

Savonarola Supreme:

Florence's New Constitution

F INDING themselves their own masters again after seventy years
of Medicean dictatorship, the people of Florence were not unlike
the forgotten prisoner in the Bastille who, upon his release, was
blinded by the light of day and would have fallen had not a sympathetic bystander caught him up. The Florentines knew not what
to do with their new-found freedom in an environment where all
things had worked or were working themselves loose from their
habitual moorings. Since the old institutions were devoid of vitality
or had grown obsolescent with time it was hopeless to think of re-
viving them. Nor was there any longer a patrician class in existence
fitted to take the lead in public affairs. The ancient trade corporations and guilds, once the centers of industrial and political life, had
lain dormant and impotent for half a century. All through the years
of their autocratic preponderance the Medici imprisoned, banished,
or otherwise eliminated every man or body of men bent upon or
likely to challenge their usurpation. New men, new parties, or
schools whose rule would be "conscience and the public weal" were
not available. Lorenzo and Piero had allowed the business of state to
be dispatched according to routine by ill-paid but punctual clerks.
As a result, no man with the requisite training or experience was in
sight to conduct the lengthy, intricate, and exasperating negotiations which must of necessity precede setting the new order on its
feet.

153

Irascible, indomitable Francesco Valori, who had incited the street mobs against the Medici, still went around haranguing the crowds. But with him it was all sound and fury. His proposals alternated from day to day; one afternoon he was for laissez faire, on the morrow he favored pouring oil on the conflagration and letting the evil burn itself out. "I love the smell of gunpowder," said Valori.

An enormously fat individual, Ippolito Pompini by name, a circus clown by profession, but a doughty jawsmith withal, dressed in his weirdest costume, his face powdered with flour, occupied a permanent stand in a corner of the Piazza where he talked inanities about catching the sun's beams and preserving them for the purpose of roasting the Medici should they venture to return. As he read the names of the proscribed from a prepared list, he mimicked the gestures and grimaces of the imaginary victims of his proposed heat test.

Hard by stood thunder-voiced Piero Capponi who had won renown by his defiance of the King of France. Scowling, fists clenched, he announced with fierce eloquence his willingness to take the lead. But if eloquence can do much it cannot do all. Work was to be done, and talk is not work. Both Valori and Capponi lacked the patience and the statesmanlike qualities indispensable in the conduct of the national business. The Florentines bethought themselves of the horse and the man in the fable. In despair the horse asked the man to punish an old enemy. The man mounted and dispatched the enemy swiftly enough, but then unhappily refused to get off the horse's back. Would it be prudent, the wise old citizens asked themselves, to hoist a hotheaded patriot like Capponi into power? Of heroic valor he undoubtedly was, but did he not also advocate a system of iron discipline without respect of persons? Could a man with such ideas be trusted?

In the crowds that inundated the Piazza like a sea of troubles, listening to tireless, brass-lunged orators, contending and haggling, shouting and gesticulating till everybody was ready to drop from sheer exhaustion, certain young and rising politicians made a favorable impression with the reasonableness of their propositions and their sharp tone. The most listened-to was twenty-five-year-old Niccolo Machiavelli, a light, thin man, who looked down on the passions seething around him with cold indifference. Able he was, talented in statecraft and diplomacy, much to be heard from in days and years and centuries to come. Instead of speaking directly to the understanding of the people Machiavelli philosophized about principles and theories, and, although generally far above the crowd's head, one of his sayings flew from mouth to mouth: "Man's greatest happiness on earth consists in having a share in the government of his own country." There wasn't a Florentine who didn't agree with him. Every respectable citizen, the gaping crowd understood the young diplomat to say, should not only have the right to vote in the election of his rulers, but also enjoy the bliss of filling a public office for a short time. Though this was not exactly what Machiavelli meant, his pronouncement was taken as an incentive to proceed from vain palaver and hubbub to action.

And high time it was! A tempest which might wrench all asunder was rising. The state was rocking on its foundations. After languishing for months, commerce and industry now stood stock-still. Burghers had not the elementary confidence to reopen their stalls, shops, and countinghouses. Victuals were coming in but slowly. Factions were arming. Never much of one heart and mind, the Florentines were now splitting into opposing camps. Like the ravages of a swift wasting disease, intrigue, revenge, rivalry, and feuds ate their way into all layers of society, turning the city into mutually hostile cabals, families into adversaries, and all men into enemies. As always when signs of hurricane appear in the sky, the fishers in troubled waters and the rumormongers worked overtime. Long-haired brigands in rags, armed with clubs which they smote against the side of buildings, filtered into Florence. Three of the customs booths at the city gates went up in flames without anybody able, or willing, to identify the incendiaries. The number of assassinations, as old scores and rivalries were settled, grew to frightening dimensions. Every morning dead bodies were fished from the Arno. Only the taverns, the gambling houses, and the bagnios were open. There, too, not surprisingly, brawls and fights were the order of the day and night. Since most of Piero's old gendarmes were dismissed and no new police force as yet appointed public order was at the mercy of the slightest incident. One chronicler reports gleefully that in some boroughs it became quite a sport "to hunt the guard." Instead of peace, an era of lawlessness, of nonlaw or mobocracy seemed to have dawned for Florence.

To make things worse, information came that Pisa had risen in revolt. Gathered on the common under their famous Leaning Tower, the men of that city voted to go their own way now that the Medici ruling house was abolished and banished. Couriers went to and fro, ambassadors and bishops had their try at persuading, all to no avail: the Pisans vowed never again to stick their necks into the Florentine yoke. Several other subject cities in Tuscany threatened to follow Pisa's example. Arezzio and Montepulciano, encouraged by a financial subsidy from Siena, and the arrival of military experts from that city, did not hesitate to declare war, and Pisa promptly joined the alliance. Pisan troops were already on the march, scorching the earth, driving off the cattle, and burning the peasants' huts in the republic's territory. On top of it all, the Most Christian King, who had just sworn eternal friendship to Florence, gave a new sign of his benevolence. Though payment wasn't due for another three months, Charles VIII demanded remittance of the second installment of the 120,000 ducats pledged. Failing compliance *Carolus Major,* "Charles the Still Greater," as his chancellor betitled him in a dispatch from Rome, threatened to return and hand the city over to his lust- and loot-crazed ruffians to do as they please.

Florence was hard-pressed as consternation piled upon perplexity. Everything had to be done at once: recruits levied, captains engaged, heavier taxes imposed on the already overburdened people, and above all some semblance of law and order introduced if anarchy were not to become the gravedigger of the republic.

In that hour of mounting confusion and failing hearts Savonarola spoke the first word of common sense: he advised the convocation of a *Parlamento,* an assembly of the whole body of the people. Not the alarm tocsin this time, but the tolling of the great bell called the citizens into the Piazza. Two of Lorenzo's old councilors—there wasn't anyone else with authority to mount the speakers' rostrum—appeared on the *ringhiera,* the ramplike platform in front of the palace gate (it no longer exists), to propose the revival of an ancient custom.

One of these men was Paolo Soderini, former ambassador to

Venice, who had a vast knowledge of the ways and methods of
government in other parts of the world. Soderini proposed that a
Committee of Twenty, the *Accopiatori* as they were called, should
take charge with the right of *Balia,* that is, to govern temporarily
by decree. The Twenty were to elect the members of the Signoria,
the supreme legislative body, and to appoint a new set of officials
for the different departments. The Twenty were to be changed
every year, and the Signoria every two months. Though admittedly
falling far short of the unviersal franchise the people half expected,
it was said to be the only practical measure that could be thought of,
and would at any rate be superseded by more satisfactory arrangements the moment the crisis abated. Soderini's proposals which,
incidentally, were dropped and forgotten in less than a month, were
adopted with heaven-rending acclamation, followed by an order to
illuminate the city once more, but this time with a right good will
inasmuch as the circumstances fully warranted "a jubilee of freedom."

Savonarola refused to sit either in the Signoria or on the Committee of Twenty. But he got busy in another direction. He was at
last able to carry his great gifts into the full stream of the city's
life, and he seized his chance. "Our first task," he said, "should be
to relieve the distress caused by the general suspension of business."
He suggested the banks issue a kind of script money that could be
called in as soon as the emergency was over. "We must go to work
and put an end to the idleness which is halting the normal flow
of activity."

Too much time, he said, was wasted in talk, in wrangling, and
chatter. It only increased the suspense and made action the more
difficult. Action would never start of itself, unless it be an explosion
of the misery of the poor stored up in vast sordid volume since the
beginning of time. "Christ began with the poor," he told the citizens.
"Christ cared for the poor and never left off caring for them . . .
The lesson is clear: we, too, must forsake pomp and vanities, sell
all superfluous things, and bestow the money on the poor . . .
Let us collect alms in every church in this city and outside the
walls . . . Let us take the church plate and decorations, and I will
be the first to set you an example. But above all, pass a law to open

the shops and to provide work for the populace now idling in the streets. . . ."

He went on to describe what he had seen in the popular quarters: raggedness and wretchedness at every step, faces haggard with hunger, women in tears, children sitting silently in doorways, too weak and undernourished to run around and play. "And yet at the same time," he added, "the flood of sin and shame is not abating, but every hour rising higher, revealing behind the flimsiest veil a bottomless abyss at our feet." Outside the city, amongst the refugees, he declared, the situation was still worse. There lay piles of unburied corpses. Hungry and wounded men, poor mortals robbed by passing bands of soldiers, subsisting on meal husks and boiled grass, sat staring vacantly at the walls of Florence, which kept its doors tightly shut. "O *Firenze,* O *Firenze,* O *Firenze!* This must not be, this is unworthy of you! Citizens! Christian men and brothers, this situation is intolerable . . . It cannot and must not endure! . . ."

The text of his discourse was: "Let us sing a new song unto the Lord!" He repeated it over and over again and expounded its meaning: "It is the Lord's will that you, Florentines, renew all things, that you wipe out the past so that none of the old evil customs, the evil laws and evil governments remains. The time has come for deeds to take the place of words and meaningless formalities. Let us from this moment onward discard vain ceremonies and celebrations, and, as honest men, give expression to our real feelings. The Lord said to those he rejected: 'I was hungry and ye gave me no meat; I was naked and you clothed me not.' He did not say: 'Build me some fine churches and beautiful convents.' He exhorted us to works of charity. For through charity, that is love, all things can and shall be renewed."

In the course of his address urging the people to put charity before everything else, Savonarola avoided the one subject for which everyone eagerly waited. Whenever he felt that he was coming too close to politics, he stopped short, hesitated, and his old trouble of stuttering returned. With Savonarola it was either a case of letting his words flow freely and even tempestuously or else remain altogether silent. With him there was no middle way. Having the dark and mysterious blood of Italy in his veins, he could not possibly follow the calm didactic manner of exposition which comes almost natural from men of the phlegmatic temper and cold logic of the Northern races. The sight of a congregation set Savonarola on fire. Then the flood gates of eloquence opened by themselves. He spoke as "a dying man to dying men," as if it was his last chance to speak and theirs to hear. And there was no stopping him till physical exhaustion compelled him to sit down. But he spoke well only when and if he was wholly free in his own mind from limitations set by caution or expediency. The moment he put a hushcloth on the inner voice or wandered from the fount of inspiration, deep ceased to call unto deep. Then he floundered like a novice who has mislaid his notes.

Although a citizen, he was also an ecclesiastic, and while history records many instances of ecclesiastical intervention in the business of state, Savonarola tried as long as he could to keep politics out of the pulpit. Even now, when it was clear to everyone else that he was destined to be the saviour of Florence, Savonarola still held aloof. He struggled against his fate as all the prophets of all times struggled till the day when the word of God was in their hearts like a burning fire and they could no longer be silent. "O Florence!" he cried out, "I cannot express to you all that I feel. Could I but tell you all, you would see in me a new vessel, a sealed vessel, full of boiling ferment that vainly seeks to force its way out!"

This was the end of Savonarola's hesitations and wavering. On December 12—we are still in the year 1494— he pronounced his first political discourse which led step by step, on succeeding Sundays, to the formulation of a new constitution for the Republic of Florence. It was afterwards published in his *Treatise respecting the Rule and Government of the City of Florence,* a document which no less an authority than Machiavelli praised as "the noblest and godliest set of rules ever laid down for the government of a state."

In order to keep the record straight, it should perhaps be added that Machiavelli revoked his commendation of Savonarola the moment the Friar lost his influence in Florence. Such a complete change of attitude was habitual with that master theoretician of statecraft. One of the most abominable criminals of the age, Cesare Borgia, who lied, murdered, and pillaged as no other tyrant, also carried away the approbation and admiration of Machiavelli. But that support was also withdrawn when Borgia fell. Whether good or bad Machiavelli applauded a statesman only as long as he was successful. Machiavelli could admire the promotor of liberty, the founder of the republic, but not the Friar, the preacher of morality. In his book *The Prince,* that vademecum of all dictators and totalitarianists, Machiavelli declares that a moral and a political state are too far apart ever to meet save as adversaries. Morality is the business of priests and philosophers, not of politicians. A moral government should be cast aside as rubbish the moment its inherent inefficacy becomes apparent. If morality interferes with good government it must go overboard at once.

On December 12 the Friar began explaining the political program he had in mind. As he started his sermon it sounded as if he were merely going to repeat the propositions of St. Thomas Aquinas. "An absolute monarch," he said, "is the best of all governments under a good prince, but the worst under a bad one, inasmuch as it is the strongest and most united both for good and evil. . . ." This was the language of the schools. But after briefly referring to the familiar doctrine he cast the old formulas aside. "These principles," he said, "should be modified and adapted to the nature of the people and the climate of the times. Among northern nations," he went on to say, "where there is great strength and little intellect, and among southern nations where there is, on the other hand, great intellect and little strength, the rule of a single despot may sometimes be the best of governments. But in Italy, and above all in Florence, where both strength and intellect abound, where men have keen understanding and restless spirits, the government of one can only end in tyranny.

"The sole government suited to our needs in Florence is a civil and general government. Do not choose a chief of government to dominate and oppress all the rest! From such leaders come all the evils by which cities and states are ruined . . . *Wherefore, let this be the first of your laws, that no man shall be sole head of your city.* Those who want to rise above others and cannot tolerate civic equality are generally exceedingly wicked. They are the destroyers of souls and of states.

"You know that I have always refrained from touching on

political questions; do you think that I would broach them now if I did not think it necessary for the salvation of souls? For a time you would not believe me, but now you have seen how all my words have been fulfilled. They were not uttered of my own will, but proceeded from God. The Lord desires nothing but your salvation . . . Purify your hearts therefore, pay attention alone to the common good, forget private interests. If you reform your city with this intent, you will reap greater glory than in all past times.

"In this way shall you usher in the reformation of all Italy, and spread your wings over all the earth to bring reforms to all nations. Remember that the Lord has given you plain signs of his purpose to renew all things and that you are the people chosen to begin a great world-wide enterprise provided you follow the will of him who calls and invites you to the spiritual life. Your reform must indeed begin with spiritual things. All temporal things must be subordinate to the moral and religious . . . If perchance you have heard it said that states cannot be governed by the Lord's prayer [Cosimo de' Medici once said: 'you cannot run a government with paternosters'] remember that this is the maxim of tyrants, of men hostile to God and the public welfare.

"There is nothing a tyrant hates so much and persecutes so cruelly as a truly pious soul. A true Christian is a perpetual living reproach to the tyrant's own shameful, vice-sodden way of life. Our past tyrants were so jealous of anyone who proved their superior or merely their equal in such minor and childish things as cardplaying, gymnastics, racing, or reciting poetry, that they never ceased hounding him till they got the better of him. How many righteous men, how many honorable citizens, fathers of families, benefactors of the poor, fine Christian gentlemen were foully done to death in the last two or three decades here in Florence? . . . The rule of the Medici was a rule of oppression, not for the relief and liberation of the city. If you want a good government you must submit it to God.

"When you shall have purified your hearts, rectified your aims, condemned gambling, sensuality and blasphemy, then set to work and frame your government, first making a rough draft, afterwards filling in the details and making the amendments.

"And let your first draft, or rather the model and basis of government be conceived thus: *that no man occupy any office or receive any preferment save by the will of the whole people. The people must have the sole right to create magistrates and enact laws.*

"Before any other measure is taken, let there be a general amnesty, a full pardon for all political contraventions. An invitation to return should be extended to all who were banished. Nor should fines or penalties be imposed for the nonpayment of taxes in hard times like these. Let the tax collectors be prudent and merciful and never forget that all men are brothers.

"I would like to see the entire population of Florence assembled in the Duomo, but since not all can find room, the women and children should remain at home. The men are to assemble under the sixteen *Gonfaloniers* (the heads of the reconstituted guilds and corporations). Let each corporation propose a form of government. From the sixteen forms of government thus obtained let the Gonfaloniers select four, and present them to the Signoria, who, after first earnestly engaging in prayer, will choose the best of the four forms. And whichever will be chosen in this manner, you may rest assured that it comes from God. . . ."

Before closing Savonarola recommended that the Venetian method of government be investigated. "You have seen," he said, "how, since the present government of Venice was established, no factions or dissension of any sort have arisen. Therefore we must believe that it exists by God's will. With certain modifications it could very well be a model for Florence. However, beware of one thing: there must be no Doge at the head of your government (as they have in Venice). A Doge leans naturally to self-rule, autocracy, tyranny. Let it not be so with us, let us learn from experience."

Savonarola's recommendation of the Venetian system modified in accord with Florentine conditions and in line with the city's historical evolution, led to a speedy acceptance of his proposals. It should not be thought that like some conjurer he produced a constitution from his hat on the spur of the moment. Few constitutions are known to have dropped ready-made from heaven, and fewer yet from the pulpits of cathedral churches. Being the basic law of the land and intrinsically a life and death question for the State, the drawing up of a constitution is a process requiring close scrutiny at every step of the way; a constant checking and re-checking, a long period of incubation. In the case of Florence it was a slow unfolding process, worked out little by little with much shifting and halting, amending and deliberation. . . .

But the guiding spirit, the presiding genius in that process of laying down the fundamental law of the Republic of Florence was Girolamo Savonarola. Every fresh measure adopted, every additional clause inserted in the great document was preceded by one or more sermons in the Duomo in the presence of immense congregations. After passage by the Signoria of any bill whatsoever, Savonarola's first question in the pulpit would be: "Do we clearly understand the significance of the measure just adopted by our lawgivers?" Again and again he warned the people to allow nothing to be coded or inserted that would afford a loophole or subterfuge for aspirant dictators to reach for personal power. The establishment of an oligarchy, the rule by a privileged few, an intellectual or financial elite, was to be avoided as a noisome pestilence. There was nothing Savonarola hated and feared more than tyranny.

He has been called a Jacobin, a radical and revolutionary. Mussolini bestowed the title of "forerunner of fascism" on Savonarola. The Friar was none of these. He neither romanticized about the past nor indulged in dreams of empire. Later he based himself on a political party drawn from the petty bourgeoisie. There was never any question of instituting something like a dictatorship of the proletariat. According to Machiavelli, the one great failing of his policy was his neglect to set up a pretorian guard for his own protection. He was the first monk to assume the role of political director of a state without in any way selling short his ecclesiastical vocation. And that role, it should be added, was not self-chosen—at heart he did not like politics—it was imposed upon him by a combination of circumstances, by a conjuncture of historical events, or, as he said himself, by God. It was in the name of God, in the name of the highest justice, that this pastor laid down and guided the policy of the State from the pulpit. It was also the first time in the history of Christendom that any man took up such a role. But there was not a shred of narrow ecclesiastical professionalism attached to his manner of procedure. Since he knew himself summoned to speak, he felt it imperative to speak out. He was not an authoritarian, not even a ruler, but an explicator, a trend spotter, a guide, a counselor, a good shepherd. Savonarola presided at the birth of a new era. It is nothing less than a miracle, it was said by a modern Italian statesman, that a preaching friar whose vocation afforded no special training in politics, should have been the moving spirit in the reorganization of the Florentine State on lines so sagacious and, at that stage of history, so sound.

This evaluation of the man, conspicuous and valuable as it is, falls short of the whole truth. It leaves out of consideration his intense study of the Holy Scriptures. To Savonarola the Bible was the sole authoritative textbook and source of all knowledge and wisdom, religious as well as secular and political. The Bible was Mount Zion whence divine instruction and illumination goes forth to all nations, a deep sea wherein all the rivers of philosophy and policy finally lose themselves. Once he said that even the Eucharist is not more sublime than the Word of God. "For, even as in the form of bread and wine God is present, so is the Holy Spirit manifest in the words of Holy Writ." Whoever wants to penetrate the secrets of the Scriptures, must be enlightened by the same spirit which inspired them. "Whoever searches the Scriptures merely for curiosity's sake, be he learned or uneducated, he dies, that is, he falls away from the teachings of the Church and becomes entrapped in errors like Origen and many other heretics." Indispensable for a profitable study of the Bible, according to Savonarola, are not learned books and dissertations but a pure heart, humility, the subordination of passions, prayer and meditation, solitariness and study. "In all ages and in all circumstances," he said, "the Bible supplies an answer to the question: what does God demand of us?"

When he preached those political sermons, his principal aim was to bend the sentiments of individuals and of the collectivity towards the life of God. Man alone and unaided could never transcend his egocentric existence and enter into willing co-operation with others. Savonarola wanted to see Florence a commonwealth based on Christian principles. His extraordinarily keen insight into the moral forces at work in society, his never-flagging vigilance against abuses stamped him as a man of prophetic caliber. His superiority derived from his study of history and prophecy. With that marvelously retentive memory of his, he reviewed day by day

and far into the night all he had read about the making of laws
and ordinances in Sparta and Athens, in the ancient Roman republic and the empire. He had at his fingertips Moses and the
Prophets, Solon, Plato, St. Thomas, Dante, and Joachim of Floris.
Omnivorous reader as he was, he made his ground sure at every
step.

The first measure the Florentines adopted on Savonarola's recommendation was the dismissal of Soderini's Twenty and in
their place the establishment of a *Consiglio Grande* or *Consiglio
Generale,* a Great or General Council. It was but subsequently and
gradually, by successive elections and infinite debates and elabora-
tions, that the functions and prerogatives of the Grand Council
were defined and agreed upon. Membership in the Council was open
to all citizens over twenty-nine years of age who had themselves,
or whose fathers had paid taxes, or who ranked as so-called
benefiziati, men who in their own person or in the person of their
immediate ancestors enjoyed a *benefizio,* the privilege of holding
or having been proposed for high office.

Under these conditions but 3600 individuals in Florence were
found eligible. The 3600 were divided into three equal groups of
1200 each. Each of these groups made up the General or Grand
Council for a term of two months. By this rapid turnover Savonarola
expected to keep abreast of changes or fluctuations in public opinion
and to widen the range of political privilege and public responsibility. In addition it was enacted that sixty citizens who were not
benefiziati should be given membership in the Grand Council, plus
twenty young men of the age of twenty-four. The sixty represented
the proletariat, so to speak, the underprivileged and nontaxpayers,
while the twenty were introduced as apprentices of political science,
in other words, the youth group. The sessions of the Council were
at all times to be open to the public. Nonmembers were, in fact,
invited to scrutinize the voting.

The next step, Savonarola pointed out, should be the building
of an assembly hall befitting the august dignity of the popular
representation. There wasn't a single room in the whole city large
enough to contain all the members of the Grand Council at one
time, not to speak of eventual joint sessions of its three rotating
sections.

Messer Simon del Puajola, an architect of renown and the Friar's close friend, was charged with building an addition to the signorial palace and to employ as many workers as possible, not only to reduce the number of unemployed, but in order to complete the project as quickly as possible. The addition took the form of a magnificent hall which till this day attracts hundreds of thousands of visitors annually because of its fine coffered ceiling and the paintings and other treasures on view. At first it was called the *Sala Savonarola,* but since becoming the meeting place of Florence's municipal council, in 1865, it bears that body's name.

Then the corporation known as the *Ottanti* the Eighty was set up. Its membership was drawn from the Grand Council and consisted of good and prudent citizens no less than forty years of age. Membership in the Eighty was renewed every six months. They met once a week and dealt with matters of high policy. They were the equivalent of an Upper House or Senate and discussed at leisure any moot point on which the Council could not immediately come to a decision. The Eighty also performed the functions of a foreign relations committee for they handled such matters of diplomacy as did not lend themselves to discussion by all the members of the Council for *raison d'état.* Its sessions were secret. By the Eighty's side stood two committees of eight members each; the departments of justice and war.

What labors, we may well ask, did this extraordinary man not perform in the establishment of law and order in Florence? Rest he never sought, but light he always spread. He interviewed and chose the judges, he looked for the ablest military men in the country to offer them positions of command. The foreign relations committee was in constant touch with him. In addition he drew up in his cell and proposed to the Grand Council a "law for revision of the taxes."

"Levy taxes on real property alone, abolish loans, abolish arbitrary imposts," was his advice. To the people assembled in the Duomo he said: "Citizens, I would have you steadfast in your devotion and help to your community. The son owes so much to his father that he can never do enough for him. Wherefore I say to you: your community is your father and thus each of you is bound to give his assistance. And if you should object by saying, 'I get no good out of it,' know that you may not say this, inasmuch as the community protects your property, your household and your children. Rather you should step forward and say: 'Here are fifty, a hundred ducats, a thousand.' Thus do good citizens who love their country."

The system of taxation under the Medici was most unjust and in such disorder that no greater confusion could be imagined. The Medici taxed on the fluctuating incomes derived from industry and commerce and these were assessed at a fixed rate. This system roused such tremendous discontent in Florence that many citizens entirely withdrew from trade. In this way the Medici killed the goose that laid the golden egg and brought the state to the verge of bankruptcy. They scraped through by contracting loans from the rich, but for years no loans had been repaid.

Savonarola's new law of taxation was laid before the General Council on February 5, 1495. It was drawn up on such "prudent, sound, and sagacious principles" that until recent times the taxation of Florence remained unchanged from the regulations introduced by the Friar. For the first time in Italy the new law established a general and regular tax on property, abolishing all loans and arbitrary assessments, and obliging all citizens to pay ten per cent on all income from real property without any right to repayment. A new office was also created for the just valuation of property. Taxes were to be paid regularly in the first month of the year.

Next Savonarola was instrumental in having a right of appeal inserted in the judicial code. The ancient statutes required a two-thirds majority before a severe sentence could be pronounced. This was known as the Law of *Sei Fave,* the Six Beans, beans being the method by which voting was conducted in Florence. Henceforth, a person condemned by the lower court had the right to appeal to the General Council. Savonarola motivated his demand for a change by pointing to the numerically small size of the lower courts and the possibility of the judges being influenced by political considerations or personal feelings. Accordingly, from the lower court of nine judges a condemned person now gained the right to appeal to the Council's full session of 1200. Theoretically the whole nation now sat in judgment.

A final suggestion by Savonarola in the adoption of which he took great pride, was a decree ordering all documents of state, court judgments, laws and bylaws, proclamations and departmental reports which were formerly drawn up in Latin, from this time on to be written and published in the people's own language, Italian. Such a measure grandfather Michele had advocated a quarter century before in Ferrara.

It cannot be said that the new constitution was extravagantly democratic. It was a timid transition to civil liberty. That Savonarola's judgment should have been final in all matters or even coherent, was impossible, but he took an essential step. For that age his constitution meant an innovation of revolutionary import, a complete renewal. While men are feeling their way to a new understanding of themselves and a surer control of the public weal, there are of course many fumbling attempts and more or less complete failures. One of the most baneful clauses in the constitution was the change in the personnel of the legislative body every two months. Such a rapid change broke the sequence of policy and made continuity virtually impossible. Before long we will find the one government after the other undoing or annulling what its predecessor has enacted or accomplished.

It is perhaps unfair to subject a fifteenth century document to comparison with standards prevailing in the twentieth. But contemporaries and also historians of the following epoch highly approved of Savonarola's measures. His system of taxation remained in force till 1865. The historian Giovanni Nesi feels that "Florence owes Savonarola more than any other man." By his constitutional reforms the Friar "won over some who had been amongst his bitterest enemies." He put an end to the bloody quarrels of the factions. He pacified the city and restored peace. His chief merit, according to Nesi, lies in having purified the judiciary and to have established the right of appeal from the courts to the Grand Council. Guicciardini, in reviewing Florentine, Italian, and Roman history, comes to the conclusion that the constitution of 1494 was the best of all the systems of government in Italy over the centuries. Of Machiavelli we know that he initially highly approved of Savonarola's "most godly set of laws." A comparison of Machiavelli's *Prince* with Savonarola's laws will show that Machiavelli copied a number of the Friar's recommendations almost word for word. The aged Bartolomeo Scala, who was chancellor to Cosimo de' Medici and afterwards Lorenzo's closest adviser, wrote a treatise one year before his death in 1497 in which he defended the new constitution against its detractors. To the objection that the new constitution had been largely the work of a monk, he replied by asking "whether so remarkable and useful an institution loses in value by reason of its having been established by an ecclesiastic?"

Savonarola expressed himself pleased with the new arrangements and the speed with which the change had come about "without the shedding of one drop of blood." He regretted that his proposal to recall all the exiles was not acted upon. In a sermon delivered before the Grand Council he pleaded with his hearers "to lay off the yellow and green spectacles of passion and envy and to put on the clear white glasses of truth and mercy." Exile, he said, was the most horrible penalty that could be inflicted on a native Florentine. Why not allow the Medici to come back on their solemn promise not to trouble public order and henceforth to obey the law like everyone else. "Certainly," he exclaimed "the Lord Cardinal Giovanni de' Medici has done Florence no wrong." Why could Giovanni not be approached to ask his brother, Piero, to make a formal act of abdication?

As he spoke, some Council men shook their heads, others followed till at last the entire assembly signified its disapproval of the Friar's suggestion. The hatred of the Medici family had too deeply penetrated into men's hearts than that it could be eradicated at one stroke by Savonarola's moving plea.

The Friar even seems to have rendered himself suspect with his plea for reconciliation. Everybody knew that Piero was in the French King's camp, in the immediate vicinity of Rome, where he moved heaven and earth, the college of cardinals included, to help him make preparations, warlike if need be, for his return to Florence. Savonarola was charged with having sown discord amongst the Florentines with his show of leniency towards the former ruling family. "But," he objected, "I always preached and I still preach only concord, peace and forgiveness. If you do not want these, do not accuse me, but rather look into your own hearts."

It was no use: by a narrow margin, the Council defeated a

motion to hire a gang of murderers to go after the Medici. The minority demanded that the hated family be exterminated root and branch, men, women, and children. As a result of this public display of hatred two members of a younger branch of the Medici, who still remained in Florence, changed their name to Popolani, meaning as much as the people's friends or partisans of the popular cause.

The opposition to Savonarola did not in the long run remain confined to would-be exterminators of the Medici. The wealthy families on whom the new tax on property weighed heaviest blamed the Friar for the law's passage. Some of these were in close touch with the banished Medici through the courier service of the banks. In the course of time the pro-Medici crowd received the nickname of *Bigi,* the Grays. Others called *Bianchi,* the Whites, later opposed Savonarola for a different reason. They held that the State's business should not be handled or influenced by a monk or by any other ecclesiastic. They may be said to have been the anticlericals of the time, the champions of the separation of church and state though the heavens fall. Another faction which grew into a strong political party was that of the *Arrabbiati,* the Furious, the Enraged. They were the aristocrats, bankers, real estate operators, the grand moguls in general and constituted the backbone of the reaction. The *Arrabbiati* favored going back to the ancient aristocratic regime which preceded the Medicean epoch. The leaders of the popular party which identified itself with Savonarola's program and aspirations, and therefore called *Frateschi,* the Friar's men, were reviled by their opponents as *Collitori,* literally neck-wringers, muggers, and also as *Piagnoni,* crybabies, snivelers.

The new machinery of state was set in motion in February 1495, with a solemn service of laud and thanksgiving in the Duomo.

Chapter VII

The Converted City:

Christ The King of Florence

A PROPHET is not a soothsayer. He does not foretell what will happen. He is a realist and reveals to men the pattern of their own existence as contrasted with their dreams and illusions. He stands for a world order where God rules and all the divine possibilities and potentialities latently present in man and humanity are quickened, stimulated and made operative. The prophet is therefore not a utopianist, nor a dreamer about a never-never land, but a man who believes that a task is to be carried out, a good fight to be fought, a revaluation of all values to be brought about by faith in the final triumph of the Kingdom of God and its righteousness for this earth. It is the prophet's aim to actualize the righteousness of the Kingdom of God by bringing it down from the clouds of abstraction and theorizing, and make it penetrate every phase and sphere of human endeavor, social conditions and politics included. For whoever preaches the Kingdom of God must also preach freedom, equality, and brotherhood. He must demand that the sacred rights of the human person, of man the brother, of the poor and weak, be respected. He must bring judgment to bear on the false gods, Mammon and Moloch, money and violence, or under whatever other guise these idols operate. He turns against the enslavement and degradation of the human personality through economic exploitation and moral impurity. He aims at liberation from injustice, violence, sickness, sin, and death by holding high

171

the vision of freedom, purity, justice, love, and brotherhood. His is the revolutionary vision of new heavens and a new earth wherein dwelleth righteousness.

No doubt a world full of prophets would be a madhouse, but a world without prophets is a world that knows not its signs. It is like a ship without rudder or compass floundering about helplessly, aimlessly drifting toward perdition. . . .

A unique concurrence of circumstances placed Savonarola in a logical but sometimes uncomfortable position. Fully involved in the social and political struggle of his day and yet strangely above the battle, conscious of participating in the opening of a new era, he was led to envisage a strictly Christian state which should have its roots deep in the hearts of the citizens. Only convinced and true Christians, he felt, could build a commonwealth not only Christian in name or principle, but in deed and reality.

Some historians use the term theocratic sovereignty to designate Savonarola's brief ascendancy in Florentine national affairs. This is a misnomer. Savonarola at no time pushed himself to the fore. He sought no public office and he occupied none. He gave his opinion on public affairs very reluctantly, only when pressed to do so and then only in fear and trembling, that is, after days and nights of prayer, meditation, study, and great anguish. Only after a hard inner struggle of self-searching and -communing, did he venture to speak out in the belief that he interpreted the will of God. Any idea that Savonarola assumed or usurped the sovereignty in Florence rests upon a misreading of history and a misconception of the role of a prophet. For though it often lay within their grasp, none of the prophets ever sought personal power.

But Savonarola did look on the Florentines as a chosen people with a particular task to perform in the general scheme of things. They were the people of the covenant through whose deeds and influence God was to make his will known to others. The first time he broached this subject publicly his discourse gave rise to an extraordinary scene of enthusiasm. When he referred to the preference some of his hearers might have for a monarchical form of government, he threw the congregation into perplexity. Holding his audience in suspense for a few moments, he suddenly veered around saying with great solemnity: "God is willing to give you a king to govern."

Then, returning to Florence's potential influence in Europe, he delineated the role the Republic could play in the christianization of the world. By starting to live pure and holy lives the Florentines would become a model for other cities and states to follow. All Italy and beyond Italy, the unbelievers, the Turks, the Saracens, and the Tartars, would hear of Florence's example and develop a longing to follow in its footsteps. Nothing would have such persuasive power as to show the world what could be done in one place on earth when brethren dwelt together in unity, when they bore each others' burdens, and served each others' needs without price and without money.

"Florence," he said, "Jesus Christ who is the king of the universe, stands before the door and he knocks. He wants to come in. He wills to become your king in this very hour. Will you have him as your king?"

From thousands of throats roared the answer: *Si! Si! Noi voliamo!* Yes! Yes! We will! *Viva Gesù! Cristo nostra re!* Christ is our king!

This motto Christ the king, became the watchword of the new dispensation. In order that it should not remain a mere pious aspiration, or an upsurge of momentary enthusiasm, Savonarola launched a program of activity calculated to translate the idea into actual fact. The cathedral could no longer take in the multitudes streaming in from far and near. Not only the Florentines, but the Sienese, those of Fiesole, San Gimignano, and other Tuscan towns and villages marched in large numbers to the Cathedral of St. Mary when Fra Girolamo preached. And he preached every Sunday. Wooden galleries had to be erected inside the cathedral in the form of an amphitheater to accommodate the crowds. Even this enlargement proved insufficient. Burlamacchi, the author of *The Life of Blessed Girolamo Savonarola,* says that it was "a bewildering sight to see that mass of people coming with jubilee and rejoicing to the sermon as to a wedding feast."

With the first rays of daylight the people began gathering in the Piazza del Duomo waiting for the cathedral's doors to open. Meanwhile they stood closely packed together for hours on end—till eleven o'clock in fact—between the octagonal Church of John the Baptist, known as the Baptistry, and St. Mary of the Flower. At last the doors opened and the throng pressed in. "Great was the silence in the church," writes Burlamacchi, "each going to his place, and he who could read with a taper in his hand reading the service and other prayers. And though many thousand people were gathered together not a sound was heard"—a miracle if ever there was one in eternally babbling Italy—"till Savonarola appeared." As he entered from the sacristy, the Friar was preceded by a choir of girls dressed in white singing a hymn under direction of Fra Girolamo Benivieni, the music master at San Marco's convent.

We have the deposition of Lorenzo Violi, the shorthand writer and printer, that the congregation often showed signs of deep emotion at the mere sight of Savonarola. A vast murmur *"Padre, Padre,* Father, Father, *Nostra Girolamo,* Our Girolamo," swept through the crowd. And when he then, hearing them whisper his name, opened his lips and showed his dazzling smile, it was "as if a breeze from heaven passed over the earth."

"My children," he said, for thus he always greeted the congregation, "let me first of all bless you." Holding high the wooden crucifix he repeated the Saviour's comforting words: "Peace be unto you and mercy and joy in the Holy Spirit!"

Not only the common people and the women, but educated persons of rank, artists, scholars, and architects of renown and genius, bankers, magistrates, captains, and foreign ambassadors, all have testified to the tremendous triumph of Savonarola's eloquence. In Violi's notebooks which are preserved in Florence's Laurentian Library, in the midst of his incomprehensible hieroglyphics, there occurs not once but ten times a sentence in plain script: "At this point in Fra Girolamo's sermon I was overcome with weeping and could not go on!" We may forgive Violi for interrupting his outlandish scrawls, for no other Christian preacher, to our knowledge, ever carried his audience so wholly with him as did Savonarola. While preaching he was sometimes carried away by an overmastering exaltation, a circumstance which goes far to explain his physical exhaustion after two hours in the pulpit. It took him never less than two, some say three days, to recover. But those who heard him with an open heart and mind were never the same again. Lorenzo Violi appends a remark at the end of his illegible scribbles to the effect that "not a few tore off their jewels and ornaments upon leaving the church or took them to the magistrates to make their value available to the poor." Others went home "singing hymns and praising God with a loud voice . . . A new spirit had come to dwell in Florence's darkest slums and in the palaces as well. Men read the Bible again as a result of Savonarola's urging."

About that time—spring of 1495—there also circulated a curious little book by an anonymous author entitled: *The coming of the Angel-Pope*. Zenub Acciajuoli, later librarian at the Vatican under Leo X, and Prosper Pitti, whose name is perpetuated in the great palace (now a museum) across the Arno, "a saintly person endowed with the gift of prophecy," assured the world of the authenticity of the Angel-Pope document. They had discovered the manuscript in a Venetian monastery. The Angel-Pope was to make his appearance at the end of a time of troubles. The new Pope would bring about the conversion of the whole world, and usher in an era of unprecedented well-being and godliness. And—this was the nexus of the prophecy—the redemptive movement would start from Florence. It was almost inevitable that simple souls, learning of the new era about to dawn, should see in Savonarola a beginning of the mysterious prophecy's fulfillment.

At first the Friar paid no attention to the booklet and the speculations to which it gave rise. But when he noticed that people here and there began to address him as "Your Holiness," falling prostrate at his feet or trying to kiss his hands, or, as happened on one occasion when he passed through the Ognisanti quarter, men hoisted him on their shoulders shouting: *"Habemus papam angelicum. We have the Angel-Pope,"* he tore himself loose from the crowd and fled as fast as his legs could carry him.

"His Holiness Alexander VI is our Pope, the Father of the Church and the Vicar of Christ," Savonarola wrote to the presiding officer of the Grand Council. "Let there be an end to these superstitions and false rumors. The Holy Spirit, as he has always done and will do till the return of Christ, will designate the next Pope when the time comes . . . I am but a lowly friar without the least qualification or ambition. I am the obedient, respectful son of the Lord Pope Alexander VI and of our Mother, the Holy Roman Catholic and Apostolic Church."

The spurious veneration gradually abated, although there were many who were ready to swear of having seen an aureole around Savonarola's head. Others saw the Blessed Virgin and John the Baptist stand by his side in the pulpit. One rumor, which could not be laid, had it that Christ himself had been seen placing a golden crown on the Friar's brow at the moment when he pronounced the benediction.

Even if the Florentines flocked to his sermons in undiminishing numbers, Savonarola soon realized that the fight was far from over. The hardest struggle lay ahead. If man's ultimate goal lies in his union with God through love it also requires the fullest assimilation possible of the human to the divine in everyday life. In order to attain this goal man must try and live in the greatest simplicity. The simplicity of Christian life can only be expressed and carried out through disinterestedness, with a pure heart, and in the actual practice of love of God and man, for what in the final analysis makes man good is solely his good will and intention.

Evidently the heart's simplicity, if it is not to remain a dream wish or a beautiful abstraction, must be reflected in man's way of life, in his conduct in private and public, in his relationship with others, and also in his clothing, in the kind of food he eats, and in the kind of house he inhabits. This simplicity is not incompatible or irreconcilable with culture, with knowledge or even with refinement. But what Christian simplicity can neither tolerate nor ignore is filth. Under the rallying cry "Only a good Christian can be a good citizen," Savonarola launched his campaign to clean up the Arno city.

The widespread moral turpitude and depravity were the first evils to be attacked. Whether right or wrong, Savonarola attributed the prevalence of unnatural vice to the social elite's predilection for the poetic and theatrical works of ancient Greece and Rome. We know that the Florentine intellectuals went into ecstasy upon the discovery of a Ciceronian manuscript, a play of Plautus, or a scroll by Lucian. In Homer and Hesiod they read of the adulterous gallantries of the gods, of expressive mimic entertainments with flute accompaniment relating to the intercourse of the sexes and represented by dancing men and women. In Xenophon they read of the loves of Aphrodite with Mars and Adonis, the lustful adventures of Ganymede, Danaë, and Leda. Arnobius informed them that in pagan Rome the sacerdotal colleges and authorities, augurs and chaste vestals, senators and consuls took their seats in the theaters where Venus, the mother of the Roman race, was danced to the life, and in shameless mimicry was represented as reveling through all the phases of meretricious lust. Jupiter, the supreme ruler of the world, was brought in to play the part of an adulterer, masking himself in order to deceive chaste wives, and take the place of their husbands in the nuptial bed. From recently recovered works of antiquity, the Florentines learned of men prostituting themselves in the ancient pagan temples and boasting of their shame afterwards.

There was a society or club of wealthy young men in Florence, who called themselves *Compagnacci,* the Good Companions, fast and free livers, whose leader Doffo Spini sponsored the reenactment of the most notorious plays and rites once practiced in pagan Rome. This Doffo Spini followed the emperor Nero's example by marrying a man, and even several men, who accompanied him on the streets in the evening, dressed in feminine clothes with veils covering their faces. In his mansion the banker Spini had a chamber modeled on the gloomy interior of a Roman temple where the altar was sprinkled with blood and vilest impurities were committed amidst clouds of incense. The walls of his house and the houses of his friends were covered with a profusion of lascivious paintings. Children were made acquainted far too early with things that would otherwise have been hidden from them. The general moral condition of Florence was so low that other reformers before Savonarola had given up in despair or passed the evil under silence. Savonarola did not condemn classical learning per se, but he saw in the preference given by the best educated circles in Florence to lewdness and obscenity, a revival of paganism and a threat to the common people's traditional piety.

"You have fallen into idol worship," he said, addressing himself to the aristocracy and the wealthy. "Your male and female harlots, your filthy panderers, your concubines have become your gods . . .

Girls and young men are debauched in the streets of Florence in sight of all. Even the Cathedral, this house of God, is not immune, but daily besmirched by your abominations. This very week a young girl was assaulted by a gang of well-dressed men and boys in the Duomo, and the beadles who came to the child's assistance were beaten up."

The Friar did not mince words: turning to the upper-class women he charged them with bearing a heavy share of responsibility in the rise of the flood of slime. Strutting around in scarlet- or gold-lacquered shoes, wearing gowns cut down to the waistline or transparent skirts and tunics, affecting a lascivious gait, they were guilty, he said, of arousing the basest instincts and lusts. While admitting that things were just as bad in Bologna, Genoa, Venice, and other large cities, Savonarola declared that in one particular vice Florence surpassed all others. "Sodomy," he said, "is Florence's besetting sin."

Judging by numerous plaints uttered by secular and priestly moralists living in that era, Savonarola did not exaggerate. "The prevalence of the practice of sodomy is more destructive of Florence than armies of rapacious mercenaries," writes one contemporary historian. Another says: "Every social class is infected with this evil, the clergy not excepted. Even children indulge in this unnatural impudicity to which the city destroyed by the divine wrath gave its name." Parents saw no wrong in it. Worse than that, parents and teachers encouraged the young inasmuch as sodomy obviated the danger of pregnancy. It was said that parents advised their boys to become acquainted with elderly rich men so as to relieve them of the burden of paying for their education. Savonarola insisted again and again that elderly men were the worst abusers of the youth in this respect. "Into what an abyss of wickedness has this city sunk!" exclaimed the Friar. "A young boy cannot walk in the streets without danger of falling into evil hands. Mothers, I pray you, do not send your boys out on errands, rather let the girls go out. The girls run no danger comparable to that which the boys encounter on every street corner."

When the Friar turned next to the gambling mania, he was joined by many Christian laymen in attacking games of chance and lotteries. "The man who gambles," said Savonarola, "does not love his neighbor, but causes damage to his victim and the victim's wife and children . . . Away with the usurers!" he cried. "Away with the counterfeiters and those who falsify the weights and balance scales in their shops and warehouses! . . . To ask thirty and forty per cent interest on a loan is an outrage which the Signoria should forbid. . . Whoever keeps his business open on Sunday, desecrates the Lord's day. He should be hailed before the magistrates and forfeit the earnings of an entire week. . . ."

His first step in combating the gambling evil was the establishment of the *Monte di Pietà*. This institution was designed to liberate the poorer classes from the usurious exactions of the moneylenders. At the Monte di Pietà, people could obtain loans at a reasonable rate of interest. The Monte di Pietà was really a peoples' bank and it was Savonarola who went around getting subscriptions to its capital fund.

Sometimes Fra Girolamo was carried along by his zeal till he landed in the inhuman and incoherent. For sodomites caught in the act, who were generally dismissed with a light fine, he demanded a revival of the punishments devised by Blessed Jordan of Pisa and St. Bernardin of Siena who, in their time, required the magistrates to burn the offenders alive. Savonarola compromised by urging garroting or stoning. Those guilty of blasphemy or of using the Lord's name in vain were to have their tongues pierced with a nail and attached to a block of wood. But for incest: death! For gambling: death! For theft: death! For homosexualism: death! Any show of clemency in such cases he denounced beforehand as insane leniency, an act of judicial aberration. Had not Moses prescribed the death penalty for adulterous women? Had not God blotted out the city of Sodom for demanding that three strange men be handed over to the local lechers? Was not Phineas deemed worthy of God's approval for killing a fellow Israelite who had taken a heathen woman into his tent? "Would you be wiser than Moses, than God, and let all these miscreants go scot-free?" asked the Friar.

Fortunately for Savonarola, as well as for the possible victims of his fanatical vendetta, nothing or hardly anything came of these threats. When his demands for punishment came before the Eight of Justice and then were referred to the Grand Council, one member asked coldly if the Friar had gone out of his mind. Another man rose to pour ridicule on one of Fra Girolamo's sermons wherein he commended abstinence from sexual intercourse for married couples. "What does this friar expect us to do; become the object of mockery and derision in the whole world? Wouldn't our Pisan and Venetian enemies rejoice if they learned that we had stopped going to bed?"

Just about this time, the spring of 1495, Savonarola preached a sermon in which he applied the prophet Amos' designation of Samaria's women as fat cows to certain females of Florence. "Hear this word, ye kine of Beishan, that are in the mountains of Samaria, which oppress the poor, which crush the needy, which say to their masters, move over and let us drink." Translated into Savonarola's language, this word of Tekoa's angry man became: "Big, flabby hunks of fat you are with your dyed hair, your high-rouged cheeks and eyelids smeared with charcoal. Your perfumes poison the air of our streets and parks. Not content with being the concubines of laymen and debauching young boys, you are running after priests and monks in order to catch them in your nets and involve them in your filthy intrigues." He called for the closing of the *casolini,* "the little houses," the private love nests, so to speak, as being breeding holes of the worst perversities. But he did not say a word about the big houses, the licensed brothels whose number was legion in Florence. What occurred at this point to curb the prophet's zeal?

This is what happened: Fra Antonio Benivieni, the same friar who had criticized his preaching in the early years, said to him: "You are not following Christ when you threaten the whole city with direst punishments. Our Lord did not condemn the adulterous woman when her judges wanted her stoned. Jesus simply said to her: 'Daughter, go home and sin no more.' From Mary Magdalen the Lord threw out seven devils and she became Saint Maria Magdalena who is now interceding for all her wayward sisters before the throne of the heavenly grace. Think deeply, Father Girolamo, before you condemn the harlots in general. Many girls, now steeped in sin, would gladly turn new creatures. Go and speak with them. Touch with a loving hand those who have probably never known genuine love in their lives. Awaken them by kindness.

Do not scold or threaten them. Try to persuade them! Try to make them see the evil of their ways. Humble yourself and ask them if you may pray for them.

"Are you aware that since you began to hurl your imprecations to left and right men and women run for cover when they see a man in the Dominican habit coming their way? Would they run if our Lord Jesus Christ came into their poor hutches and hovels? Are we not Christ's messengers and should the people not see and hear us gladly as they once saw and heard the Lord?

"All Florence approves of the changes you have brought about so far. It is true that our Lord commands us to 'compel them to come in,' but not by violent measures, not by compulsion or physical constraint or by holding a threat of punishment above their poor heads. The Saviour always began by forgiving sins. He was never angry with the poor and the outcasts for he knew himself what it meant to be poor and to have no place to lay his head.

"Reform there must be," continued Fra Benivieni, "reform of Florence, reform of Italy, reform of the Church, all things must be made over. But I warn you that the Kingdom of God cannot be forced. 'Not by might, nor by violence, but by my spirit shall it come to pass, saith the Lord'. . . ."

Convinced that he acted in the spirit of St. Thomas, who made "brotherly reproof" a duty of love, Fra Benivieni spoke "long and earnestly" to his superior. And Savonarola never forgot the lesson. He revoked the resolution which his followers, the Frateschi, had introduced in the council to punish certain crimes and offences with death. The brothels were not closed, not even when a delegation of respectable matrons brought their complaint to San Marco that the two thousand licensed streetwalkers were growing more arrogant and impertinent every day. "Ladies," replied Savonarola, "let your first concern be not to resemble the prostitutes in dress and deportment. Some of you here present are by far too lavishly gowned. I pray you, rub the paint off your faces. Do not wear jewels. Dress modestly. Walk with dignity. The harlots who imitate readily, will soon leave off molesting you when they see your superior manners."

The upshot was that no streetwalking or soliciting from doorways and windows would be allowed during Lent with the exception of the day known as Mid-Lent, Mardi gras, fat Tuesday, when all rules were relaxed for twenty-four hours.

Now comes that era of transformation in the social and religious life of the people of Florence which has led foreign and Italian historians and sociologists of the most diversified schools of thought and confession to declare that Christ's Kingdom, albeit for a short time, was once a tangible reality in the city on the Arno. Nor was it ushered in or enforced by clerical or secular authority. Tens of thousands of Florentines chose to walk the strait and narrow path voluntarily. Throughout Italy and in foreign lands, men and women, lay and clerical alike, looked up with great reverence to Savonarola. But the entire movement of moral, spiritual and political renewal which he inspired ran its course within the bosom of the Church. There was no break, no secession, no interference or censure by competent ecclesiastical authorities. The later conflict between the Pope and Savonarola derived from causes which had nothing to do with the Friar's revivalism and his placing ethical values before politics and social reform.

Where St. Thomas Acquinas subordinated the State in all things to the Church, San Marco's Prior did not take the opposite point of view in seeking to make the State subservient to the Church. He placed both on an equal footing, side by side, neither one to dominate over the other, but to complement each other, each in its own sphere in the pursuit of the goal held up to mankind in the Lord's prayer: to do God's will on earth as it is in heaven.

Since this is and has been, in theory at least, the desideratum of Christian social movements and schools, both before and after the Reformation, Savonarola is often spoken of as the initiator of modern democracy. There is an element of truth in such an evaluation. It is indisputable that he founded a stable government on a popular basis. The political tendencies of Savonarola, as well as his religious ideas, survived him during several centuries. The German historian, Leopold von Ranke, continually recurs to the idea that Savonarola's political and social prescriptions were based on the moral law "which gave a permanent value to his political ideas."

Savonarola was instrumental in putting a democratic constitution in the place of the Medici's dictatorship and instituting a far-reaching moral reform. Yet for this reason to hold him up as a unique and exceptional figure, a singular enlightened religious and political thinker, a lone pioneer of freedom in an age of reaction and obscurantism, is to overstep the bounds of historical truth. What is overlooked here is that every reformer stands on the shoulders of his predecessors. In his conception of the Kingdom of God and its righteousness for this earth, Savonarola was not an innovator. He expressed the spirit of the age in which he lived. Perhaps he did it more vigorously than others, but the hope of Christ's reign lay as deeply anchored in the hearts of St. Francis, Bernardin, Joachim of Calabria, Dolcini, St. Dominic, and Aquinas as in Savonarola's. Had this hope not been shared by the common people of Florence Savonarola could not possibly have risen to the height he occupies in history. He was borne upwards by spiritual currents which had lain dormant during the first centuries of the Renaissance. It is true that he did a very great deal to awaken them.

Fra Benivieni's solemn warning that the Kingdom of God cannot be forced made so deep an impression on Savonarola that for weeks on end he neither preached nor was seen in public. He spent his days and nights in prayer in his cell at San Marco's. It was a spiritual wrestling bout in which he engaged, and like the wrestling of Jacob with the Man in the night at the brook of Jabbok, Savonarola came out of the struggle blessed indeed, but with his health permanently impaired. Fra Antonio Benivieni, the monastery's physician, dates Savonarola's physical decline from his solitary retreat in the early months of 1495. He fasted, it is said, forty days and forty nights, yet in order not to appear to have striven for equality with the Master's forty days and nights in the Judean desert, the Prior ate a crust of bread every seventh day. It is not surprising to find Doffo Spini and his Compagnacci later citing the Friar's fast as an indication of mental disturbance.

Though the loss of weight made him look like a ghost, he returned to work with as great a zeal and intensity as he exhibited before. The children now became Savonarola's first and foremost preoccupation. In this respect he went back to one of the oldest and finest traditions of St. Dominic's Order. Instead of asking parents to bring their children to Mass, he organized special services for the youth. This departure from common practice produced in the young an enthusiasm which by far surpassed the fervor of the elders. The first children's sermon brought out two thousand youngsters, the second four thousand. When Savonarola appeared in the pulpit on the third successive morning, the Duomo was crowded to the bursting point, for the parents had accompanied their children and not vice versa as formerly. When at the appointed time the Friar's head appeared above the pulpit's edge, all present rose and spontaneously sang the hymn: *Ave Stella Maris* (Hail, thou Star of the Sea). In a contemporary work entitled *The Simplicity of Christian Living,* it is written that "everything went off with such good order and taste that those looking on thought themselves transported to paradise and from emotion could not hold back their tears."

Savonarola asked the young people not to confine their interest in religion to an occasional visit to church. Religion was not merely a brief intermission in everyday activity; it was life. It had to be lived, nourished, developed, and to be manifest in an all-encompassing reform. They were to organize themselves on a permanent basis in clubs and associations. A few such youth companies, as they were called, existed already in Florence, though their activity had for the most part degenerated into gaming, drinking, vice, and delinquency. Since nothing was to be forced, Savonarola asked the children to carry out the necesary reforms themselves. Two of San Marco's monks were attached to each company, one as *guardino* or supervisor, the other as *corretore* or proctor. The platform or program of activities was drawn up in mass meetings and ratified by the civic notaries. Every boy made a pledge not to use the Lord's name in vain, not to listen to the solicitations of the sodomites, not to wander in suspicious neighborhoods, not to gamble, not to carry knives, to be kind to animals, to treat his elders and teachers with respect, to go to church on Sunday, to confess once a month, and tactfully and kindly to point out their offensiveness to public morality to girls and women who wore immodest or indecent clothing in church or on the streets.

And then the old lute on which Fra Girolamo hadn't played since the last evening at home before his flight from Ferrara, was brought out again. He became an instructor of singing in two or three of the youth companies. In the meantime the number of monks at San Marco increased to nearly three hundred. To house the novices the adjacent building of La Sapienza was obtained from the government and connected with the convent by a passage tunneled under the Via del Maglio. Several of the new friars were sons of the leading families of Florence, as for instance, the six Strozzi brothers and the three Salviati. Other newcomers at San Marco were persons of high standing in art and letters, such as Rucellai, Georgio Vespucci, uncle of the celebrated navigator Amerigo Vespucci, who gave the American continent his name, and Blemmet, the Jewish scholar who taught Hebrew and cognate languages.

The most sensational conversion was undoubtedly that of Bettucio, a young man about town who led a life of frivolous gallantry. The son of a famous goldsmith and himself a painter of miniatures, a poet of distinction, a singer, and raconteur, Bettucio was the most favorite guest in society circles. He wrote about himself in a clever poem: "I wore so much perfume, such gaudy finery, lace and frippery, that my head flew without wings."

When peasants and nobles journeyed by night to be in time for Savonarola's morning sermons, some coming from as far as Bologna to spend the Lenten season in Florence, Bettucio scoffed at the Friar as a *masticapaternostro,* prayer mumbler. He frequently joined with a company of licentious youths who made it a habit to jeer at Savonarola as he made his way from San Marco to the Duomo to deliver his sermon. One day, however, Bettucio was persuaded by a noble lady to accompany her to church. He described his feeling of embarrassment on entering the Duomo and finding himself among so many of the faithful who stared at him with astonishment because of his foppish garments. He felt like running away, but could not move on account of the pressure in that sea of humanity. As soon as Savonarola mounted the pulpit everything changed in Bettucio. He could not tear his eyes away from the preacher. His mind was captivated, his conscience was touched by the Friar's words, and, he says: "At last I knew myself to be as one dead rather than living." It is as if we read Bunyan or Wesley or Spurgeon in going over Bettucio's recital of his conversion.

Bettucio had a hard struggle breaking away from his former habits and friends, and "a still harder struggle with my own passions." He discarded his fine clothes and roamed the countryside as a vagabond. At last he called at San Marco and threw himself at the Friar's feet, but he trembled so violently in the presence of the man whom he had formerly mocked that he could not say a word. Savonarola, who never pressed any man to join the brotherhood, sought to dissuade him and asked him to try and lead a Christian life in the world for a time before crossing the monastery's threshold. This advice Bettucio took, but in November, 1496, he made his vow and put on the robe of St. Dominic and assumed the name of Fra Benedetto. Fra Benedetto nourished an admiration bordering on worship for the Friar who had been the instrument of his spiritual regeneration.

Savonarola made his friars what we would call today youth counselors in different wards of the city. Some were entrusted with the role of *pacieri,* or peacemakers. They were to see to it that there be an end to fighting by street gangs. Others became *limosinieri,* alms collectors. Several youth companies called *lustratori* or cleaners, devoted themselves to keeping the shrines and statues on street corners in good repair and fresh-looking with flowers. Fra Bartolomeo, the celebrated artist, took charge of a whole battalion of these youngsters. Every day he could be seen with his boys lugging ladders, paint pots and brushes or standing on a scaffold touching up one of the corner statues with his marvelous blues and golds. Still other groups manufactured banners and flags to be borne in processions and church festivals, stitching the emblems, mottos and iconical images on them with gold and silver thread. The marble exterior of the Baptistery was given a bath, the Cathedral and all the other churches in Florence had their windows washed once a month. They looked like new after the lustratori went over them with scrubbing brush and wet ashes and lye.

In striking contrast with the overgreat majority of his countrymen, and, we may safely assume, with the commonality of his fellow Europeans in the fifteenth century, Savonarola was a man of meticulous bodily cleanliness. He got the habit from his grandfather, old doctor Michele, who attributed his success as an accoucheur to "clean hands and nothing else." The Friar urged the Signoria to purify the city of Florence by washing the streets regularly on Saturday afternoons. There was no reason in the world, he said, for the streets to remain dirty and untended. An abundance of water was available, the Arno flowed right through the middle of town. The Florentines could not invoke the excuse of the Ferrarese who were forced to go three miles to the banks of the Po for their water supply. The lustratori, the youths of the cleaning company, would set the example. Brother Anton of Zwolle, a towheaded Dutch monk with rosy cheeks, upon whom the generally swarthy Florentines looked as a creature from another world, assumed the superintendency of the street-cleaning department. With hundreds of youthful assistants he made Florence look as spick and span as the cities in his native Holland.

Water was also brought inside the houses. Savonarola encouraged the manufacture of ewers and basins and hanging lavabos so that these utensils should no longer serve the exclusive comfort and hygiene of the rich. Except for the palaces of the great families, the thing known as sanitation in our day was unknown, not only in Florence, but in the whole of Europe. "Personal and private functions," says a historian, "were pursued after the manner of cats and dogs." Savonarola advised against drinking the water from the river. Wells were to be dug in the courtyards and at the end of every street. To the Florentines this was a highly amusing idea, but they dug the wells nonetheless when Savonarola linked bubonic plague with drinking contaminated water. It might be said that he frightened the people into cleanliness as he had done his best to frighten them into godliness with his terrible sermons of the wrath to come. There were men then living in Florence who remembered how an epidemic of plague wiped out a full third of Europe's population in less than a decade. . . For bathing the body Savonarola recommended the use of sweet herbs, glasswort and alkaline which were the substitutes for soap. But no perfume! Perfume, as we shall see, was taboo on the Friar's list.

For the public festivals once organized with such sumptuous display by the Medici the Friar substituted simple folk dancing in the evening in the Piazza San Marco, right in front of the monastery where he could personally keep an eye on things. The monks supplied the music and the words for the new melodies. Fra Girolamo Benivieni was in charge of this phase of endeavor. A huge tree was put up in the center of the Piazza and thousands, old and young, came to see or to participate in the joyous ring dances. Those of the monks who wished, could take part in these harmless diversions. . . .

But there were troubles, too. Doffo Spini's Compagnacci more than once broke up the ring-around-the-rosies. The appearance of a squad of youth proctors in a gambling den or bawdy house, for the purpose of admonishing the inmates, was fiercely resented and led to brawls and forcible ejection of the pious intruders. "What are we to do, Father Girolamo?" the boys asked him. "In passing through the Via de' Martelli we were attacked. Ordure and garbage were poured over our clothes and heads. Near the Church of Santa Croce we were met with a hail of stones. Some of us were injured. Knives were used against us. What are we to do? Resist, run, or bear up under these humiliations and outrages?"

"Do as I do," advised Savonarola, "when the bandits stand waiting for me to hurl insults and to throw stones and filth, I say to them: 'In the name of Jesus Christ, the King of our city, I summon you to give up your bad habits and to come with me to hear Mass at the Cathedral.' Sometimes that admonition has effect, but sometimes not, I am afraid."

But this was no solution! Nonresistance lies not in the Italian character. Moreover, Savonarola did not follow his own advice either. When he went to the Duomo following an attack by some Compagnacci, a bodyguard of friars accompanied him, unarmed to be sure, or, perhaps, hiding some stout cudgels under their garments. He petitioned the Council to be allowed to form a children's police. The Council turned him down on the motion of Francesco Valori, who happened to be presiding. One of Savonarola's boys, known as a petty thief, a burglar, and a fighter asked and was granted permission to address the Council. Everybody knew the young man as the Tiger. "The Tiger behaved like a lamb."

"Christ, the King of Florence," he told the Magnificent Signori, "and Mary his glorious mother, have freed our city from the bondage of sin. A prophet has arisen amongst us who has kindled hearts and minds with the pure light of the spirit. . . Fifteen thousand boys and girls are organized in companies which form a new Christian militia. We have sworn an oath not to rest till we have spoken to every youth and maiden wherever they may be of the

love of Christ, and God's promptitude to forgive all transgressions. . . ." The Tiger got a standing ovation. Savonarola himself
was moved and surprised at the faultless language and the noble
sentiments of a boy who had never gone to school, whose parents
were drunkards, and who had but recently learned to read and
write.

The number of adherents to the youth companies grew by leaps
and bounds. Exceptionally fine work was done by the girls' brigade
in what in a later age would be called rescue work. The female
youth societies were led by ladies belonging to the most prominent
families in Florence. On Savonarola's request, the Archbishop of
Florence admitted about one hundred of them to the religious
orders. Their special task was to visit the brothels and by prayer
and admonition to seek and persuade the inmates to give up their
evil way of life. "You are Christ's dearest children," the harlots
were told. "God loves you as much as the wealthiest women in the
community."

To the surprise of everyone, the rescue mission met with startling success. In two months' time an entire red-light district was
deserted. In other streets, too, the houses of ill fame closed their
doors one after the other. When at Easter time, 1495, Savonarola
held a procession of all the youth companies and they, with flags
unfurled and singing hymns marched through the streets, all Florence turned out. In front of the youth army, under the blue and
silver banner of St. Mary Magdalen, dressed in white, all paint and
powder removed and, by common consent, singing best of all,
walked the erstwhile prostitutes, seven hundred strong. "Some of
the girls wept," says an eyewitness of this "marvelous scene," as
they heard the waves of applause that greeted their appearance.

In the course of spring and early summer of 1495 the aspect of
the city was completely changed. National and foreign historians,
ambassadors, Roman prelates, members and officers of religious
orders who visited Florence, did not recognize the place. Florence
had become a city of brotherly love, of peace and concord. Political agitation and turbulence had abated to a point where they were
no longer noticeable. From a people given over to unbridled libertinage and shameless flaunting of morality, the Florentines were, to
all appearances, transformed into sober, religious-minded men and

women. Riotous young men, once in avid pursuit of pleasure and vice, had turned to a life of decorum and devotion. So pleased and proud was the Grand Council that an invitation was sent to the Pope and the College of Cardinals to pay a visit to what was called "our converted city." Completely restored following the pillage and destruction by the French troops and tastefully refurbished with great works of art, the Medici Palace was placed at the Pope's disposal for the length of time he was hoped to spend in Florence. Had Alexander VI accepted the invitation, which he did not and could not, because he was preoccupied with the French invasion of Rome, he would have seen "wondrously new and strange things."

Florence was the only city in Italy, perhaps in all Christendom, where on Sundays the shops remained closed till an hour after noon. The cabarets, bagnios, and gambling houses had gone out of existence, not by signorial or ecclesiastical decree, but by the former customers staying away. The roads leading to Florence from Bologna, from Rome, Genoa, Milan and, of course from Ferrara, and all intervening points, were continually crowded with parties of pilgrims as if the Holy Year's celebrations had been transferred to the city on the Arno. Peasants with their families walked in from neighboring provinces and the mountain regions to the east and north. Prominent Florentine ladies supplied them with food and drink. At each city gate canteens and barracklike hostelries were erected to provide the poorer visitors with food and lodging at no cost. Every Florentine family took in visitors. There were homes where ten or twenty guests were a daily occurrence. The palaces of the Strozzi, the Ridolfi and other magnates often harbored as many as a hundred visitors over the weekend.

The times of the primitive Church seemed to have returned when St. Paul and his companions were met by enthusiastic new congregations at the halfway point between city and city and triumphantly brought within the walls. Laymen lived like monks, and it is said on the authority of trustworthy sources that housewives rose in the night to say their prayers. "In those days the Florentines behaved like angels," a contemporary historian exults. No more obscene songs were sung by the peasants working in the fields as formerly had been quite common and almost customary. Spiritual songs, hymns, and lauds had taken the place of Lorenzo's indecent carnival songs. No blasphemies were heard in the smithies, the bakeries, and the warehouses. Sometimes the market place spontaneously turned into an open-air religious song fest. In the evening families could be seen by torchlight and candlelight, sitting around, listening to a friar speaking an edifying word. The priests were kept so busy hearing confessions, performing marriages, administering the sacraments, preaching, and saying Mass, that Savonarola, speaking for all the Orders and the clergy in the city, asked the faithful for a two weeks' suspension from all these duties since the monks of San Marco, as he could see, were physically exhausted. The churches, all of them, were crowded day and night. Nor were the poor forgotten; never were the Florentines so generous in the giving of alms.

The historian Pacifico Burlamacchi writes: "Women threw aside their jewels and finery, dressed plainly, bore themselves demurely, and licentious young men seemed as by magic transformed into students of religion. And most wonderful of all, bankers and tradesmen, impelled by scruples of conscience, restored ill-gotten gains amounting to many thousands of ducats." The Prior himself spoke of the changes one Sunday. He said that the number of Bible students who flocked to San Marco after a hard day's work had grown so large that no more could be accommodated, neither in his own monastery nor in the other places of assembly. It was a source of great satisfaction to him that all the children were now receiving religious instruction and this not only in the city, in the rural regions functioned a growing number of prayer circles. "There is joy in heaven," said Fra Girolamo, "for the people of Florence who have returned to Christ and Our Lady. . . You can tell when a man is a Christian if he shows pity, when he shares what he has with others and especially with the poor for they are Christ's own family."

Savonarola performed a splendid spiritual work. He sensitized the consciences of men, he lifted up their hearts. He stirred the Church to a new sense of responsibility and made religion a nobler and more vital force in the life of Florence and all Italy. Christ's law, at least for a time, was supreme in one place on earth.

Every man has two countries, his own fatherland and the City of God. Of the first he is an inhabitant, of the second a builder.

That the walls of the City of God in Florence rose higher under Savonarola's impulse cannot be denied. But it is like trying to measure the immeasurable to attempt an objective evaluation or speak of success or nonsuccess. In these matters another norm, the norm of God's Kingdom itself, enters into operation. The Kingdom of God does not come with outward display. It is not of this world in the sense that it proceeds along the world's lines or can be placed on par with the world's ways. It advances from fall to fall and from minute obscure gain to minute obscure gain. It is only from those who believe in man and have faith in the new and better world which man in co-operation with God can build here on earth that help can come in making us move towards the lands of promise. With men of this kind, as Jacques Maritain once said: "The principal question is not success, for that never lasts. The principal thing is to have been, that is ineffaceable."

Chapter VIII

The Pope Faces the French Army:

Savonarola Offered a Cardinal's Hat

WHAT became of the vainglorious ambitions of the King of France, Charles VIII, during the winter and spring of 1495 while Savonarola pushed his political and moral reforms in Florence with quiet caution and dexterity?

Early in December, Cesare Borgia, the commander of the papal troops, withdrew from the region of Bologna before the superior armament of the Seneschal de Beaucaire who had marched southward on the eastern side of the Appenines. The two divided sections of the French army were reunited and on December 31, 1494, Charles VIII entered Rome without firing a shot. On the advice of Cesare, Pope Alexander VI quit the Vatican and shut himself up in the Castle of Sant' Angelo. The fleur-de-lis banners went up over the Apostolic Palace and the silver trumpets played the royal hymn: *Où peut-on être mieux qu'au sein de sa famille,* "Where can one be better than in the bosom of one's family."

The hour had struck for which Juliano Cardinal della Rovere, who accompanied the French expedition, had waited nearly three years. The Pope's downfall now seemed as certain as the morrow's sunrise. He was a virtual prisoner; his ally, King Alfonso of Naples, shivered in his boots, the papal troops had laid down their arms. Nothing remained but to convoke an Ecumenical Council, convict the Pope of having obtained the tiara by fraud, and send him and his family on "a long, long journey." Della Rovere had King

193

Charles' word for it that he would reform the Church in its "head and members," which meant in the Cardinal's calculations that his hated rival Alexander VI would be removed and he himself placed in St. Peter's see. As if the change was already an accomplished fact, the Cardinal invited five members of the Curia: Sforza, Paraudi, Savelli, Colonna, and Sanseverino, to join him in taking over the provisional government of the Church.

There had been many delays on the arduous trek from the Alps, many hardships encountered, stores had been lost, provisions wasted, some cannons were spoiled, a deal of tergiversation and squabbling in the French high command had repeatedly held up the triumphant march, but all was now forgotten in the bright Roman sunshine as the Cardinal della Rovere installed himself in Donna Vannozza's palace and the French troops were quartered in the houses of the Roman populace.

There was but one further obstacle, a Council of the whole Church could not be called without the Pope's consent. But this last impediment would now also be swiftly overcome as the French artillery wheeled into place and trained its guns on the papal fortress. The Pope would be forced to surrender and abdicate. If he escaped with his life, which would not happen if Della Rovere had his way, he might call himself fortunate. The Cardinal predicted that the white flag of surrender would go up the moment that the Pope, whom he branded a great coward, realized the danger he was in.

As we see it today, the Castel Sant' Angelo is but the core of the magnificent sepulchre of the emperors. What is left of the original gigantic structure which Hadrian raised as a mausoleum for himself and his successors, are the quadrangular basement and the lower mass of the round keep. Deep in the basement were placed the golden funeral urns, enclosed in alabaster, of six Roman emperors. At the time when Pope Alexander took refuge in the castle, four great turrets stood at the four corners of a system of walls, bastions, and outworks making the papal stronghold virtually impregnable. These towers and walls then touched upon the Tiber and remained there till the year 1890 when the Roman municipality, over the indignant protests of all Europe, leveled them with the ground and drove a road between the castle proper and the river.

When Alexander VI retired into the fortress and Cardinal della Rovere expected his momentary surrender, a strange thing happened: a section of the castle's walls suddenly collapsed and slid into the Tiber so that a breach was opened for the French troops to enter at will. The Pope was still more helpless now than he had been before. But the white flag did not go up nor did the French soldiers march or storm forward.

In the breach occasioned by the slide appeared the Holy Father. Vested in his pontifical robes, crowned with the tiara, six loyal cardinals by his side, Alexander carried the Sacred Host in his covered hands. Though not a word of command was given the French army dropped to its knees. The King of France, his Chancellor Cardinal Gurgins, the Seneschal, the princes of the blood, the Archbishop of St. Malo, all bowed their heads and remained in that position as the Pontiff solemnly pointed the monstrance to the four corners of the earth and then withdrew with his cardinals as silently as he had come. . . .

After four days of wrangling the French troops were persuaded to make a second attempt. The artillery again moved up and the infantry brought its scaling ladders, battering rams, and other formidable engines of war. Cardinal della Rovere, who appeared personally on the scene, assured the artillerists that but one salvo would bring the castle down in ruins. But the artillerists, protesting that such action might cause injury to the Pope or worse, refused to fire. The Scottish archers made about turn, followed by the Swiss, the Flemings and the Gascons.

Some of the Church's most precious relics had been exposed on the castle's wall, the skulls of the martyrs, the lance of Longinus with which Christ's side was pierced on Calvary and a portion of the True Cross encased in gold. By the side of the relics stood Alexander VI, bareheaded, dressed in a simple white cassock, one unarmed man face to face with the most powerful army of Europe. Guillaume Brissonet, Archbishop of St. Malo, warned a remaining company of musketeers: "If you fire on the Holy Father and the relics, you will commit a mortal sin!" The troops did not need to be told twice. They downed their arms and fell to their knees as the Pope lifted his right hand in benediction. The Cardinal della

Rovere ran around in hot rage, but his chance to eliminate the Pope and seize St. Peter's chair had passed.

Following these incidents, Charles of France announced a postponement of the Church Council for which Cardinal della Rovere had already set the date and the place; February 1495 in Ferrara. First, declared the King, he would deal with Naples, conquer that kingdom, chase out the reigning sovereign, Alfonso II, and build a fleet of transports at Amalfi and Sorrento to ferry his troops to the Holy Land. When Alexander learned of the King's intentions he sent him a blessing for the undertaking against the Turks and, as a token of his esteem, a golden medallion inscribed *Carolus Imperator,* Charles the Emperor. The new title sent the King into transports of joy. He dispatched a letter of thanks to the Pontiff and marched off to Naples. The Holy Father quietly walked back to the Apostolic Palace along the covered viaduct known as *lo andare* which connects the castle with the Vatican, and resumed his daily rounds of duties as Father of the Universal Church.

Halfway on the road to Naples, the King of France on the advice of the Seneschal de Beaucaire, halted and bethought himself to exact some guarantees from the Pope to keep the peace. Cesare Borgia was seized as a hostage and also a person with the Arabic name of Djem. This man was a brother to the Sultan of Turkey, Bajazet II. He lived at the Vatican where he had fled to escape his brother's vengeance. The Sultan paid the Pope 25,000 gold ducats a year to keep Djem from starting trouble. But now the French King took him under his protection and in addition appropriated Djem's savings account of 100,000 Turkish pounds. However, before the French reached Naples, Cesare Borgia escaped from the French camp and Djem died of poison, administered, it was rumored, by his fellow hostage.

Charles VIII made his entry in Naples on the first of May, 1495. Seated on a white horse, an ermine cloak draped around his shoulders, a glittering crown on his head, in his left hand the scepter and in the other the golden apple of empire, he had been made up to look like Charlemagne, the Emperor of the Franks. "The incredible has become a fact," exclaimed the Archbishop of Naples in his address of welcome. "We have an emperor again! The Infidels tremble! A new crusader, a new Richard the Lion Hearted, a new St. Louis has arisen! The Saviour's tomb will be wrenched from the hands of the Unbelievers and a great cathedral will be built in Jerusalem to commemorate the victory over the unspeakable Bajazet." God, said the Archbishop, was clearly guiding His Imperial Majesty's footsteps. Neither Alexander the Great, nor Julius Caesar had marched as swiftly as Charles VIII.

All this was said in the Citadel of Naples, more than five hundred miles distant by water from Jerusalem, with no ships available to carry the French troops across and no money in the royal exchequer to finance the crusade. But the King of Naples had fled to the isle of Ischia. The Neapolitan granaries were filled to the nooks with last season's superabundant harvest. There was money in the banks, treasures in the palaces, wine in the cellars, girls in the streets, smiles on all faces, victory arches in the squares. What had Charles to fear? Pope Alexander leaned over to Cardinal Caraffa when the dispatches of the French King's triumphant entry into Naples were brought to him. "The man is trapped," commented the Pope. "There never was a greater fool than Charles the still Greater."

The French King came to Italy as a liberator, he behaved like a common bandit or holdup man. None of the tyrannical governments in the various Italian principalities which he had promised to abolish or at any rate to curb, suffered the least interference. The Italian governments were terror-stricken at the sight of the perfectly drilled and equipped foreign host marching through their country in triumph. Charles took no advantage of the awe he inspired to effect the least reform. In Florence, where his advent was initially hailed as the coming of a messiah-liberator by Savonarola, Charles contributed nothing towards eliminating the hated Medicean dictatorship. After the Medici were ousted the King clearly showed on which side lay his sympathies. He took Piero de' Medici under his protection. Piero lived in his camp, sat at the King's table, and together with his royal host drummed up scheme after scheme to effect his return to power in Florence.

While the King of France was occupied in Naples in feasts and banquets and endangered his health by consorting with the lowest class of women, the Pope quietly organized a League of Italian states, ostensibly in support of Charles' crusading project, in reality to check the French, end their occupation of Italy, and break their hegemony. In this attempt he succeeded. He communicated first with Ferdinand and Isabella of Spain, then with the German emperor, then with the ruling house of Portugal. When these princes agreed it was high time to check the French domination and promised their support to frustrate Charles' further insane ambitions, the Pope by the same stroke, rallied all Italy to his side with the exception of Florence.

Alexander persuaded the Duke of Milan, Ludovico Sforza, to occupy the passes of the Alps in order to prevent the French from receiving reinforcements from their own country. Naples mobilized 10,000 men, Ferrara 2,000, Genoa 5,000, Venice 5,000, and so on. In no time Cesare Borgia stood at the head of a well-equipped force roughly estimated at 40,000 which, though dispersed through the length and breadth of the peninsula, presented such a threat to the French King's lines of communication that he forthwith abandoned thoughts of a crusade in the far-off East.

In a fit of fury he swore that he would march on Rome, depose the Pope, execute Cesare Borgia, and set the city on fire. It was pointed out to him that armies were on the march throughout Italy. Spanish warships patrolled the Italian coast preventing the landing and even the departure of reinforcements from Marseille. The German emperor was known to be negotiating with Venice for a fleet of transports to sail through the Adriatic and around the Italian peninsula with the object of attacking the French in Naples. Charles was trapped indeed. For a time he consoled himself with the thought of shutting himself up in Florence and defying all his foes from the walls of the Arno city, till it dawned on him that Florence might not even let him in. What then? There was no other way out but to fight his way back to the Alps. If he was driven to this extremity, however, he threatened to devastate every town and village on the way, leaving Italy a succession of smoking ruins.

In this perilous state of affairs, with Italy on the verge of a roaring blaze, Pope Alexander VI, militarily speaking the weakest of the Italian princes, easily showed himself the most resourceful and the strongest. His thirty-three years in the diplomatic service of the Curia gave him the edge of a practical mind over the stupid intriguant notions of King Charles and Cardinal della Rovere. When all combined against him and his situation seemed hopeless beyond recall, the Pope, quietly, without any fanfare, gained the upper hand.

Look at the man, for he is well worth a glance: six weeks after being a helpless prisoner in the Castle of Sant' Angelo, threatened and vilified by Juliano della Rovere, who hurled imprecations from the moats, the Pope's situation is completely reversed and he commands the world scene with his indomitable sangfroid. He has turned the tables on Charles of France. He is the recognized head of an Italian confederation. He has a powerful army in the field and has gained the good will and support of mighty ruling houses abroad. By cheerful adroitness, patience, and sheer force of character he, singlehandedly and almost bloodlessly, now sets about to appease the universal riot.

As Charles' plight became known and visible in Naples the city was thrown into convulsions. The conduct of the French troops in the Neapolitan Kingdom had not been any better than in the Florentine Republic. The soldiers had devastated the countryside for miles to the south and the east, pillaging, ravaging, maiming, and killing. The King himself had plundered the banks. Wherever they went his men left only corpses and ruined villages behind. The Neapolitans were so disgusted with the French that they openly clamored for the return of their legitimate monarch from his hiding place on the island of Ischia. The street mobs began to attack the French troops which were thereupon confined to barracks in that huge citadel by the seashore, which serves no other purpose today but to obstruct the view of the never enough praised Bay of Naples.

Alarmed by these signs of a coming debacle, Charles in all haste sent his historian, Philippe de Comines, a man of world renown, to consult with Savonarola. Did Savonarola advise retreat or facing up to Cesare Borgia in a pitched battle? Would he, Charles, be able to cut his way out of Italy? And if, by God's grace, he should be successful in escaping the trap would he safely reach home or was he destined to perish in the attempt?

"Thus it came to pass," writes De Comines in his *Memoirs,* "that I was sent to Florence and became acquainted with the prophet whose fame filled the whole world. Where I had expected to find a remarkable man, I found a marvel. Savonarola spoke far better of what went on in the Vatican and in the French King's privy council than myself who had just come from Rome and Naples."

De Comines looked around in Florence for ten days and reported on the general condition of the State and the people: "What Savonarola has accomplished in Florence is almost beyond belief. His sermons against vice have established good morals in the city and in the entire province of Tuscany. Savonarola treats politics with an extraordinary knowledge of men and things. All his thoughts are expressed with a clarity and perspicacity that stem from the purest of lives and the most guileless of consciences."

But what did Fra Girolamo reply to the panicky King's questions? "He took a solemn tone," says De Comines, "and began to recapitulate the faults and errors committed by the King of France." Charles VIII, said the Friar, had made a pledge to carry out a mission entrusted to him by God to effect a great and necessary political and religious reform. But he had broken every vow. He had pillaged the cities and villages of Italy. He had robbed the poor. He entirely disregarded the promise he made before God and men to reform the Church.

"Your king," said Savonarola to De Comines, "is in grave danger, and still worse scourges will be visited on him if he goes on flaunting the divine will and does not return to the ways of truth . . . As regards the future, His Majesty the King will have to fight hard, but he will safely return to Paris and see his wife again . . . That much I can promise but no more. . . ."

For a second time in less than a year the French army, having disgusted friends and foes alike, marched through Italy, but now in the opposite direction. At its approach from the Naples' side, the Pope, fearing to be seized as a hostage, took the precaution of withdrawing into the fortified town of Viterbo. He needn't have gone to the trouble; the King passed through the papal territory by forced marches. He was in too great a hurry to reach the Alps and be safe on home soil again. The French army halted at Siena on June 13, 1495.

One incident in this hurried retreat must not be left unmentioned. Before quitting Rome in Charles' train, the disgruntled Cardinal della Rovere gave one more token of the malice with which he pursued the Pope's person. He led a French troop in raiding the palace of Donna Vannozza which the Pope had built for that lady who was the mother of his children. By this action, Della Rovere not only gave vent to his bitter disillusionment as a beaten man but proved himself a vandal at heart as well.

Florence, which was still loyal to the French alliance, sent an embassy to Siena to inquire by which road the King intended to pass through its territory in order to furnish the necessary supplies. The ambassadors received a rough answer: "Furnish your whole territory. I and my men intend to have a great feast in your city." As they came away from the King's presence, pondering this enigmatic reply, the Florentine ambassadors noticed one large tent which flew the Medicean colors. Upon inquiry from soldiers loitering in the vicinity they learned that Piero de' Medici was in the royal camp with about 2000 hired soldiers of his own.

No sooner was this intelligence forwarded to Florence when all flew to arms. In a few days' time 11,000 foot cuirassiers were collected from the neighboring villages while the city was stocked with war and food supplies. Every citizen gathered his friends and domestics around him and turned his house into a fortress. All the fighting towers were furnished with missiles and in every house the pots were put in readiness to boil water, pitch, and oil to be hurled into the streets in the event of entry by the French. The Signoria decreed a state of war. All males above the age of sixteen were mobilized and set to build barricades, reinforce ramparts and bastions, and patrol the roads in the neighborhood. Piero Capponi was appointed commander in chief and Michelangelo, much to his disgust, was placed in charge of the fortifications.

At this show of hostility the French King took offense. He sent a letter to the Signoria charging the city which called itself his friend and ally with treachery. He threatened to unleash a twenty-four hour bombardment with red-hot cannon balls and set Florence on fire. The Florentines had to make a choice: either allow the "eternal friend," Charles VIII, to enter their city in which event he would almost certainly reinstate the Medici, or be blasted with a rain of fire. In this extremity the Signoria decided to send Savonarola once more to the royal camp to speak to King Charles "with firmness but without exciting his wrath."

And so Fra Girolamo went to Poggibonsi on the road to Siena where the French army lay encamped. When introduced in the royal presence he assumed his old commanding prophetic tone for which Charles entertained an almost superstitious respect. "Most Christian King," began Savonarola, "you are now returning to your country almost as a fugitive. You are beset by perils which I have foretold you. You have provoked the Lord's anger by breaking your word with the Florentines. You have forsaken the task of reforming the Church, which the Lord has imposed upon you by my lips, and for which you were chosen by many manifest signs.

"It is God's will that the Florentines remain the allies of Your Majesty, but He wills that your protection should serve to extend their freedom and not the power of a private citizen (Piero de' Medici) now in your camp. The Divine Providence has ordained the overthrow of all tyrants. If you should fail to resume your abandoned task, if you should disobey the commands of the Lord, now repeated to you once more by the voice of His unworthy servant, I must tell you that still greater misfortunes shall befall you."

The King trembled violently as he listened to Savonarola. He swore that he would return to Italy to finish the task imposed upon him by Almighty God. In a year's time at the latest he would be back with a still greater army and do all the things which he had now failed to accomplish. He ordered an instantaneous breakup of the camp, and continued his march to Pisa, but ordered Piero de' Medici to stay behind. Before pulling out of Tuscany, however, he committed one more act of perfidy: he did not, as had been agreed, return the Florentine fortresses; he sold them for 50,000 ducats to the Genoese and left his artillery in Pisa on a cash payment of 30,000 ducats.

Then he marched north with all speed. In the foothills of the Alps the army of the Holy League under Ludovico Sforza, the Duke of Milan, intercepted his retreat and he was forced to give battle at Asti, the same town where he was so sumptuously entertained by Sforza a year before. Outnumbered ten to one, he nevertheless succeeded in breaking through, but saved only 1000 of his troops. The rest was slain or taken prisoner. Scarcely had he crossed Mount Genèvre and set foot on French soil when a messenger arrived to inform him that the Dauphin, his only son, was dead. Overcome with grief, Charles VIII threw himself on the ground weeping: "Oh, Savonarola, oh! Had I only listened to you!"

Thus ended in shame and tragedy the French expedition which had been undertaken to set a new king on the throne of Naples, to reform the Church, to chase the Turks from the Holy Land, and to establish the hegemony of France over all Christendom. Not one of these objectives had been even partially attained. By their criminalities the French troops, which were at first received with the cry "France Forever," had made the name of their country odious from the Alps to Mount Vesuvius. Charles, who still clung to the title Carolus Imperator which the Pope had shrewdly bestowed on him, had become the whole world's laughing stock.

Even so, there was no cause for rejoicing in Florence yet. New dangers threatened. Not only did the other Italian powers reproach the Florentines for letting the French King depart in peace, but the Pope resented the fact that the Republic still remained aloof from the Holy League. The Florentines would probably have joined the League, too, were it not that Piero de' Medici, after the French King's departure, took up residence in Rome where he busied himself, with the Pope's approval, in recruiting an army for the purpose of eventually making an attempt to regain his lost position in Florence. To complicate matters further, the German Emperor, Maximilian, summoned the Florentines to join the League and solicited their help to eliminate the last vestiges of French power by attacking the French garrison left behind by Charles VIII in Pisa.

On Savonarola's advice the Signoria refused, saying that Florence was at peace with the whole world and intended to remain loyal to the French alliance. Fra Girolamo still entertained hopes, which were probably fortified by a secret communication from France, that Charles VIII would soon return. But the German emperor expressed his dissatisfaction with the Grand Council's reply and added that if the Florentines remained loyal to the French alliance, he would make war on Florence also. "Nothing will give me greater pleasure," wrote Maximilian, "than to put an end to the radical, popular government sitting in your signorial palace."

The emperor's bark was worse than his bite. A whole year

would go by before he made a move to expel the French garrison
from Pisa, but in Florence the Arrabbiati demanded that the Republic sue for peace with the emperor, join the Holy League, and
support the League both with money and troops against the remaining French garrisons at Pisa and Naples. At the same time they
informed the Pope by letter that Savonarola was the chief obstacle
to the city joining the League and requested the Holy Father to
transfer the Friar to the Dominican monastery of Lucca. The Pope
acceded to this request by return courier and Savonarola was
ordered to leave Florence.

"You must know," Savonarola told the Grand Council, "what
this means. The moment I leave, the Arrabbiati will seize power
and invite the Medici back. It is Piero de' Medici himself who
suggested my removal to the Holy Father."

Fra Girolamo produced evidence that he knew better than anyone
what was in the wind, what intrigues, organic and inorganic, were
being spun without and within. He told the astonished Signoria
that but recently at a social gathering Piero de' Medici showed his
Roman friends a list of Florentines whom he intended to execute
in the event of his reinstatement. The names of scores of members
of the Grand Council then listening to Savonarola figured on that
list.

"I advise you," continued Savonarola amid deadly silence, "not to
wait till Piero's executioners start cutting off heads here in Florence.
There are clearly traitors in our midst. . . There are men who are
in daily correspondence with the Medici. . . They are plotting your
downfall and the return of tyranny. Yet the first law of our constitution forbids any single man to rule over all the others. Those who
would bring the Medici back are trampling on the constitution
which you have sworn to uphold. . . .

"There are men here in Florence taking steps for departure,
asking passports, safe conducts for themselves, for their families
and their funds. Where do they wish to go? Are they off to join
the Medici? Do not let anyone depart! Close the gates! Place the
traitors under arrest. Judge them fairly before your august body and
let those who are found guilty pay the price. Do not show any
mercy for they are even at this moment moving heaven and earth
to bring about the destruction of your liberties and the restoration

of the ungodly, murderous Medicean tyranny. . . As to the German emperor," he continued, "do not be afraid! He will accomplish nothing. He will not take your city. God will not abandon his beloved Florentines. We have an invisible king who watches over us.

"And now," Savonarola wound up his oration, "I must leave you. I must obey the Pope, our Holy Father, and, as you know, move from here to Lucca. . . ."

"At these words of the Frate," says stenographer Violi, "a great sadness fell on the assembly. . . Many burst out in lamentation, all pleaded with him not to leave Florence in its hour of need. . . ."

An ambassador was sent to the Pope to ask for a revocation of the order of Savonarola's transfer. The ambassador carried a letter setting forth what San Marco's Prior had wrought in the reform of Florence's morals. "Fra Girolamo is a holy man whose prayers and admonitions have saved the Republic from great peril. He has proclaimed Christ the King of our city. He spends his time in prayer and meditation. He is disinterested, asks no reward for himself, but only that God's name be revered in our midst and in all the world." A covering letter was addressed to Cardinal Caraffa urging him to persuade the Pope to reconsider. With this letter went a bundle of Savonarola's printed sermons.

The result was that Alexander rescinded his Brief. He replied that he had once again read Savonarola's sermons and that he was deeply impressed with the Friar's learning and piety. "If any more sermons are available," wrote Cardinal Caraffa, "the Holy Father will gladly receive them from Your Serene Highnesses. . . ." On July 25, 1495, Alexander VI dispatched a personal letter to Savonarola conceived in the mildest terms: "To our well beloved son, Girolamo Savonarola, Vicar-General of the [Dominican] Province of Tuscany, Prior of San Marco, greetings and our apostolic benediction. We have learned that of all the workers in the Lord's vineyard, you are the most zealous, at which we greatly rejoice and give thanks to Almighty God. We have also heard that you assert your predictions of the future not to come from yourself but from God. For this reason we desire, as befitting our pastoral office, to speak with you personally concerning these things, so that hearing from your own mouth we may be better informed and be better able to fulfill God's will. To this end therefore we enjoin you, by virtue of your vow of holy obedience, to come to us without delay, and we shall welcome you with loving kindness."

Though suffering from a severe intestinal malady, Savonarola, as a loyal son of the Church, seemed at first inclined to heed the Pope's summons. He was so weak physically that he could scarcely mount the pulpit stairs. He had in fact been compelled to give up his preaching in the Duomo where one of his friars, Fra Domenico Buonvicini, now took his place. "Nonetheless," he said, "when the Pope calls, I must obey, and I will obey."

Others took a different view of Alexander's invitation. Fra Girolamo's friends at San Marco and in the Grand Council suspected a trap. Might not Piero de' Medici who was in and out of the Vatican every day have suggested to the Pope these means to lure Savonarola away from Florence? How did the Friar expect to proceed to the Eternal City? On foot, as required by the rules of St. Dominic, carrying only his staff and his wooden water bottle? In that case how easily would he fall victim on the long road to Rome to highwaymen and cutthroats in the service of the Medici?

Savonarola deprecated these warnings which were after all but based on suspicions, till he learned that the party of the Arrabbiati were already rejoicing at the prospect of his leaving Florence. They figured that without its spiritual leader and guide the popular government could and would soon be destroyed.

Fra Girolamo was in a sore dilemma; he had either to disobey the Pope's mandate or fall prey to his wrath. He decided to place his problem before the people and expressed a desire to mount the pulpit once more. Over the strong objections of Fra Antonio Benivieni, San Marco's physician, who told him frankly that his illness might be fatal, Savonarola was literally hoisted into the pulpit. He still wanted to go to Rome he told the congregation but before departing he desired to leave a simple word of advice. "To four things I have exhorted you," he said, "to the fear of God, to peace, to the public welfare and to the reform of the government. I am able to tell you today who are the authors of the new perils menacing Florence, but I will do no man any harm. . . Let there be union and concord among you. Let there be an end to these names Bigi, Bianchi, Arrabbiati and Frateschi, this party strife which is the ruin of your city. Let the Council remain steadfast and become better and purer. I advise you to encourage labor in all possible ways, to promote public works, to care for the sick, and for the proper authorities to be on the alert for plots and conspiracies. . . .

"When I stand in this pulpit," he continued, "I feel strong, but when I descend these stairs I feel that my pains will return. I must try to recover my health. Then I will return and preach to you again. I am very weak at the present moment. I have probably shortened my life by many years by preaching so often and fasting so hard. But however much the wicked rage, the seed I have sown will bear fruit. Of this I am certain, for it is God's will. You are Christ's own people, and you will be rewarded with peace and prosperity. . . ."

After this sermon his monks lifted him down and carried him back to San Marco where Antonio Benivieni forced him to dictate a letter of reply to the Supreme Pontiff. "Most Blessed Father," wrote Savonarola, "my most ardent desire is to behold the shrines of the apostles Peter and Paul and venerate the relics of those great saints, and still more willingly would I go now that the Holy Father deigns to summon his humble servant. But I am seriously ill. I have been forced to suspend both preaching and study, and my life is still in danger. Since I am bound rather to obey the benign purpose of your command than the mere words in which it is framed, I would ask Your Holiness to consider that although the Lord, by my means, has saved this city and subjected it to good and holy laws, there may still be many enemies both inside and outside Florence, who, having sought to enslave it, and having been confounded instead, now seek my life and blood. I cannot depart without manifest risk. The government is not yet firmly rooted and is visibly in danger without continued assistance. Wherefore, in the judgment of all good and experienced citizens, my departure would be of great hurt while of scant profit to Rome. I cannot suppose that my superior would desire me to ruin a whole city, and therefore beseech Your Holiness graciously to accede to this delay and accept my very true and plain excuses, and to believe that it is my ardent desire to come to Rome whither I will travel as soon as possible."

The Pope did not reply by letter, but sent a special messenger to inform Savonarola that his excuses were accepted. And herewith

the incident was closed or seemed closed to the Friar's and the
city's entire satisfaction and reassurance. Fra Benivieni ordered
Savonarola to bed and prescribed a nourishing diet with the result
that Fra Girolamo recovered his strength so fast that soon those
monks who encountered difficulties in their theological studies were
permitted to visit him in his cell. It is not unlikely that this was a
little stratagem thought out by Savonarola himself in order to have
Fra Domenico Buonvicini constantly by his side. Fra Domenico
replaced him in the Duomo pulpit and Savonarola simply had to
hear what his replacement intended to say on the following Sunday.
The congregations and the members of the government understood
full well that Domenico was Savonarola's mouthpiece, if not his
alter ego. Although quite unequal to the Friar in eloquence and
energy, the people went to hear Domenico in great numbers. "When
Fra Domenico speaks," the Florentines said, "it is Fra Girolamo
who gives us his opinion."

In this way the month of August passed quietly at San Marco
when a thunderbolt struck as from the blue shattering its peace for
ever. On September 8, a new Brief arrived from Rome threatening
Savonarola with excommunication. This missive was not, however,
addressed to San Marco, but to the Franciscans of Santa Croce,
whose prior was known to be insanely jealous of Savonarola's
reputation as a theologian and pulpiteer.

Savonarola was designated in the Brief as *"a certain Fra Girolamo, a seeker after novelty, and disseminator of false doctrines.
This man's wits,"* the papal Brief went on to say, "have been so
unhinged by the changes in Italian affairs, that he seeks to make
the people believe that he has a mission from God and holds discourse with God, although he is unable to prove this, either by
miracles or direct evidence from Holy Writ, as the canonical law
prescribes. We have shown great patience towards him in the hope
that he would repent from his transgressions by making submission
to us and desisting from the scandalous severance from the Lombard
congregation, to which our consent was extorted by the specious
devices of certain monks."

This reference to the separation of the Tuscan from the Lombard
province of the Dominican Order was absolutely incomprehensible
to Savonarola and his friars inasmuch as it was through Cardinal

Caraffa, and not "by the specious devices of certain monks," that it had been brought about with the Pope's full consent. The Pope's private seal was on the document.

The Brief wound up by ordering Savonarola to recognize the authority of Fra Sebastiano Madiis, the Vicar-General of the Lombard congregation and "to go without delay" wherever this man would direct him. He was furthermore ordered "to refrain from every description of preaching, whether public or private." He was demoted from his position as Prior, and San Marco's convent was declared to be joined to the Lombard congregation. And all this under pain of excommunication.

In less than a hour's time after receipt of the papal Brief all Florence was astir. The people ran into the streets. At every corner stood groups discussing the latest news from Rome. The Signoria went into secret session to consider the matter with the ambassadors and the foreign relations experts. Why should the Pope have veered around after graciously accepting the Friar's excuses but a month earlier? What had happened in the meantime to have kindled the Holy Father's anger? And most puzzling of all: why should a communication, solely concerning Savonarola and San Marco's convent, have been addressed to Santa Croce, where, to everybody's knowledge, prevailed a decidedly anti-Savonarola sentiment?

Nobody knew the answer, Fra Girolamo least of all. Only gradually did the truth dawn on the Florentines. By addressing the Brief to Santa Croce, the Vatican undoubtedly wanted to prevent concealment and assure immediate and wide publicity. But why? In the Grand Council they reasoned this way: the Pope wants to silence Savonarola since Fra Girolamo is the most outspoken opponent of the Holy League of Italian states over which His Holiness presides. And besides, isn't Pope Alexander entertaining the hated Medici at his court? Doesn't this raise suspicions that Piero de' Medici is plotting and scheming an attempt to regain power in Florence?

By guessing and conjecturing the Signoria came close to the truth, though not quite the whole truth. The whole truth would perhaps never have been known had not the Duke of Ferrara intervened at this point. Ercole I of the House of Este, who was an admirer of Fra Girolamo, sent a secret message to the effect that

Pope Alexander planned to divide the territories of the Florentine Republic amongst the members of the Holy League. But this was not the whole extent of the Pope's plan; there was one reservation or stipulation in the scheme to which Ercole alone was privy. The League members, Milan, Genoa, Naples, Venice, the Medici, and the rest, were only to think that they would share in the spoils. Alexander intended to excite their lust for plunder and power in order to speed their attack against Florence. When victory came, the Pope had confided to Ercole, he would sow discord amongst the conquerors, set them at each other's throats, and then have his son Cesare Borgia step in with the papal forces, ostensibly to restore order, in reality to attach the Florentine Republic and all its territories to the papal domains.

Savonarola, the recipient of Duke Ercole's confidences, was placed on his honor not to disclose the Pope's scheme to the people of Florence lest they fly to arms and precipitate the entire country into civil war. Still, everything was clear now: with his Brief of September 8, the Pope made it appear that the severance of the two Dominican provinces was uppermost in his mind. If the congregation of San Marco was dissolved Savonarola's authority would be at an end. If he left Florence on orders of his newly appointed superior, the Vicar-General of Lombardy, an eventuality which was plainly hinted in the papal document, the Republic would lose its guide and director. To Florence Savonarola's sagacity and diplomatic acumen were worth more than an army with banners. Once deprived of the Friar's counsel the Florentines would be lost. They knew it, Savonarola knew it, and the Pope knew it best of all. . . .

What was the Friar to do? He had given his word of honor to Ercole not to talk or write to anyone of the Pope's plot. On the other hand, the conditional sentence of excommunication, he realized, would be turned on full force against him the moment he refused to obey the Pope. Yet he was also determined not to allow the Republic to be crushed without warning the people and preparing them for resistance.

He was thrown into a further quandary when upon examining the papal Brief closely, he discovered no less than eighteen gross errors in syntax and etymology in its Latin composition. Whatever else might be said of him, Pope Alexander was certainly not deficient in Latin grammar. Fra Girolamo concluded that the Pope could not have written the Brief as it was in an elementary school-boy's style.

Had it been a question of dogma or Church doctrine, Savonarola would unhesitatingly have made his submission to the Holy See. His conscience was clear; at no time in his life had he preached heretical doctrine, nor had he said or written anything contrary to the teachings of the Church. But the Pope's astuteness in cloaking his political intentions with the veil of a religious dispute nevertheless placed him, Fra Girolamo, at a distinct disadvantage. The difficulty of his position resided in the fact that by virtue of his priestly vow he owed the Supreme Pontiff strict obedience. Once more, however, he extricated himself from his predicament by writing to the Holy Father. In a detailed reply the Friar first of all lamented the success of his enemies in deceiving the Pope. He did not name any names, but he made it known to the Holy Father that he was fully aware of what had transpired in the Sistine Chapel when Fra Mariano da Gennazzano preached a sermon before the Pope and the resident cardinals.

Fra Mariano, the one-time favorite of Lorenzo de' Medici, had spent the last four years in Rome. He was introduced to the Pope by Piero de' Medici of whose reinstatement in Florence he was one of the most ardent promoters. He had lost none of his charm and eloquence and when he began his sermon, Alexander VI, who had a fine ear for poetry, nodded in approval as the Augustinian friar declaimed from Virgil and Horace. Gradually, however, Mariano changed his subject and began to attack Savonarola.

"Savonarola," he said, "that braying ass who has thrown so much discredit on the fair city of Florence, is chiefly responsible for keeping the Florentines from joining the Holy League . . . And this is not all: the monkish ignoramus preaches against the Pope. Inspired by the most ignoble ambitions, one of them being to ascend the throne of St. Peter himself, this monstrous half-breed drives the people of Florence to distraction with his insanities that pass for sermons . . . These sermons, it should be known by all present here, are infected with the vilest heresies. Savonarola utters blasphemies against Christ and the Mother of God. . . ."

At this point in Mariano's homily, the Holy Father, who had just read several sermons by Fra Girolamo, looked around in surprise and shrugged his shoulders in a questioning gesture at the cardinals. Why hadn't the Archbishop of Florence, the cardinals whispered among themselves, or the General of the Dominican Order, who visited San Marco regularly, ever breathed a word of these heresies of which Mariano now accused Savonarola? The Pope called for silence and bade the Friar continue. But Mariano did the same thing he once did in Lorenzo the Magnificent's presence; he lost his head and grew more and more intemperate. "Savonarola is a drunken Jew," he shouted. "He is the devil in human guise. He has enriched himself to an incredible extent with funds extracted in the form of penance from wealthy women who come to him for confession and absolution. . . .

"Savonarola and his friars," he went on to say, "recognize no authority but their own. They hold the Pope's sacred person in contempt. The head of San Marco's monastery publicly besmirches the Holy Father's character. San Marco is the nightly scene of orgies so unnatural as to be unmentionable." Mariano's tongue refused to go on. When he, Mariano, then accompanied his diatribe with indecent gestures, the Pope with indignation written on his face, rose to his feet and, followed by his cardinals, left the church.

This scene Savonarola had in mind when he wrote that his enemies deceived the Pope with their slanders. "As to my doctrines," he went on to say, "I have always been submissive to the Church. With regard to prophecy, I have never absolutely declared myself a prophet, although this would not be heresy, but I have undoubtedly foretold certain things, of which some have already been fulfilled, and others will follow. Moreover, it is known to all Italy how solely by means of my words, peace has come to Florence and greater woes have been prevented."

He then ventured to remind the Pope that the decree of separation of the Tuscan from the Lombard province had not been extorted by his monks, but had been granted after full debate before the Holy Father and the college of cardinals. The Pope had freely given his consent and approval by stamping the document of separation with the papal ring.

"Inasmuch as Your Holiness now desires the reunion of the two congregations [Lombard and Tuscan] so as to prevent others from falling into my errors and inasmuch it is now most plain that I have not lapsed into error, the cause being nonexistent, neither should its effect remain . . . Since I have proved the falsity of all the charges brought against me, I pray Your Holiness to reply in my defense, and to grant me absolution. I preach the doctrine of the Holy Fathers, I have departed in nothing from their precepts. If I am in error on any point, I am ready not only to correct myself, but to make public avowal and amends before the whole people. Once again, Blessed Father, I repeat what I have always said, that I submit myself and all my writings to the correction of the Holy Roman Church."

The next move was up to the Pope. To everyone's surprise Alexander assumed a conciliatory tone. All at once the matter which had scandalized him so much in the Brief addressed to the monks of Santa Croce, vanished into thin air. No further mention is made of the reunion of the two congregations. In his reply to Savonarola the Pontiff rejoices over the recovery of a lost sheep. "In other letters," he writes the Friar, "we have expressed our sorrow concerning the disturbances in Florence of which your sermons were the chief cause since you did not preach against vice, but predicted the future. This gave rise to discord among the Florentines in whom there are many seeds of discontent and party spirit. These were the reasons that we bade you to come to Rome, but now that by your letter and the testimony of our cardinals we find you prepared to yield obedience to the Holy Church, we do greatly rejoice, feeling that you have erred rather from simplicity than from badness of heart. Therefore, in virtue of your vow of holy obedience, we command you to abstain from all sermons, not only in public, but in private also, so that no man may say that, after ceasing to preach in the pulpit, you had recourse to illegal gatherings and conventicles. If, as we doubt not, you will obey, we shall revoke all our preceding Briefs, so that you may tranquilly attend to your own spiritual welfare."

Savonarola understood perfectly well that all this paternal suavity had but one purpose: to seal his lips and to weaken the spirit of resistance to the Pope's designs on the Florentine Republic's security and the popular government. From the General of the Dominicans, Turriano, to whom the Pope had in the meantime submitted some volumes of Savonarola's sermons came the reply: "Most Holy Father, this friar says nothing that is not wise and honest. He speaks against simony and against the corruption of the clergy which in truth is very great. But he respects the dogmas and the authority of the Church. For this reason I would rather make him my friend, even, were it needful, by offering him the cardinal's purple."

Evidently, the Pope, who consistently operated on the hypothesis that every man has his price, thought this a good idea. Alexander VI decided to make Savonarola his friend. According to Violi, the stenographer and publisher of Fra Girolamo's works, Cesare Borgia came to Florence incognito to offer the Friar a cardinal's hat on condition that he cease opposing the League and abstain from criticizing the Vatican's international policy.*

Never in his life was Savonarola so shocked as when he received the Pope's offer. He was surrounded by all his friars in the chapter hall when the papal message was delivered. Amazement, even horror, was written on every face. Some could not believe their own ears and asked Cesare Borgia to repeat what he had been charged to say. Here was proof that the Supreme Pontiff was not in the least concerned about the religious aspects of the dispute, but trafficked like a vulgar peddler in the most exalted ecclesiastical positions if it suited his purpose. Savonarola informed Cesare Borgia that he was unable for the moment to reply to the Holy Father's offer, but that he would, in all likelihood, give his answer from the pulpit "within the hearing of all Florence," as soon as he recovered his health. After Cesare Borgia's departure, the Friar said to his companions: "A cardinal's purple will not be bestowed on us, but of a martyr's gown drenched in blood I am absolutely certain."

* According to Lord Acton Cesare Borgia was accompanied by Ludovico di Ferrara.

Chapter IX

Florence In Deadly Peril:
The City's Miraculous Deliverance

KING CHARLES of France was so overwhelmed with grief over the death of the infant Dauphin that he completely neglected the business of state. He took no measures to reinforce or even supply the garrison he left behind in Naples with the result that these troops were shut up in the Citadel and in acute danger of falling into the hands of the Neapolitan king who had returned from exile in triumph. In Florence the death of the little Dauphin—the child was but three months old—was regarded as fulfillment of Savonarola's prophecies. In the rest of Italy, amongst the members of the Holy League, the French King's sorrow was thought to have unhinged his mind to such a degree as to render him unfit to govern and to make it most unlikely that he would ever return and renew his campaign. This feeling of relief at once slackened the eagerness of the allies for the German Emperor's arrival. Why, it was asked, should the "stinking Germans" * be brought in now that the French "barbarians" had happily passed beyond the Alps? Only the Duke of Milan, in fear of a resurgence of Neapolitan power, encouraged the Emperor Maximilian to make all haste and come to restore order in Italy. But the Emperor took a long time to make up his mind.

* Thus they are already called in a thirteenth century popular song by Cecco Angiolieri.

The Pope took advantage of the delay to make war on Florence to force the Republic into the Holy League. However, the papal troops proved no match for the Florentine citizens' army. They were repulsed and routed at Siena on the Republic's borders. Driven in chaos towards Montepulciano, they entered that city, closed its gates and made ready to withstand a siege. The Florentine army, however, did not pursue its victory; it returned to the siege of Pisa.

Since the French King's departure Florence was seeking to recover Pisa, which since time immemorial had been part of the Florentine Republic's territory. In order to drive off the papalists the Republic had weakened its forces before Pisa to a point where the Pisans, by making two or three successful sorties, chased the Florentines into the hills.

In the meantime, a monthly subsidy of 40,000 ducats having been pledged by Milan, the Emperor did indeed cross the Alps. He came to Venice and there embarked his forces on Venetian and Genoese galleons, sailed around the Peninsula, and landed at La Spezia. From La Spezia Maximilian marched south to Pisa, a distance of 35 miles, and the Pisans opened their gates. The small French garrison was taken prisoner, the statue of Charles VIII thrown down and one to the Emperor Maximilian raised in its stead. Pisa now had capable military leaders, ample supplies of money and provisions, and the backing of the German empire. A large number of Florentine soldiers immediately went over to the Pisan side because of the higher pay offered.

On the advice of Savonarola the Great Council of Florence abandoned the siege of Pisa and concentrated all its attention on Livorno (Leghorn), Florence's harbor city through which all supplies and chiefly wheat from France entered Tuscany. Should the Emperor take Livorno Florence would be forced to capitulate. Accordingly Livorno's defenses were greatly strengthened. Abundant supplies were poured into the city. Bettino da Riascoli, a man noted for his energy and military talents, was appointed governor and Count Cecco, a daring young officer, placed by his side as second in command. Appeals made to Florentine merchants living abroad to do everything in their power to hire soldiers, send wheat and other food supplies and arms, brought in enough money to pay the troops their back wages and even a month ahead.

By request of the Signoria, Savonarola urged the wealthy to make a voluntary financial contribution to the war effort, and thereby make a new tax levy unnecessary. This task the Friar carried out most willingly, but when pressed to stimulate the people's courage by a new course of sermons in the cathedral's pulpit, he refused. He foresaw that his preaching would instantly bring a sharp reaction from the Pope. He would not, he said, in the hazardous circumstances, provoke Alexander VI to further severities against his person and the city.

With Savonarola silent, the affairs of the Republic went from bad to worse. The new troubles seemed beyond the Republic's capacity to cope with. The exorbitant subsidies paid to the French King, the repulse of the papal invasion, the attempt to bring Pisa back into the old obedience by force of arms, had proved too great a strain on the public resources. In February, 1496, credit was so low that a city bond of 100 ducats was only worth 10 in the market. Public and private funds both were exhausted, taxes were left unpaid, in a word, the Republic was on the verge of bankruptcy. To make things still worse famine made its appearance.

There remained an ample food supply in Florence itself, but the rural districts were cruelly pinched by hunger. The peasants flocked into Florence by the thousands. According to the old law they would have been expelled as foreigners, but Savonarola had seen to it that this law was abrogated as unworthy of a Christian commonwealth. Under the new "rule of charity" the refugees from the war zone were given a brotherly welcome though not, it must be added, without a heated discussion in the Council. Members of the wealthier classes opposed the admission of the foreigners on the ground that their presence would in a short time exhaust the available food stores and thus expose the Florentines themselves to hunger and privation. Savonarola's adherents who were nearly all drawn from the popular classes, carried the day, and many of the poorest citizens— how faithful are the poor!—gave shelter in their own houses to the refugees. But still the peasants kept coming and misery increased. Maddened by hunger, roving bands of country folk, whose fields had been ravaged by two years of war, boldly attacked the Florentine military camps in the immediate vicinity of Livorno with such fury that the Republic's troops were temporarily expelled and their stores thoroughly pillaged.

Thus went by the first six months of the year 1496. Florence was in a bad way. The churches and monasteries were crowded with refugees, the infirmaries full of sick people. In every doorway and courtyard, on the steps of churches, in the piazzas, and in the parks peasants and their families were camped, but dying of hunger and exposure. For in February it started to rain as it had never rained before. The rains continued all through the summer and far into the autumn of that year. The Arno overflowed its banks and not only the bridges in Florence stood under water, but the flood entered the cellars of the houses along the quays. Heaven and earth seemed to conspire to bring about the doom of the Lily-City. On top of these disasters a mysterious disease made its appearance. In the diary kept by a citizen named Landucci, it is said that the plague broke out in March, 1496. But Savonarola writing in that month to his brother Alberto, the physician of Ferrara, did not think it was the plague. He calls the spreading disease *bolle franciose,* French boils, and asks his brother if he can provide or suggest a remedy. "More people are dying," he writes, "of certain malignant fevers than of the real plague." Alberto Savonarola's reply has not been preserved. Before long, the Friar had to admit that the epidemic of French boils was the harbinger of a vicious outbreak of bubonic plague.

Now began an exodus of the rich who sought to escape the plague by retiring to their country houses or moving to other cities. Some wealthy antirepublicans took advantage of the opportunity to join Piero de' Medici in Rome. Distress and dread were written on every face. Many died of fright as the number of plague victims rose to a hundred a day. Drawing on his medical knowledge Savonarola wrote and quickly printed a pamphlet "On the Prevention of the Plague" which was distributed in thousands of copies. The burden of Fra Girolamo's advice was bodily cleanliness and the extermination of the rats which, carried from far and wide by the flood waters, had come to nest and breed in the inundated sections of the city. Yet, sensible as the advice may have been, it did not provide an adequate remedy. The plague got worse, one neighboring county after the other was contaminated. Unwittingly, the people themselves were responsible for spreading the contagion.

To avoid panic in daytime, the dead were collected in the night. After sunset carts circulated through Florence with attendants ringing a bell and calling: "Throw your dead into the street!" When corpses were brought to the door, the bearers picked them up with thongs and trundled them off to the riverside. For those whose relatives or friends insisted on a decent Christian burial the disposal was not different. The corpses were indeed placed in coffins and laid on a bier, but the coffins had trap doors in the bottom. The trap was sprung and the bodies were dumped into the Arno. The river carried them away to spread the contagion even as far as Pisa.

Savonarola had no fear for himself, but he wrote Alberto in Ferrara that their brother Marco, who had become a Dominican under the name of Fra Maurelio, had been sent to a dry clean place up north along with a number of the younger friars after ten of San Marco's community had succumbed to the pestilence.

Bad as the situation was inside the city, outside in the war zone Fortune seemed to have forsaken the Florentines entirely. The commander in chief of the militia, that valorous old republican, Piero Capponi, fell on the battlefield the 25th of September. He was laying siege to the Castle of Soiana which was occupied by the Pisans when a shot from the walls struck him down. On the previous day his biggest siege gun burst and this seemed so evil an omen to Capponi that he wrote to Fra Maruffi, Savonarola's beloved disciple, asking to commend his soul to God.

The news of Capponi's death spread a nameless terror both in the camp and in the city. His soldiers fled in panic and refused to continue the siege of Soiana. The body of the commander was brought by barge to Florence and a splendid funeral decreed at the State's expense. For three days the body lay in state at Capponi's house near the Trinity Bridge. It was then borne to the Church of San Spirito and, in the presence of the magistrates, the clergy and a vast multitude, laid in the family tomb by the side of his distinguished ancestors.

Hardly was the funeral over when a new alarm seized Florence. A greater danger to the life of the Republic than any previous threat arose when the allies, Milan, Rome, Venice, Naples, and the others, sent ambassadors to Florence to present an ultimatum: either Florence break with France and join the League, in which case the allies promised to help in the reconquest of Pisa, or, failing that, they threatened to make war on the Republic.

The ultimatum threw the Signoria into unprecedented perplexity. The councilors realized that Florence would be no match for the unified armies of the allies and on another front battle the emperor for the security of Livorno. But they had to make up their minds quickly: Milanese forces were reported already on the way and a fleet of Venetian galleons had anchored before Livorno to blockade the port and prevent the entry of a dozen French ships out of Marseille carrying the long-awaited cargoes of grain.

The Council voted to ask the advice of Savonarola. The Friar came down from San Marco and disclosed in a full session of the supreme governing body that he was the recipient of an offer of 5000 ducats from Ludovico Sforza, the Duke of Milan, to induce the Council to join the League. From the Vatican had come an offer of double the amount with the same condition. But from Ercole, Duke of Este, Savonarola's devoted friend, came a warning in cipher against accepting the bribes and under no circumstances to join the League. His Holiness Alexander VI was said by Ercole to be fully determined to abolish the republican form of government in Florence, and put his son Cesare in the place of the execrated Medici.

"Have no fear," Savonarola told the Signoria, "the Duke of Milan will not come to this city. His threats are mere bluff. On the other hand, the papal troops are in no condition to embark on a serious campaign. The danger lies in the opposite direction. The emperor must be driven from Livorno. Let this be your chief task. . . ."

The Signoria was silent. Several members of the aristocratic party stood up to say that Florence, brave and energetic though her soldiers were, had evidently come to the end of her resources. "The pestilence is raging. There is hardly any bread in the city . . . The peasants in our midst are growing restless and may at any moment take the upper hand . . . We have allowed these vipers into our own houses . . . If we are not vigilant they will presently murder us in our beds . . . To what a state have Fra Girolamo's reforms and policies brought this fair city! What a happy future we face! We have our choice: death by starvation, death by the plague or death at the hands of brutal assassins! . . Let us end our troubles forthwith and accept the Holy Father's offer and enter his League . . . Then we will have peace. . . ."

Leaving the assembly hall some of the Arrabbiati went outside to harangue the people who had congregated in the Piazza in large numbers, as was their wont in days of stress and national peril. They went about crying: "At last we can all see plainly how the Friar has deceived us! This is the happiness he predicted for Florence; enemy armies are bearing down on Florence, the plague is snatching away more victims every day, the scarcity of food is robbing us of our strength to perform our everyday duties!" They spoke openly of surrender, censuring the government for remaining in power when all its policies had failed.

In the confusion the Signoria did not know what course to adopt. Savonarola proposed to bring the miraculous image of the Madonna dell' Impruneta within the walls, because the people had always venerated the statue in days of adversity and drawn great comfort from its adoration. The proposal was not rejected, but from the clamor arising in the streets the Signoria learned that the people first and foremost desired to hear the Friar himself. "Only Fra Girolamo," the crowds insisted, "can bring us real comfort and raise our spirits."

Accordingly, a delegation called at San Marco's convent, and first beseeched and, when the Friar still proved adamant, sternly commanded him not to remain silent any longer, and thus deprive the people of the consolation of his words, Savonarola gave away before their entreaties when an immense throng of citizens collected before the convent and called on him to come out and speak.

On the 28th of October Savonarola re-entered the pulpit. A sea of faces turned to him waiting for his first words. The atmosphere was tense with expectation, for the general feeling was that time was running out for the popular government and that the triumph of the Arrabbiati was near at hand. What this meant for the leaders of the Frateschi, the Savonarola party, so to speak, was evident to all. There would unquestionably come a bloody purge. Hundreds would be executed or sent into exile and, most likely, the Medici recalled to power.

"I am here in obedience to the Signoria," the Friar began. "I was not to speak to you any more by order of my ecclesiastical superiors. But I cannot be silent when I see so much distress all around me and dread of the future written on every face. Citizens! There is no denying the fact that our city is in dire tribulation. But *figliuolini, fratellini,* my little children, my little brothers, let me tell you. . . ." He could not continue. On all sides men and women broke into sobs and laughed through their tears at the sound of the words overladen as they are in Italian ears with endearment and sympathy. "Let me tell you this," he began once more, "I have not the least fear. No more evil will befall you. I believe that God has some great token of his love in store for us. We need not stand in fear of anyone. Yes, may my very robe be forfeited if we do not drive off all our enemies. I will be the first to go out against them, crucifix in hand, and our foes shall fly before us even to Pisa and beyond."

Again Savonarola had to wait till the thunderous acclamation died down. "First of all you must lay aside the idea that had already been conceived amongst you of changing the form of government. You must reject the suggestions to surrender. Surrender will bring not peace, but a more bloody persecution than this city ever saw. . . .

"What must we do then? We must take every human precaution to help ourselves. We must begin lending our money to the city to the full extent of our means. Be united, maintain justice, let there be an end to the spirit of factionalism upon which our enemies depend to overwhelm us . . . There are three kinds of citizens to whom I address myself in particular: first there are those who were exiles under the old government and yearned in vain to return to their country. Now they are back, so let them be quiet. Secondly, those who had the halter already around their necks. Now they enjoy both safety and liberty, so let them be quiet also. Third, there are those who are plotting. These must be watched. They must be prevented from carrying out their knavish conspiracies. . . .

"But above all, let us return to the Lord. Florence still clings to its vices. There is still a great deal of gambling and blasphemy in our midst. Do you not realize that these things draw the scourge of God upon us? Cleanse your city! Purify your hearts! Remember the many tears you shed in this church on the sixth of November two years ago, and how the revolution took place the same day, and you were made free [He refers to the expulsion of the Medici]. Remember how I prevailed on King Charles to depart from Florence, and when he returned from Naples, how I went at full speed to his camp and threatened him, for which reason he left us unharmed . . . Have the same faith again which you showed two years ago. You need fear nothing if you return to the Lord. Arrange for a great procession in which you will all be united and give the world a mighty sign of your devotion to Christ the King of Florence, and to all our enemies an assurance that you are one people whom nothing can divert from doing their duty. . . ."

Although the danger was still great, the people were mightily encouraged by Savonarola's words in spite of the fact that the Arrabbiati dismissed his sermon as demagogy and rabble-rousing. It seemed as if they actually took delight in stressing the dangers in which Florence found itself by pointing to the fact that the food supply was now totally exhausted. The Venetian galleons prevented the entry into Livorno of the French grain ships and, most perilous of all, the road between Florence and its harbor city had been cut by the military forces of the Emperor Maximilian. Florence was isolated and Florence was starving. The popular government's fall could not much longer be delayed, certainly not by what the Arrabbiati called "the meaningless, asinine discourses" of Fra Girolamo.

In these circumstances the authorities, as a last resort, decided to bring the statue of the Madonna dell' Impruneta within the walls. This was a serious step which all Florence knew should not be taken lightly or frivolously. Only when they found themselves in the direst extremity and were at the same time in a deeply penitent mood had they a warrant to disturb the Madonna dell' Impruneta and ask her to plead for them in heaven to turn disaster away. The historical records showed that on three or four occasions during the past two centuries, when Florence suffered flood or pestilence or threat of war, the Gracious Mother had brought help and healing. When were the Florentines in more need of her pleading than now?

On the evening of the 29th of October the tabernacle containing the miraculous image was taken from its chapel at Impruneta, six miles on the road to Rome and brought to the Church of San Gaggio outside the walls near the San Piero gate. During the night that followed the heads of the most prominent families stood guard over the tabernacle with drawn swords while priests and acolytes in unbroken sequence chanted prayers of intercession.

Morning broke on the dreariest scene ever witnessed in Florence. The pestilence had snatched away an unusually large number in the night. Everywhere the monks could be seen carrying off the corpses to purify the city in anticipation of bringing in the statue of the Madonna. The sight of so many dead horrified the people who began gathering early to witness the procession. The rain came down in torrents. Thunder rolled incessantly as if a mighty cannonade roared on high. Sheet lightning colored the murky atmosphere with a lurid glow. But worst of all was the intelligence which spread rapidly from street to street and from house to house: the grain ships had been driven off by a stormwind.

"Should we not postpone the procession till tomorrow?" Savonarola was asked. "Heaven itself seems to order us to delay."

"No," replied the Friar, "it is in the greatest need that the divine power draws nigh. We will bring in the Madonna now and, believe me on my word the whole aspect of the city will change. The sun will come out to greet the Queen of Heaven. Before noon all dangers will be dissipated. . . ."

"But Fra Girolamo," the people objected, "what good will it do even if the sun shines, the French grain ships are far out at sea. Perhaps they are wrecked or sunk. We are without bread. We have lost hope. Nothing can save us now!"

At nine o'clock sharp the procession entered the San Piero gate. First came, borne by four angels, a delicate marble statue of the infant Jesus, carved by Donatello and supported by twelve strong men. The statue's right hand was raised in benediction, the other hand pointed to the cross and the crown of thorns and the nails lying at its feet. As far as the eye could reach, beyond the river and the gardens of the Pitti Palace, could be seen a procession of monks, nuns, priests, the guilds and corporations, walking four abreast. Not a word was spoken. Not even a chant was heard. In deference to an ancient tradition the procession was to be held in perfect silence.

As the statue came upon the bridge, and thereby entered Florence proper, the rain suddenly stopped. Before it was halfway the

Ponte Vecchio, the clouds parted and the sun shone forth in all its golden brilliance.

Following the statue came the mysterious-looking Companies of Discipline, all wearing a garb which concealed the whole head and face except the eyes. These disciplinarians were private citizens who had made a vow to perform acts of charity and to praise God by their works. There were many wealthy persons amongst them and a great many youths who had been organized by Savonarola into companies and clubs. All wore the same white shroud on this occasion and were in this way unknown even to those walking by their sides.

Then came the Franciscans, clad (in that age) in grey, the knotted cord around their waists and the wooden sandals under their feet. Following the Franciscans, the Carmelites, and the Servites walked the Dominicans. Those of Fiesole passed first. Then those of Lucca, a long train of black mantles over white scapularies. When the Luchese had gone by, the friars of San Marco, about three hundred in number, hove in sight. At the end of this group appeared Fra Girolamo Savonarola, alone, eyes cast down, his hands deep in his sleeves, his mantle worn quite threadbare, nothing really remarkable about him, just one more monk among thousands of others. But the deep silence of the onlookers was broken. A murmur passed through the crowds: "Fra Girolamo, Fra Girolamo!" Many bent the knee at his passage, but there were also some hisses and catcalls as he turned up the Por' Santa Maria, the street which leads directly into the Piazza della Signoria. At this point a group of Arrabbiati had taken up their position to watch the procession. Some of the boldest ran up to the Friar and spat upon his clothes and his face, but he, as if he noticed them not, continued on his way unperturbed and imperturbable.

Then more monks, Humbled Brethren from All Souls' Convent, white-garbed Benedictines, Vallombrosans, Augustinians from San Spirito and San Gallo, till at last there followed the secular clergy and the members of the twenty-one corporations and guilds, all under their own banners, and finally the Canons of the Duomo.

At last came the mysterious image of the Madonna dell' Impruneta. At its approach all the people knelt down or prostrated themselves by touching their heads on the pavement. The statue was invisible. Enclosed in a tabernacle which had not been opened for 500 years, the boxlike shrine was borne on the shoulders of twelve carriers by means of long staves of silver passed through rings in the manner of the Ark of the Covenant which the Jews under Moses and Joshua brought from the Sinaian desert into the Land of Canaan. Not only was the miraculous statue invisible but the tabernacle in which it was enclosed was also hidden from view by veils and curtains and mantles richly stitched with gold and set with precious stones.

According to tradition the costliest of the veils enveloping the tabernacle was woven by a poor abbess and her nuns who, having no money to buy brocades, embroidered it and adorned it with their prayers. One day, a thousand years before, two beautiful angels brought the prayers back from heaven in the form of an incredibly gorgeous veil, draped it around the tabernacle in full view of all the people gathered in the Piazza della Signoria, and then spreading out their wings vanished in the blue.

In the inner shrine of the tabernacle stood the statue which was found ages ago in the soil of Impruneta. But no man now living had ever touched it or seen it. In fact there was a saying current that whoever touched the statue would be instantly killed.

Before every church the tabernacle stopped a minute. There was difficulty at times to advance through the close-packed multitudes who deposited their alms on the altars erected in front of the churches. But when the head of the procession had crossed the Piazza della Signoria and was about to turn into the Via Calzaioli leading to the Duomo Cathedral, progress became quite impossible. The procession virtually broke up as men and women crowded forward to meet a man on horseback who came riding down the street waving an olive palm above his head.

"I have news! I have good news!" shouted the rider. He was instantly surrounded and compelled to dismount. But he would not answer the people. Not until he was brought to the Loggia de' Lanzi, where the Gonfaloniers, the chief magistrates, sat watching the procession, did he speak: "Magnificent Signori! I have to deliver you the news that the road to Livorno was opened by the Florentine troops and that the emperor's army is in full flight . . . And that is not all! . . . Magnificent Signori, the galleys from France loaded with grain, men and weapons, have safely arrived in the port of Livorno last evening. The enemy's fleet was driven off by a strong wind. . . . The first wagonloads of food are on their way to Florence. They ought to arrive here in a few hours' time!"

The news spread like wildfire. The people, as far back on the route of the procession as the Arno bridge, broke into song . . . and dance. The tumult was densest around Savonarola. A heaven-rending shout went up: "Fra Girolamo to the head of the procession! Fra Girolamo to the front! Fra Girolamo in the lead!"

Tears streaming down his face, Savonarola urged the people to proceed with dignity and calm to the Duomo for a service of thanksgiving. When the Friar passed the Loggia, the Gonfaloniers and the Syndics rose to their feet, swept off their hats, and bowed low.

Immediately after the service, while the people streamed into the streets to rejoice and sing and dance, the Friar and his monks returned to San Marco. On their way to the convent they were inundated with dirt thrown by a band of Compagnacci, Doffo Spini's ruffians, who had climbed on the roofs to carry out their ignominious depradation and to vent their disappointment over the city's deliverance, on the man whose prediction had come true.

Chapter X

The Pyramid of Vanities:

Tragedy in the Vatican:

Savonarola Excommunicated

A SCHEME of political reconstruction apart from religion was inconceivable to Savonarola. There could be no lasting change for the better, he felt, no life-giving impulse to the new order of things without a living faith springing up in the hearts of the citizens. If such an all-pervading faith did not come into existence and manifest itself in deeds and action, the mass of the people, he feared, would be in grave danger of slipping back into moral numbness and lethargy.

The first thing needful therefore was individual conversion, personal regeneration. Each soul must be sought, and was sought by Savonarola, lest it be shipwrecked. The flower of personal faith was to blossom forth first in the individual, then in the family, then in the commonwealth and ultimately in the whole world. Savonarola looked upon the Florentines as a people with a peculiar destiny, as a nation set aside to be an example in righteous living to all Italy. For this reason individual faith must not quietistically or self-indulgently be allowed to rest in God or itself. It must be given collective meaningfulness by being integrated with contemporary social responsibilities. People who were not believers must be able to learn and to assess the character and the purposes of the Christian man's God by the way his followers behaved as a group

228

and by the contribution they made to the welfare of the community. Christian thinking and planning must be given a sense of direction. In order to merit the name of Christians the people must be confronted with Jesus' own searching question in the Sermon on the Mount: "What do ye do *more* than others?" There must also come some judicious stimulation. Savonarola had brought the horse to the water, so to speak. He will now take a further step. He will "put the horse's head into the trough in the hope that it will like the water after drinking deeply of it."

Whether he made a mistake in doing so, is not for us to say. Savonarola belonged to an age which was ill-furnished with knowledge and instruments. There is no doubt that he was very confused at times in that great confused gulf stream of humanity and history called the Renaissance when the whole intellectual fabric of the time was shaken to its foundations. But he was ahead of his time in an intuitive sentiment that the Christian life must rid itself of the dichotomy of sacred and secular. He saw the contrasts between the ways of the world and the way of Christ, and the contrast frightened him.

In taking the next step Savonarola was aware that a hard struggle loomed ahead. It was more than a presentiment. Through all his thoughts was woven the absolute certainty that a dire, harrowing fate awaited him. Terrible must have been the wrestlings and questionings of this strong-fibered intellect, alone and disinterested save in the triumph of right. He nevertheless stood forth manfully, through and through illumined by the Spirit's reckless courage. Now at last he became the true prophet. For what matters it, in the last analysis, if the prophet goes down in the struggle for the people's souls? So long as the fire of God is thrown into the world!

Obedient to the Pope's injunction not to preach, Savonarola was replaced in the Duomo's pulpit by his disciple Fra Domenico Buonvicini. In the course of January, 1497, Domenico called on the citizens to give conclusive evidence of their resolve to make Florence the cleanest, most Christian community in the world, both outwardly and inwardly. This could be accomplished, said Fra Domenico, by ridding the city and its homes of smut, vanity, and frivolity of which there was still known to be an inordinate amount hidden in secret places.

Florence was asked to make a great and solemn sacrifice. Obscene literature, pornographic pictures and paintings, marble statues of lewd posture, mechanized dolls of impure gesturing, as well as all articles apt or calculated to excite lust, perversity and evil thoughts were to be collected in the middle of the Piazza and given over to destruction. As the date for this display of mass austerity, the last day before Lent had been selected. Formerly on that day all moral restraint was thrown to the wind. A wave of licentiousness and immorality swept the city involving high and low, rich and poor, old and young in an unbridled twenty-four-hour orgy of dissipation. Through his spokesman, Savonarola invited the citizens to make a voluntary repudiation of this ancient erotic paganistic festival. He wanted the people to make an act of affirmation.

The response to the Friar's call was favorable beyond all expectations. Members of the disciplined youth squads went from house to house, the mansions of the rich not excluded, collecting the offensive articles. The objects were loaded in baskets and carried to the grand square where a guard was placed over them till the day of the holocaust. In the event of compliance with a request to surrender sundry vanities, Fra Girolamo authorized his young men to pronounce a benediction of his own composition on the houses they visited.

With the approval and support of the Grand Council, where his friend Francesco Valori was presiding, Savonarola caused an enormous octagonal-shaped pyramid to be erected in the Piazza, 60 feet high and 240 feet in circumference, divided into fifteen stories or superimposed compartments. This was the famous pyramid of vanities, which, when seen retroactively, also represents the highwater mark of Savonarola's reforming endeavors. Into the pyramid's compartments went the collected vanities: mirrors, love philters, aphrodisiac herbs, masks, false hair, rouge-pots, beauty lotions, face powders, perfumes, transparent garments, costumes used in masquerades, playing cards and dice, and certain musical instruments whose tone was deemed to be of an excitant nature, furthermore: some illustrated works by Boccaccio and Petrarch, books on astrology, witchcraft, necromancy, and devil worship, amulets of indecent shape and pile upon pile of immodest pictures and paintings of prominent Florentine ladies in the nude, some, it is said, by the greatest artists of the age.

On top of the pyramid stood a huge canvas called "Carnival," probably from the hand of San Marco's monk-painter, Fra Bartolomeo. It showed a hideous, unclean monster representing in its traits and posture all the abominations, blasphemies, vice and iniquity which formerly held the Florentine people in thrall.

Long before the appointed day of the holocaust all the pyramid's compartments were crammed from top to bottom. The structure and its contents looked so impressive—and valuable—that the Venetian ambassador on behalf of his city's merchants offered Savonarola 20,000 gold ducats. It goes without saying that the offer was indignantly rejected. In fact to shame the ambassador his own portrait was added to the pile.

At last came the day of the sacrifice. On Shrove Tuesday, February 7, 1497, the Duomo's doors opened at the crack of dawn and Savonarola celebrated Mass in the presence of thousands of persons. After breakfast, the sacrifice of the vanities got under way. A vast host of children, singing a new hymn specially written and set to music for the occasion by Fra Benivieni, led the way to the Piazza. Young men and boys belonging to the youth companies went around among the spectators with collection plates taking up contributions for the charities of the Good Men of St. Martin, a society of laymen which devoted itself to helping the poor. Mindful of the slanders circulated by Fra Mariano about Savonarola enriching himself with money obtained for priestly absolution in the confession booth, the Friar had issued strict orders not to ask for anything in support of his own convent of San Marco or any of its eleemosynary enterprises. All the contemporary historians report that the alms collectors got more gold on that day than throughout the whole year.

When the procession reached the Piazza, the *regulatori,* or traffic cops, members of one of the youth organizations specially trained to handle large crowds, ranged the public in front of the Signoria Palace and in a quadrangle along the other sides of the square. The smallest children were given seats in the Loggia de' Lanzi so that they might look over the heads of the crowds at the unusual pyrotechnical show about to commence.

At a given signal the guards advanced with flaming torches, the militia's silver trumpets sounded the charge, the bells in the Signoria tower began to peal, and the pile of vanities was set on fire. As the pyramid's crossbeams had been copiously sprinkled with gunpowder and smeared with pitch, the smoke and flames shot up instantly and a mighty shout went up from the multitude.

It was indeed a grandiose spectacle. Each time the flames reached a higher story, the people waited breathlessly for the combustibles to explode. When they did there was a new bedlam of jubilation and so fifteen times in succession till the whole structure was one crackling, roaring, exploding pillar of fire.

Such was the burning of the vanities or, as they were also called, the *anathemas,* because of their forbidden nature and evil influence. Even if it was a day of feasting and rejoicing for the Florentines, it stood in stark contrast with the explosion of ribaldry and vulgarity formerly associated with Shrove Tuesday's public celebrations. Not once, it is said, were Lorenzo's vile ditties heard in the streets where formerly they were on everybody's tongue. No blasphemy, no fights, no drunken brawling, or any untoward incident marred the day. . . .

But there is also a less happy side to that seventh of February. When Savonarola and a handful of his friars made their way back to San Marco after attending Vespers in the Church of Santa Maria Novella, a band of young men attacked them. The ribalds followed the monks home and hung around the convent singing obscene songs far into the night and did not leave until they had sprinkled some evil-smelling concoction which diffused an offensive odor inside San Marco's monastery and throughout the neighborhood.

Under the same heading falls the denunciation of Savonarola as a fanatic and a barbarian by his enemies and by certain modern *Kultur* historians. He has been placed on a par with the Vandals, with the iconoclasts of Byzantium, and with the image breakers of the Netherlands of Reformation times. For what he did in February, 1497, some historical critics have not hesitated to call Savonarola a "trail blazer for John Calvin."

If the Prior of San Marco, for destroying the vanities, is a forerunner of Calvin, so must be Bernhardin of Feltre, John of Capistran, St. Bernardin of Siena and their disciples who destroyed the vanities of Bologna, Perugia, Siena, Rome, Erfurt, Magdeburg, Breslau, and a dozen other cities in precisely the same manner and, of course, many years before Savonarola fired his pyramid in Florence's principal square. Savonarola set no precedent; on the contrary, he followed an old custom.

It is true, the position of Calvin in Geneva was somewhat similar to Savonarola's. Like Savonarola, Calvin fiercely cracked down on luxury, fine clothes, rich food, cosmetics and elaborate church ceremonials. But Savonarola never denounced any man for heresy, nor did he stoop to invective or compare persons who dared to disagree with him on doctrine with dirty dogs, vile pigs, theological abortions, and similar uncouthness. No doubt Savonarola kept a watchful eye on general conditions in Florence. But he did not go as far as Calvin "whose spies controlled the merchant in his shop, the laborer at work, the fishmonger in the market, the housewife preparing the family meals, the bride and groom in their nuptial chamber and parents in their conversation with their children."* At nine o'clock in the evening all candles were ordered extinguished in Geneva. Only Master Calvin permitted himself to keep one burning on his desk throughout the night. He had youngsters under the age of ten snatched away from their play and young girls from the side of their swains for such crimes as wearing a silver buckle on their shoes or a piece of lace around their necks . . . During the four years of Calvin's dictatorship, there were between 800 and 900 arrests in Geneva, 76 banishments, 58 death sentences were carried out.

Savonarola went to the gallows for his opinions, Calvin sent others there.

There is a good possibility that the references to Calvin as a follower of Savonarola and the Friar as a trail blazer for Calvin, relate to something entirely different than the moral reforms they carried out. None of Calvin's biographers makes mention of the fact that John Calvin lived in Savonarola's birthplace of Ferrara in the year 1536 as a guest at the same Castello from which young Girolamo fled in disgust in 1472 at the time of Duke Ercole I's wedding. In 1536 the Duchess of Ferrara was Renée of France, a sister to King Francis I. Her husband was Ercole II of the House

---

* *Jean Calvin et sa Dictature,* Jean Schorer, Pasteur à la Cathédrale de Saint-Pierre, Genève.
Imprimerie P. E. Grivet, Genève, 1948.

of Este, himself a son of Lucrezia Borgia, Pope Alexander's insignificant and much maligned daughter. The lady Renée called a number of scholars to her court to discuss questions of theology and church reform. Calvin, who was an itinerant exhorter in Italy at the time, accepted the invitation. He stayed but one month and took the road again when the Inquisition broke up the Huguenot circles meeting at the palace. Most likely Calvin's stay in Ferrara in February 1536 escaped the attention of Protestant historians by reason of the fact that in Italy he walked around in the disguise of a Renaissance dandy and used the pseudonym of Charles d'Espeville. . . .

Johan Huizinga, the renowned medievalist, claims that the burning of the vanities in Florence in 1497 caused "incalculable damage to art." In that pile of vanities were indeed some paintings by Lorenzo di Credi and a large number of compositions by the maestro Sandro Botticelli. But Botticelli surrendered the paintings himself. Those he piled on the pyramid were all of a lascivious nature. He had been converted when Savonarola began his sermons on penitence in the Duomo. He expressed deep regret for having contributed to the decline in Florentine morals by his works. On some of the pictures which had passed out of his possession, he painted drapes and veils. It's the same with the books of Petrarch and Boccaccio. Quite a few copies of the *Decameron* and of *Laura* were fed to the flames. But they were all illuminated copies, i.e., illustrated by miniatures of a salacious character. The Friar objected to that form of art which comes in conflict with purity, ethics, and morality, that is to say, all forms of art which were not an expression of the positively religious. There is, to be sure, an element of sensuousness in all art, but pornography is not art even if it surpasses in craftsmanship the fleshy nudes of, let us say, a Peter Paul Rubens. But Rubens is art. Huizinga implies that Savonarola was an enemy of art and letters. Art and letters are very important, but exploited, starving and oppressed people can be forgiven for not putting them first. It was with such people that Savonarola was primarily concerned. Besides, the Friar never inveighed against Boccaccio's text, the manuscript of which lies in the library of the Franciscan monastery in Florence. Most likely there was a copy of the Decameron in grandfather Michele's study back home in Ferrara. At any rate, Father Niccolo knew all the stories, and the whole family admired the literary excellence of the author who, it should not be overlooked, was generally regarded in that time as a fine moralist.

Rather than being inimical to art and letters, Savonarola's sermons on the prophets and other biblical subjects, which his lifelong friends Bartolomeo, Michelangelo and Botticelli heard and read many times over, continued to exercise a marked influence on the evolution of Florentine art long after his death. This is most clearly discernible in the works of Michelangelo whose greatest single composition of the Last Judgment in the Sistine Chapel is essentially a Savonarolian sermon in color. We are told by the French historian, Michelet, that Michelangelo spent five years of his life in the Sistine Chapel, eating and sleeping there with no other company but the sermons of Savonarola. "It is as if the hand and mind of Savonarola steered Michelangelo's brush in the execution of this mighty, breath-taking mural." In the Last Judgment we actually find a pictorialization of Savonarola's Christ concept. Here is not the "Jesus meek and mild" of the evangelical hymnbooks, but a stern, dreadful, godlike figure. In Christ's terrible, almost vindictive gesture of rejection of his enemies, in his facial traits and attitude, Savonarola's penitential preaching, magnified to sublime proportions, comes to life again. Savonarola's sermons made the Florentines tremble, Michelangelo's painting sends a shudder through five centuries of human history.

There is no doubt, on the other hand, that the Friar like all the prophets before and after him was too drastic. Strict compliance with the prescriptions of an austere and high-pitched morality such as Savonarola advocated and sought to enforce may be looked for and indeed expected in a convent or in the ranks of a religious order. In the tumultuous social life of the Renaissance city like Florence it must, by its very nature, remain confined to the inner chamber of an occasional mystic or theologian. To the great majority of the people of Florence the yoke of Savonarola's asceticism became unbearable in the long run. His attempts to have his proposals and suggestions of reform placed on the statute books as laws and bylaws with binding force on all were more and more resented as interference in state affairs, as a form of ecclesiastical authoritarianism or priestcraft.

When shortly after the burning of the vanities the Friar proposed to abolish horse racing and betting as a soul-destroying business, he not only stepped on the toes of the owners of the racing stables he angered the common people whose sole diversion and hope of a winning number came on the day of the weekly track events. Most of the horse owners were aristocrats belonging to the party of the Arrabbiati. These men were consumed with nostalgia for the times of Lorenzo the Magnificent when public entertainments were the order of the day. Thus far they had left Savonarola alone, taking him and his Dominicans for eccentrics twisted with a queer religious streak. Now that he threatened to strike them where it hurt they took a different view of things.

The Arrabbiati looked on Savonarola as an enemy, a menace to the existing social order. In their opinion he was a prig and a crank, and he . . . was bad for business. A man who could cast doubt on the divine origin of property, as the Friar did by saying that most of the wealth in Italy derived from robbery of the poor —thus anticipating Proudhon's "property is theft" by four hundred years—such a man, priest or not, was not to be trusted as a counselor of the Signoria and mentor of the people. He might have made a vow of poverty, but that vow related strictly to himself and his monks. St. Francis of Assisi, and even more the followers of Petrus Waldus, got into serious trouble with the Inquisition over their severe strictures on property.

Fortunately for Fra Girolamo the Grand Council rejected his proposal to abolish horse racing and betting. Not only the Arrabbiati, but many of his own followers in the popular party voted against the bill. He had been warned that a vote in the opposite direction might bring an attempt on his life by assassins in the service of Doffo Spini, the head of the Compagnacci. When Savonarola burned the vanities these men made no bones about it that they would, at the earliest opportunity, do away with the puritanical spoilsport who had so much influence on the government. What alarmed them most of all was the great likelihood of Savonarola, with his well-known aversion to riches and luxury, following up his moral reforms with measures designed to assure a more equitable distribution of wealth.

By way of precaution, the Friar armed a number of San Marco's monks and organized them into a bodyguard to accompany him wherever he went. But against the spreading lampoons and the posting of insulting and filthy slanders by the Compagnacci, Savonarola did nothing. The placards often referred to his prophecies concerning the King of France's declared intention to reform the Church. These prophecies had not been fulfilled and Savonarola was derided as a false prophet, a would-be soothsayer who had been corrupted by French money.

During Lent, 1497, the Friar antagonized a segment of the upper classes by preaching against the wealth of the Church and particularly the monasteries. "Should the Church not have temporal wealth?" he asked dramatically. "To say that would be heresy. We cannot believe that St. Silvester accepted riches for the Church or St. Gregory confirmed her in possession of them had it been unlawful to do so. For this reason we submit ourselves to the Church of Rome. But, let me ask this, which is best, that she have riches or that she have them not? This is a serious question for we all know and see that by wealth the Church has been led to evil. Of this we require no further proof . . . The Church would be better without riches since she would thus be drawn closer to God. To my own friars I always say what St. Dominic taught us: seek to adhere to poverty, for where riches enter amongst you, death enters also. . . ." He appealed to the priors and abbots of other monasteries to follow his example and dispose of their properties. "Give the proceeds to the poor," he advised them. "There is no canon law which opposes such action, for no canon of the Church of Christ can be opposed to charity."

And then came the charges which angered a number of high ecclesiastics both in Florence and Rome. "The priests have withdrawn from God," declared the Friar. "Their piety consists in spending their nights with harlots, and all their days in chattering . . . Some priests affirm that God does not take care of the world and that everything is dependent on blind chance. Many priests do not believe in the doctrine of transubstantiation. They say that Christ is not present in the Sacrament . . . The Lord has given the Church beautiful vestments, but the clergy has made idols of them and uses the sacred vessels for its own glory and the Sacraments for simony. Once the Church was ashamed of her sins, but now she is shameless. At one time anointed priests called their sons nephews, but now they speak no more of their nephews, but always and everywhere as their sons. . . .

"O you prostitute Church, you have displayed your vile nakedness to the whole world. You have multiplied your fornications in Italy, in France, in Spain and in all parts . . . But the Lord will put forth his hand. Earth and heaven, the angels and the saints accuse you and your house of shame . . . O you priests and friars whose evil example has entombed the people in the sepulchre of ceremonial, I tell you the sepulchre shall burst asunder, for Christ will revive his Church. Do you think that St. Francis, St. Dominic and the other saints have forgotten their creed, and no longer intercede for it?"

*   *

At first the Pope paid no attention to this violent diatribe which by its reference to sons and nephews clearly aimed at His Holiness. The Pope's attention was preoccupied with considerations of a different nature. His ambassador in Florence informed the Signoria that the Pontiff was quite willing to help the Republic in bringing the city of Pisa back into the Florentine obedience. The Holy Father had been negotiating with the Pisans, it was said. He had an important communication to make to the Signoria. Accordingly, an embassy headed by Ser Alessandro Bracci was sent to the Vatican to learn of the Pontiff's proposals.

His Holiness, Messer Bracci wrote back to the Signoria, first of all deplored the French expedition which had been the cause of all the woes in Italy and led to dismemberment of the State of Florence by the loss of Pisa. "We are once more seeking to unite all Italy in one body," continued the Pope. "After great difficulty we have persuaded the Holy League to bestow Pisa on you. That city will be restored to you on one condition: that you act as good Italians and make no further efforts to bring the French back."

The Florentine ambassadors were too astonished to reply at first. They knew that certain members of the League, notably Venice and Milan, were supporting Pisa and that in these circumstances there was no chance of that city's return to the Florentine fealty. Bracci told the Pope that the Florentines were not just good but excellent Italians, and that they owed France so many obligations that they could not break off relations. He assured His Holiness that this should not be understood to mean that Florence wished any harm to the League and least of all to its leader and organizer, the Pontiff himself.

"Messer Ambassador," the Pope interrupted, "you are as fat as ourself, but you have come on a lean mission. If you have nothing else to say, you may go." But the Ambassador did not go and the Pope did not stop speaking. He threatened Florence with a new war. "We will force you to do what we now gently ask you to do; we will bring you into the League . . . We know where your opposition comes from. It all stems from your trust in the prophecies of your monstrous idol, that pulpit prattler whom you allow to lacerate us, insult us, threaten and trample upon us, upon us who occupy the Holy See of St. Peter."

"I tried to calm the rage of His Holiness," writes the Ambassador, "by saying that Savonarola was full of goodness and modesty, that His Holiness was misinformed about the Friar insulting the Holy Father, but the Pope would not listen. I then remarked that it was useless to talk about the surrender of Pisa without the consent of the governments of Venice and Milan who were opposed to it. Then the Pope grew still more inflamed. He stormed back at me: 'The League will bring you to your knees! The League will bring you to your knees! You will regret your stubbornness. You will repent when it is too late.'

"There was no earthly use continuing the conversation," Messer Bracci winds up his letter. "The one moment the Pope screamed at me, the next he stopped his ears when I ventured to remonstrate with him. But," he adds, "this the Signoria should also know: the feeling against Savonarola is on the increase in Rome. Some cardinals who were hitherto favorably disposed towards the Friar, are now turning against him. . . ."

*　　　*　　　*

Before the Pope's wrath turns into a bolt of lightning we must bide a while with Alessandro Bracci, the Florentine Ambassador, as he gathers some highly important information in Rome on the daily life and the scheming of Piero de' Medici, the head of the former ruling family of Florence. Piero resided in the San Severino Palace and had in his service a certain Lamberto dell' Antella, a Florentine citizen who participated in all the plots and intrigues set on foot by the Medici. Some historians suspect that Dell' Antella also took money from the Florentine Republic to watch over and report on all of Piero's moves and plans, in other words, that he was *un agent double.*

Dell' Antella informed Ambassador Bracci—the document lies in Florence's National Library—that Piero, ruined, hopeless and without friends, found an outlet for his bitterness and frustration in a life so sordid and brutal that the Romans, who were not easily scandalized, felt nauseated by his conduct. "He rises about midday," Dell' Antella reports, "he eats some tasty dishes and passes the rest of the afternoon in seclusion with some courtesan or other. After a sumptuous banquet, he roams the streets in search of adventure and generally finds his way to one of the most notorious dives in Rome's Old Quarter. Blear-eyed, disheveled and exhausted he is carried back to San Severino at daybreak. Thus," says Dell' Antella, "Piero de' Medici spends his time and strength in gluttony, gambling, lewdness and every description of unnatural vice."

According to Dell' Antella, Alexander VI despised the Medicean chief mainly because of his vulgarity of speech. Once or twice, Piero did not scruple to insult his brother, the Cardinal, so viciously, that Giovanni withdrew with tears in his eyes from the Pope's apartments. Piero treated his servants worse than dogs. Men who had grown old in the Medici service, who had known Lorenzo's and Clarissa's gentleness and courtesy, and who still held Piero in high esteem for his parents' sake, he callously caused to be poisoned when old age or illness rendered them of no further use to him.

Lately, Bracci's report goes on to say—and this was the most alarming part of the intelligence transmitted to the Signoria—Piero had pawned the family plate, jewels and tapestries, and borrowed a large sum of money at 20 per cent interest. He had, moreover, prepared a list of Florentine families he intended to crush if he succeeded in being re-instated. The list included hundreds of names of prominent Florentines, supporters of Savonarola and the popular party. Discussing his chances of recapturing power in Florence, Piero had told Dell' Antella: "Once back in Florence there will not be a soul left to threaten my mastery of the city. Heads will fall like ripe apples and blood is going to flow like water."

When Ambassador Bracci's report came before the Signoria it so happened that the Arrabbiati were in the majority in the Council, and had elected one of their own partisans Gonfalonier for the months of May and June. This person was the seventy-five-year-old Bernardo del Nero, who had always been a creature of the Medici and upon whom Piero could therefore rely to open the gates should he succeed in raising an army and appear before the walls.

On April 20, Piero de' Medici started from Rome with a force of about two thousand mercenaries, a motley crowd of cutthroats, highway robbers and bandits avid for loot. At Siena he received word from Bernardo del Nero urging him to delay the enterprise as the suspicious Florentines had lately doubled the guard at the city gates. Piero cast Del Nero's counsel to the wind. He would not wait an hour longer. He marched to within sixteen miles of Florence halting at a place called Tavernella on the 27th.

As the name indicates Tavernella had a tavern. It was a stopping place for travelers and a meeting place for the peasants of the neighborhood. Piero's men surprised a wedding party at its meal in the tavern. After robbing the guests and giving them a beating, they threw them out on the road. One old peasant, however, who had recognized Piero de' Medici amongst the cavaliers, ran across country to Florence where he was immediately taken before the Council and told what he had seen. The information the man brought spread like wild fire through the city. But there was no panic. All citizens ran to the arsenal to get their weapons and everybody stood ready in the Piazza to receive orders.

Fra Benivieni, San Marco's music master, who happened to be on an errand in the neighborhood of the Signorial palace, rushed back to the monastery with the grave tidings. He relates that the moment Savonarola saw him enter, and before he, Benivieni, had time to speak, the Friar exclaimed: *Modicae fidei, quare dubitasti?** "O ye of little faith, why have you doubted? . . .

"Go at once to the Council," Savonarola ordered, "and say that Piero de' Medici will ride up to the gates and will ride off again without accomplishing anything!"

And so indeed it came to pass. At daybreak on April 28, Piero and his troops halted at the monastery of San Gaggio, less than a mile from Florence's Gattolini gate, now called the Roman gate. He expected the gate to be opened at sunrise and to be back in his residence, the Palazzo Medici, in the course of the morning. But the gates remained closed and the first wan rays of a sickly sun revealed to Piero's astonished eyes a row of cannons mounted on the walls and directly pointing at his men. Instead of welcoming him with shouts of deliverance, the Florentines stood on the ramparts mocking him and daring him to advance. The cannoneers loaded their culverins and stood ready to fire their first salvo.

This was too much for the profligate son of the fearless Lorenzo. He spurred his horse and galloped off at full speed, dismounting only when he was sure to be out of gunshot. He held a council of war and waited the whole day looking at the ramparts through a cut crystal which served him as a telescope.** When he became convinced that nobody inside Florence would lift one little finger in his behalf, he gave the order to retreat. His bedraggled army dispersed before he reached Rome leaving him without a cent to his credit.

In the afternoon of the day when Piero stood outside the walls the Council, which had recessed in the morning, met in extraordinary session, and on the motion of Francesco Valori at once deposed Bernardo del Nero as Gonfalonier. The man's movements had aroused the people's suspicions. To allay their distrust, he had busied himself, too ostentatiously perhaps, about the defense. Once or twice he had been observed changing certain banners on the ramparts giving the impression, erroneous or not, that he

---

* Words spoken by Jesus to his disciples on a ship in the midst of a storm on the Sea of Galilee.
** All the Medici were myopic. Leo X, Giovanni de' Medici, holds a magnifying glass in his hand in the famous painting by Raphael.

was signaling to Piero's troops. But he was not arrested or troubled in any way. When Bernardo del Nero left the Signorial palace, the Council went into secret session and appointed a committee headed by Valori and Tosinchi to inquire what threads of conspiracy had been woven inside the city. The Arrabbiati vociferously denied complicity in the Medici plot now that Piero's attempt had turned to failure. The Council nevertheless decided to investigate and to collect all the information before laying charges.

*   *   *   *

At the same time the Council set the date of May 5 as a termination for preaching in all the churches of Florence in order to prevent the further spread of the plague which with the approach of the summer heat had recently grown more virulent. Savonarola was asked to address the people on Ascension Day, May the third. Though forbidden to preach by the Pope, he accepted, and planned to make it a day of penitence and prayer. In the presence of the whole people he would, like King David in days of yore when the pestilence threatened Jerusalem, implore the Lord to stay the hand of the Angel of Death.

An immense throng gathered in the Duomo on Ascension Day, but the service was rudely interrupted and Savonarola was forced to withdraw before he could finish his sermon. That something sinister was brewing became evident the night before. A city guard noticed light in the Cathedral just before dawn. Some men, who were identified as Compagnacci, had forced an entry and were carrying vats of filth inside. The watchman was severely beaten by the intruders and left unconscious on the Cathedral steps. Recovering his senses, he dragged himself to San Marco's monastery about a quarter mile distant and told the friar-porter what was amiss. Instantly a group of monks ran to the Duomo and upon entering discovered that the pulpit had been inundated with the contents of privies. Doffo Spini and his Compagnacci had been at work all night to make Savonarola's appearance in the pulpit impossible. In the ledge of the rostrum where the Friar was wont to strike his hands for greater emphasis while preaching, the intruders had driven sharp spikes. In the rear of the pulpit, against the pillar, stood the grinning and bloody carcass of a freshly slain donkey.

At once the monks set to work cleaning away the dirt and the rest so that by midday when High Mass was to be celebrated, not a trace remained of the odious depredation. Even so, Fra Girolamo ran into serious trouble when he came down from San Marco to begin the service. Hundreds of Campagnacci rushed at him in the Via Larga and showered him with stones and offal. With great difficulty the Friar's bodyguard cleared a path for him. When he reached the Duomo he first had to go into the sacristy to wash the blood from his face and forehead where a stone had cut a deep gash.

When Savonarola ascended the pulpit shortly before noon, a large number of Compagnacci squeezed into the Cathedral and stood apart in a compact group near the door. Burlamacchi tells us that they were all richly dressed and heavily perfumed and by their insolent behavior—they stood arms akimbo and with sneers on their faces—they produced an atmosphere of tension and nervous expectancy in the vast congregation. Everybody felt that there was trouble in the air. Alessandro Gingi who was an eye-witness writes: "I saw the worshippers tremble in fear before the service started."

The Friar appeared unruffled and perfectly at ease as he began a discourse on the power of faith. "Faith is all-powerful," he said. "It can overcome all obstacles and lead us to gain assurance of heavenly glory . . . We all need to be fortified by faith as things are about to happen in Florence and in Italy which shall make manifest who is truly on the Lord's side and who is not . . . We had the first intimation of trouble this morning. The wicked thought to prevent the sermon, but they should know that I have never shirked my duty through fear of man. No mortal on earth, be he great or small, can boast of having prevented me from fulfilling my office. I am even now willing to lay down my life for it. I call the Lord, the Virgin, and the saints to witness that all things predicted by me are revelations from God, revelations granted me during the vigils endured for the sake of the very men who now plot against me. . . .

"I must tell you, my people, that tribulations are at hand. We will be warred against by excommunications, by the sword, by martyrdom. In days to come, I feel, I shall have to support great ingratitude. The lukewarm will do to me what Joseph's brothers did to him when they sold him to the merchants of Egypt . . . The wicked cry that I am no prophet; yet they do all things to fulfill my prophecies. . . ."

At this last remark the Compagnacci began to laugh out loud and made catcalls and other unseemly noises. Turning in their direction, Savonarola said: "Lord, be thou not angry with them for they know not what they do . . . My friends, I fight you not from hatred to yourselves, but for the love of God. Why return ye not to virtue? Why do you not convert yourselves? For then peace will be with you and God will show you his grace. . . ."

As he spoke the noise of a tremendous crash resounded through the Cathedral. Panic seized the congregation. There was a wild stampede for the doors. Violi, Burlamacchi and other eyewitnesses report that there was such confusion, shouting and trampling, that nobody could hear a word Savonarola was saying. People were beating each other in order to reach the exits.

The tumult was started by one of the Compagnacci, Francesco Sei by name, who seized a large wooden collection box and hurled it to the floor. This was the signal for the others to begin yelling at the top of their lungs, to upset benches and bang upon the doors. As the people fought their way out, the Compagnacci advanced towards the pulpit, but Savonarola's monks and a large number of his partisans grouped themselves around the pulpit to protect the Friar. Other Frateschi ran out to get their weapons. When they, about a hundred strong, returned with swords and lances, pandemonium broke out anew. The Compagnacci drew their daggers and two of them, forcing their way through the cordon of Savonarola's defenders, raced for the pulpit with the intention to dispatch the Friar. At the foot of the pulpit stairs they were knocked down by one Corbizzo da Castrocaro, a member of one of Fra Girolamo's youth companies.

When the band of ruffians fled helter-skelter, the commotion subsided and the Friar came down. Escorted by thousands of his friends and closely surrounded by his bodyguard, Savonarola returned to the monastery. In San Marco's garden the crowd of his

followers raised the cry: *Viva Cristo!* as he made ready to conclude his interrupted sermon.

A full report of the Ascension Day tumult was quickly set to
print in the shop of Girolamo Cinozzi and diffused in thousands of
copies throughout Italy. Three or four days later the Pope and the
cardinals had the report in their hands. The riot in Florence's
Cathedral was the sole talk of the country. But rather than considering the fracas in the Duomo as the end of the struggle
between Compagnacci and Frateschi, everyone in Florence feared
it to be a harbinger of more trouble to follow.

*   *   *   *   *   *

The edict forbidding regular priests and friars of any Order
to preach went into effect on May 5. Savonarola seized the opportunity which this relative leisure afforded him, to bring out a
highly significant book in four parts entitled *The Triumph of the
Cross*. In this work upon which he labored for years, Savonarola
gives a full exposition of the truth of the Christian religion. He
seeks to prove the existence of God without referring to the sources
provided by the Church Fathers and the great Doctors of preceding
times. By sheer analytical power and scientific research, he dis-
penses with the scholastic arguments which thereunto had been
essential to every theological book. The truths of religion were
expounded by means of natural reason. "Not that faith, the spontaneous gift of God, can be acquired through reason," wrote
Savonarola, "but because reason is a useful weapon with which
to combat unbelievers or open to them the way of salvation. It is
an instrument to arouse the lukewarm and give strength to the
faithful."

The concluding part of the work, which should interest us most
in view of events to follow, is a definition and defense of the
Church. "The Church Militant is one," he writes, "under one
head, in the likeness and image of the Church Triumphant in heaven
under the rule of Jesus Christ . . . Yet, although Christ is in heaven
as the true and sole head of the Church, he has left St. Peter as his
representative on earth saying: 'Thou art Peter, and upon this rock
I will build my church; and the gates of hell shall not prevail against

it. And I will give unto thee the keys of the kingdom of heaven: and whatsoever thou shalt bind on earth shall be bound in heaven: and whatsoever thou shalt loose on earth shall be loosed in heaven.' "

Savonarola goes on to say that the words addressed by Christ to St. Peter do not solely apply to the Prince of the Apostles. "God has promised," he writes, "that the Church shall endure till the end of time, so the 'Thou art Peter' [formula] must be held to apply both to Peter and to the successors of Peter. It is therefore manifest that all the faithful should be united under the Pope as the supreme head of the Catholic Church, the mother of all other churches; and that whoever departs from the unity and doctrines of the Church, unquestionably departs from Christ."

The Triumph of the Cross went through numerous editions in the fifteenth century and in subsequent periods. Translations into Spanish, German, French, Hungarian, Provençal, and Flemish followed in short time. The work was thought so valuable that it was inserted in the curriculum at the College for the Propaganda of the Faith in Rome for those studying to become missionaries in foreign fields. As late as 1850 Lacordaire, the famous preacher of Notre Dame of Paris, made Savonarola's *Triumph of the Cross* the subject of a course of sermons. Lacordaire praised the Friar for the extent of his learning which "embraced nearly the whole philosophic knowledge of his time."

What was Pope Alexander to do about Savonarola when he received the first copy of *The Triumph of the Cross,* a work professing absolute submission to the Church and to the papal authority? Several cardinals read it and found not the slightest evidence of disagreement with or attack against the dogmas of the Catholic Church. "Here," Cardinal Caraffa told the Pontiff, "is a passionate, sincere, learned champion of the faith, and no heretic, rebel, revolutionary, or ignorant peddler of novelties. . . ."

Notwithstanding this favorable testimony, it is as a heretic that Savonarola will be condemned shortly after *The Triumph of the Cross* reached the Vatican. By a curious concurrence of circumstances the copy of the Friar's work destined for Pope Alexander and the Holy Father's Brief of excommunication crossed each other. Fra Mariano, Savonarola's old adversary, presented to the Pope such a false interpretation of the recent stormy events in Florence's Cathedral church, that Alexander was furious and dispatched his excommunicatory Brief on May 13. The Pontiff placed the document in the hands of Gian Vittorio, one of his household prelates. The priest was to deliver the Brief in Florence, but stopping at Siena for a few days, and reading there a copy of *The Triumph of the Cross,* he declined to carry out his mission. Gian Vittorio returned to Rome and the Brief of excommunication was put in other hands. It did not reach Florence till the last day of May.

The papal Brief was in the form of a pastoral letter addressed to the friars of the Monastery of the Annunciation. Drawn up in a strange, ambiguous tone and lacking specific charges of heresy, the document greatly embarrassed the recipients. They hesitated to publish it.

Here it is: "We have heard from many persons worthy of belief," wrote the Pope, "that *a certain* Fra Girolamo Savonarola, at this present time *said to be* Vicar of San Marco in Florence, has disseminated pernicious doctrines to the scandal and great grief of simple souls. We had already commanded him, by virtue of his vows of holy obedience, to suspend his sermons; but he refused to obey, and alleged various excuses which we too graciously accepted, hoping to convert him by our clemency . . . He has persisted in his stubbornness and thus, ipso facto, incurs our censure. Therefore, we now command you on all festivals and in the presence of the people, to declare the said Fra Girolamo excommunicate, and to be held such by all men for his failure to obey our admonitions and commands. And under pain of the same penalty, all are forbidden to assist him, hold converse with him, or approve him by word or deed, since he is an excommunicated person and suspected of heresy."

Since suspicion of heresy is something entirely different than conviction for heresy and no trial or investigation having been held, two hundred of the most prominent citizens of Florence, amongst them the Eight of Justice, the heads of such world-renowned banking houses as the Strozzi, Pucci and Tornabuoni, high-ranking military officers and diplomats—Niccolo Machiavelli's name stood at the head of the list—petitioned the Holy Father to withdraw the Brief of excommunication. The petitioners sent their document to Rome by the hand of Ambassador Becchi who told His Holiness that most of the information he had received about the disturbances in the Duomo on Ascension day, was false evidence concocted by the Friar's enemies. It was also untrue, said Becchi, that Savonarola had publicly insulted His Holiness. He had indeed preached against corruption in high places, but he had at no time mentioned the Pope or any other Italian prince or prelate by name.

"Most Holy Father," said the petition, "we are deeply afflicted to have incurred the ban of the Church, not only because of the respect our Republic always entertained for the Holy Keys, but we see that a most innocent man has been wrongfully and maliciously accused to Your Holiness. We deem this friar to be a good and pious man, and thoroughly versed in the fundamentals of the Christian faith. He has labored many years for the welfare of our people, and no fault has ever been detected either in his life or his doctrine. But, as virtue is never free from the attacks of envy, so there may be some who invert the name of honesty and think to rise to greatness by attacking the good. Wherefore we humbly and fervently implore Your Holiness, in your paternal and divine charity, to remove the ban from Father Girolamo Savonarola. Your Holiness could do no greater kindness to the Republic in this time when bans are of grave peril to men's souls."

Fra Girolamo also wrote the Pope imploring His Holiness not to give credence to the false charges brought against him by his enemies. "Everything they allege against me, Blessed Father, is refuted by the evidence of my public and printed sermons," the Friar wrote. "I humbly declare again my submission to the Church and to the Holy Father."

From Ambassador Becchi's report of his audience with Alexander VI when the petition and Savonarola's letter were discussed, it is clear that the Pope was favorably impressed. Three cardinals who were present spoke well of Savonarola. They were Cardinal Giovanni de' Medici, Cardinal Caraffa of Naples, and the Cardinal of Perugia. All three urged Alexander to revoke the Friar's excommunication. The Pope nodded his head and expressed regret that the Brief had been sent inasmuch as it did not exactly set forth what he had in mind. "The Pope is well disposed to revoke the Brief," Messer Becchi reported to the Signoria. Savonarola in turn was informed that the Holy Father was of a disposition to yield, or, at any rate, did not consider the excommunication final and irrevocable.

* * * * * *

Why then was the excommunication not revoked? For answer to this question we must shift our attention to the Vatican where precisely in the days when Alexander VI was discussing Savonarola's case with his cardinals and the Florentine ambassador, a gruesome tragedy occurred. Don Juan Francisco de Lançol y Borja, Duke of Gandia, Prince of Teano and Tricarico, the Pope's second son, whom he loved more than any other mortal, was murdered. Cesare Borgia, who passed for Alexander's eldest son, is generally held responsible for the crime, though suspicion did not fasten on him till nearly a year after the murder. There were only two persons who knew the whole truth, the Pope and the murderer himself. Neither ever spoke of what he knew. On the other hand, the circumstances preceding and following the assassination were placed on record by a dozen contemporary historians and memorialists.

Both men, Cesare and Juan, dined with their mother, Donna Vannozza dei Cattanei, on the evening of June 14. Because of the intense heat an alfresco supper had been arranged in the garden of Donna Vannozza's villa near the Church of St. Peter-outside-the-Walls. The two sons left at the same time, about ten in the evening. Juan, or Giovanni, as his mother called him, excused himself with a remark about an appointment. Cesare returned to the Vatican shortly before midnight. In answer to the Pope's questions, Cesare said that he and Giovanni had ridden through Rome together and had parted in front of the Palace on Banchi Vecchi (today the Palazzo Sforza-Cesarini) which the Pope had built for Donna Vannozza before his infatuation with Donna Julia Farnese.

At the Banchi Vecchi Giovanni took a certain "bully," probably a bodyguard, who was waiting there on his crupper and accompanied by another cavalier who wore a mask and who had visited Giovanni several times at the Vatican without his identity becoming known, turned his horse in the direction of the Piazza Giudei, the Jews' Quarter. The three disappeared in the twilight of a midsummer night. Early in the morning, the Duke of Gandia's bully was found on the Piazza Giudei severely wounded by a dagger stroke through the neck. He was unconscious and died without having spoken a word. The Pope was not told of the bully's death. An entire day passed before Alexander grew worried about the Duke's absence from the Apostolic Palace. By nightfall, the Pontiff, who seems to have had a premonition of evil, began to walk the floor of his apartment, and by midnight went over to the Castel Sant' Angelo which, on account of its thick walls, was cooler, and there tried to get some rest. At dawn of June 16, the Pope ordered the guard alerted and a systematic search of Rome was made by the papal troops, but no trace of the missing Duke could be found. Cesare took an active part in this search. Even the Holy Father himself ran through the streets questioning early morning passers-by.

About noon an old man, Giorgio Schiavoni by name, informed a party of searchers that he had seen a body thrown into the Tiber around midnight on the fourteenth. Asked to indicate the exact spot, Schiavoni pointed to a patch of yellow mud close to the left bank. And there indeed half-submerged lay the corpse. Giovanni had been stabbed through the throat and the eyes and received eleven other wounds. Since no one dared to tell the Pope that his favorite son was dead, the informant was taken to the Castel Sant' Angelo to relate exactly what he had seen.

"Two cavaliers rode up to the shore around midnight," Schiavoni told the Pontiff. "One of the riders had the limp form of a human body lying across the saddle. The two cavaliers dismounted, lifted the body down and dragged it to the Tiber. After it sunk in the water, the murdered man's cloak remained afloat. This the two cavaliers made disappear by throwing stones on it."

"Why did you wait till now before telling us what you saw?" asked Alexander.

"No one asked me, Holy Father. I have seen hundreds of bodies thrown into the river. I have been employed for years as a watchman of boats in the neighborhood. Nobody ever showed any interest in the crimes I have witnessed."

"Did you recognize the two cavaliers?" asked the Pope.

"Holy Father it was dark, but I saw that they wore masks."

At this moment the body of Giovanni was carried into the Vatican, and the Pope looking from a window in the Castel Sant' Angelo, saw the bearers and uttered a piercing scream of alarm. He ran out bareheaded, ordered all present to leave the papal apartments, and shut himself up with the corpse.

"Alexander's grief was boundless," write the eyewitnesses. Reverting to his mother tongue of Spanish, which he always did when under great stress of emotion, the Pope sat talking by his dead son's side: "Juan, Juanito, Juanito, *mi hijo, mi hijo!* my son, my son! How can I go on living without you?" Despite the fact that the doors and windows of the Apostolic Palace were tightly shut on account of the sweltering heat and the poisonous vapors rising from the river, passers-by could plainly hear the Pontiff's cries and laments. By reason of the horribly lacerated face and the circumstance that the body had been in the foul Tiber water for thirty-six hours, Don Giovanni was buried the same evening, June 16, in the Church of Santa Maria del Popolo.

Immediately after the Duke's death an accusation was launched against Cardinal Ascanio Sforza. But the Pope shook his head: "It wasn't my Lord Cardinal Sforza," he said, "for we have been always like two brothers." A grave suspicion that the Orsini were implicated in the murder came next. Their four fortresses stood in the Jews' Quarter and the adjacent precinct of Santangelo. They, an old Roman family of patricians, despised the plebian origin of the Pope and his Spanish antecedents. Alexander's troops, who were all Spanish, frequently clashed with theirs. It was rumored that the pleasure-loving Duke of Gandia had been lured by the masked panderer into the Orsini quarter to keep an assignation on that June night and fell by the daggers of a murderer or murderers in their hire.

If this version were correct, the Pope would almost certainly have declared open war on the Orsini and would not have rested till he had exterminated the family root and branch. The Pope's silence and his order not to pursue the investigation are the most telling evidence against Cesare. For long months, some say a whole year, Alexander refused to see Cesare.

There is no doubt that Cesare was intensily jealous of Giovanni whom the Pope designated as his heir and through whom he expected to found a dynasty of Borgia grandees in Spain. The rumors that Cesare and Giovanni were contending for their sister Lucrezia's favors are without foundation. They arose from the Cardinal della Rovere's never-abating animosity. Cesare, who probably knew the secret of his paternity, hated Giovanni with a deadly hatred. This was common knowledge. Cesare murdered many others in cold blood. But direct evidence of his guilt or complicity in his half-brother's assassination has never come to light.

After two days and nights of weeping, Alexander called the cardinals together to inform them that he repented of his past life. With divine help he vowed to work henceforth solely for the glory of God and the good of the Church. As an earnest of his good intentions he appointed then and there a commission of six cardinals to study ways and means to prepare for and to carry out a program of thoroughgoing reforms. This commission set to work at once and compiled two huge volumes of recommendations for the reform of the Church. These recommendations were not acted upon till fifty years later at the Council of Trent. To this commission the Pope also entrusted the case of Savonarola with a view to revoke the sentence of excommunication.

When the news of the Duke of Gandia's murder and the Holy Father's inexpressible grief reached Florence, Savonarola sent the Pontiff a short letter of condolence: "Most Blessed Father, faith alone gives us strength to bear adversity and to rejoice in adversity . . . Blessed is he that is called to this gift of faith. The Lord in his mercy passes over all our sins. Christian love and filial obedience cause me to write and to hope that Your Beatitude may receive true consolation from God. May the Lord of all mercy console Your Holiness in your present tribulation."

Savonarola's letter was read to the Pope in the presence of seven cardinals. He was deeply moved. He buried his face in his hands and fell to weeping again. At the sight of the old man pouring out his woe in heartbreaking sobs, the cardinals were moved with compassion. They stood around his chair patting his shoulders and speaking words of consolation and comfort. Cardinal Giovanni de' Medici remarked that the Lord Alexander VI P.P. till then a remarkably well-preserved and even handsome man, seemed to have aged by ten years in the few short days following the death of his beloved son. When he recovered his composure somewhat, the Pope once more instructed the newly appointed commissioners to move with due dispatch in the rehabilitation of Savonarola.

All seemed to go well for the Friar. The thunderstorm of Alexander's wrath had passed. The unfortunate part of the story is that Savonarola never heard of the Pope's change of heart and his desire to let bygones be bygones. The calm weather in the Vatican did not last. In a few hours Alexander's anger was rekindled. He spoke of Savonarola's letter of condolence as "a piece of contemptible insolence." He had been insulted, he averred, in his dignity as Vicar of Christ. The particular sentence in the Friar's missive which aroused his resentment most was the reference to God's willingness "to pass over all our sins." The Pope now saw in this sentence an allusion to his own past misdeeds. . . .

No counterorder having been issued, Savonarola's excommunication was solemnly proclaimed on June 18 in five Florentine churches. In each church the decree was read by clerics known for their hostility to the Friar. One of these, Piero Leonardo, Vicar of the Church of San Miniato, before reading the papal Brief, declared that it was "a holy delight" to be able to put his foot at last on Savonarola's neck. The reading was done by torchlight amid the tinkle of small bells. At the concluding words the torches were extinguished and the church was plunged in darkness. The people and the clergy filed out in deepest gloom.

In a very short time the ominous significance of the excommunication became apparent. On June 24, the festival of St. John the Baptist, the Augustinians, Franciscans, Servites, Benedictines, and the members of several other Orders, refused to take part in the traditional procession in honor of Florence's patron saint if the monks of San Marco participated. The Grand Council ordered Savonarola and his monks and also the Dominicans of the nearby towns of Fiesole and Lucca confined to their monasteries for the day.

Chapter XI

The Beginning of the End:
Bloody Drama in Florence: Savonarola
Defies the Pope

UNDER the terms of the Constitution a new Council entered upon its two months' terms of office on the first of July, 1497. The overwhelming majority in the new governing body consisted of popular party men or Frateschi. In pursuance of a resolution taken three years earlier, the Friar himself continued steadfast in his refusal to fill any political office and left the entire conduct of affairs in the hands of his friend, the Gonfalonier Francesco Valori. In deference to the papal condemnation, Savonarola also abstained from public preaching, though he carried on his work as Prior and Master of Studies at San Marco's convent as usual. He persisted in this attitude of obedient silence for nearly six months, till the beginning of December, when the alarmed Signoria begged and finally ordered him to re-enter the Duomo pulpit to counteract the tide of factionalism, civic strife, and public immorality which rose higher with every passing month that Savonarola's voice was hushed, and he and his Dominicans were virtually cut off from the main stream of Florentine life. In December, too, word got out that Charles VIII, King of France, planned to return to Italy with a freshly trained and newly equipped army, this time for the openly avowed purpose of marching straight on Rome and deposing the Pope, Alexander VI. This news threw the whole of Christendom into consternation. Savonarola felt that in those circumstances he no longer could remain silent. The return of the French army was a matter that affected the whole Catholic Church and every Christian man in Europe.

However, in the interval, during July, 1497, the city of Florence will be the scene of a bloody drama which sends a shudder of horror through the Peninsula. Although Savonarola who lived almost like a hermit at San Marco's, was not directly involved in these tragic events, he has been charged with lacking in Christian charity for remaining a passive onlooker as five of the most prominent members of the political opposition were done to death on the flimsiest evidence by the Gonfalonier of Justice, Valori, and the Frateschi majority. This particular charge against Savonarola has not been allowed to sleep or slumber during five hundred years of history and was brought forward again by the opponents to the Friar's beatification as recently as February, 1959.

Let us see how this grave accusation originated and whether it can be substantiated from and by the evidence or should rather be discounted as the calumny and false charges which have not ceased to assail the Friar's memory till this very day.

The first act of the Council which took over in July was to order the arrest of Lamberto dell' Antella, the friend and confidant of Piero de' Medici, who, as we have seen, secretly informed the Florentine ambassadors in Rome of Piero's plan to make an attempt to regain power in the Republic from which he was banished. At Dell' Antella's house—the man had returned to Florence following the Medici fiasco—the investigating magistrates uncovered a number of letters which formed part of Piero's correspondence with several prominent citizens.

Asked why he no longer was in the Medici service, Dell' Antella replied that he feared Piero's vengeance for the failure of the military expedition in April. This reply was deemed insufficient and Dell' Antella, in accordance with the barbarous legal procedure of those days, was put to the torture "in order to make him confess the pure truth." The bailiffs led him into the Bargello's torture chamber and tied his hands behind his back. One end of a long cord was attached to his wrists, and the other end was flung over a beam or passed through a ring in the ceiling and held by the official torturer. Then "the witness," for such he is called in the examining magistrates' record, was hoisted up to a height of about twenty feet. After he hung there for a time by his wrists, which were strained backward and upward, he was dropped to within 2 feet from the floor so that his body was brought up with a frightful jerk which dislocated both his arms at the shoulder. When he had been dropped four times Dell' Antella volunteered to tell everything. He was then unbound and the magistrates questioned him closely, although he could not stand up because of the pain and lay writhing on the floor. The notaries wrote down Dell' Antella's answers.

He began his deposition by revealing that Piero de' Medici was hatching a new plot to seize power in Florence. On the night of the following August 15 the Medici chief was to be brought secretly into the city. Once in Florence, Piero expected to raise a general revolt by distributing bread and money among the populace of the slum quarters and allowing them to plunder the houses of the rich. In the resulting general confusion he planned to seize the Palace of the Signoria and take the reins of government in his own hands.

"Who are Piero's principal agents inside the city?" Dell' Antella was asked. Without a moment's hesitation he named five: first, the seventy-five year old Bernardo del Nero who was Gonfalonier at the time of Piero's previous attempt on Florence, and who had aroused the suspicions of the citizens by changing the banners on the ramparts. Secondly, Gianozzo Pucci and Giovanni Cambi, both of noble birth and wealthy merchants, highly esteemed in Florence society. The next implicated were the heads of two families of bankers, Niccolo Ridolfi and Lorenzo Tornabuoni, both related to the Medici by marriage.

The five citizens named by Dell' Antella were immediately taken into custody. On the basis of the incriminating correspondence —some of the discovered letters were in the handwriting of the accused and underwritten by their signatures—they were found guilty of high treason by the Eight of Justice and sentenced to be executed forthwith. However, in view of the prominence of the prisoners, the Eight hesitated to carry out their own sentence, though the Gonfalonier of Justice, Francesco Valori, insisted that they be done to death without further ado. Moreover, two of the accused, Pucci and Tornabuoni, it was pointed out, were not Medicean partisans or even Arrabbiati, but ardent sympathizers of the popular cause. Both men had for years given evidence of their democratic inclinations by assiduously attending Savonarola's sermons.

Seeing the gravity of the charges, the Eight of Justice proposed that the case be referred to the Grand Council for trial. But on this point the advocates for the defense demurred. While recognizing the Council's competence as a court of last resort under the Law of the Six Beans, the defense argued that "it would be unwise to communicate secrets of state to so great a multitude."

From its side the Council refused to take the case under consideration on the ground that the first trial—which was no trial at all—had been valid and just. In the meantime great anxiety spread through the city. Dell' Antella's disclosure of a new attempt to be made by Piero de' Medici caused the Signoria to reinforce the city ramparts. The civic guard was mobilized, a system of fire signals installed on the hills in the vicinity to notify Florence of the eventual approach of a hostile force, and, of course, every arrival and his baggage were thoroughly searched at the city gates. Letters from Rome and Milan poured in urging a delay in the execution. The Pope wrote, the Duke of Milan, the Lord of Bologna, and very many others. The Duke of Este, Ercole I, interceded for the prisoners by pointing out that Tornabuoni and Pucci had, with Machiavelli and two hundred other prominent Florentine citizens, but recently signed the request for clemency to the Pope on behalf of Savonarola.

The five condemned men, barefooted and in chains, were brought into the full session of the Council to soften the hearts of the members. They made a pitiful impression. For a moment it seemed as if the thirst for revenge might give way to a feeling of compassion. But Francesco Valori was on his guard. He took the floor and in a fiery discourse denouncing the five accused as traitors to the Republic, demanded that the lower court's death sentence be carried out at once. He did not read the incriminating correspondence but gave detailed information as to what each of the five accused had expected to gain or was promised in the event of Piero's re-instatement. Valori deplored and denounced the letters from the Pope and the Dukes as "unseemly inmixture by foreign potentates in the internal affairs of the sovereign Republic of Florence."

Still the Council would not order the execution. Some of the members suggested that Savonarola be brought down to give his opinion. To this Valori objected by saying that the Friar was neither a member of the Council nor exercised any public function. "Let justice be done!" he exclaimed. "Do you not see that by your delay you are opening the gates to Piero de' Medici? The Republic is in danger! And these are the men responsible!" he added pointing to the accused. "I demand their immediate execution and the confiscation of their properties."

While he was speaking a new batch of letters arrived from foreign ambassadors and private persons. All these dispatches contained appeals for lenity. They were read to the Signoria by the clerks, but instead of dampening the heated atmosphere, they aroused Valori and the Frateschi to a new outburst of fury over outside interference in Florence's affairs of state. In the meanwhile an immense throng had collected outside in the Piazza della Signoria shouting: "The fatherland is in danger . . . Let justice be done! Let justice be done!"

"Can Your Serenities not hear the people's cry?" Valori roared above the tumult. "Your Serenities should remember that you are placed here by the people of Florence to defend the liberties of Florence. If you betray your duty in order to favor traitors, you may be sure that there will be plenty to defend so just and sacred a cause to the peril of all who oppose it."

With a resolute gesture he passed the ballot box and not a single vote being cast in favor of the accused, the bailiffs were ordered to proceed to the Bargello to make arrangements for the execution. Under heavy guard the prisoners were conducted to the Bargello which is situated directly behind the Signorial Palace. While in the street they tried to stir the crowd's commiseration by appealing for leniency. But the mob was not in the mood for mercy. The people's rage was aroused to such a pitch that had the guards not protected them, the prisoners might have become victims of the hate-boiling multitude.

The five citizens, who by birth and influence ranked amongst

the first in the Republic, were executed in the course of the night
in the courtyard of the Bargello. All submitted to their fate with the
utmost fortitude. The last one to lay his head on the block was
Bernardo del Nero, who had pinned his hope till the last on a
message from Savonarola. The message came, but Valori did not
permit the messenger, who was one of the Dominicans of San
Marco, to present Fra Girolamo's appeal for clemency.

Fra Mariano, who to everyone's knowledge was deeply implicated in the Medicean plots, had fled to Rome. He was sentenced
to perpetual banishment and Dell' Antella who had turned state
evidence, was acquitted. He lived to a ripe old age, but was never
again able to use his arms, crushed in the torture. On the morning
after the execution Valori sent a message to Pope Alexander:
"The whole city of Florence was united in its abhorrence of these
five traitors and parricides whose execution was demanded even
by their own kin. It is now hoped that the State may be sound and
healthy for a time. May God have mercy on the souls of those
men, for as traitors to their fatherland they most certainly stand
in need of divine aid."

At the time of his own trial a few months later (in April, 1498),
Savonarola denied all responsibility for the death of the five by
deposing that he had tried to influence Francesco Valori with a
suggestion that banishment would be sufficient punishment. He had
made a special plea to spare the life of Bernardo del Nero because of the former Gonfalonier's venerable age and exemplary
life. On behalf of Tornabuoni and Pucci, the Friar had assured
Valori that they were heart and soul attached to the democratic
cause. But Valori would not listen. . . . At Savonarola's trial, it
should be added, Valori could not be called to confirm or deny
the Friar's statements. For he and his wife had by then been
assassinated by relatives of the five executed citizens.

Although the Signoria, with its majority of Frateschi, did not
pay much attention to Savonarola's excommunication, chiefly because the Pope himself did not seem to attach a great deal of
importance to it, there were others in Florence who took a different
view of the matter. In several churches the faithful were warned
to avoid all contact with the brethren of San Marco and their
Prior. The sermons of Fra Piero Leonardo in the Church of San

Miniato against Savonarola became more and more violent. There scarcely passed a day without some monk or priest denouncing the Friar as an enemy of Christ and the Church. Savonarola was said to be consumed by an insane ambition to raise himself into the papal chair, or, failing this, to set himself up as a counter or anti-pope.

Savonarola and his brethren were treated as outcasts. They were isolated in their convent and seldom ventured into the streets where their appearance invariably gave rise to quarrels and unseemly incidents. Doffo Spini's Compagnacci made it their business to be on hand whenever the Friar came out to hurl scurrilous epithets at his head. Sometimes they launched more than mere verbal assaults. At nights San Marco was literally besieged by Compagnacci who painted the outside walls with inscriptions and pictures of the most sordid kind. One night a band of Compagnacci broke all the windows at the convent. Some of the most insolent got inside the chapel where they did a great deal of damage to the furniture, not even respecting the sacred vessels on the altar. From these same rioters went letter upon letter to the Pope informing His Holiness that the city of Florence was in open rebellion against the Holy See.

In these circumstances, the restraining hand of Savonarola having been removed, the moral condition of Florence sank to a point scarcely distinguishable from the old state of affairs prevailing before the Friar began his reforms. "Righteous living," declared one of the Signoria members, "is menaced from all sides since the Prior of San Marco and his monks have been deprived of their freedom of speech." The red lanterns re-appeared above the doors of bawdy houses. The taverns filled as formerly. Loose women brazenly paraded the streets half-naked or dressed in immodest clothing. The upper classes reverted to their customs and habits of flaunting arrogance and dazzling luxury. All that Savonarola had so laboriously and hopefully built up in the preceding years seemed about to go by the board.

Notices appeared on the walls warning citizens not to entrust their children to Savonarola and his brethren for religious instruction or for gymnastic exercise in the youth clubs because San Marco was said to be a breeding ground of perversity and lewdness. Nardi and Parenti, two contemporary historians, tell us: "On every street corner and on the façades of public buildings, churches not excluded, appeared pictures of Savonarola in the most obscene attitudes in the company of young boys." No weapon was too base or too dastardly. One notice in flaming red letters accused the Friar of being a sodomite.

Savonarola's excommunication had been proclaimed in only five out of Florence's thirty-six churches. The churches where the excommunication had not been read, were frequently made inaccessible by young aristocrats of the Compagnacci type. Women and girls, who were about to enter, were held back by Doffo Spini's men shouting indecencies. Girls were asked if they were prepared to go into the confession booths where "the Jew Savonarola" or his "lecherous friars" were waiting to subject them to shameless indignities. Many times the services in the pro-Savonarola churches were interrupted and the clergy and the faithful driven into the streets by cudgel- and dagger-wielding terrorists.

In the course of November Fra Girolamo was urged by the Signoria to go into the pulpit to make an attempt to raise the drooping spirits of the devout who attributed the glaring increase in vice and turbulence to the restrictions placed on the Friar's preaching. Savonarola consented on condition that the Signoria make an effort through diplomatic channels and the intermediary of friendly persons in Rome to bring the Pope back from his decree of excommunication. The Signoria promised and did in fact send a special ambassador to plead with the Pope.

About that time Savonarola seems to have received confidential information from Paris that the canonists of the university in that city, after deliberating for a whole year on the validity of Pope Alexander's election, were about to make known their decision. Who communicated this information to him is not known, but a month before the Paris verdict was released, Savonarola knew that by unanimous decision the Pope's election had been found invalid. The charges of simony and bribery were deemed proven beyond any peradventure of doubt. The University of Paris deplored the fact that Alexander VI had not followed up his good intentions, expressed at the time of his son's murder, by deeds, which were to include a reform in his family and his court as well as renunciation of all favoritism in the disposal of ecclesiastical benefices.

In the first week of December, 1497, the Friar announced his intention of going into the pulpit once more at the express invitation of the Signoria. Immediately the Vicar-General of the diocese, Leonardo de' Medici, countered by posting a notice on the Cathedral door that Fra Girolamo, being under sentence of excommunication, would not be allowed either to preach or to enter the church. In view of the Signoria's official invitation, this move by the Vicar-General was rejected as interference in the affairs of State and Leonardo de' Medici was summoned to appear before the Eight of Justice.

The Gonfalonier of Justice, Francesco Valori, told Leonardo that he had just one hour to withdraw his prohibitory edict and to apologize to Savonarola, failing which he would be escorted to the city gate and expelled from Florence. The Vicar-General was reminded that his Medici name was the most execrated word in human speech. Valori expressed surprise that a member of the former ruling family should still be living in Florence. "Every member of your family is outlawed," he exclaimed. "You will go their way in an hour's time unless you publish a counterorder. . . ." Leonardo de' Medici complied and was allowed to remain.

Savonarola was asked not needlessly to arouse the Pope's anger, seeing that Alexander could retaliate not only against the Friar's person but against the whole city of Florence. In this respect Savonarola disappointed the Signoria. On Christmas he celebrated Mass three times and then entered the pulpit to launch a course of sermons on the Book of Ezekiel. He was, however, painfully ill at ease. Knowing his canonical law as well as the next man, he was deeply aware of the ambiguity of his position. He was not only preaching—which was forbidden him completely—he was preaching under the wrong aegis, that of the secular power. Nevertheless, he dwelt at length on the corruption of the Church and called for a General Council to reform the entire ecclesiastical organization.

Though he did not as yet mention the Pope by name it was quite evident what Savonarola had in mind, namely the deposition of the reigning Pontiff and his replacement by a worthier man. This was not a crime of lèse-majesté or insubordination. It was not then, nor at any other time, considered a breach of church discipline or an act of schismatic design to call an unworthy Pope to account through and by the convocation of a Church Council. But Savonarola had neither the authority nor the standing to do so. He was free to make suggestions, but no more. But to whom were his suggestions addressed? Not to Alexander VI, surely. Pope Alexander, in whom was vested the sole authority to convoke a Council of the whole Church, was not likely to heed the advice of an excommunicated preaching friar in Florence to call a Council that would tell him, Alexander, to pack his belongings and vacate the Chair of St. Peter.

The situation changed a month later when the verdict of the Paris canonists was officially communicated to the heads of all Italian states and the ruling houses of Europe. The Paris verdict called Alexander "an unworthy man," "a scandalous priest," who had "desecrated his sacred office by simoniacal practices." He was accused of having acquired the tiara by bribery and corruption. The Cardinal Juliano della Rovere dispatched a covering letter to the Signoria from his place of self-chosen exile near Paris, stigmatizing the Pope as a heretic and a heathen. According to the Cardinal, Alexander's election to the supreme pontificate, having been obtained by simony, was null and void and could not be considered as validated by the act of homage of the cardinals after the Pope's elevation.

These dispatches from Paris decided Savonarola in facing the shock of Alexander's wrath. In February he said in a sermon delivered before a formidable congregation that his own excommunication was invalid in the sight of God and man in that it was based on false reasons and accusations devised by his enemies. He repeated that he had always and still submitted to the Church. "But no one," he declared, "is bound to yield to demands opposed to charity and God's law. In such cases our superiors are no longer the representatives of Christ."

Savonarola quoted from the learned canonist and chancellor of the university of Paris, Jean Charlier de Gerson, to the effect that in order to escape from unjust excommunication a Christian does not commit a sin in accepting the aid of the secular power. "Unjust sentences are mere violence and the law of nature prescribes that we should repulse force by force. We are specially justified in so doing," Savonarola continued, "to enlighten the fainthearted who believe the Supreme Pontiff to be almost as God, having power over both heaven and earth. It is indeed needful to show him reverence and humility, but when humility fails then we must assert our freedom of conscience.

"Yet so great is the ignorance of mankind," he continued, "that many would not only hold me excommunicate, but all those who frequent the convent, while others, being still more ignorant, would add that it is necessary to avoid attending our Church of San Marco. They do not know what was said by Pope Martin V at the Council of Constance, afterwards confirmed by the Council of Basel: 'We are in no wise bound to shun the excommunicated unless *expressly and personally* commanded so to do.'

"My excommunication is therefore powerless in heaven," exclaimed the Friar. "For me it is enough not to be excommunicated by our Lord Jesus Christ." On the two following Sundays his tone became more vehement and more personal. "Nominally the Vicar of Christ," said Savonarola, "Alexander cannot be regarded as a true spokesman of the divine will. My excommunication by the Pope is hostile to godly living and therefore must be considered as having proceeded from the devil." The Friar called it a mockery to suppose that Alexander, "a notoriously unspiritual man who had disgraced his position as head of the Church by the shameless immorality of his life, spoke in the name of God. It was he Alexander who should be excommunicated forthwith.

"The temporal power of the Popes," he went on to say, "is at the bottom of all the evils and abuses which have slipped into the Church. When the Church was poor, she was holy, but when she gained temporal power, her spiritual power collapsed. She fell into the dust of riches and earthly things." How could this evil inflicted on the Church and countenanced by bad Popes, be remedied? There was, Savonarola contended, but one remedy: the Council. "The Councils of yore punished bad priests, they deposed schismatic bishops and prelates engaging in simoniacal practices . . . We must pray the Lord that a Council of the whole Church at last be called in order, once and for all, to help the good and fight the bad."

In saying these things Savonarola was clearly out of order, canonically speaking. No one denied Pope Alexander's immoral conduct or his trafficking in ecclesiastical benefices. But he was still the Pope. He had not been deposed. Even an unworthy Pope had to be obeyed. For the Pope's holiness resided not in his person, but in his office as Vicar of Christ, just as the efficacy of the Sacraments depended not on the actor but on the act. Alexander, however, did not greatly mind the attacks against his person. What he dreaded was the King of France and the preparations that monarch was rumored to be making for a second military expedition into Italy. So long as Savonarola thundered against luxury and immorality Alexander deemed him harmless. There were countless other preachers in Christendom saying the same things. But the moment the Friar mentioned the King of France in the same breath with a Council the Pope was filled with apprehension.

He sent his son Cesare to Florence to ask the Signoria where Florence would stand in the event of a second descent into Italy by the French army. Cesare was to make the Signoria an offer of territory and money if Florence would decide to abrogate the French alliance and join the Holy League of Italian states over which His Holiness still presided. In the course of his visit to Florence, Cesare Borgia called on Savonarola and offered him a large sum of money, 10,000 ducats it is said, if the Friar would bring his influence to bear on the Signoria either to break off relations with France or at least to advise the French King that he could not count on Florence's co-operation in the plan to march on Rome.

As might be expected Savonarola rejected the bribe and told Cesare Borgia frankly that his most ardent wish was to see the French army return and the French King proceed without delay with the convocation of a Council.

"Do you realize what will happen in that event?" asked Cesare. "It can easily be foreseen, a Conclave will be held, but the Conclave will split into two or even more factions. There will be a Pope and an anti-Pope and the Church will be torn in twain as in the days of the Avignon schism. If you do not wish to contribute to such a calamity, and I do not see how you can favor such an issue, your best course is to advise the Signoria to break off with France. If the King of France is informed that Florence plans to join with all the other Italian states in the Holy League and oppose his passage, he will abandon his projected expedition, and the Church may tranquilly put her own house in order."

But Savonarola would not budge, although new and still graver doubts now assailed his mind. The King of France, Charles VIII, had reverted to his old policy of tergiversation. One day he let it be known that he was already on the way, the next day he would notify the Signoria that he might be compelled to postpone his expedition for a month or a year and even longer. His vacillations had all Europe on edge. Savonarola, on the other hand, could not wait. He wanted to force the issue. If the King of France feared to go it alone, perhaps a pledge of co-operation by the other European ruling houses might put an end to his halfheartedness and inconstancy. After consulting with two of his brethren, Buonvicini and Maruffi, and with the Cardinals Della Rovere and Caraffa, Savonarola addressed personal letters to the sovereigns of Spain, England, Hungary, Germany, and France urging each of them [as was their right if the Pope refused] to summon a Council "with the utmost speed in some fit and free place."

"The moment of decision has arrived," Savonarola writes in his 'Letter to the Princes.' "The Lord commands me to reveal new secrets, and make known to the world the peril by which the bark of St. Peter is threatened owing to your long neglect. The Church is teeming with abominations from the crown of her head to the soles of her feet. Yet, not only do you apply no remedy, but you do homage to the cause of the woes by which she is defiled . . . Now, I testify, God being my witness, that *this Alexander is no Pope,* nor can he be held as one. Leaving aside the mortal sin of simony by which he obtained the papal chair and daily sells the benefices of the Church to the highest bidder, and also leaving aside his other evident vices, I declare solemnly that *he is no Christian and believes in no God.* Infidelity can go no further."

In the second part of his letter, Savonarola outlines a plan for a speedy convocation of a Council, the mode of procedure to be adopted in deposing Alexander VI, and the election of a new pontiff, whom he did not, however, identify, a circumstance to be noted inasmuch as at his trial in the ensuing month of April, he will be charged with having conspired in favor of Cardinal Juliano della Rovere. In his missive to Ferdinand and Isabella, who had just liberated Spanish soil from the 500-year-long Moorish domination, Savonarola appended a postscriptum: "Of what avail are your victories over the Infidels? You raise an edifice without, while within the foundations of the Church are crumbling, and the whole building falling to ruins."

To King Charles of France he sent a reminder of the death of the Dauphin: "Remember, God has given you the first sign of his wrath . . . You bear the title of Most Christian King whom the Lord has armed with the sword of his vengeance, will you consent to the ruin of the Church by your constant hesitations?"

It is at this point, February, 1498, that Savonarola commits a blunder which will swiftly undermine his position and influence in Florence and Italy and send him careening headlong to ignominious death two months later. What was the Friar's error? Before dispatching his letters to the sovereigns, he sent copies to a number of trusted friends with a request to back him up in the tremendous enterprise of trying to oust the Supreme Pontiff of the Universal Church. One copy went to Simone del Nero who was asked to forward it to his brother, the Florentine ambassador at the court of Ferdinand and Isabella. Domenico Mazzinghi was asked to write to the ambassador in France; Giovanni Gambi, the Florentine ambassador at the court of St. James, was to approach Henry VIII; while a friend at Savonarola's old convent in Bologna, was to write to the King of Hungary. These ambassadors were urged to request the sovereigns to whom they were accredited, to write the Pope of their full agreement with Savonarola's denunciations and proposals.

The monarchs never received Savonarola's missives. The ambassadors did, but they took no action and did not even deign to acknowledge receipt of the Friar's letters. One letter only went through, that to the King of France to whom Savonarola wrote directly. It was, however, intercepted in Lombardy and fell into the hands of Ludovico Sforza, the Duke of Milan. Sforza immediately forwarded the document to his brother the Cardinal Ascanio Sforza in Rome, and the Cardinal hastened with it to the Pope.

What impression it made on Alexander can be imagined. He is said to have turned as pale as death when Cardinal Sforza read him the contents of Savonarola's letter to Charles VIII. Then he rose to his feet and went around the chamber beating his fists on the tables and chairs. When his temper cooled off, Alexander remarked: "Now we have proof of this monk's audacity and treachery. We have so far dealt very leniently with him. But now the cup is full. Such a challenge will not be passed over. After this Savonarola will be made to feel the full measure of our wrath!"

Chapter XII

Ordeal by Fire:
The Mob Attacks San Marco's Convent:
Savonarola Surrenders

ZEAL for religion was not the motive which brought the tension between the Pope and Savonarola to a head in the course of the month of March, 1498. At all times there have been men, resolute and relentless in the pursuit of their aims, whose ardor was too strong to be restricted by moral barriers or the instinct of humanity. Against the Pope's intoxication of authority was pitted the Florentines' fanaticism of freedom. The rivalry and animosity between the Florentine Republic and the Papal State went back for hundreds of years. Alexander VI was not the first Pope to be told that Romans, any Romans, were expected to keep their hands off Tuscany. The Florentines tolerated not the slightest inmixture in their affairs of state by the head of another Italian principality. What they resented in Alexander was not his censure of Savonarola, but his unceasing efforts to have them change their foreign policy in favor of the Holy League. They had been the loyal allies of France for a hundred years. They intended to remain so and denounced the Pope's opposition as a perversion of his spiritual power.

In March King Charles VIII announced that he was ready to lead his army into the Peninsula to give suit and service to the findings of the canonists of the University of Paris. The French were now coming to Rome for the avowed purpose to depose the Pope. If Florence merely accorded them unobstructed passage, the Pope's chances of survival were extremely slim. How Alexander could extricate himself from this predicament was a puzzle which held all Europe in ferment and suspense during the first three months of the year 1498. By astute maneuvering and an unexpectedly favorable concurrence of circumstances, Alexander VI once more succeeded in saving his life and his throne. It was Savonarola who got under the wheels, for the Pope made his moves pivot on the Friar's position in Florence.

On March 9, Alexander sent the Signoria a Brief highly approving that body's decision to forbid Savonarola to preach in the Duomo. He made no mention of the excommunication which he had but recently pronounced. He had no quarrel, he declared, with the Friar's doctrines or theology, nor did he doubt Savonarola's orthodoxy or his fidelity to the Holy See. He deemed it a most salutary measure for the maintenance of public tranquillity to impose silence on a monk who was, as he said, "undubitably the cause of the revival of factional strife in Florence." In the same Brief the Pope chided the Signoria for not extending the ban on preaching to include all the brethren of San Marco. They, and especially Fra Domenico Buonvicini, went on as before and used even sharper language. For the sake of civil peace, the Pope urged the Signoria to send Savonarola and two other Dominicans, Domenico Buonvicini and Silvestro Maruffi, to Rome. Nothing untowards, Alexander assured the Signoria, would happen to the friars, either on their way to Rome for which he would provide an armed escort, nor at the Vatican, where he merely "intended to speak to them in a loving paternal fashion and persuade them to mend their ways."

Nobody in Florence believed the Pope's benevolent assurances. The popular party men, the Frateschi, saw in the Holy Father's latest maneuver but an attempt to drive a wedge between the Friar and the Florentine people. By getting Savonarola in his hands, Alexander would moreover remove the most outspoken champion of the French intervention in the affairs of the Church. The Frateschi notified the Pontiff that they were not afraid of anybody, not even of the Holy Father himself or the Roman Curia. That Alexander had condemned Savonarola was his right, but no Roman, even be he the Supreme Roman Pontiff, was going to tell them what to do in a purely Florentine question of policy. The Pope was reminded that he had just excommunicated Savonarola and had forbidden all citizens to hold converse with him or assist him on pain of incurring the same rigors. It was easy to imagine, the Frateschi replied, what would happen to the Friar in the event of his being taken to Rome. Certainly the most lenient punishment he could expect was imprisonment in the lightless dungeons of the Castel Sant' Angelo where so many of the Pope's enemies had already perished. The message of the Frateschi to Alexander VI left no doubt as to their feelings; Savonarola would not be delivered up.

During the month of March, messengers from Rome were continually coming and going. Some were secret agents who told a different story. These men said that the Pope's real views on the matter could not conveniently be disclosed to the common people. The leaders of the Arrabbiati were informed of the Pope's below-the-surface rage and his determination to put an end to the scandal of the excommunicated Friar's defiance of the Holy See. If Florence refused to hand over Savonarola, the Pope would be forced to place the city under the interdict. If the interdict did not bring the Florentines to their senses, the Pope disposed of still sharper weapons in his arsenal. He warned that he might be compelled to close all Florentine business houses in Rome and confiscate the deposits of Florentine citizens in Roman banks.

Here was a most striking instance of the mixing of the temporal with the religious power of the Holy See and making the Catholic Church subservient to the politics of one particular state. The distinction between the Pope as supreme bishop and the Pope as a temporal prince was intelligible in theory, but was hard to maintain in practice. Alexander VI, for one, never observed it.

The Arrabbiati, the party of wealth and property, were not so much frightened by the Pope's threat to cripple their business as by a great struggle of developing social thought which they saw looming ahead. The next phase of Savonarola's reforms might well bring an attempt to introduce a more equitable distribution of wealth. Certain historians aver that Savonarola was trying to force new ideas on minds totally incapable of appreciating them. This was not the case. The reactionary and antidemocratic forces knew very well what the Friar aimed at. When the Arrabbiati fought

Savonarola, they were fighting for their existence, power, wealth, splendor, all which made life valuable. Although they agreed with the Pope to put Savonarola out of the way, they dared not say so openly in the sessions of the council. They confined themselves to asking questions: were their warehouses to be closed, Florence's trade and commerce to be ruined for the sake of that braying ass of a monk? Was Savonarola worth the sacrifice of prosperity? One doesn't ruin a whole city for the sake of one yapping false prophet. The money market has always been a sensitive barometer in the spiritual world as well as in the temporal. Florence's credit was falling fast in the markets of the world. The Arrabbiati were growing desperate. Come what may, there must be an end to Savonarola's sway over the minds of men.

The Frateschi, on the other hand, who were simple and forthright people for the most part, were terror-stricken by the mere thought of an interdict. For an interdict was a measure designed to punish a whole population for the faults of a few of its members who could not be reached separately. Till the Pope lifted the interdict, public worship would be strictly curtailed. No bells would ring. The sacraments would not be administered and ecclesiastical burial would cease. In that age—and for another fifty years—the common people dreaded an interdict more than war or pestilence.

On account of Savonarola's popularity with the common people, the Arrabbiati dared not introduce a motion recommending surrender to the Pope's demands. They were, to be sure, in the majority in the Council which sat during the months of March and April, but they were vastly outnumbered in the city and the country districts. They realized that they would first have to compromise Savonarola, show him up as a false prophet and a misleader, before they would be able to proceed with full force against him. Savonarola was to be trapped into committing some blunder or other, or, by forcing him to lower his guard, furnish the political reaction with an opening to make a direct assault.

The task of destroying Savonarola was entrusted to Doffo Spini who, it need hardly be said, required no prompting or persuasion. He looked upon the Friar as a personal enemy because of his campaigns for moral purity and his preaching against the unnatural vice in which the leader of the Compagnacci indulged on his own admission. At one of the lavish banquets which he and his Compagnacci held periodically in the Pitti Palace, it was decided to launch a war without scruple or mercy. Since attempts at assassination had been frustrated by the vigilance of Savonarola's bodyguard and his Frateschi followers, other more subtle and subterranean methods were to be employed.

The Compagnacci seized upon a rather banal incident which had occurred in the Church of Santa Croce to launch their drive to bring Savonarola to a fall. In that church a certain Fra Francesco di Pulia of the Order of St. Francis in the course of a Lenten sermon had attacked Savonarola with singular vehemence as a heretic, a schismatic, and a false prophet. Not content with this, Fra Francesco challenged Savonarola to prove the truth of his doctrines by submitting to an ordeal by fire. Such challenges had previously been made, but the Friar had always treated them with contempt. When Fra Domenico, Savonarola's faithful disciple and dearest friend, learned of Pulia's challenge, he let it be known that he was willing to take it up. When the challenger heard this, he quickly left town. And there the matter would have rested, had not the Compagnacci brought Francesco di Pulia back to Florence and urged him to launch his challenge anew, and in addition heap the vilest insults on the Friar's head from the pulpit of Santa Croce.

The accusations were accordingly repeated in the presence of a large congregation. They brought about the desired effect. Fra Domenico of San Marco fell into the trap. Without Savonarola's knowledge he printed a document known as the "Conclusions" in which he refuted the allegations of heresy and declared his willingness to go through the ordeal by fire in Savonarola's place since the Friar must reserve himself for greater things.

Savonarola severely reprimanded his friend for his folly, but the affair had gone too far with the publication of Domenico's "Conclusions" for the trial to be prevented. Only at this point, Francesco di Pulia withdrew his challenge. He claimed that he had no quarrel with Domenico, but only with his superior, Fra Girolamo, whom he stigmatized anew as an "excommunicated spreader of false doctrines." Again the matter seemed about to be dropped when the Compagnacci applied to the Grand Council, and found that body willing to assume direction of the contest. The Council caused the disputed "Conclusions" to be transcribed by the government notaries and invited the signatures of all citizens who favored their maintenance as a declaration of faith or their opposition by an ordeal—in other words, a referendum.

Fra Domenico was the first to affix his signature to the petition for an ordeal. His opponent did not appear to sign till the Compagnacci pledged him their protection. They promised that no evil would befall him. They would cause a public commotion on the occasion of the ordeal and thought they could manage to pitch Savonarola into the flames. On this promise Francesco di Pulia signed that he would enter the contest with Savonarola, adding expressly that he acted "on the desire and request of the Magnificent Signoria."

The instrument setting the date for the contest on April 7, 1498, may be consulted in the Archives of the City of Florence. It is hard to believe that the government lent itself to the organization of so shameful a business which could result only in the shedding of innocent blood, and was moreover a degradation of the dignity of the Exalted Signoria. But then it must be taken into account that the Arrabbiati were in power during the months of March and April and that they grasped at the opportunity to bring about Savonarola's discomfiture and possibly his death in this surreptitious manner. If Fra Girolamo enters the fire, they calculated, he will undoubtedly be burned; if he refuses, he will lose all credit with his followers.

On March 30, the ordeal was debated in a full session of the Council. Several members expressed disgust with the Signoria for even discussing such a ludicrous measure. Giovanni Canacci said: "I truly believe that if our forefathers, the founders of this city, could have divined that a like question would ever be discussed here, and that we were to become the jest and opprobrium of the whole world, they would have indignantly refused to have anything to do with us . . . I implore Your Serenities to deliver our people from all this wretchedness at any cost. Let Your Serenities' main concern be the saftey and well-being of our city." Another member said: "It seems to me that too much noise is made about this trial by fire. The only point of importance to us is to be rid of all friars and nonfriars, Arrabbiati and non-Arrabbiati, and to keep the citizens at peace."

"This is a church affair," declared still another man, Rucellai by name. "What do we care whether Franciscans or Dominicans are right. The question is for the Pope to decide. Nevertheless, if it is thought that this trial will restore concord to the city, let those monks not only go into the fire, but into the water, up in the air or down into the earth. Our care should be for the city, not for the monks." Filippo Giugni tried to ridicule the whole thing: "I think," he said, "there should be a trial by water rather than by fire. It's far less dangerous. If a monk can walk through the Arno without getting wet, I am willing to subscribe to his doctrines. I believe in Moses. Did he not walk through the Red Sea dry-shod?"

When it came to the voting there was no serious opposition. All agreed that the ordeal should take place. The historian Villari says: "It was truly an afflicting sight to see the inhabitants of the most cultured and civilized city in the world in solemn assembly of their parliament seriously discuss the advisability and then decide upon lighting so barbarous a pyre." The stipulation was made that if the Dominican contestant perished in the fire, Savonarola would be exiled. If the Franciscan contestant was burned, their leader would be banished. Piling ignominy on folly, the Signoria voted that if both contestants perished, only the Dominicans should be punished by having their monastery closed and the brethren dispersed throughout Italy.

What did Savonarola himself think about this utterly nonsensical project? He opposed it. Pope Alexander VI also notified the Signoria that he did not approve of ordeals by fire. Savonarola indignantly condemned the Compagnacci and the Arrabbiati for "hatching a diabolical plot" and for "disguising party passions under cover of religious zeal." His own followers, however, the Frateschi, were decidedly in favor of the contest. They believed that when the critical hour arrived, the Friar would be unable to restrain himself from entering the fire and that a miracle would be accomplished. Savonarola had himself to blame for this strange expectation. He had frequently declared that his words would be confirmed by supernatural evidence. And so the people were taking him at his word. All Florence, Savonarolians and anti-Savonarolians looked forward with almost frantic eagerness to witness the ordeal.

How else can events in April, 1498, be explained than that an entire nation, just like a single individual, may suddenly go stark mad? Everything that happens in the course of that month of April is bereft of rationality and common sense. Did anyone ever believe that a human being could walk through a fire of flaming fagots and come through without a blister? And even if a man should somehow or other traverse the burning pyre unscathed, what did it prove or establish, or disprove or refute? They called an ordeal by fire a religious test in those days. Great questions of controversy were submitted to God's direct judgment. As in the case of the Baal priests on Mount Carmel with whom Elijah contended for the honor of Yahveh, God was expected to speak his opinion, to render a verdict in such disputed questions as the validity of Savonarola's excommunication, the correctness of Florence's alliance with France, and the city's refusal to enter the Holy League, and also the need of convoking a Church Council for the purpose of examining the Pope's conduct. If Savonarola perished in the fire, it would be tantamount to his designation as a false prophet by the divine majesty. If he came through alive, the opposite was true. Savonarola may have opposed the ordeal, but he had not the slightest doubt that if it took place he would be completely vindicated. Of this opinion were all the brethren of San Marco. Every Dominican volunteered to take the Prior's place in the ordeal. There was even talk of all the brethren walking into the flames together.

The challenger, Francesco di Pulia, was extremely ill at ease, despite the assurances by Doffo Spini that he would never let it come to an ordeal. On April 4, the Signoria received a letter from its ambassador to the Vatican saying that the Pope was "rather more fearful and embarrassed than irritated or dissatisfied." The Holy Father had told the Florentine ambassador that he feared the contest would turn out in favor of Savonarola. If that happened Alexander told the ambassador, he would feel obliged to abdicate. The Pope believed in the authenticity of the ordeal as an expression of the divine will, and so wrote the ambassador, "gravely worried lest heaven opt in favor of so righteous a man as Savonarola."

Many in Florence hoped that Rome would issue a decree forbidding the contest. But they were disappointed.

At dawn on April 7 the Piazza della Signoria was occpuied by a vast multitude. In the middle of the square rose a scaffold, four feet from the ground, ten feet wide and fifty feet long. To prevent the flames from attacking the wooden structure itself, the scaffold and its supports were covered with plaster and wet clay. On top of the bridgelike contraption lay piles of dry fagots, rags soaked in oil, resin and gunpowder. Between the fagots on the platform ran a narrow pathway, not wider than two feet, where the two contestants were to walk towards each other after mounting small ladders placed at the two opposite ends of the scaffold.

The Loggia de' Lanzi was divided in two parts by a partition. On one side the Franciscans were to take their seats and on the other the Dominicans. A small altar had been erected just in front of the partition. All the streets leading into the square were closed by barriers. Three hundred soldiers under Captain Maruccio Salviati stood in front of the Loggia. The Compagnacci, five hundred strong and heavily armed, were under command of Doffo Spini and had taken up their position in front of the Palace of the Signoria. Niccolo Machiavelli, who was in the crowd of spectators, noticed that Savonarola's followers, although present in their thousands, had not brought their arms along. "This is bad business," he remarked. "It is not God who is going to decide here, but the daggers of the Compagnacci."

At eight o'clock the Franciscans were admitted into the Piazza and without ceremony took their seats in the Loggia. The Dominicans were still at San Marco attending a Mass celebrated by Fra Girolamo. Thousands of Frateschi stood outside waiting to escort the Friar to the Piazza della Signoria. Before starting for the square and the ordeal Savonarola prayed: "Thou knowest, O Lord my God, that I have not undertaken this thing in vain presumption. Thou hast willed it thyself. I pray thee therefore to show the people of Florence that thou art he who reigneth in heaven and on earth, so that they may believe that thou hast sent me, and that they may all return to the way of righteousness and praise thee with their lives. Lord, hear us and show Florence that we have verily preached and taught thy truth."

Then two hundred of the brethren formed a procession and walked down to the Piazza. At the end of the procession came Fra Domenico Buovicini dressed in priestly vestments and a cope of scarlet. Behind him, Savonarola, in a white mantle, bearing the Holy Sacrament in a silver monstrance. Following the Friar came a vast crowd of men, women and children, carrying lighted torches and tapers. A great silence fell on the Piazza as the Dominicans entered and began to sing the Psalm: "May God arise and disperse his enemies." The historian Guicciardini remarks that the arrival of the Dominicans made a tremendous impression. "All their partisans were confirmed in their faith of Savonarola's triumph, and their opponents were sorely troubled in mind by the simplicity and the greatness of the procession." Instead of taking their seats in the Loggia, Savonarola and his brethren prostrated themselves before the altar. For ten minutes not a sound was heard in the Piazza where no less than 50,000 people stood uncomfortably packed together.

At about ten o'clock when the crowd began to show signs of weariness, a messenger issued from the Palace and approached Savonarola to say that all was ready. The Friar replied that Fra Domenico would be the first to go into the fire, but not before the challenger, Fra Francesco di Pulia, had put in an appearance. The messenger informed him that a certain Fra Juliano Rondinelli would take Francesco's place.

But Rondinelli, who was inside the Signoria Palace, did not come out. An hour went by, two hours passed. Finally at noon Rondinelli sent out word that he refused to enter the fire if Domenico wore his priestly vestments and the scarlet cope. Savonarola ordered Domenico to go inside the palace and change his clothes. When he emerged, he wore an ordinary tunic.

Again the Franciscans objected: where did the tunic come from? Fra Domenico said a member of the Signoria had loaned it to him. Was he sure? Couldn't it have been the devil who had passed him the tunic? Once more Domenico went back to change his clothes, and this time came out dressed in the ordinary garb of a Dominican, white robe with black mantle over the top and carrying a crucifix in his hands.

"This crucifix has been bewitched by Savonarola!" Fra Rondinelli exclaimed. "He has put a hex on it. There is a demon hiding in this crucifix!" These words brought on a violent dispute between Franciscans and Dominicans as to the possibility of the devil taking possession of or moving into a sacred object. All four hundred monks talked, shouted, and gesticulated at one time. To the thousands of spectators who could not understand a word of what was said, the quarrel raging in the Loggia de' Lanzi was a perfect nonplus and bafflement. Once more Fra Domenico gave in. He placed the crucifix on the altar and took the monstrance in his hands with the words: "I am ready to begin the test." But now the opposition rose in a body and began hurling accusations of blasphemy and desecration. The wrangle became so violent that Captain Salviati of the civic guard stepped in between the two contending parties to prevent them from coming to blows. But the quarrel did not subside. Fra Domenico was howled down as a damnable defamer of the Body of Christ by seeking to use the Blessed Sacrament as a shield to protect himself.

Savonarola walked up to Fra Domenico and was seen to take the monstrance from his hands and replace it on the altar. "Can we start the contest now?" he asked the Franciscans. "No," they roared. "You have touched Domenico's hands in taking the monstrance from him. God only knows how many of the devil's amulets you carry on your person. By touching Domenico you have put him under a spell. The devil has him in his power now and will keep him from burning."

While the brethren were arguing at the top of their lungs, the patience of the spectators was entirely exhausted. It was close to five o'clock in the afternoon. Tens of thousands had been without food or drink from early morning. They had come to see a miracle, what they saw were two groups of monks spitting insults and defiance at each other, haggling and wrangling on points of theology, canon law, liturgy, the history of ordalia, and every other subject under the sun. Being for the most part out of earshot of the disputants the crowd could make no sense out of what was going on. Men began to press the police cordon. "Let's be done with these deceivers!" the people shouted. "They have no intention of walking into the fire. Put the torch to the fagots and throw all the monks into the fire!" Captain Salviati drew his sword and scratching a line across the pavement immediately in front of the Loggia de' Lanzi, warned: "I will run through the first man to cross this line!"

Hearing these words the Compagnacci drew their daggers. Their main body stood in front of the palace, but hundreds of their agents and provocateurs had mixed with the crowds and now set up a clamor: "Savonarola is causing the delay. He is afraid to walk into the fire! Death to the Friar! Death to the Friar!" In an instant the Piazza turned into a screaming howling bedlam. Fights broke out in half a dozen spots. In the confusion, some of the boldest of the Compagnacci forced the police cordon and ran towards Savonarola who sat quietly in the front rank of his monks in the Loggia waiting for the signal to start the ordeal. The desperadoes came quite close to the Friar who did not budge an inch. Captain Salviati, however, caught up with the dagger men and slashed at their legs, mowing them down as if he were using a scythe on the tall grass.

The fighting became general. Doffo Spini was heard to order his Compagnacci: "Get the Friar at all costs! Death to Savonarola! Death to the false prophet! Death to the devil's magician! Death! Death! Death!" Many of the Frateschi hurriedly left the square to fetch their arms. The Compagnacci redoubled their efforts to reach the Loggia. Savonarola's situation became more perilous with every passing moment when nature magnanimously intervened with a sudden downpour of rain. It was more than a shower, more than a rainstorm, it was a cloudburst. In the twinkling of an eye the Piazza was deserted. Frateschi, Compagnacci, Arrabbiati and all the rest ran for shelter, leaving the Dominicans and the Franciscans alone sitting side by side in the Loggia staring at the downpour.

After a quarter hour the rain stopped as suddenly as it started. The multitude streamed back into the Piazza and the monks resumed their dispute. The Signoria sent a messenger from the Palace to suggest a convocation of learned men, bishops, and theologians, to decide whether the consecrated Host could burn without the transubstantiated Body of Christ being destroyed at the same time. The Franciscans agreed to the proposition. Savonarola, on the other hand, favored staging the ordeal at once. After deliberating for another hour, the Signoria announced that the ordeal was postponed. In the same moment a thunderstorm broke over the Piazza. "There is your miracle!" shouted the Frateschi. "God has decided against the ordeal!"

"Not so," retorted the others. "This is not the Lord's doing. This is Savonarola's devilish magic at work. He has bewitched the weather! Death to the devil's magician! Death! Death!"

The Friar and his monks walked back to San Marco's monastery with a howling mob at their heels. In contrast with their solemnly impressive arrival in the Piazza early that morning, their retreat cannot be called other than precipitate flight. Captain Salviati and his men were compelled to draw their swords in order to save Savonarola from being assassinated. "Death to the deceiver! Death to the false prophet!" From all sides, fiercer and fiercer, rose the menacing cry. Egged on by the Compagnacci, the mob, amongst whom were thousands who had but a few hours earlier been counted ardent Frateschi, made attempt after attempt to break through the armed cordon and the two hundred monks who protected the Friar with their bodies. Savonarola reached San Marco in safety. But, even so, the Compagnacci were victorious. They had achieved their end, Fra Girolamo was thoroughly discredited. And he had no one to blame but himself. He had not entered the fire and the people were bitterly disappointed. Their prophet had failed them. They had expected a miracle. Savonarola was a deceiver.

In the convent chapel Fra Girolamo explained to a thousand women, who had spent the entire day praying for his safety and triumph, what had happened. He did not interpret the heavy rainfall as a sign from heaven. He was profoundly saddened. "By the fault of those who feared the triumph of the truth," he said, "the proof of divine protection has been prevented." Everything was in doubt now, he added. The quarrel with the Holy See over the French alliance would start all over again. The solution, which an ordeal by fire would have furnished, was postponed. Nobody knew whether it would ever take place.

While Fra Girolamo was speaking, the Signoria went into secret session and decided not to hold the ordeal on the following day. The city was too excited. If another attempt was made, there would undoubtedly be a tumult, perhaps a new civil war. As a precautionary measure and to put an end to the tension, the Council

voted the banishment of Savonarola. He was notified in the middle
of the night that he must leave Florence within twelve hours.

On that same afternoon when the Florentines were gathered in
the Piazza, their ally, King Charles VIII of France, lay on a dung
heap half an hour's walking distance from the town of Amboise,
southwest of Orleans. He had been inspecting his troops that day
as they were about to start on the long march to Rome. At five
o'clock in the afternoon on April 7, 1498, King Charles was seized
with a heart attack. For want of a bed or a couch, his soldiers
laid him on a manure pile where he expired after suffering atrocious
pains. The King of France was dead, the Friar had failed to produce a miracle, and Pope Alexander was safe.

The hour for Savonarola's departure was set for twelve o'clock
noon on April the eighth. At ten in the evening he had not left
yet. He was on his knees in his cell while a tumultuous mob surrounded the monastery on all sides. His followers, the Frateschi,
had vanished as if the ground had swallowed them up. Disappointed
in his failure to produce a miracle and intimidated by the aristocrats,
the nobles, and the wealthy, all armed to the teeth, the common
people who had been Savonarola's main support, miserably deserted
their leader in the hour of danger. The civic guard presented itself
at San Marco in the course of the afternoon to summon Savonarola
to come outside so that he could be escorted to the town gate.
But the brethren refused to open the door. The Friar came downstairs and informed his monks that he intended to obey the law.
He was ready to depart. He wanted them to assemble in the
chapel where he would lead them in a brief service of intercession.
They would not hear of it. Fra Domenico Buonvicini said: "You
are probably unaware of the fact, Reverend Father, that the Compagnacci are outside waiting for you." And Fra Silvestro Maruffi
cautioned: "Doffo Spini and his men will snatch you from the hands
of the guard. You will never reach the town gate alive, nor any of
us for that matter, for when you leave San Marco we all intend to
follow you. We will either live or die together."

"We will not die," exclaimed some of the brethren, "without
giving a good account of ourselves. We will hold out in the con-

vent till our partisans in the city get their arms and come to our relief. In the meantime, let us get ready!"

Fifty or sixty members of Savonarola's youth companies were admitted into the convent through the tunnel from the Sapienza building across the street. They had brought their own weapons and a hundred extra swords for the monks. The brethren now put on their helmets and buckled their armor over their white robes and took their pikes and swords in hand. The youngest monks danced for joy at the prospect of battle. They swung their muskets about their heads and handled their daggers in such expert fashion as if they had been training for the military profession all their lives.

When Savonarola came down again from his cell and ordered the brethren to put down their arms they refused. "We will be massacred if we do not defend ourselves," they objected. "Look through the spyhole in the gate. See what goes on in San Marco's piazza!" Savonarola looked out. Right before his eyes, the Compagnacci were torturing two citizens, one old man, an optician, the other a certain Fredo Pecori, whom the mob had seized as they were going to church for evening prayers. Just for the fun of it, or, as they said, to blood their daggers, the Compagnacci were literally hacking the two citizens to pieces, cutting off their limbs and throwing them against San Marco's door which was bespattered with blood.

"Put down your arms," Savonarola once again commanded the monks. "Nothing will happen to you for I am going out and place myself in the hands of the guard to take me to the San Gallo Gate. . . ."

It was too late to leave the convent. The Arrabbiati and the Compagnacci had arranged their demonstration precisely in the hour when Savonarola was to carry out the decree of banishment and leave the city. By preventing him to depart at the stipulated time they rendered him liable to heavy punishment. For failing to comply with the Signoria's decree even the death sentence might be inflicted. It was now one of two things: either Savonarola went out and surrendered and in that case he certainly would be turned over to the executioner, or he remained with the brethren and faced almost certain death in their company.

Amongst the fifty who came to San Marco's aid was the old Gonfalonier Francesco Valori. He informed the Friar that the enemy planned to attack the monastery under cover of darkness. Valori thought that if a few hundred additional armed Frateschi could be alerted in the city and brought in through the tunnel, the defense could be assured for an indefinite time, at any rate, throughout the night. In the morning, he felt, all of the supporters of the popular cause could and would be aroused to come to the Friar's aid. Old as he was, Valori himself volunteered to go out and gather and bring the first reinforcements. He succeeded in passing unseen through the tunnel and into the street. As soon as he reached his home he assembled a number of men and a quantity of arms when he noticed that his house was surrounded by soldiers of the Signoria. An usher or sheriff's officer notified him that his presence was urgently required by the Council which was in session at the Signorial Palace. Confident that with the great prestige he enjoyed, he would be able to persuade the magistrates to put an end to the tumult in San Marco's square instead of encouraging the rioters, Valori set out at once. However, as he walked behind the usher, he was set upon from behind and stabbed to death by kinsmen of the five citizens, whom he had caused to be executed earlier in the year for alleged complicity in the Medici plot. Not content with killing Valori, the assassins entered his house and massacred his wife and two of his grandsons. After that triple murder they set the Palazzo Valori on fire.

At San Marco's they waited in vain for the old Gonfalonier's return. The enemy before the gate went wild with joy on hearing that the political leader of the Frateschi was slain. The news of Francesco Valori's assassination served as a signal to open the attack. Trees were chopped down in the Piazza San Marco and used as battering rams against the convent doors. As they broke down, the mob stormed in and in a few moments occupied the refectory, the infirmary, the cloister and the cells both downstairs and upstairs. The monks retreated into the church and barricaded themselves. But the door of the chapel was soaked with oil, set on fire, and the flaming woodwork easily splintered into fragments. Though half-blinded and asphyxiated by the smoke, the monks put up a stiff fight. The first Dominican to be felled by a musket ball was Brother Panciatici. Fra Girolamo Gini, who aimed from behind the altar, put half a dozen mobsters out of action before he was himself shot down. He was carried into the library where Savonarola administered the last rites. In the meantime the monks drove the invaders back foot by foot and in a short time succeeded in clearing the church. Two or three more monks fell and twenty or more of the assailants had been put out of action when the invaders suddenly took flight. But when they were outside, a messenger from the Signoria arrived with the announcement that whoever participated in the defense of the convent, be he lay or cleric, would be expelled from the city. A second messenger, on behalf of the Signoria, promised all the besieged safety of life and limb on condition that Fra Girolamo Savonarola, Fra Domenico Buonvicini, and Fra Silvestro Maruffi, be handed over forthwith. To give greater force to this order, the commander of the Signoria troops trained six pieces of artillery on the convent from close quarters.

In this extremity, Fra Domenico proposed that Savonarola make his escape via the same tunnel through which Francesco Valori had passed to the outside. The Friar was to proceed to the house of a trusted partisan and then in disguise leave the city and walk to the Dominican monastery in Bologna where all the surviving brethren would try to join him at a later date.

Savonarola agreed and embraced Fra Domenico and all the other brothers in turn. He flung a sack of provisions over his shoulders and was about to go into the tunnel when Judas Iscariot in the person of Fra Malatesta Sacramoro spoke up: "Should the good shepherd not lay down his life for his sheep?" Savonarola appeared thunderstruck by this remark. He did not reply, but kissed Malatesta on the forehead and then taking Fra Domenico and Fra Silvestro by the hand, stepped outside to surrender himself to the officers of the Signoria. For one moment he looked around at his brethren and cried: "*Fraticelli,* be not afraid! God's work will go on. My death will certainly accelerate it!"

The howl that went up in the Piazza San Marco when Savonarola came in view was so ferocious, that the monks who stayed behind, thought he had been assassinated on the spot. But the soldiers protected him against the mob. His hands were tied behind his back. The troops closed in around him and the march to the prison began. The soldiers placed their shields between themselves and the crowd in order to prevent Savonarola from being stabbed. In spite of this, the mob jostled the Friar, threw burning torches in his face and spat on him. One man severely cut Savonarola's fingers with a pocket knife. His escort could not prevent Fra Girolamo's face being cut open by stones which were hurled at him from all sides. When he entered the postern door of the Signorial Palace the blood was streaming from his nose. In the doorway Doffo Spini kicked the Friar in the back shouting: "That's where your prophecies come from!"

Savonarola and his two brethren were lodged in three bare cells located in the Alberghettino, literally the Little Hotel as the Florentines called the top story in the tower of the Signoria Palace to which thousands of tourists turn their admiring gaze year after year without giving a moment's thought to the tortures and indignities which were once perpetrated in its gloomy interior.

Chapter XIII

A Bargain Is Struck

Over Savonarola's Life

O N THE 6th of April, 1498, Savonarola was still the effective and undisputed master of the Florentine state. He counted influential friends in the Grand Council, the magistracy, and the clergy. He had devoted partisans and admirers in the ministries of justice and foreign affairs. The overwhelming majority of the common people was on his side. Tens of thousands of adherents of the popular party in the city and the country were willing and ready to lay down their lives for him.

Twenty-four hours later, in an inexpressible whirlpool of confusion, incoherence, lies, hatefulness, and barbarism, Fra Girolamo was beaten down and delivered up helpless into the devil's tearing claws. By means of a thousand poniards made to order, the aristocrats and money bags intimidated the popular masses, stunned them into irresolution and impotence, and plunged the city of Florence into the depth of ignominy. In one single day, though be it in the comparatively microscopic area of Florentine politics, the Compagnacci achieved what in our own flat and aimless time a handful of determined men, more by browbeating and bluff than by force, accomplished on a world scale: the diversion of the course of history into channels of their own choosing with the rest looking on mesmerized or paralyzed by apathy or fear. How many are the cities, no, entire nations and civilizations which have thus stumbled blindly towards perdition and extinction for the lack of a mere whiff of daring?

Not a single voice was raised in the Friar's favor or defense. It is true that two of the pawns in what the Pope called *il giuoco del mundo*,* King Charles VIII of France and Francesco Valori, were removed from the chessboard by force majeure. But after all is said, the very much alive chiefs of the Savonarola party seem to have vanished just as effectively. In a few days' time the Friar had nobody and nothing left but enemies. As in a drama on the stage, the decor changed with the curtain rising on a new act with the actors remaining substantially the same. The same men who shouted hosannah one day, called for Savonarola's death a week, a day, no, a few hours later.

The Signoria resolved to examine the three arrested friars very closely. A rider was added that under no circumstance were they to be handed over to the Pope. In that era of endless intrigue and counterintrigue, the Signoria did not consider it politic to allow the Pontiff to put the friars and especially Savonarola to the question and thus perchance learn too much of the subterranean currents of Florentine state affairs.

To examine the friars very closely meant putting them to the torture. Only under torture were men expected to tell "the pure truth," that is, they could be compelled to say what they either did not want to say or simply did not know. All trials in those days were murder under the forms of law. No witness was examined without torture. Since the Alberghettino prison in the Signoria tower, surprisingly enough, lacked a torture chamber—every palace or aristocratic mansion in Rome had a private one—Savonarola was taken to the nearby more modern Bargello for a preliminary examination. Four members of the Signoria who had been the first to raise their hands in volunteering to examine "the witness," were appointed to conduct the investigation. Before any charge was laid or any question asked, the Friar's hands were tied behind his back and he was hoisted up by the wrists to a height of twenty feet. Four times in one hour he was dropped to within a few inches of the floor, but despite the cruel pain, not a sound escaped his lips. To the amazement of the magistrates he did not faint either, though he was weak with hunger and clearly sick with his old abdominal complaint. The examiners reported to the Signoria

* The game of the world.

that the prisoner had stared them "just as arrogantly" in the face after as before the application of the *corda*.

Guicciardini's *History* informs us that the real commissioners charged with the trial of Savonarola were not appointed till the tenth. They were seventeen in number. "All must be counted amongst the Friar's most ferocious enemies." This circumstance alone should have sufficed to invalidate the trial under Florentine law which required the judiciary to be scrupulously impartial. Among the judges were Doffo Spini, the sinister leader of the Compagnacci, and Giovanni Manetti, Giovanni Canacci, and Benedetto Nerli, three men generally known and despised for their dissoluteness. As secretary or notary functioned one Francesco Ceccone, a common criminal who had served several terms in prison and who was disinherited and disowned by his own father. Ceccone was Doffo Spini's creature in all of that blackguard's unsavory enterprises.

Another commissioner, Piero degli Alberti, was the same man who injured Savonarola by beating him on the head with a stone on Ascension Day the previous year when Doffo Spini and his Compagnacci befouled the Duomo pulpit and raised a tumult during the service. All the others, without exception, were partisans of Piero de' Medici. They had never forgiven Savonarola for his share in the expulsion of the Medicean despot and the introduction of democratic institutions.

Such were the inquisitors who interrogated Savonarola officially for the first time on April 10. That day he was brought to the Bargello on a stretcher. Not that he was unable to walk, but as a precaution against escape the irons were put on his legs in such a way as to render walking impossible. His hands were manacled behind his back. He was put to the torture three and a half times, that is, he was hoisted up and made to drop from a height of twenty feet three times and once from a height of ten feet. He was asked to tell the commissioners whether he was a false prophet or not, at least this is the sole question asked of him. At the fourth drop he cried out: "Let me down and I will write out my whole life for you."

Savonarola was taken back to the Signoria tower and wrote till sunset. At nightfall he was forced to stop, for there was neither lamp nor candle in his cell. What he wrote that day and the following two days is not included in the trial records. The commissioners divided the written pages amongst themselves and kept them as souvenirs or autographs. These documents were recovered by the Marquis Roberto Ridolfi, the distinguished Florentine historian, who spent a lifetime of research in the circumstances surrounding Savonarola's trial and death.

From the twelfth till the seventeenth, the Friar was tortured fourteen times, but the lately discovered documents disclose that he was in addition "secretly" dropped six times. Savonarola supported the outrages with superb disdain and fortitude. He held his head high though he could no longer stand erect. Not a word, not even a groan or a cry of pain could be extracted from him. As time went on, however, his nerves began to give way: the man's soul had always been more vigorous than his body. His resolution remained unshaken and his will power seemed inexhaustible, but his mangled body was now an inert bag of bones and crushed flesh. When they dragged him from his cell in the Signoria prison in the morning for another bout of questioning at the Bargello, he was but half-conscious. His eyes were closed and his head rolled impotently back and forth. He seemed to have passed beyond the capacity to experience or register physical suffering. His arms were dislocated at the shoulders and the elbows, his legs at the knees and the hip joints. He grew feverish under such unremitting barbarity. And this became his greatest fear. As a student of medicine he knew that fever might turn into delirium. He was afraid that in the overwrought state of his mind he might talk and his incoherent mumblings and stammering be noted down as confessions.

After ten days of this inhuman procedure, the commissioners read the minutes of what they called the judicial interrogations to him and asked Savonarola to sign the document. "I have never said these things which you ascribe to me. . . . I refuse to sign," he replied.

"In that case we will continue the interrogation till you confess," he was told by Doffo Spini. "You will end up by telling us exactly what we want you to say."

"What then is it that you want me to say?"

"You must recant, you must confess!"

"What is there to confess? I have always obeyed God's commands. Everything I have done was done for the love of Florence, for the love of my fellow men. I wanted Florence to be a godly city, a city of righteousness and honor. I wanted you, Doffo Spini, to convert yourself . . . It is not too late yet. I pray God incessantly to grant you his salvation. . . ."

The commissioners had not been able to fasten the least reprehensible word or action on him relative to the three crimes of which he stood accused: his political activity, his religious thought, and his claim of prophetic utterance. Not the slightest taint of heresy had been detected in his moral and philosophical treatises, in his sermons and his poetry. His teaching and preaching had always conformed to the doctrines of the Fathers and Doctors of the Church. Politically he had acted with disinterestedness and impartiality. He had never sought to push himself forward. He had sacrificed himself for the people of Florence and saved the city when the French troops were determined and on the point of putting it to fire and sword. In conformity with the moral and the natural law his politics and his religious instruction had been sound, equitable and orthodox.

The commissioners admitted as much when they destroyed the minutes of their own proceedings on April 19 and decided to start from the beginning. Francesco Ceccone was charged to draw up a second report, and he did. It lies in the Hall of Archives of the city of Florence. But it contains not a word of truth. It is pure fabrication and was in fact denounced as such by one of the commissioners, Agnolo Niccolini, a nonparty man, who was present at all the interrogations, and who later refused to sign the verdict of guilty. Thomas Ginori, also a member of the Signoria, but not a follower of Savanorola, declares in his *Book of Memoirs* that Ceccone's report is a falsification "from beginning to end," "full of arbitrary additions" and omitting "many of the most important depositions."

Pope Alexander VI, who received a daily report on the transactions in the torture chamber, wrote a letter to the Signoria complaining of the slow progress of the trial and demanded once more that Savonarola be sent to Rome. The commissioners, the Pope wrote in an irritated tone, were not getting anywhere with their inane and irrelevant questions about the Friar's prophetic qualities and the doctrines he preached. If the stubborn monk could only be sent to Rome, the Pontiff guaranteed that he would soon find the means to extract the whole truth from him. In addition the Pope insisted that San Marco's chapel be closed since it had come to his knowledge that thousands went to pray there for the Friar whom they still regarded as a prophet and a saint.

The Signoria knew full well what His Holiness meant by his reference to the inane and irrelevant nature of the questions. The Pope was not interested in Savonarola's religious doctrines or his reputation as a prophet. Alexander wanted to ferret out the precise status of Florence's alliance with France and whether others besides Savonarola were involved in what he dubbed the conspiracy to call a Church Council and a Conclave to elect a new Pope. Since the death of Charles VIII the Pontiff suspected, and had ample reason to suspect, that Cardinal Juliano della Rovere, who still resided in France, was busy entangling the new King, Louis XII, in the scheme to depose him. In their reply the Signoria pretended an artless naïveté. Their Exalted Serenities humbly apologized to His Holiness and called heaven to witness that in Savonarola they had to do with a man of extraordinary physical endurance and great strength of mind. "The Friar," they informed the Pontiff, "seems to be able to harden himself against the torture so that it has little effect on him."

In the meantime a false report was printed and spread through the city that Savonarola had confessed. He was reported to have admitted that all he had done was for his own glory. He had enriched himself enormously with money donated for eleemosynary purposes. He had accused himself of having craved a cardinal's hat and even nourished an ambition to occupy St. Peter's chair and thus become "the most influential person in the universe."

This information produced a painful shock on the Friar's adherents who were just beginning to recover from the bewilderment and anxiety in which the swiftness of events had plunged them. Many of the most loyal refused to believe in the genuineness of the confession or in the possibility of Fra Girolamo having accused himself of deception. Nevertheless, as happened more than once in history, the big lie, repeated over and over again, gradually gained the upper hand. A great number of people had been sorely disappointed in Savonarola for not producing a miracle on the day of the ordeal by fire. These grumblers now foreswore their allegiance and became even more enraged than the officially styled Enraged, the Arrabbiati.

The second trial got under way on April 21 and continued through the 25th of the month. Although the same methods of torture and falsification of the depositions were repeated, it brought the case not a whit nearer solution. A portion of the minutes of the trial were read in a session of the Greater Council on the 26th. One member raised the objection that Savonarola was not present as required by Florentine law. In reply the clerk alleged that the Friar had declined to attend for fear of being stoned by the populace. This ludicrous excuse was so much at variance with what every man, friend and foe alike, knew of Savonarola's character and fearlessness, that a roar of laughter greeted the clerk's explanation. The man never finished reading the record.

The result of both trials was a disappointment to the Signoria who either desired or were bound by political exigencies and the Pope's pressure to find a justification for proceeding to extremes. "They were completely baffled in their purpose, even Francesco Ceccone had failed to help them with his falsifications and suppression of the evidence. He was dismissed with but a fraction of the reward promised him, thirty ducats instead of four hundred."

Leaving Savonarola alone for a time, the commissioners now went to work on the other monks of San Marco to whom the Pope's letter had drawn attention. Here they had more success, if success it may be called. Fra Silvestro Maruffi soon broke down under the lacerations. The Signoria published a report stating that Fra Silvestro had wholly disowned the man whom he once called father and friend. But again, nothing was really gained by this maneuver. Maruffi was what the French call *un innocent,* a holy innocent, a fool in Christ, one of the poor in spirit. He was not a good student and had never stood in the pulpit. But he saw visions and heard voices and spoke of them as the most natural things in the world. He lived in so high a state of mystical exaltation and was so wrapped up in his visionary experiences that most times he was quite unaware of his environment. Savonarola loved him dearly and was often seen leading him by the hand. The Friar and the other brethren treated and spoke to Maruffi as to a child. And this man had betrayed Savonarola while hanging upside down in the torture chamber by making a full confession? People shrugged their shoulders and called Maruffi's evidence absolutely worthless, as indeed it was.

When Fra Domenico Buonvicini was put to the cord, he proved as steadfast as Savonarola himself. The commissioners urged him to denounce his friend as an imposter and false prophet. "I cannot say what you ask of me," he replied. "I have always believed in the Reverend Father Girolamo Savonarola, and still believe in him. I have often said to the brethren and also to the laity that if I found the slightest trace of heresy or imposture in Savonarola I would denounce him publicly and immediately. I now repeat, if I knew of any evil, deceit, selfishness, heresy or worldly ambition in Savonarola, I would say so right now."

Again and again Fra Domenico was racked but with no different results. The more the bailiffs tormented him, the more energetic and eloquent he grew in his declarations of the Friar's innocence. Three or four other monks were tortured. Their shrieks as their limbs were torn apart, could be heard plainly in the street adjoining the Bargello. The brethren waiting their turn, and hearing the wails and groans coming from the cave of torment, broke down and implored the commissioners for mercy. They volunteered to disown Savonarola formally and on the spot. It was a bitter pill to swallow for Fra Girolamo, although he had foreseen their desertion in that sermon in which he foretold that he would undergo the fate of Joseph who was sold to the Egyptian merchants by his own brothers.

Since their Prior's arrest, the brethren found themselves leaderless, exposed to the full weight of ecclesiastical penalties and public scorn. They were helpless and at bay. They declared that they could no longer acknowledge a master who, as they were led to believe, had confessed himself a deceiver. On April 21, the monks of San Marco wrote a letter to the Pope deploring the errors in which they had been drawn. They had been beguiled, they said, like many others, "by Fra Girolamo's commanding ability, by his exalted doctrines and the holiness of his life and by the fulfillment of so many of his prophecies." They asked the Holy Father's forgiveness. "Let it suffice Your Holiness to punish the head and source of this offense; we, who like sheep have gone astray, return to the true shepherd."

There are but few if any parallels in the history of Christian martyrdom to be placed alongside the almost incredible demonstration of fortitude, love of souls, and forgiveness with which Savonarola confronted his tormentors in the last weeks of his life. There he lay on the bare stone floor of a prison cell without bed, chair or blankets and the most elementary hygienic facilities. When he asked his jailer for water he was given to drink from a bowl which was first purposely befouled. He suffered excruciating pain in the abdomen. His whole body was bruised and crushed by the hideous brutality. It is almost inconceivable that he did not succumb or was driven insane.

And what were the first words the poor innocent victim uttered when he recovered his power of rational speech? He humbly requested the commissioners to spare his right arm so that he might be able to write. If there were to be any more sessions in the chamber of horrors, he pleaded that his right arm and hand be exempted from the bone-crushing and sinew-tearing punishments. The commissioners submitted his plea to the Signoria and the Signoria acceded to the request. He would in future be attached only by his left arm and would be provided with writing material. Pathetically he thanked their Exalted Serenities for their show of leniency and Christian charity.

Lying on the floor in the Alberghettino he wrote his Exposition and Meditation on Psalm 51 which opens with the word *Miserere,* "Have mercy." The booklet is a heart-searing lament consisting of prayers, self-accusations, exegesis, and praise of God. It is the last sermon or meditation he wrote and was immediately set to print and went through nearly as many editions in Italy and Germany as *The Imitation of Christ* by Thomas à Kempis which, next to the Bible, is the most widely diffused work of edification in world literature. The first printing of Savonarola's Meditation is from 1498, the most recent edition in Italian bears the date 1954 and in German 1958.

> "Where shall I turn, to whom shall I flee, I who have no one left in all the world to give me aid or solace? Who will take pity on me? I dare not lift my eyes to heaven for I have

most grievously sinned. On earth I find no refuge for I have
become an object of scandal and offense to men. What then
shall I do? Shall I give myself over to despair? No, this I
must not, for God abundantly pardons, my redeemer is full
of mercy. God alone is my refuge, He will not abandon the
work of his hands and the human being made in his image.
I approach thee, therefore, O Lord, my God, as a beaten
and defeated soul. In thee alone is my hope. In thee alone
seek I refuge. But what words shall I speak? I will plead for
thy commiseration, for thy pardon and forgiveness. . . .

"O dear Lord, my God, have mercy on me! O hidden
God, O God who canst not be understood by human intelligence, nor expressed with the words of man or of angels,
O incomprehensible God, O unseizable God, to thee I call
because thou art the reality, the sole reality, the source and
cause of all reality. Thou canst not change thine own essence and nature. Thou must carry out thy work which is to
create, to love, to forgive, to redeem, to bless . . . Look
down upon my miserable state. My misery is great because
of my sins. I have sinned against thee, against thee who so
loved me that thou camest down from heaven to be crucified for me. O Lord, my God, my Rock and my Redeemer,
forgive, forgive my sins! . . . Deep calls unto deep, the abyss
of misery calls to the abyss of divine mercy. The abyss of
sin calls to the abyss of grace. May thine abyss of mercy
devour my abyss of sin and blot it out. . . ."

Such are the opening words of Savonarola's meditation. No
more passionate expression of the love of God is to be found in
Christian literature. No greater magnificat to the Holy Trinity, no
more ardent and poignant confession of faith in the Atonement
has found a place in the liturgies and rituals of the Church. Savonarola rises to the height of the greatest Bidders of all time, Augustine, Cyprian, Chrysostom, the Venerable Bede, St. Francis, and
John Henry Newman. . . .

"Do well unto Zion according to thy promise so that the
walls of Jerusalem be built again in our day," he winds up
after sixty-five closely written pages in that ghastly prison
cell. "Zion is thy Church . . . Send the fire and the power
and the love of the Holy Spirit upon thy Church. Thy
Church is so weak and feeble, dear Lord. There are so

many millions in this world who have not yet heard the words of truth and salvation from the holy gospel. May the day not be far when all shall confess thee as their father and know thee as their saviour.

"Have mercy on me O Lord Jesus Christ, my hope and my redeemer. Take my life as a righteous sacrifice, as a pure sacrifice, as an acceptable burnt offering for thine own offer on the cross. And if it please thee, O Lord, my God, grant me to pass from this vale of tears into the glory which thou hast prepared for all those who truly love thee. . . ."

The chief turnkey to whom Savonarola entrusted his manuscript for delivery to the printer, first read the document himself and was so stirred by the Friar's passionate yet reverent pleading for more complete consecration and firmer faith that he ran back up the stairs in the prison tower and threw himself at Fra Girolamo's feet. He begged Savonarola to forgive him for the many uncalled-for hardships and vexations he had inflicted. Savonarola bade the man rise and embraced him. Upon inquiring into the jailer's family circumstances and learning that he had a young daughter, the Friar asked if it were possible to see her. When she came a few days later, Savonarola was so pleased at the sight of the maiden, that he presented her with a booklet which he had written for her in the meantime: "Rules of Life for Young Girls."

He was now also allowed to wash himself. The barber was brought into the cell and some of his friends amongst the laity were permitted to see him for an hour or so every day. They found him in as serene and kindly a mood and temper as ever he had been. Not by so much as a word did he refer to the gruesome treatment he had undergone nor did he complain or express bitterness or resentment about the commissioners. But he did learn from his visitors that everyday life in Florence had virtually come to a standstill and that large crowds assembled in the streets and in the Piazza to await the emergence of the trial judges after a day of questioning or deliberation.

His Meditation had not only been printed but transcribed by hand. Sometimes, Savonarola was told, portions of it were read to the people in the Piazza and friends and foes fell to discussing its contents. The news cheered the Friar enormously, but the Signoria soon took a different view. Sympathy for Fra Girolamo was clearly on the rise and the Arrabbiati saw to it that quills, ink and writing paper were removed from Savonarola's cell so that a treatise entitled: "In God is my trust," which he had begun to write, remained unfinished.

Though this new affliction added to his wretchedness, there was one item of intelligence conveyed to him by visiting friends which, if it did not afford him hope of seeing his life spared, at least raised his spirits for a time. A letter had been received by the Signoria from the new King of France, Louis XII, urging cessation of further disciplinary action against Savonarola. Louis XII, who, as one of the Princes of the Blood, had been in command of the cavalry in Charles VIII's Italian expedition in 1494, knew Savonarola personally from having spoken to him at the latter's embassy in Pisa. Louis XII made no bones about it that he was coming to Italy to call a Council of the Church and depose Alexander VI. On his passage through his friendly city of Florence, the King and his councilors promised to look into the charges against the Friar themselves. In the meantime, the Most Christian King urged that Savonarola be set free and allowed to return to his convent.

This information greatly embarrassed the Signoria. As King of France, Louis XII was Florence's ally and protector. He was on his way to settle the fate of Pope Alexander. The new King was known to be as resolute and determined as his predecessor had been vacillating and timid. But the Pope was on relatively good terms with the Signoria since the arrest of Savonarola. His Holiness was apprised of the new French King's plans and warned that danger loomed ahead.

Alexander replied that, since Florence refused to extradite Savonarola, he intended to send two prelates to examine the prisoner on his own behalf. A bargain was struck over the life of Girolamo Savonarola: the Pope would be allowed to send his commissioners on condition that he give the Signoria license to tax ecclesiastical property in the city. When this request was granted by the Holy Father the Signoria made a pledge to sentence Savonarola to death. Alexander accorded the Signoria the right to levy a tenth on ecclesiastical property for a period of three years. "Three times ten makes thirty," grimly remarked the Friar's friends; "Savonarola, like the Saviour, is sold for thirty pieces of silver."

In great trepidation over the French King's threat to march into Italy, the Pope allowed no grass to grow under his feet. Savonarola, the strongest supporter of the French alliance, had to be removed before Louis XII had time to cross the Alps. The bargain over the tax on ecclesiastical property was struck on the 16th of May; on the 19th the papal legates and their following made their entry in Florence with great pomp and circumstance. A crowd of Arrabbiati and Compagnacci greeted them in the Piazza with the shout: "Death to the Friar! Death to Savonarola!"

One of the papal inquisitors was Giovacchino Turriano, General of the Dominican Order, a man eighty-four years of age, highly esteemed for his learning, and a former friend of Savonarola. But Turriano was present only *pro forma,* to give a semblance of impartiality and honesty to the judicial proceedings. The other ambassador was the Bishop of Ilerda, Francesco Romolino, a countryman and household prelate of Alexander VI, and eventually a cardinal, who had a reputation of being one of the most profligate members of the Roman court. He had been the tutor of Cesare Borgia and was of as savage and murderous a disposition as his pupil. In previous trials conducted in the Pope's behalf he had shown himself to be without mercy. The presence of Romolino was a sure guarantee against any failure of vigor through the gentleness which his colleague, Turriano, might show. When the Arrabbiati shouted: "Death to Savonarola!" Romolino smiled and replied: "Don't worry. We will stoke a nice little fire under your Friar. . . . I have the death sentence in my pocket."

The papal officers and their suite were sumptuously installed in the Palazzo Medici. On the following day, May 20th, they went to the Bargello prison where Savonarola was brought before them. The result of the third trial was a foregone conclusion. Fra Girolamo was treated from the beginning as a guilty man, the sole aim of his judges being to compel him to confess himself guilty. They had no luck the first day. When the bailiffs stripped him preparatory to fastening him to the pulley rope, he held out his left arm to Bishop Romolino, showing it to be all wrenched and limp from the previous tortures.

Romolino had no pity. "I command you to tell the truth, the whole truth and nothing but the truth!" he exclaimed. "Name your confederates in your endeavors to obtain a calling of a General Council of the Church and you will not be tortured too long. Pull him up by both arms," the Bishop commanded the bailiffs in the same breath. As his body rose from the floor and was dropped from a height of twenty feet, Savonarola screamed so loud that his cry was heard by the people who gathered outside the prison.

"To whom have you spoken of a Church Council?"

"To none except Fra Domenico and Fra Silvestro."

"Did you not take counsel on the subject of a Council with any Italian princes, not with Duke Ercole of Este, not with any cardinals?"

Savonarola replied that he indeed hoped most ardently for the convocation of a Council but that his sole confidence to bring it about was vested in the King of France, the German Emperor, the King of England, and their Majesties Ferdinand and Isabella of Spain who had a right to proceed to the calling of a Council in the event of the Pope's refusal.

This was nothing new to Bishop Romolino. He wanted to know which member or members of the Curia were involved. Since Savonarola refused to name any cardinals, Romolino angrily quit the chamber saying that on the morrow the trial would resume. In the evening several prominent Arrabbiati paid a visit at the Palazzo Medici where Romolino informed them that the Pope's instructions to take the Friar's life were irrevocable. "Even if Savonarola is a saint like John the Baptist, he must die," Alexander VI was reported to have said.

A sumptuous banquet was ordered and a certain member of the Arrabbiati, Girolamo Martelli by name, presented Bishop Romolino "to his immense satisfaction," with a beautiful girl, who had been brought to the palace dressed up in boy's clothing. . . . to avoid scandal. The General of the Dominicans, Fra Turriano, whose composure was shattered by what he had witnessed in the Bargello, did not join the hilarious company in the evening, but spent his time in prayer. Yet, how Turriano, who knew Savonarola intimately and who had always encouraged him and praised the Friar's sermons and social endeavors, did not once, in the course of the iniquitous trial, turn upon Romolino with indignation and scorn, must forever remain a puzzle. The man was old, it is true, but he was no coward or sycophant. Old age confers no warrant on us to quail before a devil in human guise.

In the morning session on May the 21st Romolino pressed the Friar closely: "Who were the cardinals involved in the plan to call a Council? Did the Cardinal Juliano della Rovere not write that he would bring a large number of cardinals to Florence for a Council?"

"No!"

"Did not the Cardinal Gurgins speak to you in Pisa about the need to reform the Church and depose His Holiness Alexander VI?"

"Of the need to reform the Church, most certainly. Every Christian sees the need of it and prays God for it. As to speaking about deposing His Holiness, the answer is, no!"

"Did the Archbishop of St. Malo, Brissonet, speak evil of the Pope?"

"He did not!"

"Now, the last question: Is the Cardinal Oliviero Caraffa of Naples a friend of yours?"

"Yes, he is. His Highness* of Naples has always dealt very graciously with me and spoke well of me to the Holy Father."

"Did he plot with you against the Pope?"

"No, he did not!"

"Yes, he did! Say that he did! If you won't say that he did, I'll have you torn to shreds! . . . Fasten him!" Romolino commanded the bailiffs. "Drop him from the greatest height possible! By the right arm! Tear it off!"

The pain made the Friar delirious. "Yes, yes," he screamed. "I will tell everything. I will confess!"

"The Cardinal Caraffa is your accomplice? Do you admit?"

" *Si, si, Napoli, Napoli!* Yes, yes, Naples, Naples!"

"That is enough, let him down," said Romolino. "Now tell me: did you betray the secrets entrusted to you in the confession booth for personal gain or political reasons?"

"Never! I do not possess a farthing in the world. I am in fact

---

* The title "Eminence" was not bestowed on the cardinals till 1630 by Urban VIII.

heavily in debt for the purchase of Lorenzo de' Medici's library for my convent. . . ."

"Did you not falsely preach a high doctrine of morality in order to divert the people's attention from your own unnatural vices?"

"You only repeat what Fra Mariano mendaciously accused me of. . . ."

"No, I do not!" screamed the Spaniard, red in the face and gnashing his teeth. "You monster, you insulted the Pope's holiness time and again . . . You are a drunken Jew . . . You subjected small boys to your unmentionable lusts. This was your sole purpose in forming the youth companies. . . . Isn't that the truth?"

"You know it is not!"

"How dare you speak to me in that tone? Have you no respect? Have you no decency? Tell me, did you not murder Ridolfi and Tornabuoni and the other three noble citizens on a false accusation of conspiracy?"

"I was not the judge who sentenced them. The entire Grand Council voted their death . . . I pleaded with Messer Francesco Valori to spare their lives. . . ."

"That's easily said; Valori is dead. He got what he deserved. . . . Are you a false prophet? Remember if you deny, you will be tortured again! I charge you to tell me: does God speak to you?"

"No, I am abandoned by God. I hear no voices now," whispered Savonarola, bursting into tears and using almost word for word the defense which Joan of Arc put up when badgered by the ecclesiastical court of Rouen: "My voices speak no more to me," Joan wept . . . "I am abandoned by Jesus. . . ."

"O Jesus, O Jesus, I have denied you!" Savonarola frantically cried beating his breast. "I have betrayed my Lord! I have betrayed my Lord. O!"

Once again he was suspended and, as the record cynically adds, "after he hung for a long time" by that one bruised and swollen arm, he was dropped. When he was loosened, he lay on the floor in a dead faint. He was brought back to consciousness and told that unless he signed a confession which Ser Francisco Ceccone, who had been reinstalled as notary by Romolino, had drawn up in the meantime, the torture would be renewed. Savonarola signed.

But hardly had he appended his signature, when to the astonishment of everyone present, he rose to his feet and put on his Dominican robe: "I signed because I was afraid of being tortured anew," he said in a clear and normal voice. "I revoke my confession entirely. If I am to die, I will die for the truth. The truth is that God did speak through me to the people of Florence. I speak the truth now. I deny all your accusations. *Ecclesia Dei renovabitur*: the Church of God will be purified. *Florentia quoque post flagellam renovabitur et prosperabitur*: Florence, too, after the scourging, will be purified and prosper . . . *Infideles convertentur ad Christum*: the unbelievers will be converted to Christ. . . ."

As if he felt his old admiration for his friend returning, the General of the Dominicans, who had sat through the proceedings with head averted or with his face hidden in his hands, suddenly looked up at Savonarola. All the commissioners rose to their feet. The Friar was terrible to behold. Upon him descended in that moment the essence of that *terribilità* which does not denote horror or terror in Italian, but greatness, grandeur of soul, lofty and awesome superiority. How a man, a human being, could stand on his feet after being subjected to such wracking physical punishment, and yet speak in so forceful a way with that beautiful voice of his, is in itself something bordering on the miraculous. Savonarola's whole attitude and his proud fearless bearing in that moment of his retraction testified to the unimpeachable purity and consistency of his life.

Seizing the crucifix from the table, the old boyish smile came back to his face for an instant and spread a glow of glorification over his countenance. The Friar's moral superiority was so overwhelmingly evident that the startled Romolino blanched and backed to the wall.

"Did you then not plot at all? Have you nothing to confess?" the Spaniard gasped, changing from Latin to Italian.

"Do not wonder," Savonarola replied with great dignity, "if it seems to you that I have told few things; for my purposes were indeed few but they were great."*

---

* *Se vi pare che io abbia detto poche cose, non ve ne maravigliata perchè le mie cose erano poche ma grandi.*

Chapter XIV

"How Little a Way a Soule Hath to Go to Heaven When It Departs from the Body"

E ARLY in the morning of the 22nd of May another brief interrogation took place, but Bishop Romolino, realizing that nothing further could be extracted from Savonarola, soon broke off by ordering the Friar to appear on the following day to hear sentence pronounced. "I am in prison," replied Fra Girolamo, "I can only appear before this tribunal if I am brought here." His legs were thereupon chained together and he was carried back to the Signoria tower. In his absence the commissioners drew up the sentence. The three friars, Girolamo Savonarola, Domenico Buonvicini, and Silvestro Maruffi, were condemned to be defrocked on the morrow and to be handed over to the secular arm for execution "as heretics and schismatics and for the preaching of novelties."

That no trace of heresy had been found in either Savonarola or Buonvicini, and that the simple-minded Maruffi had never in his life so much as expressed an opinion on doctrine, dogma, or any other ecclesiastical or theological matter, was known to all present. The idea of schism, wilful separation from the Church, was so alien and abhorrent to Savonarola that it had never occurred to his mind. Nor was the charge of schism actually made at that trial which as a travesty of justice and human decency surpasses even the fiendishness of a Torquemada, who had at least the excuse of believing that he pleased the Deity by burning the Jews of Spain in his murderous autos da fé. In bringing Savonarola to the stake,

305

his enemies were tempted by an evil spirit of revenge into an act unsanctioned even by their own bloody laws. Novelties Fra Girolamo preached, that is, if it be a novelty to protest against trafficking in the sacraments and saying that the Vicar of Christ should not have a concubine.

The Eight of Justice met in the afternoon to review the sentence. Not that there was any doubt as to the finality of the commissioners verdict, or that the case would be debated with opinions for and against being heard. The Eight gathered merely to conform to custom and regulations. Confident that they would uphold the verdict without hesitation or scruple, Bishop Romolino did not even think it worth the trouble to attend. He had other equally unsavory business to transact at the Palazzo Medici that afternoon. He was incensed upon learning in the evening that one of the Eight, Agnolo Niccolini, a doctor of jurisprudence and a man of calm good sense, had dared to take the floor to make a spirited defense of Savonarola. The accusation of heresy and schismatism, Niccolini contended, was not proven at all. To be zealous for the reform of the Church could not by the furthest stretch of the imagination be regarded as criminal, contrary to the laws of Christ or subversive of the papal authority. There were tens of thousands in Italy and abroad who prayed daily that the Church might be raised from the corruption in which she had fallen. It would be wiser, said Doctor Niccolini, to keep Savonarola in prison till tempers cooled off rather than commit an irreparable wrong by putting him to death . . . "Let Fra Girolamo be furnished with writing facilities so that he may continue to write his great works for the glory of God . . . The ages produce so few men of the religious genius of Savonarola that Florence should not inflict upon herself the odious distinction of having silenced so great and holy a man. . . ."

Niccolini's argument was heard in grim silence. Rucellai, another member of the Eight, was apprehensive lest sparing Savonarola's life open the door for the popular party to stage a comeback. Within a year, Rucellai thought, perhaps within a few months, the Frateschi would secure a majority in the Council. Savonarola would in that case certainly be liberated and he and his partisans wreak dire revenge on the Arrabbiati and Compagnacci. The Gonfalonier of Justice, Messer Piero Parenti, exclaimed: "Dead men make no trouble. Dead men do not come back. Let the Friar be executed without delay and the strife and factionalism in Florence will be at an end for good." Even so, the Eight did not ratify the verdict, but voted to refer the question to the General Council which met the same evening.

At this session Bishop Romolino, who was seriously alarmed by the information concerning Agnolo Niccolini's plea for leniency, made it his business to be present. It did not take the Spanish terror long to browbeat the Council into submission. Their Serenities, he declared, had promised the Pope to execute Savonarola in consideration of the privilege to tax ecclesiastical property. Let them now keep their word or face the alternative. If Savonarola was not swiftly executed, Alexander VI would most certainly retaliate by throwing all the Florentine merchants and bankers resident in Rome in prison. Before this threat the cowed Signoria gave way immediately. After all, business is business, and human life is cheap.

"But Fra Domenico and Fra Silvestro, why should they die?" someone asked the papal official as he left the hall. "They have not even been tried. . . ."

"One dirty monk more or less, what does it matter," remarked Romolino with a shrug of the shoulders. "Burn all three of them. It will be good riddance!"

It was shortly after midnight when the three brethren were notified that they were to die in a few hours. Savonarola was found kneeling in prayer when the message was brought to his cell. He nodded his head and went on praying. Fra Domenico became strangely excited. He gave a shout of joy and leaped in the air at the prospect of becoming a martyr. He asked permission, and was granted permission, to write a letter to the brethren of St. Dominic's convent at Fiesole of which he was the prior. In that letter he advised his friars to collect all of Savonarola's writings and put them in a safe place. "For a brief time," he wrote, "the books of the noble servant of God, Fra Girolamo Savonarola, will be hunted and proscribed. But not for long. Soon every man concerned with the condition of the Church and the good doctrines of our teacher will want to read his books. Do you, therefore, collect his works, have them printed and bound in the right sequence, and you will render the Church and mankind invaluable service."

When Silvestro Maruffi heard that he must prepare for death, he began to weep. "Why?" he asked. "What wrong have I done? I am so young (he was but twenty-four years of age), I do not want to die." He recovered his equanimity somewhat when he was promised that Savonarola would shortly come into his cell to comfort him.

This promise was not kept. The Signoria which remained in session all during the night, gravely deliberated for more than an hour on the propriety and the advisability of allowing Savonarola to confer with Domenico Buonvicini and Silvestro Maruffi. Why this sudden concern for correct procedure? We are still in the fifteenth century, let us remember. Their Exalted Serenities were seriously perturbed lest Savonarola bewitch his brethren, cast a spell over them, perhaps with his diabolical powers cause wings to sprout on their backs or after etherealizing them make them fly out through the barred windows. At last permission was given for the three condemned men to meet for an hour, but "no longer," and only in the presence of the whole Council so that all could witness and perhaps frustrate any demonological trickery or magic to which Savonarola might have recourse.

Accordingly, the three friars were brought down to the *Sala Savonarola,* the hall which the Friar himself had caused to be built in the first years of his mission in Florence. When they met they fervently embraced, and Savonarola who sensed what went on in the minds of his companions, gave his instructions. To Fra Silvestro, who was resolved to cry out his innocence on the way to the place of execution, Savonarola said: "You must be silent *figliuolino mio,* my dear little son. Follow the example of our Lord who did not protest his innocence on the cross." Fra Domenico he reprimanded for being in so joyful a mood. "I know that you desire to be burned alive, but that is not correct . . . You have no right to desire death. Besides, do we know how we will feel in a few hours, whether we will be resigned and steadfast as it behooves Christians? This does not depend on us, but on the grace which God accords us in the hour of death."

Astonished that he perceived their secret thoughts so accurately, the two knelt before their Prior who gave them his blessing. Then the allotted hour having passed, they were taken back to their respective cells, accompanied by a heavily armed guard. Fra Domenico ate a hearty meal and promptly fell asleep. Savonarola declared that his soul alone needed sustenance and that he would seek it in prayer. When one of the guards looked through the spyhole of Maruffi's cell a few moments later he saw that the monk slept like the innocent child he was.

At one o'clock in the morning the workmen got busy erecting the scaffold in the Piazza della Signoria. With a characteristic touch of cruelty, Bishop Romolino ordered the carpenters chosen from amongst the followers of Fra Girolamo. The scaffold went up in approximately the same spot where the structure prepared for the ordeal by fire stood a month before, and where today lies the bronze memorial slab in front of Ammannati's fountain. Fagots were heaped up to the height of a man's shoulder. They were liberally sprinkled with gun powder, resin, and oil. In the midst of the fagots stood a tall gibbet thirty feet high. The ends of the crossbeam protruding on either side of this pole were purposely made of uneven length in order not to make the stake resemble the cross of Christ. From the crossbeams hung three chains with three iron collars attached. A ladder reached to the top of the cross for the victims to ascend and the executioner to perform his grisly task of choking the three monks to death from behind by twisting the noose through holes in the iron collars.

Further, three separate tribunals were erected in the space between the main entrance of the Signoria palace and the funeral pyre, one for the lay commissioners who had tried Savonarola, one for the papal officers and their suite, the third for the Eight and the members of the Council. Nothing was overlooked to increase the festive solemnity of the occasion. The different stands were draped with velvet cloth, black, gold and crimson in color, and the banners of the guilds and corporations were displayed as for a great state ceremonial. The cavalry and the civic guard, armed with pikes and short swords, moved into the square at five o'clock in the morning making their way with difficulty even at that early hour through the dense mass of spectators. All Florence was taking the day off to be on hand to watch the spectacle. The eyewitness accounts state that "the people fought ferociously to be as near the woodpile as possible."

At dawn the turnkey awakened Savonarola. He had fallen asleep with his head resting on the knees of the Benedictine monk who heard his confession. It was to this man, Jacopo Niccolini, that Fra Girolamo told of events long ago in the church of Faenza when, upon hearing a sermon on the text: "Get thee out of thy father's house," he decided to consecrate his life to the service of God.

"Do you know that you talked in your sleep and that you pronounced the word '*Roma*' several times?" asked Father Niccolini.

"I did not know that I spoke out loud," replied Savonarola, "but I did dream about Rome. I scarcely dare tell you though what I dreamed, because Rome is the dear city of your birth."

"Tell me nonetheless," urged Niccolini.

"I dreamed," said the Friar, "that a frightful disaster descended on the city. It was revealed to me that this will come to pass in the reign of a Pope named Clement. It will be the worst scourge with which any city has been visited since Jerusalem was destroyed. . . ."

Niccolini, who did not belong to Savonarola's friends or followers, wrote down what the Friar told him the same day. The prediction is therefore not a post-mortem insertion in Savonarola's biography or an attempt to bolster his reputation as a seer. It was first published in 1502, four years after Fra Girolamo's death. Confessor Niccolini went on to live through the pontificates of Alexander VI, Pius III, Julius II, Leo X, Adrian VI, and saw Julio de' Medici ascend the throne of St. Peter under the name of *Clement VII* in A.D. 1523. Father Niccolini did not, however, live to see the disaster which Savonarola foresaw in his dream. But the sack of Rome in 1527 by the army of the Emperor Charles V, was an event which for ruthless inhumanity and wanton destruction has few parallels in world history. Never since Attila's time had Rome witnessed such a scene of havoc and woe.

Fra Girolamo's face was calm and he smiled when he said: "Today is the day when I go to meet my Saviour." He asked permission to say Mass. The other two condemned men were brought into the chapel of the Signoria. While they lay prostrate before the altar, witnesses heard Savonarola say in his usual clear voice: "O Lord, my God, I know that thou art the true God, the creator of the world and of human nature. I know that thou art the perfect Holy Trinity, invisible, inseparable, God the Father, God the Son, and God the

Holy Ghost. I know that thou art the eternal Word descended in the bosom of the Virgin Mary, and that thou didst go on the cross to shed thy precious blood for us miserable offenders and to wash away our sins. I pray that thy blood, O Lord, may not have been shed in vain for me. I humbly ask forgiveness for my sins and for all the damage and offense I have committed in this city. Turn thy face with love on Florence and all its people. I ask the forgiveness of those who stand about here in this hour. I pray thy divine pardon for my errors if there are such of which I have no knowledge. I ask this for myself and for my two brethren here with me prostrate at thy feet. Grant us the courage of thy saints and martyrs in the supreme hour so that the enemy may have no power over us . . . Hear me, O Christ! O Saviour! O Love immortal. . . ."

Scarcely was the Mass concluded when the bailiffs took the brethren by the arm to lead them downstairs. As they descended the staircase of the Pallazzo della Signoria, they were stopped by two priests, Thomas Sardi and Sebastian Buontempi, who informed them that they were to be divested of their white Dominican robes and black mantles. When one of the priests tore his garb roughly from Savonarola's shoulders, the Friar protested: "For the sake of the sufferings I have endured, allow me to hold my cloak in my hands for one instant!"

"Oh, sacred gown," he said, "how ardently I desired you. God gave you to me and I can say with all my heart that I have kept you unsullied and holy. I still hold you pure in my hands and I would willingly always hold you. But you are taken away from me. . . ."

He kissed his old tattered robe and the three men continued downstairs in their hair shirts, out of the palace gate into the Piazza. When the three monks appeared on the palace steps, an immense silence fell on the multitude. Before approaching the first tribunal, the friars were dressed again, but this time in their priestly vestments. Piece by piece these symbolical garments were taken away from them by Bishop Paganotti to whom the unconquerably malignant Romolino had assigned the task of performing the rite of desecration for no other reason but that he, Paganotti, was a former monk of San Marco, one of Savonarola's ablest students and greatly liked by him. Paganotti scratched the fingernails

of the three condemned men with a piece of glass, denoting that the
sacred oil with which they were anointed when consecrated to the
priesthood, was now removed. Then a barber destroyed the tonsure
on their heads by shaving off all the hair, and the Bishop proceeded
to read the prescribed formula of desecration.

As he read, Paganotti dared not look his old Prior in the face.
He swallowed hard and stuttered and was so nervous that he had
to correct himself several times. When he said at one point: "I
separate you from the Church Militant and Triumphant," Savonarola gently interrupted him: "Not from the Church Triumphant, my
dear son, for the Church Triumphant is in heaven . . . You have
neither the right nor the power. . . ." The Bishop corrected himself,
but then, overcome by emotion, he did not finish reading the formula. He hid his face in his hands and broke into a violent fit of
sobbing.

These formalities lasted more than two hours. It was now one
o'clock in the afternoon. The three monks were taken before the
tribunal where sat the papal legates, and Bishop Romolino read
the entire minutes of the trial, including the so-called confessions
and the verdict. Savonarola listened attentively, but Fra Domenico
had his eyes turned on the gallows. Like a somnambulist Fra Silvestro seemed totally oblivious of his surroundings. Mentally, the
dreaming mystic had already passed the bourn separating life
from death.

All at once Bishop Romolino departed from the written text in
his hands and spoke these strange words: "I have received word
from His Holiness Alexander VI this very day that he grants you
a plenary indulgence-in-the-article-of-death with release from all
canonical censures and excommunications. His Holiness sets you
back into your original state of sinlessness . . . You will not undergo
the punishment of purgatory. . . . Do you accept?" All three
gravely bowed in assent. The Bishop's announcement signified
that by virtue of the power of the Holy Keys vested in St. Peter and
his successors, the Pope now threw the gates of heaven wide open
to the three men about to die.

The suspense was not over yet. From the papal tribune the
monks were led to the stand where sat the Eight of Justice. Here
Piero Parenti, the Gonfalonier of Justice, read the verdict of the

secular court which found Savonarola guilty of having fostered civil strife, been instrumental in driving out the Medici and having connived at the death of the five prominent citizens who were executed for high treason and conspiracy.

At last the ordeal was over. It was three o'clock. The formalities had lasted from eight in the morning. Fra Silvestro Maruffi, who was the first to be hanged, almost ran up the ladder. At the top, as the executioner fastened the iron collar around his neck, he called down to Savonarola: "Father Girolamo, see how a knight of Jesus Christ dies with joy in his heart. . . ." He wanted to say something more, but the executioner pushed him off the ladder and the body swung free. For a few moments Silvestro's pitiful cries resounded through the Piazza: *Jesu, miserere! Christe, miserere!* "Jesus, have mercy! Christ, have mercy!" Then only did the executioner apply the garrot.

Fra Domenico Buonvicini came next. As he walked to the stake he intoned the psalm: "In thee O God, I have trusted." A priest walking by his side cautioned him: "Do not sing so loud, it is unbecoming!" Halfway up the ladder, Domenico turned to the crowd and called out: "I assure you that all of Fra Girolamo's prophecies will go into fulfillment . . . The Church will be purified. The Holy Spirit will send his heavenly fire. . . ." The executioner ordered him to stop talking. When Domenico dropped from the ladder he died instantly. The bodies of the two monks hung at the two extremities of the crossbeam. The place of honor, in the middle, was reserved for the greatest offender, the heresiarch and arch criminal, as the verdict called Fra Girolamo.

While Savonarola walked slowly to the stake, some Compagnacci broke through the police lines and slashed at his bare legs and feet with their knives and daggers. He paid no attention and probably did not even feel the injuries.

A poor old woman came close to him and offered a crust of bread. "Take and eat, Blessed Father Girolamo!" He smiled broadly at her and said: "Thank you very much, my dear daughter, but I need no food now. I have so little a way to go. In a moment I will be in the mansions on high having sup with my Lord and Saviour."

Before ascending the ladder he asked the executioner to be so kind and tie a rope around his shirt "for modesty's sake." The executioner harshly refused. Not even the humiliation of appearing naked before the people was to be spared him. At the foot of the ladder he was assailed by the cry: "If you are able to perform miracles, now is the time to show us!" The executioner tied his hands behind his back and pushed him towards the Compagnacci to give them an opportunity to spit upon him and strike and scratch his face. When he climbed the ladder his face was covered with blood. On the top rung he stood still, turned around and faced the awe-stricken crowd. How often had he not seen the Florentines gather at his feet in the great Duomo? His eyes traveled over that sea of humanity from left to right and back again from right to left. He tugged at the rope around his wrists as if he wanted to free his right hand in order to raise it in blessing as he had always done when facing a congregation. But the executioner struck him a blow from behind which caused him to fall. Savonarola was dead at once. To amuse the Compagnacci the executioner raised the dead man's shirt with a stick and committed other vile indignities on the body.

At precisely 3:30 in the afternoon the huge pile of fagots was set on fire and the smoke rose in a thick column hiding the three suspended bodies from view. When the flames leaped up they burned the rope around Savonarola's wrists. In the same instant a strong breeze blew into the Piazza. The flames were dispersed and the smoke wafted away. The bodies of the three monks which had been hidden by the curtain of smoke and flame, became visible once more.

Whether it was the temporary cessation of the heat or a last spasm of life which shook Savonarola's frame, the fact remains and is attested to by a number of eyewitnesses, that all at once the dead man's right hand with two fingers uplifted in blessing, rose to the height of his shoulders.

"*Miraculo! Miraculo!* A miracle! A miracle!" roared the crowd scattering in all directions. Pandemonium swept the Piazza. A wail as of a thousand damned souls went up. Women screamed and sobbed. The Compagnacci filled the air with curses and execrations. Men, women, monks, and nuns fought their way out of the Piazza. In the stampede many children were trampled. The halberdiers were pushed aside and the horses of the lancers reared in panic. The members of the Signoria and the papal legates, Romolino in the lead, climbed down from their tribunal and scurried for safety into the palace.

Then the wind subsided and a crepitating pillar of black smoke and flames shot upward removing Savonarola forever from the eyes of men. . . .

Thus went to God the boy from Ferrara whose mother predicted that his mission in life would be a terrible one.

Thus the people of Florence rewarded the champion of popular liberty who had overthrown the Medicean tyranny, who gave them a modern constitution, and who more than once saved their republic from dire peril.

"What constitutes a great life?" once asked Alfred de Vigny. "An idea conceived in youth and carried out in maturity."

Judged by that test, Savonarola's life was of the greatest. We cannot lament his fate. His body they could kill, but not his soul. The martyr's death suffered by Savonarola was a proper and fitting climax to his life as a prophet. He ran his course as by special providential arrangement. His belief that the world and all men in it are at the disposal of a transcendent power was never shaken. What he desired most ardently, and also clearly foresaw, the renewal of the Church of God, became a glorious reality a few decades later.

Epilogue

WITH Savonarola out of the way the Florentines were in a mood not unlike that of the ancient Israelites when the man Moses ascended the mountain and tarried so long that they compelled Aaron to make them a golden calf in order to prostitute themselves in lascivious adoration of the beast. The Friar's death opened the sluice gates to a wave of filth and slime which changed the noble city of Florence from a tranquil house of religion and piety into a vile lupanar. But whereas Lorenzo de' Medici had encouraged libertinage and debauchery as a counterrevolutionary prophylaxis to demoralize the common people and prolong his own tyranny, the erotic frenzy of 1498 appears to have been more in the nature of a spontaneous combustion. It came on, partly suggested by the example in bestiality set by the Compagnacci, and partly in reaction against the iron discipline of the cloister which Savonarola sought to impose on the whole populace. The Florentines were swept along by a *mystique* which modern psychoanalysis may well qualify as mass hypnosis, but which looked more as if the devil got them in his grip and shook them till they grew nauseated with their own depravity.

"Now has come the happy time," remarked Benvenuto del Biancha in a session of the new Eight of Justice, "when we may freely revert to the practice of sodomy."* Rapine, fornication, and the abomination which brought down the divine fire on the cities of Sodom and Gomorrah, were publicly indulged in. As if Savonarola had not been enough sinned against in his lifetime, the smuttiest pornographic pictures and paintings were exhibited on the walls and doors of churches and convents with the Friar as the chief object of vilification. Literally thousands of harlots walked about in broad daylight, naked, unashamed, and with them heavily perfumed males with painted faces, travestied in women's garb and

* *Chronicles of Florence* by Filipepi.

316

wearing false hair. There were so many desecrations at San Marco's convent that a protecting wall had to be put around the buildings. The Duomo pulpit and even the high altar in the Cathedral where Savonarola preached and officiated so often, were smeared with the most loathsome filth day after day. When the priests entered to start the service, ribald youths and girls prevented them by forming an indecent saraband and carousing in the holiest place. The jeweled crown on the great statue of the Madonna was stolen and found on the head of a drunken whore who paraded with it from one brothel to the next. The woman was not even reprimanded but applauded wherever she went. The delirium of salacity and satyrism reached a paroxysm on Christmas eve when instead of a Mass in celebration of the birth in Bethlehem, a "Devil's Carnival" was staged by torchlight in the Cathedral of St. Mary of the Flower. The apotheosis in this satanistic rite came with the introduction of a number of horses which were tied down to the sanctuary rail and then slowly tortured to death in a manner too unspeakably lewd and horrid for words. Florence, the city of philosophy, taste, and culture, seemed to have fallen into a ritualistic savagery not far removed from that of cavemen and cannibals. . . .

The Frateschi were hounded from pillar to post. The new Signoria decreed that to have been a follower of Savonarola or merely to have been assiduous in attendance on his sermons, was tantamount to high treason and a sentence of fifty years banishment was imposed. The absurdity of this measure became at once apparent when it proved unenforceable on so large a number. But many prominent Frateschi left voluntarily. Amongst these was Francesco Pico della Mirandola who had retrieved portions of Savonarola's skull and right arm from the ashes in the square. Another was Fra Pacifico Burlamacchi. Burlamacchi and Pico set to work, each writing a *Life of Blessed Fra Girolamo*. The three distinguished Benivieni brothers shook the dust of Florence from their feet. Their example was followed by the six Strozzi who had been converted under Savonarola's preaching and received the tonsure at San Marco's. Women who braved the vindictiveness of the new Signoria by praying on the spot where the Friar and his companions were executed, received a beating and were threatened with immurement should the offense be repeated. It was dangerous to life and limb merely to be heard pronouncing the Friar's name. To sing his favorite psalm: "How good and beautiful is it for brethren to dwell together in unity" was deemed defiance of the Exalted Signoria and punished with the strapado followed by exile. Savonarola's books were proscribed in all Italy. His younger brother, Fra Maurelio, was declared an outlaw and vanished without leaving a trace. But the Friar's sermons were read by more people and in more countries than he could ever have hoped. The number of miracles attributed to touching his relics also multiplied. Burlamacchi collected these instances of supernatural intervention in a huge tome which went through a dozen editions in the decade following Savonarola's death and was reissued as recently as 1937 by the Prince Piero Ginori Conti.

In the meantime the Mass of Savonarola was celebrated in secret in a growing number of churches, convents, and private houses. The more it was forbidden, the more it flourished. When an instance of this surreptitious veneration came to the notice of the authorities the participants were punished with the confiscation of all their goods. Six of the nuns of St. Ann's convent on the Via San Gallo, who claimed to have seen the shade of Savonarola officiate at the altar of their chapel and to have received Holy Communion from his hands, went stark mad. People grew hysterical when contemplating the portrait of Fra Girolamo around the head of which Fra Bartolomeo had painted a golden aureole. Another painting entitled St. Peter Martyr, but endued with Savonarola's features with the index finger pressed to the lips in a gesture cautioning silence, sent men and women away screaming in remorse and self-accusation. When the rumor got around that Savonarola could be seen and heard ringing the bells of San Marco at night, the Signoria could think of no other remedy to counteract the ensuing mass hysteria but to remove the bells to San Miniato's spire where they hung for twenty years till Pisa returned to the Florentine obedience, as Savonarola had foretold.

By that time Alexander VI was dead and all those who had taken a leading part in Fra Girolamo's trials had descended into their graves. Doffo Spini and Giovanni Manetti, the two presiding judges at that iniquitous trial in the Bargello, succumbed to the ravages of venereal disease. The record of their last days has been preserved, but the details are too loathsome to bear repetition.

"Even if you take my life, I will come back!" Savonarola predicted.* Under the pontificate of Julius II, the Friar came back in the teeth of a mass of slanderous pamphlets and sermons of his own which teemed with falsifications. When Burlamacchi presented his work *Blessed Fra Girolamo* to the Pope, Julius II told the author: "There is not the least doubt in our mind that Savonarola is a saint. . . . When he is canonized it is not the Friar who will be honored, but the Church will honor herself." Cardinal Giovanni de' Medici at last read Fra Girolamo's sermons and remarked: "I have learned more good about the Christian religion from the Friar's works than from all other sources." He nonetheless advised Julius II against an early canonization since the Friar's rehabilitation could easily be used to renew factional strife in Florence where the Medici had returned to power. But he raised no objection to his friend Raphael placing Savonarola in the august company of Pope Gregory the Great, St. Jerome, St. Augustine, Dante, St. Thomas, and others in the great painting *Disputa,* which has been called "the most beautiful representation of the Christian world in existence," and which may be seen on the entrance wall of the Hall of the Segnatura in the Vatican till this day.

In 1516, eighteen years after Savonarola's death, twelve cardinals with the Spaniard Bernhardin Carvajal at their head, convoked a Council in Pisa for the reform of the Church. Julius II, who had clamored for a Council so long as it was to be an instrument to remove his rival from the papal throne, did nothing about it once he obtained the tiara. Leo X (Giovanni de' Medici) was too busy building St. Peter's and selling indulgences to discuss the reform of the Church with a Council. Twelve cardinals broke away from him and came to Florence to seek the co-operation of the Frateschi and the Dominicans of Tuscany with a promise to place the canonization of Savonarola as the first item on the Council's agenda. In spite of this tempting offer, the followers of Savonarola could not be moved to join the twelve schismatics. They informed Cardinal Carvajal that they intended to "remain loyal to the See of Peter, as our dear Father in God, Savonarola, has taught us."

* Savonarola, *Discorsi,* No. XXIII, p. 67.

The Florentines had long ere this freed themselves from the erotic neurosis which forced and dragged them into shame. With a feeling of guilty embarrassment they returned to honor Savonarola. His Mass was sung everywhere, and his sainthood was taken for granted. On successive anniversaries of the Friar's death, the people brought flowers into the Piazza, till 1789 when those heaps of roses and gladioli assumed such mountainous proportions that General Bonaparte in a fit of anger forbade the practice. But in 1901 people spontaneously went back to decorating the memorial slab, albeit in a more modest way.

Schiller wrote: "After being tossed to and fro by waves of jealousy, hatred and obscurantism, Savonarola has at last come to rest in the haven of peace." Although the Friar was still attacked as a heretic as late as 1924, the volumes in his favor by Catholic scholars declaring him "a fit ornament for the altars of the Church," "absolutely free from heresy and schism," and honoring him as "a doctor, virgin and martyr," form a library by themselves which grows steadily in size and importance as time goes on.

Whether these recommendations will ever lead to more than pious enshrinement in the Christian people's hearts, is doubtful. There still remains a great deal of historical ignorance and some religious-dogmatic prejudice as well on the subject of Savonarola. Rehabilitation of Savonarola, one hears it said, would automatically involve a condemnation of Alexander VI. A Church which claims infallibility cannot permit such a measure to pass. But the present reigning Pontiff has done so nevertheless, by assuming the name of John XXIII, which was also borne by an earlier Pope or rather antipope (Baldassaro Cossa), who sat (illegally) in St. Peter's chair from 1410 till 1415.

Nor was the claim to infallibility and perfection invalidated by a confession of the Church's share of guilt in the breaching of Christian unity at the time of the Reformation. In the message which the last non-Italian Pope, Adrian VI, sent to the Diet of Nuremberg in 1522 we read: "The Holy Scriptures make it abundantly clear that the sins of the people have their origin in the sins of the clergy . . . We know only too well that many abominable things have happened in the Curia, abuse of spiritual matters, breach of the divine commandments . . . It is not surprising that the disease has spread from the head to the members, from the Popes to the prelates . . . You must therefore promise in our name," wrote Adrian to the Nuncio Chieregati who conveyed the pontifical message to the German princes, "that we shall employ all our zeal in improving the Roman court whence perhaps all the evil came forth, so that the disease which started here may also be healed from here."*

This mea culpa on the part of the Church was the first world-historical step on the road to recovery and healing. "It is sin that dishonors," wrote Adrian VI, "not confession of sin. . . ."

From the days and nights in grandfather Michele's study we have seen how strangely Savonarola was fitted for his great task. His passion for Laudomia Strozzi was strong enough to let him into the great secret of human happiness, but did not lead him too far from his predestined functions. Both she and his grandfather were the appointed instruments of fate. He was not an enemy of art and letters, but he was not a Renaissance man either, nor a prodigy of impossible perfection. He and his grandfather and men of their stamp were leftovers from the age of faith when the great cathedrals went up in Europe and great religious figures such as Anselm, Bernard, Domenic, Francis, Thomas and Catherine walked the earth. He had no deep insight, it is true, into the forces crushing or remolding the old order. The tremendous issues which were shaping up in his day were but imperfectly visible to him probably because he was an actor in the drama himself, and his view of men and events was from too close a perspective. He nonetheless became a pioneer of the modern era with his extraordinary faith in civic freedom, the moral role of the state and his deathless devotion to the fatherland.

He was "tenderhearted, forgiving, kind in all great matters," and to charge him with lack of charity—anonymously and 500 years after his death—is the most contemptible accusation ever brought against him. To be sure, the man was opinionated, impatient, and even intolerant. But behind these contradictions stands a person of integrity, simplicity and great courage. The light of heroic sanctity remained undimmed in Savonarola. Fierce and immoderate he was too at times in his denunciations of corruption and sin in high

* In J. Lortz, *Die Reformation in Deutschland*, 1949, pp. 101, et seq.

places. In fact immoderateness is the quality which he has in
common with all the prophets. Those men of old were governed
by the same laws which are operative now. A prophet who is not
immoderate, not uncompromising and not inflexible is not a true
prophet. The fate of the true prophet is to suffer for the cause of
God's Kingdom and to go down to ignominious defeat covered
with the world's opprobrium. On the other hand, the unmistakable
sign of the false prophet is that he flourishes like a green bay tree,
is everywhere received with open arms, and garners in the world's
acclaim. . . .

Savonarola had a message to deliver in which he profoundly believed. He wanted to instill a sense of moral responsibility in the
individual and gradually built this up into a collective national
and international force. In the belief that the Florentines were
destined to demonstrate the primacy of social justice to the nations
of the earth, he wanted first of all to develop to the maximum the
potentialities of the individual for the good life in a society of
freedom and justice.

"The Kingdom of God has entered history," he announced. "You
may belong to it whenever you wish." It was to be a communion
in which all contradictions would pale and vanish before the sacred
oneness of God and of humanity. The high and the low, the near
and those far-off, the rich and the poor, the learned and the un-
sophisticated, all were to be united in one community under God.
Nobody was to be despised because he owned no property, and
nobody to be honored for the reason that he possessed much. In
one word, Mammon was not to rule the world. Everything was to
be enlisted in God's service, hearts and hands, houses and fields,
energy and money. Life was to be spent in the service of God and in
"love of the brethren."

The youth problem, he held, could not be detached or seen as a
separate entity from contemporary society. He realized that, like
an individual, society carries in its own blood stream the noxious
waste matters which make for social arteriosclerosis, decay and
death. When youth feels itself reduced to an infinitesimal small cog
in a gigantic piece of soulless machinery and sees its elders and
society worship the golden calf of materialism, that is to say all
things which are spiritually dead, a disillusioned, frustrated, "beat"

generation becomes as inevitable as toadstools in the forest after a night of heavy rain. Savonarola sought to remedy the evil of youthful delinquency, crime, and vice not by repeating the hollow phrases habitually employed by "God's ground crew" in such circumstances. Savonarola looked upon the plunge into vice and crime in his day as basically a revolt against a society which arrogated to itself the virtue of perfection. The rulers of Florence claimed that the apex of well-being, prosperity, sophistication, wealth, and power had been attained under their aegis. Savonarola led the people to revolt against such a world from which the Spirit of God had been forced to depart.

He sought to give the youth a common task to perform, a definite goal to pursue, a common ideal to hold high, something to strive for, something to lift them out of themselves and beyond themselves. A people may have all the comforts and amenities that a given civilization provides. But without vision the people perish and the future hangs before them, not as a banner inscribed with the message of messianic hope, but as a dirty rag flapping in the wind. . . .

The last evil word spoken of Savonarola in the city of Florence itself occurred in the year 1527. In order to counteract the growing influence of the Friar's printed works, a young member of the Signoria thought fit to rake up all the old slanders and scurrilities once more. He had not spoken long when the aged and arthritic Machiavelli struggled painfully to his feet and with that ice-cold voice of his which penetrated to the very marrow of men's bones, interrupted the orator:

"Of such a man as Savonarola one may speak here with reverence only!"

Finished writing on the Festival of
All Saints, November 1, A.D. 1959.

Index

325